797,885 Books
are available to read at

Forgotten Books

www.ForgottenBooks.com

Forgotten Books' App
Available for mobile, tablet & eReader

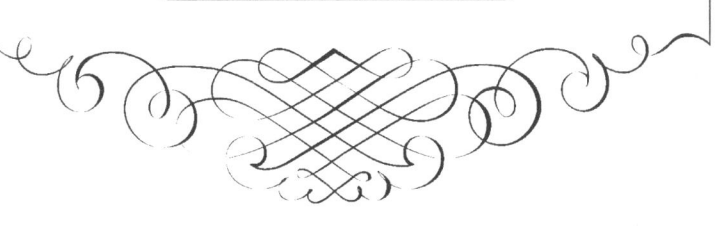

ISBN 978-1-330-95698-4
PIBN 10126233

This book is a reproduction of an important historical work. Forgotten Books uses state-of-the-art technology to digitally reconstruct the work, preserving the original format whilst repairing imperfections present in the aged copy. In rare cases, an imperfection in the original, such as a blemish or missing page, may be replicated in our edition. We do, however, repair the vast majority of imperfections successfully; any imperfections that remain are intentionally left to preserve the state of such historical works.

Forgotten Books is a registered trademark of FB &c Ltd.
Copyright © 2015 FB &c Ltd.
FB &c Ltd, Dalton House, 60 Windsor Avenue, London, SW19 2RR.
Company number 08720141. Registered in England and Wales.

For support please visit www.forgottenbooks.com

1 MONTH OF FREE READING

at

www.ForgottenBooks.com

By purchasing this book you are eligible for one month membership to ForgottenBooks.com, giving you unlimited access to our entire collection of over 700,000 titles via our web site and mobile apps.

To claim your free month visit: www.forgottenbooks.com/free126233

* Offer is valid for 45 days from date of purchase. Terms and conditions apply.

Similar Books Are Available from
www.forgottenbooks.com

Beautiful Joe
An Autobiography, by Marshall Saunders

Theodore Roosevelt, an Autobiography
by Theodore Roosevelt

Napoleon
A Biographical Study, by Max Lenz

Up from Slavery
An Autobiography, by Booker T. Washington

Gotama Buddha
A Biography, Based on the Canonical Books of the Theravādin, by Kenneth J. Saunders

Plato's Biography of Socrates
by A. E. Taylor

Cicero
A Biography, by Torsten Petersson

Madam Guyon
An Autobiography, by Jeanne Marie Bouvier De La Motte Guyon

The Writings of Thomas Jefferson
by Thomas Jefferson

Thomas Skinner, M.D.
A Biographical Sketch, by John H. Clarke

Saint Thomas Aquinas of the Order of Preachers (1225-1274)
A Biographical Study of the Angelic Doctor, by Placid Conway

Recollections of the Rev. John Johnson and His Home
An Autobiography, by Susannah Johnson

Biographical Sketches in Cornwall, Vol. 1 of 3
by R. Polwhele

Autobiography of John Francis Hylan, Mayor of New York
by John Francis Hylan

The Autobiography of Benjamin Franklin
The Unmutilated and Correct Version, by Benjamin Franklin

James Mill
A Biography, by Alexander Bain

George Washington
An Historical Biography, by Horace E. Scudder

Florence Nightingale
A Biography, by Irene Cooper Willis

Marse Henry
An Autobiography, by Henry Watterson

Autobiography and Poems
by Charlotte E. Linden

THE

LIFE, LETTERS, AND FRIENDSHIPS

OF

ICHARD MONCKTON MILNE

FIRST LORD HOUGHTON.

BY

T. WEMYSS REID.

IN TWO VOLUMES.

VOL. II.

CASSELL & COMPANY, LIMITED;
LONDON, PARIS & MELBOURNE.

1890.
[ALL RIGHTS RESERVED.]

PR
4808
R4
✓ 2

CONTENTS.

CHAPTER XII.

FRENCH AND ENGLISH SOCIETY.

PAGE

Disappointment of Milnes at his Father's Refusal of Peerage—R. P. Milnes's Account of House of Commons—Miss Nightingale's Description of Milnes—Close of Crimean War—Visit to Paris—Leigh Hunt—George Hudson—The Search for Sir John Franklin—Milnes Asked to Stand for Manchester—Stays at Guizot's Country House—The Indian Mutiny—Visit to De Tocqueville—Death of R. P. Milnes   1

CHAPTER XIII.

THE FRIEND OF MEN OF LETTERS.

Letter from Matthew Arnold—Carlyle—Demands upon Milnes's Purse—A Peep at his Letter-Bag—A Poet and Mendicant—David Gray—"The Luggie"—Milnes's Sympathy—A Painful Story—David Gray's Death—Milnes and the Poet's Father—Article on De Tocqueville—The *Cornhill Magazine*—American Civil War—Prince Albert's Death Mason and Slidell—Illness of Milnes—Tennyson at Buxton   36

CHAPTER XIV.

THE PEERAGE.

Rumours of the Peerage—Marriage of Prince of Wales—Illness of Lord Ashburton—Mrs. Carlyle—Milnes Raised to the Peerage—Comments of the Press—Speech to his Constituents—Congratulations—Landor's Last Letter—Thackeray—His Affection for Milnes—His Death Carlyle's Last Sight of Thackeray—"A Literary Squabble"   91

CHAPTER XV.

FRIENDSHIPS OLD AND NEW.

Visit to Broadlands—Goes to the Riviera and Italy—Death of Lord Ashburton—"Essays and Reviews"—Houghton Attacks Convocation—Lord Westbury's Memorable Speech—Death of Sir Charles

MacCarthy—Houghton Seconds Address in House of Lords—Mr. Swinburne—Houghton Reviews "Atalanta in Calydon"—Letter from Swinburne—Charles Dickens—Houghton's Friendship for Henry Bright—John Bright—Carlyle's Lord Rectorship—Visit to Fryston—A Distinguished Party—Mrs. Carlyle's Last Letters—Death of Mrs. Carlyle 118

CHAPTER XVI.

THE FRENCH EXHIBITION.

Politics in 1866—Houghton's Genuine Liberalism—Correspondence with Mr. Gladstone—Houghton at Vichy—Count De Montalembert Biarritz—The Imperial Family—The Cambridge Union—Houghton Opens the New Rooms—His Speech—The French Exhibition—Houghton Accepts Presidency of Group of Liberal Arts—His Stay in Paris—Distinguished Acquaintances—A Pleasant Dinner—The Sultan in England—Female Suffrage—Letters from Mr. Mill—The Great Review at Paris—Meeting with the Queen of Holland—Speech on the Roman Question—Goes to Rome—Longfellow in England—A Catholic Breakfast-Party and a Narrow Escape—The Queen and Carlyle—Lord Houghton visits the Queen of Holland—Attends the Opening of the Suez Canal—The Ecumenical Council . 150

CHAPTER XVII.

"MONOGRAPHS: PERSONAL AND SOCIAL."

The War of 1870—Letter from the Queen of Holland—A Minister without Disguise—Dinner to Tennyson—Landor and Blake—"Lothair"—A Literary Dispute—Letters of Anthony Trollope—Death of Charles Dickens—His Funeral—The War-Feeling in Germany—Besieged Paris—Letter to Mr. Gladstone—An Autumn in the Highlands—Dunrobin—"The Complaint of Glenquoich"—Guests at Fryston—Carlyle and W. E. Forster—Mr. Edmund Yates and Lord Houghton—The Alabama Arbitration—Visit to Venice—Publication of the "Monographs"—Presides over Social Science Congress 219

CHAPTER XVIII.

VISIT TO THE UNITED STATES.

Death of Lady Houghton—Goes to Vichy—Correspondence with his Children—Lady William Russell—Sir William Stirling Maxwell—Sir Richard Burton—Lord Houghton Visits Canada and the United States—Extracts from Diary—Goldwin Smith—Robert Collyer—General Sherman—An "Interviewer" at Work—A Speech "On Change"—Friends at Boston and Cambridge—Longfellow and Emerson—"Uncle Sam"—Speech at the Century Club 287

CONTENTS.

CHAPTER XIX.

FAILING HEALTH.

Return to England—The Bulgarian Atrocities Agitation—Letters to Mr. Gladstone—Accident to the Hon. Robert Milnes—Fire at Fryston—Lord Houghton's "Cheery Stoicism" — Sympathy of Friends—Restoration of the Hall—Life at Fryston During the Re-building—Unveiling of Burns Memorial at Glasgow—The Home of Mr. and Mrs. Fox—Lord Houghton and the Prince of Wales—Meets with Accident—Death of Thiers—Failing Health—His Regard for Journalists—Appreciation of the Provincial Press—His Handwriting—Death of Stirling Maxwell—Lord Houghton Succeeds Him as Foreign Correspondence Secretary of Royal Academy—"George Eliot" . . 336

CHAPTER XX.

LAST YEARS.

Marriage of his Son—Letter from Miss Nightingale—The Passion Play at Ober-ammergau—Visit to Berlin—Conversation with the Austrian Crown Prince—An Annoying Incident—Algernon Swinburne and Landor—Death of James Spedding—Assassination of the Czar—Houghton and Panizzi—Houghton Becomes a Trustee of the British Museum—Marriage of his Elder Daughter—Visits Her in Egypt—Returns by Athens—Serious Illness at Athens—Kindness of Mr. Ford—Increasing Difficulty of Literary Work—Illness of Henry Bright—Visits Him at Cannes—Mrs. Carlyle's Married Life—Lord Houghton Proposes to Visit India—The Project Abandoned—Death of Henry Bright—The Last Gathering at Fryston—Another Accident—Last Days in London—Death at Vichy, August 11, 1885 . 381

CHAPTER XXI.

LITERARY AND PERSONAL CHARACTERISTICS.

Lord Houghton's Poetry—His Prose Writings—Contemporary Criticism—The Ultimate Judgment—His Best Poem—Reminiscences of Mr. Locker Lampson—Mr. Venables on Lord Houghton—Grillion's Club—The Philobiblon Society—The Newspaper Press Fund—An Epitaph which Does Not Lie 437

APPENDIX.

Extracts from Common-place Book 469

THE LIFE OF LORD HOUGHTON.

CHAPTER XII.

FRENCH AND ENGLISH SOCIETY.

Disappointment of Milnes at his Father's Refusal of Peerage—R. P. Milnes's Account of House of Commons—Miss Nightingale's Description of Milnes—Close of Crimean War—Visit to Paris—Leigh Hunt—George Hudson—The Search for Sir John Franklin—Milnes asked to Stand for Manchester—Stays at Guizot's Country-house—The Indian Mutiny—Visit to De Tocqueville—Death of R. P. Milnes.

IN the opening chapter of this biography the story has been told in brief of the life of Mr. Pemberton Milnes, and mention has been made of the fact that in February, 1856, he received from Lord Palmerston the offer of a peerage. His refusal of that offer without consultation with his son, and for reasons which seemed to the latter to be altogether inadequate, though it led to no estrangement between the two, was none the less distasteful to Richard Milnes. Perhaps the reader who has followed the course of this narrative to the present point will find himself better able to sympathise with Milnes's disappointment at his father's action than when he read of the incident in the introduction to my story. The brilliant social success which had characterised Milnes's entrance upon public life in London, a success in its way almost unique, had been followed by that which can only be described as a disappointing career in Parliament. The very brilliancy of those gifts which made Milnes a man of mark in every circle which he entered had militated against his success in the Parliamentary arena, and the year 1856 found him a disappointed man, so far as his own position and prospects were concerned. That his disappointment had not soured his temper or warped his sympathies, but that his heart was still as full of kindness and goodwill as it had ever been; and that his chief delight in life was still to help others—sometimes with his purse, sometimes with his overflowing sympathy, and always with a whole-hearted unselfishness too rare in this world of ours—are facts which no one can dispute. But the disappointment of his early ambition was not the less severe because it was borne with a cheery stoicism, and was not allowed to influence his bearing towards the world at large.

The offer of a peerage to his father, which Lord Palmerston designed largely as a compliment to Milnes himself, was one of the first real compensations he had found for his many disappointments in public life; and the fact that his father turned aside from this distinction, as in his youth he had turned aside from the great office offered to him by Mr. Percival, was felt deeply and even bitterly by Milnes.

R. M. M. to C. J. MacCarthy.

Crewe Hall, Feb. 21*st*, 1856.

DEAR FRIEND,—Parliament is in abeyance; while the conference lasts, we may wander at our own sweet will, and I am in the country with my children—an odd plural that, and hardly yet realised.* Amicia is getting companionable and amusing; a large light-hearted cherubic-looking child, excitable and intelligent, wilful and yet sensible. Mrs. Milnes is slowly getting better of an influenza, which followed her confinement. I am glad to hear that Hawes † is to be K.C.B. He has, fortunately for him, not been sufficiently conspicuous in the civil administration of military matters to have shared the disgust and obloquy that has fallen on more notorious men. The distrust of the military authorities themselves still continues. Whatever they do *seems* ill done, and generally is so. Want of harmonious working, and the divided responsibility of the War Office and Horse Guards, are likely to produce considerable changes. It is, after all, the Nemesis of those poor fellows left to starve on the grim shores of Crim Tartary. My father has just refused a hereditary peerage from Lord Palmerston, owing to a crotchet of his own importance as a Protectionist. I take it easy, but am not the less annoyed, more for my wife and children's sake than for my own. I think, too, that the severe dulness of the House of Lords, which Lord Grey used to call "speaking to dead men by torchlight," would have suited my nervous temperament. I told Canning ‡ to make acquaintance with you, and hope he has done so: he has got his honours early enough in life to enjoy and make use of them. Your old acquaintance, Baron Parke, is making a great disturbance with his life peerage. Alderson says he has been so fond of precedents all his life that he could not die without being a precedent himself.

Yours affectionately,

R. M. MILNES.

* His second child, Florence, had been born in the previous year.
† MacCarthy's father-in-law.   ‡ Lord Canning, Viceroy of India.

The Same to the Same.

March 3rd, 1856.

I do not mind ——'s not having paid me—that may be almost impossible for him to have done—but he might have sent me the interest, and asked me to let the principal stand over till better times, which I should have done at once. As one gets on in life, one of the most annoying reflections is the little good one has done by what people call benevolence; in fact, how little man can be benefited by others. On the other hand, it is just the best men who can be benefited, as one feels in the life of Goethe. How different his development would have been under adverse circumstances! and how much Carl August had to do with his genius in giving it the peaceful prosperous air in which it delighted to grow! I have had a domestic grievance which has given me much vexation. Lord Palmerston, for my sake, has offered my father a peerage, which the said father refused without consulting me, thereby affronting the Premier, and disappointing my fair claims. I care about the social position for the sake of my wife and children, and I should be glad of a quieter and less confused sphere of political action as I get older; and then it distorts the relation between my father and myself in a very uncomfortable manner. As we do not live in Abrahamic times, Isaac may be permitted not fully to appreciate the merit of the paternal sacrifice. Peace is inevitable. Russia acts on a well-settled principle of interest, and cares little about honour. The Czar saw he must be a loser, and bravely submitted to necessity. Consoled with the notion that he had aggrandised France as against England, he will make no small difficulties.

—— has nearly got himself into another scrape about this foreign enlistment, but his chief is in a worse one, which will get him off. He worries my life out with his askings, and has quite caused a coolness between Clarendon and myself.

I remain, yours ever,

RICHARD M. MILNES.

One of the consequences of the offer of a peerage to Mr. Pemberton Milnes was the re-appearance of that gentleman in society for a brief period during the season of 1856. It was his duty to show his gratitude to the Queen and her great Minister by presenting himself before them; and thus, for the first time during the present reign, the brilliant "political meteor" of half a century earlier attended a Levée, and did homage to his Sovereign, his own son presenting him. He saw Lord Palmerston, too, and had an interesting talk with him over their early days, and the many events which had occurred since they ran neck-and-neck in the race for Parliamentary distinction; whilst, at not a few dinner-tables, he was looked upon with interest and curiosity as the survivor of a great past, and his opinions asked upon the present condition of the world, to which for a brief moment he had returned.

R. M. M. to his Wife.
Upper Brook St., 3rd (? May).

. My father goes to-morrow, and returns next week to go to the Levée. I dine with Lord Lansdowne to-day, and took him to dine at the Dilettante yesterday (Stirling in the chair), and he breakfasted here on Saturday, when my father sat between him and Lord John Russell. The conversation was lively, though both my talkers, Vandeweyer and Macaulay, failed me, and Granville had the gout. Lady Palmerston has been very poorly with the influenza, and made it worse by going to the House of Commons on Friday to hear Fred Peel compromise the Government. The rumours of a dissolution increase. Some fine morning we shall find ourselves sent to the right-about. I am strongly tempted to give up political life altogether, and enjoy home and art, and literature and travel. What say you? After this checkmate is it not ridiculous to continue the game?

Writing to his sister, Miss Jane Milnes, Mr. Pemberton Milnes gave an interesting account of one of his own experiences during this visit to town.

Did Richard intend what he said on the length of debates to apply to Palmerston—he whom Gladstone poetically described as having spoken from the setting to the rising of the sun, unto his own endless fame? The Speaker sent Waddington to me at Boodle's, requesting me to be introduced to him. He asked my impression of the speaking; I told him frankly that in no one of the leading men did it come up to my expectation. He asked how the looks of the men were, as contrasted with those of yore. I told him it was visible they were not men of the substance we were—half the House in top-boots—nor yet as Norman, those dressed (Mr. Pitt always) in nankeens and *blue* silk stockings. I said the most remarkable-looking was Fox, the M.P. for Oldham. The Speaker answered, "And he is as remarkable as he looks, and I always like to hear him." And certainly, in that conversation on the time wasted in long speeches, Fox hit the point when he said it was owing to the leaders waiting to trip each other. I was taken with Frederick Peel. He has a conceited look, but in answer to Graham as to officers from Sandhurst being put upon half-pay, he spoke admirably, in fewest words, but so pertinent as to settle the matter.

During this Session Milnes was much engaged with the question of the treatment of juvenile offenders, one that was always near his heart, and on which he was able to accomplish some real good for his fellow-countrymen. The establishment of reformatories was a work in which he took the keenest interest. Indeed, in connection with his public life there was no question which touched his sympathies more acutely than did that grave problem of how children born in the midst of temptation and want are to be saved from lives of crime. Like every true poet, the cry of the children was one to which he could never close his ears. The pathos of youth was always visible to his eyes, and he was never so happy as when he could stretch forth a helping hand to those who had all the struggles and trials of life still before them.

Miss Nightingale, between whom and the subject of this memoir so deep and true a sympathy existed in connection with all efforts for the amelioration of the social condition of the poor, writing, after his death, to his sister, said something of Milnes's love for little children.

His brilliancy and talents in tongue or pen—whether political, social, or literary—were inspired chiefly by goodwill towards man; but he had the same voice and manners for the dirty brat as he had for a duchess, the same desire to give pleasure and good · for both were his wits and his kindness. Once, at Redhill [the Reformatory], where we were with a party, and the chiefs were explaining to us the system in the court-yard, a mean, stunted, villainous-looking little fellow crept across the yard (quite out of order, and by himself), and stole a dirty paw into Mr. Milnes's hand. Not a word passed; the boy stayed quite quiet and quite contented if he could but touch his benefactor who had placed him there. He was evidently not only his benefactor, but his friend.

These "little unremembered acts of kindness and of love" were constant in the life of Milnes. No biographer can record them, for no record remains, save here and there, when some chance eye-witness, like Miss Nightingale, with an eye to see and a heart to feel, noted that which to him was a mere matter of course, and treasured up the recollection; but I feel, when speaking of his political labours on behalf of the children, I should do him wrong if I were not to make the reader understand that in what he did in this matter—in Parliament, through the Press, and on many platforms—he was prompted, not by personal ambition, but by the purest and tenderest love for the forlorn creatures for whom he worked.

The year 1856 saw peace proclaimed, and the Crimean war terminated, much to the dissatisfaction of English politicians, who felt that hostilities had been prematurely closed at the very moment when the policy of England was on the eve of securing a triumph, in order to serve the views and necessities of our ally.

Milnes went over to Paris for a few days in the spring, and encountered some of the celebrities of the campaign.

R. M. M. to his Wife.

Boulogne, Thursday.

I got here almost without knowing it, leaving London at half-past three, and dining here as early as I ever wish to dine. Remember, when there is an east wind, always to go by Boulogne; when there is a west wind, by Calais. Don't ask me why, for I don't know; but it is so. I am now going to visit the *belle sœur*, and rail to Paris at four o'clock. There was an illumination here for the birth (or, to speak more reverently, the nativity) of the *fils de France* (did you read the Bishop's sermon?), but the rain spoiled it. Other natural phenomena may prevent a great many more things that men expect, and, instead of this poor child being a harbinger of peace, who knows that he will not be an author of confusion and discord, a Pretender the more? *Hélas!*

Paris, March 19*th.*

There is little society here, and a great deal of rain. All the Magi, in full dress, went round the cradle yesterday, and the *fils de France* was decorated with the Legion of Honour and the military medal. The Pope is coming for the christening of his god-son; so the happiness of mankind must be complete. . . . I dine with the Hollands to-day. H. Greville is staying with them. I was told that Strutt was to be offered a peerage, and now see he has refused it. The disease seems catching; and if the Lords cannot be recruited either from the Conservative or the Democratic side, what will they come to? My pleasantest encounter here is with old Rio, so fresh and young! With all his misfortunes—crippled and ruined—he is the liveliest creature I have seen in France, and with such a charming overgrowth of prejudices of all kinds—religious, political, personal, and what not, no one of them rooted an inch deep. There are not many English here—Danby Seymour, Arthur Russell, and the young Foreign Office gents with Lord Clarendon I see most of. Pourquoi l'Empereur s'est embelli depuis la naissance du Prince? Parcequ'il a un nouveau-né. (He has a very ugly one.)

R. M. M. to his Wife.

Paris, Saturday.

I was at a very pretty ball last night, when I saw General Bosquet, and had some talk with him. He said it was quite true that the French army were suffering frightfully for want of provisions, as the *Times* says. Montalembert gave me a breakfast this morning with some interesting people, and I dine to-day with the Barings, and to-morrow with De Tocqueville, whom

I am fonder of than all the *hommes d'élite* together. M. de Flahault would not dine at the Cowleys' the other day, because Layard dined there; and half the society at Lady Holland's got up and left the room when M. de Flahault came into it; so that, you see, things are on an agreeable footing. A Legitimist lady yesterday told me she did not know what to do with a page, so she had advised him to try for the throne of France, for which he was as fit as anyone else. Was Amy surprised at the sea? I fancy I remember being disappointed that it was not bigger.

Wednesday.

The weather is now as brilliant as it was dull—indeed, nothing can be brighter. I shall be in London on Monday, and able to see you as soon as you like to come. The Review yesterday was very fine, and I rode yesterday the same horse of my friend M. Vatry as I did last year. It was curious to see the Emperor exhibiting to Count Orloff the identical troops that had taken the Malakhoff. Lady Monson and I gave a little dinner here yesterday between us—the Sartorises, Lord Holland, Count Cavour, George Sand, Mignet, Browning, &c. It was not as pleasant as it ought to have been. Lamartine and Tocqueville were both too unwell to come. We dined in the room *we* occupied when here. All the world is curious to hear the Duc de Broglie's reception at the Academy to-morrow. The great thing in the theatres is the *Paradis Perdu*, which begins with the fall of Satan, and ends with the Immaculate Conception. There is such a rush for places I shall probably not see it. I have been all this morning in the Paris prisons and reformatories, and find the difference between them and ours still greater than I supposed.

On July 18th Milnes gave one of his literary dinners in town, the guests being Mr. Thackeray, Mr. and Mrs. Browning, Mrs. and Miss Procter, Mr. Venables, and Mr. Spedding. Leigh Hunt had been invited, and in reply wrote as follows:—

Leigh Hunt to R. M. M.

Hammersmith, July 17*th*, 1856.

MY DEAR SIR,—Your letter dated the 15th reached me only last night. Its doing so was no inconvenience to myself; I only mention it to account for your not having a speedier answer. An invitation to your house in connection with nothing but its owners would at any time have made me desirous to come to it, whether able or not. I have always had the same feeling with regard to that of my dear old friend Procter, and to these attractions for their own sakes are now added those of the Brownings. Judge then if I am disposed to resist all three united. Dinner, however, has long been an achievement quite beyond me, Indeed, I do not recollect that it was ever much otherwise, glad as I should have been to enjoy every good thing which nature has been pleased to set before us, with a sneaking reserve as to the right of wondering (also her gift) why we should at once like and dislike to eat flesh. But I sit at a dinner-party with the power of eating nothing but a piece of the mutton or so, which is distressing both to myself and others, and this mutton itself does me harm unless I take it when other people take their lunch. Allow me to say, therefore, that instead of being in Brook Street to-morrow (Friday) at 7.45, I will be there at 9, by which time I shall probably find the dinner-cloth removed, and so be able to be as long with you as I can without feeling myself so much *de trop*.

With best respects to Mrs. Milnes,

I am, dear Sir,

Most sincerely yours,

LEIGH HUNT.

Although he has made no figure in the pages of this narrative, George Hudson, the well-known Railway King, was one of the men with whom Milnes had once been intimate. The latter, according to his wont, had enjoyed his hospitality in the days of his glory at Albert Gate, and had acquired a fund of good stories regarding the "Financial Meteor's" wonderful career, which served him to the end of his days; but, unlike most of those who crowded Hudson's drawing-rooms when he was at the zenith of his fame and prosperity, Milnes did not desert him in the days of his adversity. To the very end of Hudson's life he befriended him and his family, and I think that some of the most touching letters which were found at Fryston, after the death of its owner, were those in which the wife of the ex-Railway King thanked Milnes for little acts of kindness and goodwill to one who had long before fallen out of the favour of the world. Milnes had written (September, 1856) to Lord Palmerston, asking him to do something for one of Mr. Hudson's sons.

Lord Palmerston to R. M. M.

Piccadilly, September 21st, 1856.

MY DEAR MILNES,—I will bear in mind what you say about Hudson's son, but I cannot say whether I may be able to do what you wish. Hudson's history is like what is found in a story-book. I am glad you found him straight in his transactions; it is not everybody, I imagine, that can say as much; but Horace's saying may not apply to this family.

Yours sincerely,
PALMERSTON.

R. M. M. to C. J. MacCarthy.

Crewe, Sept. 22nd, 1856.

DEAR FRIEND,—I have little doubt that Labouchere intends to offer you the government of the Mauritius. I own I would not have asked for it for you, but I should not venture to counsel you to refuse it; on that point you must really judge for yourself, and I will approve of either decision. I suppose the climate is held to be, at least, as healthy as Ceylon, and that your insurance would be rather lighter than heavier. You would have, no doubt, to increase it in prudence. I have been agitating, this year, to get the question of Pensions for Colonial Governors put upon a sound footing; but now that the burden of the Government is thrown upon the Colonists themselves, it becomes every day more difficult. If the Mother Country is not to pay the salary, why should it pay the pension? Yet all parties agree that there ought to be some pension if the Colonists are to get the best men. I am in mourning for my father's elder sister, Mrs. Wyvill. You remember her son, the M.P. for Richmond. I do not know why Labouchere delays the gazetting of your knighthood. I have told nobody of it, except the Cardinal, whom I saw at some public place some months ago. His grandeur has ended in quite excluding him from general society; he lives in a little Court of his own.

Two notable events in the history of England marked the year 1857—the defeat of Lord Palmerston in the House of Commons on the question of our relations with China, by a combination of men so differently constituted as Mr. Gladstone, Mr. Disraeli, and Mr. Bright, together with the subsequent General Election, and Lord Palmerston's triumphant return to power at the head of an increased majority; and the outbreak of that mutiny of the Sepoys which for a time shook the British Empire to its very foundations, and absorbed public attention to a degree which was not equalled even during the days of the Crimean war.

From Milnes's letters to his wife during the year we get only momentary peeps at the course of public events, whilst his correspondence with Sir Charles MacCarthy sank during the twelve months to a minimum of one letter. Here and there, however, in his reference to public affairs are passages which are worth preserving, as the views of such a man upon any question of permanent interest always must be.

Palmerston [he writes on the day following the defeat of the great Minister in the House of Commons] was weak in body and in mind; Gladstone superb in extravagance and injustice. The Cabinet ladies were all there, and the scene very exciting. The expectants (in all senses) out of doors took up the cheers which went far down the street. So much for the combination of Galway,* Gladstone, and Cobden, and my father's sacrifice to party opinion.

An effort was made during the year to obtain help from the Government for a final attempt to solve the mystery of the fate of Sir John Franklin and the crews of the *Erebus* and *Terror*, who had sailed to the Arctic regions on an expedition for the discovery of the North-West Passage ten years before, and of whose fate no certain news had been obtained, though again and again the ice barriers of the Polar Sea had been attacked by gallant men striving to learn the truth. Milnes supported a motion in the House of Commons on the subject, and warmly advocated the case of Lady Franklin and the other wives and relatives, who were left in agonising ignorance of the fate of the lost seamen.

* Milnes's brother-in-law.

Lady Franklin to R. M. M.

60, *Pall Mall, Feb. 25th* 1857.

DEAR MR. MILNES,—I trust you will allow me to offer you my grateful acknowledgments for the able support you have given to Mr. Napier's motion. Not one of the many friends I have seen to-day but has assured me (though the assurance was not necessary) that yours was the most effective speech in aid of his representations. I am sure you do not require to be told that I shall not shrink from the alternative now forced upon me, of completing the search by my own resources. But I have suggested to Mr. Napier whether it might not be urged still upon the Government that they have adopted unprecedented responsibility in announcing their adverse decision without having previously summoned to their aid a committee of experienced Arctic officers, best fitted to advise on the subject. Such a council has always hitherto preceded every decision that has been made. If this be denied, it might still be pressed upon them that the aid they have encouraged me to expect should be freely granted. It was *pecuniary* assistance that Lord Stanley of Alderley spoke of to Lord Wrottesley; but this I do not require, since if I can get the loan of one of the Arctic ships now lying in ordinary, and fit for no further purpose, her fittings completed in the dockyard, and some of the stores purchased which are now lying waste, my resources will be relieved as much as by money. Some concession, I think, is due to me in consideration of that cruel suspense in which I have been kept ever since the return of the last great Fish River Expedition, extending for a period which has made me lose three consecutive seasons while still in doubts as to what answer I should get to my repeated applications as to the memorial of my friends. This state of suspense, ending now in fatal certainty, after preliminary circumstances which, a few days ago, seemed to promise quite a different result, has seriously affected my interests in many ways.

I was extremely pleased to see your mention of the *Resolute*, and am sorry that Mr. Napier did not make use of a document I sent him, which has not anywhere met the notice it deserves. I mean, the Resolution of Congress when it voted the money for the purchase and equipment of the ship. The resolution expressly stated that the object of this noble gift was, not the exhibition of national goodwill, but simply of sympathy with the cause to which the ship had been devoted. I am glad to have an opportunity of telling you that Captain Hawkstone, of the *Resolute,* has placed his services in the most spontaneous and unconditional manner entirely at my disposal for the command of a private expedition, in the event of my being driven to this painful alternative, and in case of his not interfering with any English officers. I shall accept his generous offer only in case Sir Charles Wood refuses to fulfil his own written pledge (communicated to me last year by order of Prince Albert) that willing permission should be given to any naval officer volunteering for my private expedition.

I do not know whether I may ask of you to communicate with Mr. Napier upon the possibility of any further movement in the House. I am afraid of appearing to expect too much, and would rather assure you how much I appreciate what has already been done for me.

Yours very truly,

JANE FRANKLIN.

When the Dissolution took place, Milnes was approached by influential persons in Manchester with a view to his contesting that city against Messrs. Bright and Cobden, but he declined to entertain this proposition, as well as another which reached him from Chester to the same effect; and standing once more for Pontefract, was again re-elected. He only consented to abide by his old constituency, however, on the understanding that the election should be a pure one—a fact which hardly suggests that the political morality of his favourite borough had been quite above reproach previously

In April he went to Liverpool to speak at a banquet connected with the foundation of the Free Library and Museum.

I had my usual good fortune yesterday [he writes to his wife], having to speak when everybody was tired to death and quite out of humour. If people do like " litery gents " to come and amuse them, they ought to give them a fair stage. The stone-laying was a very pretty spectacle; the procession through the crowded streets, with the spontaneous interest, flags flying, guns firing, &c., all in honour of plain old ugly Mr. Brown.*
St. Paul could not have prayed better than the Bishop of Chester. *Perhaps* ———'s sorrow will make him think of other people; but very few are bettered by misfortune.

The Manchester Fine-Art Exhibition was one of the attractions of the year, and of course Milnes went to see it.

Nobody can be disappointed at the Exhibition [he writes to his wife]; it is the finest picture gallery in the world, and, just because one knows so many of the pictures, less confusing and distracting. The English School comes out wonderfully. The other works of art are also an agreeable change from the incessant upward stare which tires my eyes very soon. Many of the best modern pictures belong to Manchester men, one of whom said the other day he was getting tired of them now, and should go into orchids instead.

In August he went to France, and visited, among others, M. Guizot.

* The donor of the Museum.

R. M. M. to his Wife.

Trouville, Thursday [*August*, 1857].

I had a good passage to Havre, and got here by noon. A curious-looking place, like a sea-place on the stage. All the houses run up for the summer, and let at fabulous rents. I have seen no Englishman I know, and one or two Frenchmen only. One told me that L. N. made as much fuss of his son as if he was the Messiah. . . . I go to Val Richer on Wednesday to stay till Saturday. Such a characteristic letter from George Bunsen, asking us all to his farm-house for as long as we can stay. I daresay I shall manage to spend five or six days with him. I saw General Barnard at Mrs. Lane Fox's two or three days before he left. He has a very attached family. But Sir Henry Lawrence is the great loss; he was one of the few great men in India whom people really trusted. How will all this end? Our Indian Government was, no doubt, the most useful, the most really civilising thing that England was doing in the world, and this hideous catastrophe comes on it. The old Chancelier Pasquier gave me an account yesterday of the death of the Duc de Praslin. He took such an immense dose of arsenic that it did not kill him at once, but after seven days' horrible suffering. This was what gave rise to the rumour that he had escaped. .

Val Richer, August 27*th*.

This place is much better than I expected—quite a country-house, with a well-kept garden, and a good deal of land about, which one of the De Witts manages. It was an old abbey, which M. Guizot bought for an old song, and gutted entirely, except a long gallery (now full of books), into which all the rooms open, and which has given me the notion of putting bookcases in the gallery at the top of the stairs at Fryston, where George III. and his "bad, ugly" women now stand.* M. Guizot is in great force, and full of political and literary gossip.

* An idea subsequently carried into effect.

He had a letter yesterday from Prince Metternich, recounting the visit of the Prince of Wales to him. "Le jeune Prince plaisait à tout le monde, mais avait l'air embarrassé et très triste." There are four children here, from four to nine. The elder dines at table at seven o'clock, and has everything handed to her, like any other *convive*. She asked for currant jelly twice with her hare, saying it was the best part of the dish. All the others come to dessert, and taste everything. We have coffee here in our rooms, breakfast at eleven, lunch at three, and dinner at seven—nearly as much as an English servant. The country is very rich, and thinly peopled, so that wages are high and the peasantry prosperous.

Val Richer, Friday.

. . . I am much amused at the difference of these children from English ones. They all crowd round me, and try to attract my attention, asking me to walk with them, &c. One said to me, "Je n'aime pas le lait, mais j'aime le rhum." Madame de Witt says all the English children she saw were starved, or had nothing but bread to eat. These live a very healthy life, out of doors all day. The weather has been beautiful, setting off this thickly-wooded landscape to great advantage.

From M. Guizot's, Milnes went on to Heidelberg, to stay with his old friend Baron von Bunsen.

R. M. M. to his Wife.

Heidelberg, Sunday.

Thanks for your good news of self and bairns. In this glorious sunshine I can hardly imagine you on your Arctic coast, so I must just come and see you, though it is difficult to get away from this friendly place. Oddly enough, I cannot in the least recall what *we* did here. I remember all about Frankfort, and all about Baden; but where we lodged, and whom and what we saw here, has quite vanished from my memory—and yet you call it a good one! Bunsen was delighted at Amy's sayings, and cited, in his turn, one of his boys saying, "What is the use, papa, of God's promising not to drown the world again if He is going to burn it?" You should see Bunsen playing at bowls without his coat, which he does every day in the afternoon.

R. M. M. to C. J. MacCarthy.

Brighton, Oct. 24th, 1857.

DEAR FRIEND,—We are still on tiptoe about India, but in a mood rather too confident of universal success and general triumph. We assume Lucknow to have been saved, Delhi to have been taken or evacuated, and nothing left to do except a *chasse aux hommes* all over Bengal. This may all happen; but I think there will be still some shades over the landscape. What does remain is a strong, indefinite feeling against the East India Company; and I have a notion that the Government will not stand by them, and that there will be a considerable alteration of the system. All I hope is that it will be in the direction of making India more, and not less, independent of English interference, and that we shall have no more "rising statesmen" for Governor-Generals. I have no very near relatives to regret in these late calamities, but I have an image of a pretty girl some four years ago singing and dancing in a large family connected with me, and who has died at Cawnpore, with two little children. There was great grief at Manchester (where I have been lately for the Art Exhibition) for Mrs. Ewart and her husband, whose noble letters have been eminent amongst so much nobleness. I hear the Queen is in great admiration of Sir George Grey at the Cape having sent his carriage-horses to India, and going afoot. Why have you not sent a pony or a baggage-horse, and carried your own portmanteau? We are staying in the South. . . . I was at Heidelberg with Bunsen when he got a letter from the King, earnestly entreating him to come to Berlin, which he will now be very glad he did, as he stayed a month with him at the Schloss (an immense honour), and was fully reconciled. In the new state of things I do not think it likely he will be politically employed; but it is on the cards that he may be Minister of Cultus, which would suit him very well. The Catholics have got themselves into great odium through the blundering of your eminent relative. When people were so excited as about this affair, what folly to try and mix up other things with it, even though just! If they could not join in the general sympathy, why could they not stay quiet? The War Office still *enjoys* the worst repute, but the head is made to bear most of the blame.

I am yours affectionately,
R. M. M.

Among the letters to his wife from various country-houses which he visited during the autumn are a few from which extracts may be made:—

Gunnersbury, Sunday Evening (Baron Rothschild's).

Nobody here but the family and Bernal Osborne. Very pleasant, though a rainy day. We went to the farm and inspected the poultry, and in the afternoon we drove out (four such greys!); and then I went and sat with some old Italian acquaintances, the B——s, who live close by, and are great in the artistic line. Madame M——'s little girl rode out with a groom in the morning. She began her lessons in the riding-school at four, and now is afraid of nothing; but she does not write well yet, though she has been learning six months, and has a master every day. The youngest boy here is the most beautiful Eastern child I ever saw. We had music and whist last night. The Rothschilds were delighted with Scarborough. They were a month at the hotel we were at, and quite contented. Fancy that last Sunday—the day I proposed to come here—was their great *Fast;* they eat nothing from five o'clock on that day to seven o'clock the next evening. The Baroness, quite in confidence, read me one of the sermons she has written for the Jewish schools; it was on the deception of Jacob, in very good

English, and quite above the level of ordinary sermons in thought.

Bowood.

Lord Lansdowne has pressed me to stay and go up to town with him on Thursday, and I do so. The fate of our dinner is what gratifies my father so much, civility without consumption; but I do not see why you should not have ——, and I may pick up a man. Would you like to ask ——? If so, do it. Lady Shelbourn has had a long letter from Lady Canning, evidently inclined to diminish the horrors, and to make the best of the thing, which I have no doubt is the tone that infuriates the Calcutta people. Mr. Temple, the new Rugby master, and Mr. Greg came yesterday. Pray cut out the story of the Relief of Lucknow in the third page of yesterday's *Times.* It is a capital anecdote—indeed, much too good to be true.* . . . I saw Thackeray yesterday; his story is to be all about the American War, written something in the manner of "Esmond," with his own drawings.

Southampton, Wednesday.

Just arrived from the Island. I went to Ryde yesterday; dined at Colonel Harcourt's. Went to a dance on board the Actons' yacht with the young Thornhills; and had an early dinner to-day with Sir Augustus Clifford. There was Lady Jersey and the Dudley Carletons on the pier. The Harcourts' and Cliffords' villas are the prettiest things I know in England. The Bishop of Oxford told a delightful story of the Dean of York being present when his son was examined for ordination. Archdeacon Wrangham asked him who was the father of David, which the young man could not answer; and then the Dean began whistling "The Flower of Dunblane," to suggest the name to the son. And when this was all in vain, he said, "Now, sir, do you suppose that our excellent friend, the Archbishop, could answer such a question?"

* The fabulous story of "Jessie of Lucknow."

Ashridge.

I found a large houseful here—all the Cambridges, Clarendons, Manchesters, Cravens, Granville, the Poodle, a dozen young lords, and as many young ladies. There was to be a play to-night and a ball to-morrow, which I did not care for, so was going away; but the Princess Mary said she could not learn her part before Friday, so the ball is to-night and the play to-morrow, which I stay for. This is an inconvenience to some eighty people who were asked for to-morrow; but it is an advantage of entertaining Royalty that you need not care for anybody else. Mr. Manager Stafford is in great force, with not only a princess in his troupe, but the President of the Council, a live duke, and any number of inferior peers. Lady Marian* is a charming easy hostess, taking her dinner of forty as easy as you could yours of eight, with a pleasant word for everybody. The house is hideous and handsome; the place very fine, long grassy glades full of deer, with immense beech-woods.

R. M. M. to Miss Jane Milnes.

Woburn.

I got on very well with Lady John, as she takes a real interest in foreign politics. We had a sermon at Woburn to-day for the pastoral aid, in which we were told to imitate Stephen, who, though deacon, took all other offices on himself; to imitate Paul in turning the world upside down; and to follow Lord Ashley, "whose praise was in all the churches;" and a paper was placed in the pews, mentioning that one young lady had put a gold ring in the plate, and another her watch. I could not, however, get Miss —— to deposit her bracelet, and Lord Foley his studs.

R. M. M. to Miss Caroline Milnes.

Woburn.

You will have seen my note to my father, and now I send you the play-bill of last night to forward to Edinburgh. The

* Lady Marian Alford.

thing went off very well, and I had a good piece of nonsense to act, leaving O'Brien all the sentimental melodrama. Mrs. Anson acted very well, and made herself most pleasant, and her children are what decorous people would think sadly premature. Lord John was very much pleased with his little boy being made the hero of the piece; he is a short, grave, simple child of six, and strutted about the stage with entire unconcern. The Duchess wanted me to print my prologue, which I declined; it will do to read when we meet. I was precluded from a large field of jokes by the Jarnacs being here, which made French subjects delicate. Young Byng is a charming boy with real dramatic genius. A great part of the party cleared off to-day, and we are now few for the house. I go to Castle Ashby (Northampton) on Wednesday; O'Brien says all the different sects are applying to engage his uncle Baptist,* just as the theatre did with Grisi after her quarrel with Mr. Lumley of the Opera House; but he does not seem inclined to accept anybody. Lord John laughs a good deal at Cobden's budget, and says that a legacy duty on real property, levied as the present one is on personality, would bring in, not as Cobden says, a million and a half, but about £100,000. I cannot make out who recommended Baines† for Buller's place; he is a fair lawyer, with a conciliatory manner, and that is all. It is one of the few places that would, I think, be better for having a Lord in it. The respectability of this house is not convenient—the servants, mostly about sixty, hobbling along and waiting detestably.

Your affectionate
R. M. M.

During the autumn and winter Milnes was busily engaged in speaking at various gatherings of a literary and social character in different parts of the country.

---

* The Hon. and Rev. Baptist Noel, who had seceded from the Church of England.

† Matthew Talbot Baines, who had just been made Chancellor of the Duchy of Lancaster.

The Social Science Congress had been formed, and he took a deep interest in it, attending the inaugural meeting at Birmingham to support Lord Brougham and give his own views to the world on the questions with which the Congress specially dealt. In February, 1858, he was at Sheffield, presiding over the distribution of the prizes at the School of Art.

R. M. M. to his Wife.
Sheffield, Wednesday.

I had a formidable audience to address last night of ladies in crinolines and gents in white ties, enough to take the heart out of any speaker. But for the few artisans to whom I had to give the prizes, I could not have got on at all. Some of the artistic work was very good, but I could not apply Ruskin on the spot, though I did talk about "gradated surfaces."

House of Commons, Monday, May 10*th,* 1858.

There was a good party at Strawberry Hill—Vandeweyers, Gladstones, Lady A——, Edward Russells, &c., and [illegible] dropping in at all hours of the day. Plenty to talk about in these Indian matters. The Government act with such strange indiscretion in administration that every false step they make carries them fast to destruction. They threaten a dissolution in three weeks, and then I shall see whether you have been canvassing for me properly at Pontefract in my absence. Cardwell makes the move that is to eject the Government. I have the Comte de Paris to breakfast on Saturday, and a hamper will be acceptable on Thursday night. I am getting up a Committee for poor Lamartine, who is in the saddest penury, but I find it difficult to arouse any sympathy for him.*

Lady Ashburton had died in Paris in May, 1857. Carlyle tells how the news was brought to him by

* Milnes raised a subscription of more than £1,000 for Lamartine, and sent it to him as "a tribute from English friends."

Milnes, who had shared with the author of *Sartor Resartus* the friendship of that gifted lady. "She was the greatest lady of rank," writes Carlyle, "I ever saw, with the soul of a Princess and Captainess, had there been any career possible to her but that fashionable one."

In Milnes's Commonplace Books, as has already been told, many of her good sayings—not always so good-natured as they were witty—are recorded. It was not until the spring of 1858 that Milnes found himself again at the Grange, over the hospitalities of which she had so long presided.

R. M. M. to his Wife.

The Grange, 1858.

Ashburton said, "I will put you in your old room," where I was with my broken arm, and she came to read to me

"Your voices are not hushed," &c. &c.,

and there was just as much mirth and laughter as I ever heard here   Lady —— is very interesting in the account of Lady Ashburton's last days. After Locock's visit, which first revealed her complaint to her, she said, "You see, I have been crying; but tears must be good for—for—for the dropsy." Ashburton walks alone with a grave sad smile that is very pathetic.

In January his only son, the present Lord Houghton, was born. He received the names of Robert Offley Ashburton.

A. de Tocqueville to R. M. M.

Paris, April 28th, 1858.

My dear Milnes,—I think it quite right that you should have a son, but quite wrong that I should not have been told of it. We are such old friends now, and the event so great, that I ought to have been informed of it by no one but you. Now, having given you a good scolding, I want to congratulate you with all my heart, and Mrs. Milnes too—to whom, please, present my kindest respects.

Simon, who is the bearer of this letter, has promised to come and stay at Tocqueville at the end of August or beginning of September. I wish you would manage to come with him, or about the same time. Do, there's a good fellow, and then we may perhaps forgive you your long silence. But it would be the height of perfection if Mrs. Milnes would consent to come too, and see how she likes a small Normandy home in comparison with an English castle. You know how delighted Mme. de Tocqueville and I would be. I will say nothing more now. The bearer of my letter can tell you all the Paris topics, and much better than a Benedict and a bookworm like me.

I am leaving Paris, however, before him. The day after to-morrow I wend my way back to my green pastures; and if ever you answer my letter, you must address me there.

Many, many kind regards, and never forget us again.

A. DE TOCQUEVILLE.

Will you kindly remember me to Lord and Lady Palmerston?

R. M. M. to George von Bunsen.

16, *Upper Brook Street, March 2nd,* 1858.

MY DEAR GEORGE,—I am writing an article for the *Quarterly Review* on the personal narratives of the siege of Lucknow. It is possible that Lady Havelock might desire that some facts should be stated concerning General Havelock's two advances and his subsequent calamitous death. I need not say how glad I should be to aid in any way to the illustration of so great a name, and anything she sent me would be strictly confidential beyond what she wished to be said. There must be no delay, as the article must be written in the next three weeks. It will be purely personal, without politics or criticism of public events. You will have already presented to Lady Havelock the tribute of my respectful sympathy, and my hope that somewhere or other we may meet again. My wife and child are well. I should be glad to hear the last news of your little girl. Winter is come at last, and bitterly.

Yours affectionately,
R. M. M.

Lord Palmerston, at Milnes's request, presided at the annual dinner of the Royal Literary Fund in May of this year.

Palmy [Milnes writes to his wife] had a great reception at the Literary Fund, and, if he ever was obliged for anything, would be grateful to me for having brought him there. The Bishop of Oxford and Thackeray pleaded "indisposition" at the last moment. I always wonder how good men do these selfish things. I wish I could. Have you heard the last argument in favour of the Wife's Sister? It is unanswerable. If you marry two sisters, you have only one mother-in-law.

During the Session Milnes drifted further away from that political life in which he had once been so anxious to play a conspicuous part. His chronic state of dissatisfaction with both parties and with their leaders seemed to be intensified as time passed, and more and more he found himself subsiding into that position of social moderator and literary patron which the world had almost from his first appearance in society assigned to him. There is little in such a life to engage the attention of the reader, who must picture Milnes passing from country-house to country-house, everywhere a welcome guest, who brought good-humour and bright talk in his train; or sitting at the dinner-tables of the West End, capping the jokes of that new generation of diners-out which was already beginning to regard the man who had been Charles Buller's friend as a veteran. Time, indeed, had dealt lightly with Milnes himself; but, like other men who have completed half a century of life, he found the vacant chairs around him growing in number, and that natural melancholy which was always the undercurrent in his externally bright and vivacious mind was deepened by the successive losses which he had to face among his old friends. Referring to a visit to the house of O'Brien, he writes to his wife:—

There I was at the very spot where I proposed his health when he came of age, and there was he in the churchyard hard by—so men may come and men may go.

And again and again, in a similar strain of subdued melancholy, which shows how far his heart was from being hardened by the passage of the years, he dwells upon old friends who have been lost to him, and upon the qualities by which they had made themselves dear.

His father's health was at this time very precarious, so much so that Milnes felt compelled to remain within easy reach of Fryston. He found time, however, during the autumn for a brief visit to France and to his friend De Tocqueville. On his way to Tocqueville, Milnes stopped at Cherbourg, where certain great *fêtes* were in progress in connection with the meeting of the Emperor and the Queen, and the opening of new docks for the French Navy.

R. M. M. to his Wife.

Cherbourg, Thursday.

Since I wrote yesterday, there has been nothing but rowing about the harbour, visiting ships, and being deafened by salutes. (N.B.—A royal salute only costs 8s. 6d.!) I breakfasted with Lord Lyons this morning, who has got to look the image of Nelson, barring his two arms. He has been suffering frightfully from tic, and had six teeth taken out last week. So you need not make much of your wisdom one. Arthur Russell and I disembark to-morrow evening, and either go to Tocqueville or to the next town. We saw the benediction of the railway engines very well, being just opposite the Emperor and Empress. Nothing could be more official and cool than their reception. Our Queen has just gone to lunch with them at the Préfecture. The fleet was lit up with blue lights last evening when the Emperor visited the Queen. That and the entrance of the Queen were the best sights.

Tocqueville, Tuesday, July, 1858.

I have just received yours of Thursday, with the good news of your safe arrival in the bosom of your family. After my last I went to the inauguration of the statue of Napoleon I., and was close to the Emperor when he spoke. The speech was capital, and admirably received. The pacific parts were the most applauded, and Malakhoff kept nodding and winking at me at the end of each of them. The Court afterwards embarked for Brest, and must have had a rough night of it. Fifty journalists went on board the fleet, to the great disgust of the officers; this is worse than the " gilded saloons." M. and Mme. de Beaumont are here—old friends of mine; he was the Minister of the Republic in England, and refused the present Emperor a passport when he went to France. Tocqueville keeps quite apart from politics, and seems all the better for it. I never saw him better, both in body and mind. Arthur Russell is a charming companion. I am amused at the astonishment of foreigners at the *finesse* of his *esprit* and his knowledge of the languages. We go from here to the Imperialist Deputy's, the Comte de Kergolay; so direct your next to Château de Canisy, St. Lo, Manche. You would like the life here—breakfast at 10.30, dine at 6.30, and to bed at 10.30; a walk in the morning, a drive in the afternoon, and the rest of the day to yourself. Nothing can exceed the richness of the soil and the general air of prosperity in this country. A large amount of ground is wasted in hedgerows that divide the small properties, but else the cultivation seems good. As I shall see no English papers in this *tournée*, keep the *Times* for me when it has anything of interest, either to myself or generally. Tocqueville made a fine comparison of the basin at Cherbourg to an excavated pyramid; and when the *cortége* went down the steps to open it, it only wanted some Oriental dresses to represent Pharaoh letting out the Nile—or, at least, Martin's conception of such an event.

Château de Canisy, Sunday.

I rather expected to find a letter from you here, but perhaps one will come to-morrow. The Duc de Broglie is not at home, so we shall go from here to Caen, where I shall leave Arthur Russell, and go to Paris on my way to England. We had a nice specimen of French railroad arrangement yesterday, being left for seven hours in an unfinished railway station, without possibility of movement or food, and only got here to dinner at 10 p.m. This is a regular old château of the *ancien régime*, with large, grand, bare rooms, brick floors, and damask curtains, unpainted doors and painted ceilings, and a large church, where all the parish are at this moment celebrating the somewhat incongruous *fêtes* of the Virgin and the Emperor. The latter personage is at present in Brittany, and expects to make a sensation, as being the only sovereign who has ever visited that loyal province. I am disgusted at Roebuck's silly speech;* the

* It is, perhaps, hardly necessary to remind the reader that the relations of England and France were at this period somewhat seriously strained, in consequence of the plot of Orsini against the life of the

bluster can do nothing but harm here, where certainly the feeling is not much in favour of the English. I saw, from *Galignani,* that the *Daily News* alludes to Malakhoff's gestures to me during the Emperor's speech.

Bournemouth, July 21*st.*

I got here late last evening after a hideous passage from Guernsey; had wind against us; Mr. Savory's remedies all in vain. What a miserable physical weakness for a creature at the top of creation, that a little oscillation of his interior should turn him into a powerless beast! There must be some physical education which would prevent this if one only knew it. So I have a headache, and stay here quietly to-day. Weymouth was so full, the Royal Hotel without a bed, that I came on with Arthur, and delivered him to Hastings Russell, who is staying here.

I shall be in town to-morrow afternoon, though hardly in time for the post, and in the natural course of events shall be at Fryston on Wednesday evening or Thursday morning. I saw Victor Hugo at Guernsey, where he has bought a pretty house, and seems resigned to his exile. He had, however, been very ill, and thus perhaps was somewhat subdued. He still looks forward to seeing M. Bonaparte, as he calls him, at Cayenne.

R. M. M. to C. J. MacCarthy.

Fryston, Sept. 16*th,* 1858.

DEAR FRIEND,—My father's very precarious condition did not permit me to take much holiday in France, where I went *viâ* Cherbourg. I had seen the place before, but the

Emperor, and the subsequent revelations as to the preparation in England of the bombs used in the attempt upon the Emperor's life. Lord Palmerston's effort to carry a Bill which would prevent England being used as an asylum for assassins had failed, and, after sustaining a severe defeat in the House of Commons elected just a year before to support him, he had retired from office, and a Conservative Administration had come into power.

spectacle was excellent; the multitude of ships and men, and the solid Egyptian masonry dwarfing both to insignificance. The French up to this time had no port of refuge north of Brest; now they have this one, in which any fleet can find protection. This is really the amount of the menace, and it hardly adds to the danger in the chances of war. The Emperor's double game is very evident; he is sincerely anxious to keep well with England, and will make any sacrifice short of his popularity to keep so; but he keeps by all underhand means a reserve of ill-will to make use of if any serious cause of rupture arrives. As I think that with ordinary prudence any such rupture may be avoided, I do not look to the future with anxiety in this matter. I wish for your sake that Lord Stanley had remained at the Colonial Office, for you impressed him as favourably as he did you; and if anything turned up, he would readily have availed himself of you. How it will be with the great romancer (Sir Edward Bulwer Lytton) I do not know. Some Colonial servant began a despatch the other day, " Seated on a rock with a volume of *The Caxtons* in my hand." Perhaps if you tried your hand at this it might succeed. He may keep his place some time, for there is clearly no inclination in the House of Commons to bring the Whigs back again. It is really singular that no one of the official men of that party enjoys the least personal popularity, or possesses any requisite of leadership. When Lord John goes, or finishes himself (as he easily can do), the whole future of the Liberal party is a darkness which will be felt. I really think that short as has been his career, and unparliamentary as are his talents, Sir George Lewis commands more respect than any of them. Of my wife and children I have fortunately nothing to write. The eldest girl is becoming a delightful companion.

The blow which had so long been impending over Milnes, and which had prevented his leaving England for any long period during the autumn, fell somewhat suddenly at last. On the 9th of November, 1858, he received in London a telegram from his wife announcing that his father's illness had taken a serious turn, and that he must return immediately to Fryston. He did so, but arrived too late to be present at the closing scene in a long and honourable life, the remarkable character of which has already been made known to the reader.

R. M. M. to C. J. MacCarthy.

Fryston, Nov. 23rd, 1858.

DEAR FRIEND,—My dear father died on the 9th of this month, closing a long and weary illness with a peaceful and easy transit to the spirit world. I am left with a fair gentleman's fortune and a considerable amount of debt, which I hope gradually to pay off and put Master Robert in a comfortable position. . . . This event will make little difference in my course of life; it will keep me more here, as I have a large farm on my hands, and the place left in not very good condition. My wife and children remain well and promise well, learning everything with a pleasure incomprehensible to the mature mind. Montalembert's trial is the event of the hour. After having sanctioned the *coup d'état* it is impossible to look on him as a martyr to liberty, and no condemnation can quite give him the aureole. Bright's avowal of revolutionary objects much clears our political atmosphere, and parties will become more distinctly defined.

The death of Mr. Pemberton Milnes reminded many of the brilliant distinction of his early career. I have already quoted the letter in which Lord Palmerston referred to the loss of his old friend, and acknowledged the dying message which he had sent to him; and from many others Milnes received warm expressions of sympathy with himself, and of admiration for the remarkable talents of the man who had so completely effaced himself in the presence of the new generation that it was only by his surviving contemporaries that he was known at all.

CHAPTER XIII.

THE FRIEND OF MEN OF LETTERS.

Letter from Matthew Arnold—Carlyle—Demands upon Milnes's Purse—A Peep at his Letter-bag—A Poet and Mendicant—David Gray—"The Luggie"—Milnes's Sympathy—A Painful Story—David Gray's Death—Milnes and the Poet's Father—Article on De Tocqueville—The Cornhill Magazine—American Civil War—Prince Albert's Death—Mason and Slidell—Illness of Milnes—Tennyson at Buxton.

IT cannot be said that the death of his father made any marked change in the outward circumstances of Milnes's life. The former had withdrawn so completely from society, that he had never stood between his son and the world. Milnes, indeed, had been as much master of the hospitalities of Fryston during the lifetime of his father as he could have been if he had himself been the owner of the house; whilst in London it was but seldom that Mr. Pemberton Milnes appeared upon the scene, and when he did so, he came rather under the wing of his son than in any other position. In this case, therefore, the succession to his paternal estate was not attended by the usual change in outward circumstances; and Milnes's life in Upper Brook Street and at Fryston continued to flow evenly onwards, undisturbed by the loss which he had sustained. The actual possession of a large landed estate, of course, involved him in certain responsibilities, and these he did not shirk. His father's ideal of life, as we have seen, had been that of an English country gentleman. Very different was the ideal which Milnes had before his eyes; but now that fate had made him a country gentleman, he remembered the duties of his station; and though it cannot be said that he liked them, none can accuse him of having neglected them. Still, as time passed, his sympathies became more and more largely absorbed in one channel, and every year found him assuming to an increasing extent the task of protecting those men of genius and men of letters who were oppressed by adverse circumstances. Commanding ampler means than during the lifetime of his father, he was able to give a freer rein to those generous impulses which so constantly dwelt within his heart. He had now practically abandoned the active pursuit of a political life, though in the great controversy which divided his fellow-countrymen on the occasion of the war in the United States, he was moved to take an important part on one side of the conflict of opinion; but, apart from this question, the Parliamentary movements in which he took part were almost exclusively those connected with philanthropic objects, like the reformation of criminals, or with the educational and literary enterprises to which about this period of our history our public men began to devote increased attention. I bring together a few of his letters to his wife and others during the year 1859:—

R. M. M. to his Wife.

Woburn Abbey, Jan. 1, 1859.

It is like wishing myself all good things for the New Year to wish them to you, dearest, and I fear the "jealous gods."

It always seems to me that we lose the soonest the things that we hold on to the most, and I don't know that I ever got any good in the shape in which I wished it or expected it. I remember your fine quotation about anniversaries; and as I looked yesterday evening on the old Duke—much aged, depressed, fatigued—I thought of the old years' days with which to him this house must be haunted. The Parkes dined and slept; he much annoyed at having received a report from Dr. Taylor on the green papers he had put up at Ampthill. Taylor had analysed the dust in the room, and found a considerable quantity of arsenic; he sent specimens of copper arsenised by the dust.

R. M. M. to C. J. MacCarthy.

Fryston, Jan. 20, 1859.

DEAR FRIEND,—It will be very pleasant to see you again next spring; and as I hope to be at Fryston in the autumn, I shall have an opportunity of seeing more of you than London affords. Poor Colvile has just lost his mother in sight of land. I hope you may have a happier fortune. . . . I do not know whether you have come within the range of any of the peculiarities of the Colonial Minister, or whether Sir H. Ward has given his despatches a Caxtonian *tournure*. The Ionian matter has been singularly mismanaged, and Gladstone made very ridiculous. As I am a Phil-Hellene (I believe, the only one in England), I think Sir J. Young's views excellent, and, if I had been Foreign Minister, should have brought the matter before the Congress at Paris. Indeed, Labouchere proposed to do so; but Clarendon thought the spirit of the Congress so hostile to us, that he declined to enter upon any new matter. There has been a meeting between Bright and Lord John; but I don't know that it has led to anything, except a more temperate tone in Bright's last speeches. The effect, however, of this Radical *pronunciamento* has been to frighten the Whigs, and will probably keep the Derbyites in till a dissolution. You will find the state of Europe very anxious. I look upon Louis Napoleon as a true Italian Bonaparte, ready to liberate his own victim while he treats France as a conquered country. There is a curious conversation between old Napoleon and General Montholon on Italian independence and nationality, which is probably quite sincere. The bloody phantom of a united Austria has destroyed what might have been a strong federal empire. With best regards to your wife,

Yours affectionately,

R. M. M.

Extracts from Letters to his Wife.

I revoked again at whist last night—a proof, if I wanted one, that I am superannuated. I have no news, having seen nobody to-day but M. Waddington and the Bishop of Exeter; the latter quite amused at my telling him we were an old Dissenting family. He said, "I am glad I did not know it, as I might have expressed my surprise in an uncourteous way. How could you become such pleasant people?" He said my father was the greatest, shyest man he had ever met, and ended by hoping the House of Lords would throw out the Reform Bill.

I am dinner-full this week—to-day, Bernstorff's; Wednesday, the Barings'; Thursday, H. Vane's; Friday, Anne Beckett; Saturday, the Speaker. C. W. asked me to dine to-day; but I have sent her a pheasant instead, which is not very generous, as a partridge I had for breakfast this morning nearly walked away from the table by itself. There was a smart party at the Austrian Ambassador's last night, and I thought the diplomatists rather more cheerful, although Baroness Lionel says Paris is in a Reign of Terror. I have no doubt the Jews are anxious about their securities. I went up with a deputation this morning to the Bishop of London on the Wife's Sister Bill. His lordship seemed favourable himself, but fearful of his clergy. He has now got the living of Acton (£1,000 per annum) to give away, and the clergy are wild with expectation. I wish he would give it to ——. I am going to put a spoke into Captain Vyse's appointment to Japan on Friday. If I quote much of the Blue Book, they will call the speech *papier mâché*.

1859 was the year of the French war in Lombardy, which ended somewhat suddenly and unexpectedly after the Battle of Solferino.

From a Letter to his Wife.

July, 1859.

The armistice has not surprised me as it has the rest of the world. I told everyone it would happen when the French had crossed the Mincio. A pleasant dinner at Holland House yesterday with Settembrini and other Italians, who munched the macaroni most gratefully.

It is hotter than ever to-day, and think what it must be on the Mincio! No wonder there is peace! The great gainers are Austria and the Pope. Austria gets rid of her expensive provinces, and retains her hold on Italy. Pio Nono realises the dream of his early ambition.

Matthew Arnold to R. M. M.

1, *Wellesley Terrace, Dover, August* 3*rd*, 1859.

MY DEAR MR. MILNES,—I have desired the publisher to send you a copy of a pamphlet of mine on the Italian question, which embodies some of the French experiences I inflicted on you in Paris. You know, you entirely belong to the "aristocratie anglaise," in the broad (and just) French acceptance of the term. But then you differ from them by having what Sainte Beuve calls an "intelligence ouverte et traversée," and they in general have every good quality except that. I am only here for a few days on business, and return to France next week. No one knows my address, and I see no newspapers. I have so much on my hands just now. But still I have a natural solicitude to hear how "the judicious" take my *résumé* of the Italian question, which I cannot help thinking is true; and if you would let me have one line to tell me whether you have read it, and whether you agree with it, you would do me a great kindness.

      Believe me, dear Mr. Milnes,
        Very truly yours,
          M. ARNOLD.

T. Carlyle to R. M. M.

Scotsbrig, Ecclefechan, Sept. 12*th*, 1859.

DEAR MILNES,—I have, as perhaps you in some measure know, been rusticating and vegetating (latter partly in the aquatic manner) for these last two months and more on the pleasant coast of Fife, and now we are all slowly settling homewards, I by this western and my native border country, the wife by Edinburgh and the eastern on like grounds; ought all to be at Chelsea within a fortnight hence, with the small fruit of our summer's earning, whatever that may be. You may well suppose I never forgot your kind note, received just before leaving home, and am now thinking more decisively of it than ever—now, when the time is come for some hope of acting on it, or of honestly renouncing such hope till another opportunity. It is certain if there were a human roof under which I could wish to be a guest in my present mood and circumstances, that roof would be Richard Milnes's, but, alas! that helps little. I am not even certain whether a meeting with you on the route southward were now possible; and if it were, I feel in such a broken, bankrupt condition of mind (till once the Prussian horrors are got through, if they ever be) it is clearly better to postpone that pleasant operation, as I have done and do all others like it, till *after* said contingency of achievement, and keep it as a *bonne bouche* awaiting me on the further side if ever I get thither. It is needless for you to pity me (except in silence), though I much deserve it; needless for me to say anything further, especially to write it with such a *pen*, comparable to the laird of McNab's. "Wrang spelling! Wha can spell with sic a pen?" And so I bid my true and excellently human Richard adieu again. *Manet altá mente* he may be well sure if he likes.

His always,
T. CARLYLE.

Carlyle could not go to Fryston on this occasion. The invitation had been to meet Sir Charles MacCarthy, who, with his wife, spent some time under the roof of his old friend during the autumn.

Not many months after this visit Milnes was able again to render a signal service to his friend. Through his influence with the Duke of Newcastle he procured for him the post of Governor of Ceylon, one of the most important appointments in the gift of the Colonial Office.

MY DEAR MILNES [writes the Duke of Newcastle],—As I know it will give you pleasure, I write a line to tell you that I have to-day received the Queen's approval of Sir Charles MacCarthy being appointed Governor of Ceylon.

I congratulate you [said Sir Benjamin Hawes, MacCarthy's father-in-law] on MacCarthy's success, which you have done so much, and with such generosity, to bring about. All congratulations, therefore, to you. I think the people of Ceylon ought to thank the Duke and you.

Nothing could have given Milnes more pleasure than success of this kind, success which gladdened his own heart while it brightened the prospects of a friend's career. Yet it was characteristic of the man that he invariably disparaged any efforts of his own to secure the advancement of his friends, or of those in whose welfare he took an interest; and it was with a half-shrug of the shoulders and a humorous smile that in conversation he would dismiss a success such as that which he had secured in the case of MacCarthy as a job, of which he, as its author, ought to be rather ashamed than proud. Never-ending were the appeals which reached him from all sorts and conditions of men for assistance either with money, with literary advice, or with influence. Day after day the Fryston post-bag was filled with petitions and appeals similar in character to those which most public men are fated to receive, but far more various and more comprehensive than those which fall to the lot of ordinary men. Did some enthusiast propose to erect a monument over the tomb of a neglected genius, it was to Milnes that he looked, not only for advice and patronage, but for pecuniary support. Was it a broken-down man of letters whose friends believed that fate had dealt hardly with him, and that he deserved something of his fellow-men, it was to Milnes that they came to ask him to lay his case before the Prime Minister, or to beg him to put forth an appeal to the public benevolence. And the young men who were just entering the thorny path of literature, happily with no thought of the sad fate which had befallen so many of their predecessors, applied to Fryston for counsel and criticism, as well as for aid in the shape of introductions to booksellers and editors. A batch of letters which reached Milnes in a single month in the winter of 1859 lies before me as I write, and one or two of the appeals addressed to him may be mentioned to show their variety and eccentricity. First comes a letter setting forth the case of an old servant of the poet Shelley, whose distresses it is thought that Milnes will be eager to relieve. Then an appeal from one of the most distinguished of the French exiles living in London for his assistance in procuring an appointment as teacher of French in the Military School at Woolwich—assistance which was not withheld. And finally the old Radical poet, Samuel Bamford, seeks his aid in procuring for him compensation from the nation which in former days had persecuted him for opinion's sake. The confidences of the dead must be preserved as rigorously as those of the living, and in these pages at least the writer trusts that no "revelation" will be made which can cause pain to anyone. Yet a simple story relating to this period in Milnes's life may be told here, to illustrate the experiences through which he had too frequently to pass in connection with this side of his life and character.

It is all told in a series of letters in the possession of the writer. A well-known man of letters in his day writes to Milnes, apologising for the intrusion, and explaining it by stating that it had come to his knowledge that at a recent dinner party at which Milnes was present his (the author's) name had been mentioned. "I am told," he continues, "that when you, sir, were pleased to speak kindly of my poor productions, —— took it upon himself to warn you against me as a man who would not improbably attempt to borrow a ten-pound note from you on the first occasion on which we met."

Then, with natural indignation, the poet—for, alas! a poet he was—goes on to protest against the cruelty of one whom he had never injured in thus aspersing his character to a stranger, and, whilst gracefully offering to Milnes a copy of his published works, implores him to afford him an opportunity of proving that ——'s estimate of his character was entirely erroneous.

With his usual good-nature, Milnes acceded to the poet's request, invited him to dinner in Upper Brook Street, and to stay with him at Fryston. Recognising the man's real ability, he went further, and used his influence in a certain quarter to procure work for him. For a month or two the correspondence between them flows on in a smooth and pleasant current of grateful thanks on the one hand, and of appreciative criticism on the other. But the end is, unhappily, precisely that which had been foretold by the poet's first friend. There is a sudden emergency in the poet's life, and a peremptory demand, not for the ten-pound note which had been predicted, but for £50, which he must have within twenty-four hours, to stave off imminent ruin. And when Milnes, instead of sending the £50, writes kindly to him, inquiring into the nature of the emergency which has necessitated such a demand, he is repaid by a letter, modelled apparently on the immortal epistle of Dr. Johnson to Lord Chesterfield, in which his "patronage" is repudiated, his character maligned, and his pretensions to literary eminence turned to ridicule.

Such cases were happily not common in the experience of Milnes; but they did happen more than once, and it would hardly have been strange if they had led him to close his heart to the appeals of men of genius in distress. That effect, however, they never produced; and to the end of his life he continued to exercise a charity which there is now no harm in stating was greatly in excess of his means.

I have said that cases like that which I have just described were happily exceptional, and against them may fairly be set such stories as that which deals with Milnes's connection with David Gray, the Scotch poet. Ample justice has been done in Gray's memoir to the tender—one might say, the paternal—kindness which Milnes showed towards the unfortunate young genius. The story is, indeed, one of the most pathetic in the annals of our literature. It opens in the spring of 1860, when Milnes received from David Gray, a youth of twenty-two, then resident in Glasgow, a request that he would read a poem of his. In accordance with his invariable custom, Milnes wrote promising to do so, and a few days afterwards the following letter reached him in London :—

David Gray to R. M. M.

65, *Deveril Street, Boro', Feb.*, 1860.

SIR,—You promised to read my poem. I travelled from Glasgow to give it to you, and to push my fortune. Looking two days before me, I see starvation. Shall I *send* or *bring* it? I know that you do not want to be troubled with people of my sort coming about you—that is what makes me ask. Whatever you do, do it *quickly*, in God's name.

Yours here below,

DAVID GRAY.

Little did the writer of this letter know Milnes, when he spoke of his desire not to be "troubled with people of his sort." It was just such a man, a poet possessing something like real genius—a fact which Milnes had quickly perceived on reading some of the shorter pieces which Gray had sent him—just entering upon life, and oppressed by adverse circumstances which the kindly hand of a friend could remove, whom Milnes most desired to meet; and he who never turned a deaf ear even to the cries of the professional mendicants who constitute the camp-followers of the army of letters, responded instantly to the appeal of Gray. He did not write inviting him to send his manuscript to him—he did not even ask him to come to his house as a guest; but within a couple of hours from the delivery of the touching note I have just printed, Milnes himself entered the humble lodging-house in the Borough, bearing with him a load of delicacies such as he believed the writer of such a letter must absolutely need. Having made some provision for Gray's subsistence whilst he remained in London, he took back to his own house the MS. of the beautiful poem of "The Luggie," which Gray had written, and upon which he was so anxious to have the opinion of his fellow-poet. A few days afterwards, whilst he was sitting at breakfast in Brook Street, Gray was shown into his room. Milnes saw in a moment that something was wrong, and by-and-by he extracted from him the fact that he had spent the previous night in the park. There had been no actual necessity to do so—there could have been none with Milnes in London; but the young man was in a state of hysterical excitement, and to indulge some morbid fancy of his own had condemned himself to this terrible punishment—a punishment which laid the seeds of the fatal disease that carried him off little more than eighteen months later. He was warmed, and fed, and clothed before he was allowed to leave Milnes's house; and during the acute illness which followed this act of folly, Milnes visited him as regularly as a physician, and tended him as carefully as a nurse. As soon as the youth had recovered sufficiently, he sent him back to his native place, the village of Merkland, near Kirkintilloch, cheered by the fact that he had found a powerful friend to recognise his genius, and that the way to the fame which he coveted seemed to be opening before him.*

Whilst he was still ill, and Milnes was watching over him, the latter received this touching letter from the poet's father—a letter at least as honourable to the writer as to the recipient:—

* On some points the account I have given above differs from that which is to be found in Milnes's introductory notice to Gray's poems. I can only say that it is founded, first, upon original letters now in my possession, and, secondly, upon Milnes's own account given to me of his connection with Gray. That, writing immediately after the young poet's death, he should have drawn a veil over some of the incidents of his tragic story was but natural. No one can suffer, however, by a full statement of the truth. It ought to be said that Milnes from the first was anxious that Gray should return home, and should, if possible, pursue the path marked out for him by his parents. He urged this upon the youth with what the latter thought was undue persistence; but this was the only point upon which he acted in such a way as to ruffle the sensitive temperament of the young genius.

David Gray, Sen., to R. M. M.

Merkland, Kirkintilloch, June 26, 1860.

DEAR SIR,—We received your very kind letter to-day. David told us that you had always been his friend from the first time he had seen you, and told us that you had said something to him which was worth coming to London for; and when he took badly, that you had been kind to him, and sent a doctor to see him and tend him. Neither himself nor I can recompense you for it, I rather doubt; but it is a great comfort to us to know that he is in want for nothing, and he tells us that it has depended all on yourself. We hope it will not last long, but that he will be able to come home soon. I am sorry to say I can do him very little good at such a great distance, as I suppose you will know I am but a tradesman, and there are eight to the family, David being the eldest. If he were at home, he would be very well; but we cannot do him much good where he is. I cannot say any more. I feel very much, owing to the kindness you are giving him. I don't like to ask you to write me what you think about him—all I wish is he were home in the meantime.

I am, Sir,
Yours respectfully,
DAVID GRAY.

P.S.—David had always a wish for two or three years to go to London; he would not be kept back. We think he always read and wrote too much, and all the learning he has got he has done it chiefly himself. We have wished him always to be a Scotch minister, and he had not given up thought of it when he left, but said it would not be easy done. He told us you had given him advice and support every way.

The advice and support were continued after the youth had returned to his home. The next letter of the series, painful, but most interesting, from which I am quoting, is dated November 4th, 1860, and is written by an eminent Glasgow physician who had been consulted by Gray.

At the request [says the writer] of my friend Mr. Sydney Dobell, I visited poor Gray some days ago at his father's cottage, Merkland, near Kirkintilloch, and found, from the state of his general health and the physical condition of his chest, that in my opinion a continued residence there, and under his present circumstances, would give him little chance of life. . . . Although poor Gray has many bad points in his case, I should look upon it as far from hopeless, provided he could at once be removed to a more genial climate.

The kind doctor went on to say that he had already opened a subscription for the purpose of covering the cost of a voyage to South Africa for Gray.

Milnes wrote instantly, offering to do what he could in the matter, and suggesting that, pending his removal to such a distance as Port Natal, he might go to Torquay, where he would himself be able to see after his comfort.

Gray came up to London, and was placed for a time in a hydropathic establishment near Richmond. The following letters tell their own tale, and leave no room for comment.

David Gray to R. M. M.

Sudbrook Park, Richmond, Surrey, Dec. 5th, 1860.

DEAR SIR,—Four months ago I had a letter written for you which I was afraid to post, and ultimately burned, and since then I have been *going* to write you at least fifty times. I saw your name often in the news, read your speech at Pontefract and your article in *Fraser*, and what, thought I, have I, a poor, weak, diseased, far-away youth to do with you? Rightly so. Better, since I should die, to die with broken hopes, than with a letter from you which would but have made me *regret* my destiny. Therefore I burned your letter. From July to October I received numerous letters, but answered none, wishing to let the world outside go on without me, since I could not go on with it. Truly I lived a "posthumous existence," as you say of poor Keats in his biography, waiting patiently and, as I thought, bravely for death, and truly expecting it. You told me that "to be a brave man was above being a poet." I laid aside even my hopes of being a poet and *tried* to put on manhood. Have I succeeded? Alas! no. I wish yet to live, but do not greatly wish it. For God's sake let me go away—how far? For my parents' sake let me live—how long? Yet I fear not death or a future existence, but oh! I fear dying. Let these boyish words pass, and I will tell you how I am here. In October I got a kind note of inquiry from Dobell. I hesitated whether or no to answer it. He had come to me before, like the dayspring spreading joy. He had got me introductions to men in London; he assisted me when I was ill. He had followed me with a love that was a mystery to me. He had lost sight of me, he said, since I had left London; what was I doing? Was I better? Here are two guineas; and so on. I answered him, telling all. Thus commenced that interest in my affairs which has ended in Sudbrook. Dobell sent his friend Dr. Drummond: his verdict was instant removal if I wished to live. I had no money, could get no money. A female cousin of Dobell's said she thought she could get me into Brompton Hospital, but my life hung on *instant* removal. The kind, excellent Dr. Lane, of this hydropathic establishment, immediately offered to receive me as a *guest*, till a berth in Brompton could be secured; but I had no suitable clothes to start with. I got them; but how, I don't know. Somebody must have advanced the money, for I got underclothing, &c. &c., to the amount, I suppose, of about £15. A cab came to take me away, a railway ticket was put into my hand by the gentleman who had looked after the proper fulfilment of the matter and, after getting from him a small purse containing fifty shillings the train moved off, and I am here.

This morning I got word through Dr. Drummond of your many efforts in my behalf; how much I thank you, God knows. Looking, as I do, not so much at the effect as the cause—the sweet cause of your kindness—I am doubly grateful. I must say at once that I like your plan better than the other. The beautiful, mild, pleasant Torquay is surely, surely better than the dolorous, weary Brompton; but wherever I go or am taken, Mr. Milnes, I must be kept *gratis*. My family could not raise a sovereign for me; that is a *literal fact*. You mean, I think, that the subscription (how I hate the word!), with my father's assistance, could keep me at Torquay. The amount of the subscription which I possess is thirty shillings, and my father's assistance may be valued at *nil*. So that, you see, the sweet and goodly idea of Torquay must be given up, and I, a consumptive myself, cough with consumptives in the hospital. I dread it—dread it. I don't like to ask it, but if you will send me a little explanatory note—I don't mean explanatory, but just a little note with something in it—not money—for dear sake not money, I have enough—I mean, a few sentences with your name signed, I shall be very happy. How Dr. Drummond must have bothered you! It seems so cold and stiff all the gratitude one can write on paper that I hate to be grateful in a letter.

So believe me yours here below,

DAVID GRAY.

Sudbrook Park, Richmond, Surrey, Dec. 17th, 1860.

DEAR SIR,—Your letter was looked forward to with great anxiety. No one can know the fear I have to enter Brompton. Would you not think it awful to be constantly among dying or sick people, to sleep in the same room with them, to walk in the same bit of ground with them? But your kindness gives me an alternative which I accept with gladness. I shall start for the Water Hospital at Torquay as soon as you will send me a little programme of my journey. E. W. Lane, the kind physician here, authorised me to use his name decidedly

in approval of my choice. Torquay, he says, is superior to Brompton in almost every requisite for consumption, and the one dreadful idea of cohabitation of sickness is dispelled. Tell me then, my dear sir, as quickly as your numerous duties will allow you, when and how I may go there, and where I shall go when I do get there. It were better that it were got over at once. I write, you know, in a very feverish state, and may have gone wrong somewhere, being so unwell; but you will gather from my scrawl that I most thankfully take your offer, and only wish to be settled as soon as possible. That all good may surround you is the true wish of
Yours sincerely,
DAVID GRAY.

66, Upper Stamford Street, Waterloo Road, London,
Saturday Morning.

DEAR SIR,—Your letter was the most welcome Christmas gift that could have reached me. On receiving it, I left Sudbrook, to be in readiness to start when your answer and advices arrive. I think I can manage to get the money for my journey to Torquay, if you could settle all the rest. In the nomination sheet, which I return, some gentleman must lend me £3, to be drawn upon in case of ill-conduct. My conduct will surely not be of such a character; and so, if you will *lend* me the money required by the Honorary Secretary, it will be returned to you as it is returned to me by them. I know of no other party who can lend it me. As this severe weather tries me sorely, I would beg of you, dear sir, to be as quick as possible. With many sincere thanks for the trouble I have caused and am causing you,
Believe me to remain yours ever truly,
DAVID GRAY.

Remember the address.

Milnes hardly needed the last injunction. Gray had found a refuge with a friend of his, a fellow-countryman, also a poet, still happily living in the enjoyment of a well-deserved fame—Mr. Robert Buchanan; and from a letter of his, written to Lord Houghton in 1864, I may quote a line or two, which need no addition from me:—

> You will not have forgotten the melancholic young gentleman whom you were accustomed to see when you carried beef-tea to Gray at Stamford Street.

Gray was a somewhat difficult person to deal with. He was fighting death with a feverish anxiety that at times made him hardly accountable for his actions. It was an act of imprudence, for example, to leave Sudbrook Park before he was quite sure of being received at Torquay; but Milnes stood by him in spite of all his eccentricities, and having looked after him whilst he remained in London, duly despatched him to Torquay early in the year.

At Torquay were Milnes's aunts, and, at his request, they were anxious to do what they could for the young poet. But his stay at Torquay came to an abrupt end. He had hardly been in the place two days before he was seized with another fit of depression, and made a wild appeal to the medical men, to whom Milnes had introduced him, to provide him with the means of leaving Torquay and returning to his own home. The poor lad again received what he wanted, and went back to Kirkintilloch—there to die.

David Gray to R. M. M.

Merkland, Kirkintilloch, March 1st, 1861.

DEAR SIR,—Knowing your kindness, do not think I traffic on that knowledge; on the contrary, I feel much to trouble you again, engaged as you are, but I have no other hope. The poem or book I spoke of so vaingloriously is nearly finished. In my self-laudation and irreflective impulsion I forgot to ask your consent to have your name connected with it—not in a formal cold dedication, but after Thomson's manner recollect, which necessitates that the poem shall not be unworthy of the person to whom it is dedicated. Therefore, to insure thine own fame, and not to be mocked through me, you might—if not for your own sake, then for mine—read the production as I have re-written and methodised it, being all the while in my weakness spurred on by the thought that you would read it. If it is in any way unworthy, your name must not suffer; for I think that to dedicate a petty and incapable work to a famous man is an insult. Why I always cling to you I know not, except it be that you were the first and only poet that ever told me I was a poet—a keen, intense pleasure, which can never, never be forgotten. Perhaps, in my dreamy blindness, I anticipate a renewal of that pleasure. You must excuse my late race from Torquay: set it down to temper, impulse, want of reflection; *I could not help it*. No person could have been more willing to stay, but the sight of the invalids threw me into a nervous distemper. This season is very severe, and more dangerous symptoms appear; but I have myself to blame. If you read the poem, and judge favourably, I will first of all try Moxon and Co. I risk this letter, as we say in Scotland, with a happy-go-luck.

Yours truly,
DAVID GRAY.

Milnes wrote thanking him for this letter, and promising to assist him in revising his poem.

Your recognition [wrote Gray, in response] gives me confidence. Your letter outbalances drugs innumerable. With *morphia* I shall manage to transcribe what remains of MSS., and the whole shall not make much over one hundred pages of a book. It might be printed in Glasgow, but never published, because it would fall dead from the press. . . . Forgiveness shames the repentant soul. I am ashamed, for my own sake; this kindness is almost persecution. Believe me, when I say these lines of yours give me confidence:—

"I take all men for what they are;
They wear no masks to me."

So you must know me to be impulsive, foolish, burning with hectic desire, yet aiming for the best always.

"I never bowed but to superior worth,
Nor ever failed in my allegiance there."

I shall not trouble you again till considerable progress is made.

It was later in the year—not long, indeed, before the end came—that Milnes received the following sad letter:—

David Gray to R. M. M.

Merkland, near Kirkintilloch, N.B.

EVER DEAR SIR,—I know that it is a bother to receive letters neither concerning business nor from old friends, and that, too, at a period when probably you are busiest; but my case has become worse. I would have written to you immediately on the intelligence; but I grew so blunt and stupid about the heart, that I lost my spirit altogether. *It is this—my right lung is affected.* Now, Mr. Milnes, if I could get into a vessel (I would like one bound for the Mediterranean) bound to any warm place, as Persia, or anything, my life might be prolonged. At all events, I would not like to die at home, among weeping friends and all the horrible paraphernalia of the dissolution. They told me that Colonel G. wrote you a letter of thanks for your great kindness to me. He is a man who does much good hereabouts. I dreamed I was there when you proposed poor dear Tom Hood's health. The letters in the newspapers which I have read of his are as good as Lamb's. But where am I going? I wish often that I was near the calm, kind, patient skill of Dr. Tweedy. I could write a very, very long letter to you now; but I know how precious your time is, and forbear. Think of me for a moment when you receive this, and though your memory may be stored with recollections of great and more worthy men, my crown is laid in the dust, and I weep over it. I shall tremble if I receive a letter from you. *Dum spiramus speramus.*

Yours gratefully,
David Gray.

Alas! the poor boy's case was far beyond the remedy at which he thus sought eagerly to clutch. It was but a few days after Milnes received the foregoing letter, and on the very day after the first proof-sheet of "The Luggie" had been placed in Gray's hands, that the youth died.

Dear Sir [writes his father, with the stern reticence and self-repression of his race],—My son David died on Tuesday, Dec. 3rd, at two o'clock, afternoon. Born 29th January, 1838.

Your obedient servant,
David Gray.

Milnes's efforts on behalf of the young poet who had died in the very dawn of his life, did not cease at his death. He made it his business to bring his poetry before the world, writing a warm and generous critical notice of the published book in one of the leading reviews, bearing testimony not only to his genius, but to his irreproachable personal character, and the scrupulous honour and strong sense of independence which accompanied his hopeless poverty. Nor was this all; some years later he collected subscriptions for the purpose of placing a suitable monument above the grave in which the remains of the author of "The Luggie" had been placed. There were those who, knowing that Gray sprang from a humble stock, thought that Milnes's aid should have been given to the living rather than to the dead, and one letter at least lies before me in which he is bitterly upbraided by a man of letters for having provided a stone for the dead Gray when his living parents stood in need of bread. To the cheap sarcasm which was showered upon Milnes by the writer of this letter, who understood his real character just about as well as most of the casual acquaintances of that period in his life understood it, the only answer that need be made is to quote the following letter, which, as it happens, was written at the very time when Milnes was being upbraided for his indifference to the fate of Gray's parents.

David Gray, Senior, to Lord Houghton.

Kirkintilloch, 13*th March,* 1865.

DEAR LORD HOUGHTON,—You have quite astonished us this morning with your letter. It was unexpected; we are short-sighted. We send you our blessing, and there is no doubt you have God's blessing, as He does not lose sight of things given in that manner. It is true I have not been able to work for some time, and I am not getting better yet; but your good money, £10, a large sum to us, will be carefully gone about. You do not know the good it will do for a long time. My lord, as to David, you was the first that saw anything about him, and you have always kept up his reputation. I could say more, but I think it is quite needless.

My Lord Houghton, with many thanks,

I remain yours,

DAVID GRAY.

The reader will, I think, agree with the writer of this manly and touching letter that to say more of

Milnes's connection with David Gray and his family is "quite needless." Nor should I have said so much had it not been that this story is typical of a side of Milnes's character to which his contemporaries never did justice, chiefly because he himself was eager to conceal from their observation his tenderest and noblest actions.

Of course it was not always substantial help which was sought by Milnes's unknown correspondents. Almost as largely as Tennyson himself, he was made the recipient of the confidences of young poets and authors, anxious to obtain advice as to the means by which they might secure a place in the Republic of Letters. Milnes had always treated these correspondents with courtesy and kindness; but, as in the case of Gray, he never encouraged a man who was seeking to abandon his own path in life in order to follow literature alone. Here is a letter, written early in his career, to one who had sought his counsel. Many years afterwards—towards the close of his life—Lord Houghton was much gratified when this particular letter was returned to him, by the person to whom it had been addressed, with a word of warm gratitude for the excellence of the advice contained in it.

R. M. M. to ———.

House of Commons, May 9th, 1839.

Sir,—The verses you have sent me show grace and feeling, and are very creditable to you. If I could be of any use to you, I should be glad, but I have no patronage, public or private, by which I could place you in a more comfortable situation.

I doubt, also, whether you would find any mechanical employment of the pen a happier or more advantageous employment than your present one,* and I own I would rather see poetry acting as a comfort and sustainer to you in your path of life, than the inciter to worldly ambition.

I can assure you poetical sympathy is not generally to be met with in any rank or position of society, and all labour is so similar, that we none of us can quite reconcile the daily duties of existence with our wishes and ideas.

I remain,
Yours truly,
R. M. MILNES.

R. M. M. to his Elder Daughter.

Broadlands, Dec. 26th, 1859.

DEAREST AMY,—I hope all the letters I shall receive from you during your life will be as pleasant as this your first one. It was nearly quite well spelt; only you must learn that when such adjectives as "pretty," "merry," "naughty," are turned into adverbs, "prettily," "merrily," "naughtily," the "y's" are turned into "i's." Dear mamma has got a bad cold, which I think she caught shopping in London. She was quite sorry she could not go to church on Christmas Day. We had no Christmas-tree, as there are no children in the house here. We saw Florey's godmamma on Saturday [Lady Verney]. She asked a great deal about her, and hoped she would soon know how to read, and then she would write her a letter. You do not tell us whether Robin has been out of doors. The weather has been so mild we think it may have been good for him. I hope Mademoiselle has not been *ennuyée*, which I hope you will never be, and that she gets the newspaper regularly. Mamma does not send you any kisses, for fear of giving you her cold, but I do, and I am

Your loving Papa,
R. M. MILNES.

* The recipient of the letter was a joiner.

His correspondence with his wife during 1860 and 1861 contains comparatively few passages of general interest; but some of his letters, both to her and to his friend MacCarthy, throw light upon his occupations during this period.

R. M. M. to his Wife.

Brockett, Sunday (1860).

No party here, only the Shaftesburys, Lady W. Russell, the Poodle, Panizzi, Azeglio, and a doctor attending one of the Ashley girls, whose influenza has fallen on her chest, and the [illegible]. Half the party are laid up with bad colds. My lady [Palmerston] this evening was all in pink, and my lord is all *couleur de rose*. I never saw either of them pleasanter. We went to a new church Lord Cowper has just built, and where young Locock preached superiorly. It was all in open benches, and as uncomfortable as you could wish Fryston to be. Lord Palmerston has had a letter from St. Petersburg, saying that the Imperial Court there were delighted at Miss Braham's marriage, had had her to tea, and the Empress kissed her and told her she was much more fitted for a Court than for the stage. Palmerston still stands by Persigny, and says he is the cleverest and honestest Frenchman he has ever known, but he thinks the Emperor much changed for the worse.

R. M. M. to C. J. MacCarthy.

Fryston, Oct. 21*st*, 1860.

DEAR FRIEND,—I was really too anxious about your health till you were fairly off to take any pleasure in writing to you. Now I will trust that all is right, and that your home air and *otium cum dig.* will set you quite up again. I had a talk with Sir C. Ward about you and Madras. He said he thought you so fitted for Ceylon that it would have grieved him much to try to tempt you away so long as he could find anyone else.

. Lord and Lady Palmerston make a Yorkshire progress this week, and come here for two or three nights. As my liking for him has very much gone off, I take this rather as a *corvée* than as a pleasure. It will cost me some money and anxiety, and the honour does not much touch me now. I have mainly a family party to meet him. The Italian complication is working itself on, and maybe out, in a marvellous way. Many important checks and obstacles turn out to be wheels and impulses. All that is noble in the resistance is so damaged by base antecedents that it is but so much virtue thrown away. It is curious that in all the Neapolitan affair you see no one notorious name risk itself on one side or the other. Remember to do young T. a good turn, if possible. I could, if I chose, make the permission of young H. to go with you, after the refusal to T., look like a job of the old India House stamp; but I have no horror of jobs, and I like the boy and his family. We stay here till the middle of November, and then go southward, not to return till the spring. I find the continual *go* of a large country-house more than I can wisely afford, and very little pleasure out of it in comparison. Venables is here, and in such good temper with mankind, it is to me astonishing that the public men he has come in contact with, and they are many, have not thought it worth while to make use of him. Let somebody give me a monthly line to say how you get on in health and all things.

Yours and Lady MacCarthy's ever,
R. M. MILNES.

The Same to the Same.

Wilton House, Salisbury, Dec. 21st, 1860.

MY DEAR FRIEND,—I have been so uneasy about you that even the dubious news of the last mail is a relief. The Duke of Newcastle told me in town that you had been very ill, and now I have Lady MacCarthy's letters to my wife and to your boy, who has sent me what he has received. I can now only hope for some satisfactory intelligence next mail, and that the amiable goddess Nemesis has now done her worst with you. We are all well and prosperous—Mrs. M. and her children at Crewe, and I paying some visits. The Duke of Newcastle looks very well, and for once has had a fortunate expedition, having brought back the Prince [from America] not only all right, but grown some quantity. I met your eminent cousin [Cardinal Wiseman] at Harry Maxwell's last week; he talked of you with some interest, and made himself generally very pleasant. He is much diminished by his illness, and looks all the better, though they say his health is very uncertain. You will have read in the papers what a triumphal progress Palmerston made in Yorkshire. He seemed quite to enjoy his visit at Fryston, and made himself at home; but they got a damp bed at ——'s, which turned Lady Palmerston's incipient cold into something serious, from which she has only just recovered. There is a new book of Motley's out, with interesting details of the Armada, where, it seems, the Dutch and the winds saved us from an awful smash, our preparations being about as complete as those for the Crimean War. Beaumont's "Life of Tocqueville" is daily expected, and will be interesting. We intend to go early in the Session to London, and to get away as soon as possible. I must have a turn at Vichy next year. I assume Mrs. Milnes will answer Lady MacCarthy, so only say a Happy Christmas, and

Yours affectionately,
R. M. M.

Milnes made Beaumont's "Life of De Tocqueville," to which reference is made in the foregoing letter, the subject of a most interesting article in the *Quarterly Review*, in which he recalled his personal recollections of that eminent man, with whom he had long been on terms of intimacy. Speaking of his Château of Tocqueville, where Milnes had spent a part of the autumn of 1858, he said:—

We are accustomed to think of Frenchmen as only connected with towns, or specially with Paris; but here we have a picture of country life, with all its advantages of daily occupation, intellectual leisure, and social hospitality, as fully appreciated and enjoyed as they could be in any part of England. Many of our countrymen whose names are high in literature, will retain a delightful impression of the hours they have passed there, in such intercourse as recalled the age when conversation was a living art, in which the best men gave the best of their minds to those they loved and valued. There were long walks in lanes as deep and shady as those of Devonshire; there were excursions to the neglected port of Barfleur, sacred to the memory of the English monarch "who never smiled again;" to the scene of our naval victory at La Hogue; and to the lighthouse of Gatteville, from which were seen the fine expanse of sea indenting the varied coast, and the thick hedgerows making one continued wood up to the sloping hills. There were drives to the châteaux of family connections—old ladies and gentlemen, who suited the long broad alleys of the *ancien régime*; and to ruined manors, whence many generations of Clérels had gone forth to fight their neighbours and their country's foes. The guests of the autumn of 1858—the last— will not easily forget the brightness of look and heartiness of demeanour which, even after the warning of the previous month, made it impossible, either for the old friends who had never seen him gayer, or for the new ones who had never known anyone so charming, to look on De Tocqueville as a man about to die.

There were other literary interests engaging Milnes's attention about this time. The first number of the *Cornhill Magazine* had appeared, and Thackeray had invited the co-operation of his old friend, who once more took up his pen and produced a poem for the pages of that periodical, the fame of which was as brilliant as it was suddenly acquired. But later, in the year 1861, the subject which engrossed Milnes's thoughts most completely was undoubtedly the outbreak of war in America. I have spoken already of his views regarding the momentous problem which the American people were striving to solve on the field of battle. It says much, not only for his independence of character, but for the depth and reality of his sympathy with the cause of freedom throughout the world, that upon this question of the American Civil War Milnes should have broken away from his own class, and ranged himself on the side of the friends of the North, with an earnestness not inferior to that of Mr. Bright and Mr. Forster. His attitude upon this question, though it earned for him for a time some unpopularity in the circles in which he was most at home, brought with it its own reward, by placing him in sympathetic relationships with some men from whom he had hitherto held aloof —notably Mr. Bright—and by giving him a firmer hold than he had ever had before on the affections of the masses of his fellow-countrymen. Indeed, in spite of the warm interest which he had during his whole public life taken in the welfare of the people, and in the promotion of all wise schemes of social reform, he had never, until this period in his life, attained anything like public popularity. It was in society—the cultured catholic society, not of England only, but of all Europe— that he was a conspicuous and favourite figure; outside that comparatively limited circle, neither his poetry nor his wit, nor his inexhaustible kindness, had secured for him a hold on the popular imagination; but now his espousal, late in life, of that which, among the aristocracy at least, was an unpopular cause, suddenly secured for him a place in the heart of the people, and made his name a familiar one where, up to that moment, it had been practically unknown. In Yorkshire and Lancashire, where, if at all in England, the sympathisers with the North were in the majority, Milnes found himself suddenly turned into one of the popular idols, and sharing with Mr. Bright and Mr. Forster the plaudits of the multitude. There is something almost whimsical, something which at least struck this master of paradox as being itself intensely paradoxical, in the fact that, whilst the labours and efforts of a lifetime had failed to secure for him the public popularity which he coveted, the accident of his adhesion to the Republican side in the great conflict in America should have placed that popularity within his reach. But then it is worthy of note that "accidents" of this kind are, as a rule, merely the natural outcome of the man's previous life and of his carefully-formed opinions.

It was during this winter that Baron von Bunsen died at Bonn. Milnes had made his acquaintance first in Rome thirty years before, and he was one of many Englishmen who had learned to entertain no ordinary esteem for the distinguished German statesman. A few days before Bunsen's death Milnes wrote to his son.

R. M. M. to George von Bunsen.

Fryston, Nov. 12th, 1860.

MY DEAR GEORGE,—Miss Wynn tells me that even in this crisis of life and death (which may it be at this moment?) you and yours would like to hear from me. To me there is something awful, unapproachable, in such sorrows, and I shrink from them in a somewhat cowardly spirit. But what can I say? I cannot at such a time speak of myself, and what can I say of or to him that you will think worthy? I can only bid you, if he still lives, to give him my most affectionate and respectful farewell. If he is gone, I can only ask you to say to your family with what interest I have heard of all their communications and elevated sufferings, and how I earnestly feel the honour of having been the friend of such a man. Do not answer this till such time as you can do so without additional pain and trouble, knowing me,

Ever affectionately yours,
RICHARD M. MILNES.

I am indebted to Mr. George von Bunsen for the following reminiscences of his own friendship with Milnes—a friendship which began in 1843, and lasted throughout life:—

R. M. M.'s arrival at the Prussian capital in the autumn of 1843 was announced to me by an appreciating letter of my mother's. From whatever side I try to contemplate the fact, it must remain mysterious to me how it ever came to pass that his acquaintance with a lad of nineteen, differing in nothing from the average undergraduate of that age—*i.e.*, as conceited as he was diffident, and as sceptical as he was receptive—ripened within a few months into an intimacy which the blindest could have seen must endure. His friendship was all tenderness. Its reality came upon me like a revelation, in that look of sadness which refused to disappear from his countenance, even in his joyfullest sallies of wit and humour, during the hours I spent with him at the Hôtel de Rome, on the eve of his departure from Berlin. Originally, some of that curiosity might have been at play which would lead him to examine what shape ideas and things were taking on the mental retina of a son of Bunsen. Him he had learned to look up to and revere at Rome some ten years before, without ever (and this lasted through life) feeling entirely at his ease in his presence, as he did with so many of his fellow-creatures. But after the first encounters at Berlin I found nothing in his behaviour towards me but a true friend's love, nothing but pleasure in seeing himself, not, of course, understood, yet guessed at by one so much younger, nothing but a total unrestraint in giving the reins to that humour of which he has remained to the last, as the readers of this biography know best, one of the most brilliant representatives ever known.

During forty years there never was a falling-off in Milnes's affection. When he fancied himself neglected by his distant, and at times over-worked, correspondent, he would occasionally apply the severest castigation in his power, that of commencing his letters with a "My dear George Bunsen." Such periods of half-reproach, however, did not last long.

It is an observation as old, probably, as human kind, that a man's early friendships do not easily continue far into his maturity, unless shone upon by the wife's unquestionable consent and approval. Accordingly, the assurance he gave me in writing, on the eve of his wedding-day, that his wife would like to welcome me at Upper Brook Street, was fulfilled in a degree I could never anticipate. Never was it my good fortune to enjoy the confidence of a gentlewoman of more perfect equipoise, or of a nobler woman than the late Lady Houghton. In dealing with her husband's paradoxes and humorous leaps in the dark, she transferred into daily practice the inimitable apophthegm that "tout comprendre c'est tout pardonner." For behind every jest of her ever youthful, often frolicsome lord, she distinguished—and she inwardly prayed that everybody would duly distinguish—the meditative mood, the continuity of thought and of mental elevation, and the well-tutored wisdom of experience not lightly bought. She was glad, also, when others would perceive in her husband, through a charming veil of apparently half-conscious *bohème*, a powerful good sense, that gave solidity to his judgment on human affairs, and rendered his intuition of character all but infallible.

Milnes's poetry was not in 1843 very highly appreciated, even in his own country. At that time I was stupefied at the thought of how much poetical genius must be scattered, so to say, broadcast over the breadth and length of Great Britain, for one so elegant, so observant, so evidently the Muses' favourite, not to be praised to the very skies. This wonderment, in its general bearing, has increased, I need hardly say, rather than diminished, during the years that have escaped us since. But as regards the poet Milnes, it must be acknowledged that full justice is being done, both in England and abroad, to the genius, the felicity of diction, the gentle plaintiveness of him to whom I will gratefully apply the words of one of his favourite German poets, Friedrich Rückert :—

" Dein Blick hat mich mir werth gemacht."

Julian Fane to R. M. M.

29, *Portman Square, June* 30*th*, 1861.

MY DEAR MILNES,—I do not know whether you have read a volume of verse recently published under the title of "Tannhäuser." It purports to be written by Neville Temple and Edward Trevor. But as the famous prologue to be written in "8's and 6's" was to declare that Pyramus was not Pyramus, but Bottom the Weaver, and the lion no lion, but plain Snug the Joiner, so this brief note intends to explain that Neville Temple (Nevile-fano) is indeed plainly myself, and Ed. Trevor (Robert reversed) no less plainly Robert Lytton. We were anxious for many reasons to start our books with pseudonyms, but now that the start appears to be fairly made we have agreed to commit a few discreet indiscretions in revealing our poor secret to those who, we hope, will kindly take an interest in it. I could not bear that you should not be amongst the first of those who have good-naturedly encouraged my literary efforts. I remember, although you must forget, if indeed you ever knew, that the essay which gained me my declamation prize at Trinity was written on a theme selected by your instigation. I remember, too, that you were gentle and kind to a certain Queen Dowager who got drowned in a prize poem, and that you were much more than friendly in the kindness which you gave to my first little volume of verse. Add to these considerations the fact that I gratefully appreciate the warm-hearted friendship which you have always extended to me in social life, and you have a summary of the motives which impel me to communicate to you a little piece of information intended only for those of my friends whom I best love and most respect. If you have time to read our little book, and can commend it, we shall be glad and proud of your praise. But do not forget that we shall "reverence your blame," and that any strictures which you may pass on our work will be most valuable to us.

Believe me always most affectionately yours,

JULIAN FANE.

Mrs. Procter to R. M. M.

Brighton, Aug. 26th, 1861.

MY DEAR MR. MILNES,—I enclose a letter from our dear friend Browning. You will rejoice with us that he is coming back near his old friends. I have a strong belief that my sending this letter is merely an excuse to write to you to gain a reply. I want to know how you and yours are, and what happy people are at Fryston. I see the bright breakfast-room, those beautiful books, green and white, arranged so like a bed of flowers, and fancy myself once more taking away some book which I never read, because I liked the living book (in trousers) so much better. This place, which on Saturday was so cheerful, is now sadly altered; nearly all the shops have the shutters up. Twenty-two people were killed Saturday morning, and ten or twelve are in the hospital. Until we hang a few shareholders nothing will be done. These unfortunate people, these lives which were so valuable, all bread-winners. A good Tory as I am I always consider a poor man's life so much more precious than a rich man's, because so many are dependent upon him.

We have had a letter from America written by Longfellow's bedside. He will not lose the use of his hands, though he will be some time before he regains their use. His wife was burned by putting her foot on a lighted match.

Mr. Procter is wonderfully well. He is out by the seaside nearly all day. We have a good large house, excellently furnished, and lent us by Sir F. Goldschmidt. My love to Mrs. Milnes.

Your affectionate old friend,
ANNE B. PROCTER.

R. M. M. to C. J. MacCarthy.

House of Commons, June 25th, 1861.

DEAR FRIEND,—My still small voice is hardly audible in the tumult of the season and the world, and have we not scoffed at the leading articles which unwise men write to one another from different ends of the earth? We to-day are all full of the Chancellor's death,* and the odds as to his successor. Yesterday it was the great fire which has eaten up half the warehouses, and set (literally) the Thames on fire with tallow and turpentine. Last week it was the death of the great Cavour, the better Machiavel, for whom I said something that became notorious, and I have to subscribe £5 to his monument as a reward. Then that wretched America! Do you remember how all the world scoffed at the Arrowsmith hoax? What are railways in Georgia doing now? I am indefeasibly Northern, mainly from the abominable selfishness of the South in breaking up a great country. I am delighted to hear of Miss Hawes's marriage; she will make an admirable wife to any man. Your boy comes to us on the 20th, to stay till the end of his holidays. We are quite annoyed at not being able to have him before; I will write you an impartial judgment of him. I have a melancholy letter from —— in Australia. Did you carry out your intention of offering him employment in Ceylon? I can't, for the life of

* Lord Campbell.

me, understand his enforced idleness in that busy hive of mankind. I have seen little of the Duke of Newcastle lately. I have implored him to send you a reasonable creature as a bishop, and offered him one or two suggestions, which he probably will not in the least attend to. My wife is so sick and coughy that I sent her to Tunbridge Wells about a month ago. The children are with her, recovering.

I am yours affectionately,
R. M. M.

Best regards to Her Excellency.

MacCarthy's son visited Milnes, and the latter writes to his father, discussing the youth's qualities, commending his character and temperament, and promising to test his acquirements, especially in the classics, before he leaves Fryston.

R. M. M. to C. J. MacCarthy.

Fryston, August 5th, 1861.

DEAR FRIEND,— We have had nothing but tragic events. That Baron Vidil, whom we met at Spencer Cowper's; Major Murray and Roberts; and Sir Robert Peel's appointment to Ireland—the last, to my mind, much the most frightful of the three. It is tantamount to a dissolution of the Government, and Palmerston would not have dared to do it at any time but at the end of the Session. Sidney Herbert's death is a private sorrow to me; for though he only liked me in a Platonic sort of way, I had an old and deep affection for him. He was just the man to rule England—birth, wealth, grace, tact, and not too much principle. I have had some symptoms of a milder form of the same malady myself lately, which has, perhaps, increased my interest in him. I have a benefit next week; Burton, whom the Indian Government have turned off brutally because he accepted the Consulship of Fernando Po, comes with his wife. I go to Scotland next month, to see Mr. Ellice in the Highlands; and Mrs. M. and the children to Crewe. The country is looking well, but there is a singular absence of sunshine; and there are rumours of a serious disease among the potatoes in Ireland, where an immense breadth has been planted. That island will never be secure till the growth of that vegetable is made a misdemeanour. Colvile, for some reason or other, curiously avoids all his old friends. Our children are all well, and enjoy ponying and donkeying about this place. I am busy with an article on my French double, De Tocqueville, for the *Quarterly*.

With all regards,
Yours ever,
R. M. M.

T. Carlyle to R. M. M.

Thurso Castle, Thurso, N.B., August 7th, 1861.

DEAR MILNES,—I quitted London a week ago, *nolens volens*, things being very bad with me; and I received your hospitable note *here* (looking out upon the precipitous cliffs of Orkney, Dunnet's Head, the Old Man of Hoy, the Northern Ocean, and *Ultima thule*), already in slightly improved circumstances—able to sleep for one thing, the billows and the winds rocking me. Sir George Sinclair (excellent pious old gentleman), on hearing of "Mr. Milnes," wishes much "Mr. Milnes would come and join you here for a few weeks"—a most devout imagination. My wife is still in Chelsea, uncertain whether I shall be able to persuade her into Scotland at all, much more *hither* (600 and more miles away), though she, too, if she would own it, has much need of the country. If on my or our return, which is as yet quite dateless, I pass within wind of Fryston, doubt not I shall be right glad to see it again, in the name of the past and of the future—of the former, at any rate. Ah me!

Are you not a shocking fellow never to ask once this year whether I was alive or dead, or whether the devils had left me in a dog's likeness or a man's?—for shame! However, you can do nothing to provoke me utterly; and I must love R. M. actually more or less as I do no other or hardly one, however he may deserve.

With many regards to the honourable lady and to the two bairns, Yours ever truly,

T. CARLYLE.

R. M. M. to Lady Galway.

Oct. 31st, 1861.

The Blind Asylum Meeting at York went off very well yesterday. The two chief oratorical incidents were my allusion to Goethe, in which they declared I quoted " the dying words of the greatest of living poets," and Childers's illustration of the merits of blind men, as shown in Homer, Milton, and Mr. Foljambe—especially the latter   I think my article on De Tocqueville the best thing I have ever written. The editor has mauled it a little. I am busy with an article on Burton and Polygamy. Can you give me any information on the subject?

Your affectionate

R. M. M.

R. M. M. to C. J. MacCarthy.

Cambridge, Dec. 21st, 1861.

Prince Albert's death is a national tragedy. The peasants in their cottages talk as if the Queen was one of themselves. It is the realest public sorrow I have ever seen—quite different from anything else. The Queen is very resigned at present, but no one can tell what it will be when the lonely and responsible daily life comes on her. She has never done a thing alone in her life. It is like beginning to reign again, and without Lord Melbourne. Then Lady Canning! Mrs. Milnes was saying this would affect you more than the other. All your little preparations and expectancies so sadly frustrated.

Palmerston was so shocked with Prince Albert's death that we hourly expected to hear he had had a paralytic stroke; but he has got over the first impression, and will go on for a space of time longer. Your mother wrote to me a few days ago, asking me to do something for ———. I hear he is now with you. His story is very sad, but I own I don't understand his inability to win an independence in Australia. We talked about this before; but I can say no more than that I do not see my way to serving him here. Every day public life is becoming more a matter of regular routine, and you can no more get a man a competent place in the Public Service than in the Army. You have only ended at Ceylon by beginning at Turk's Island. We are to know next week whether we are at war or not. I believe the Americans must give in. The real difficulty will be to get Mason and Slidell away alive. Do you ever hear of your friend the Chinese Ambassador, who has joined the rebels; and were you not surprised at his doing so? I never see or hear of Colvile. It is rather odd that a man should ask you to write to him in India for some sixteen years, and never come near you when he is in England. I looked after him for some time; but there was so little inclination on his part that I shall quietly let him go, more regretting his wife than himself. I came up here to see about getting Palmerston made successor to the Prince in the Chancellorship, but he declines the honour.

With best regards to your wife,

I am yours ever,

R. M. M.

With regard to the Mason-Slidell affair, which so nearly involved this country in war with the United States, the reader will remember that it was when staying at Fryston that Mr. Adams, the American Minister, first received news of the capture, on an English mail steamer, of the Confederate envoys.

R. M. M. to C. J. MacCarthy.

Crewe Hall, Jan. 20th, 1862.

DEAR FRIEND,—A happy New Year to you, and a happier one than the last to the world in general. Prince Albert's death has been a great affliction to us all   I have a letter from Hawthorne, the author of "The Scarlet Letter," from Boston, in which he says that he "could not have conceived anything so delightful as civil war," and deeply regrets that his youth was cast in a quiet time   "Who cares," he adds, "about the amount of blood and treasure? Men must die, even if not pierced by bullets; and gunpowder is the most exciting of luxuries. Emerson breathes slaughter as fiercely as any of us." If this is the literary tone of the United States, what must be the rowdy? I think them all right, but I am in a minority of two or three, the House of Commons and society being all Southern. Mrs. Slidell declares that Wilkes told her at the Havannah that he was so disgusted with the Northern cause that if it had not been for his dressing-box, with all his silver things in it, being on board the *Saint Jacinto*, he would cut the concern altogether and go to England with them in the *Trent*. She says Wilkes is now said to go about New York like a "wilted peacock." This is the expression of the American papers themselves. I hear —— is with you. I shall be very glad if you could, out of your own success, do something to mitigate his defeat. I daresay it is his own fault; but that always seems to me so much worse than his own misfortune.

I have not been very well lately, and very easily fall into bad health; but I don't know that I have much to live for. It is unlikely that I should do much more, or gain much more, in life, and one may lose.

You will have read my "Tocqueville" in the *Quarterly,* and can now read my "Burton" in the *Edinburgh,* which is amusing enough. I think the book itself delightful. I have a letter from the Hadji from the "Brass River," setting forth the admiration he has excited among the faithful, who look on him as a Ulema, expressing his conviction that the conversion of

Africa to Islam and the uprooting of the Kaffir missionaries is the only hope of the future. He has asked for time to go and settle the King of Dahomey, which I fear will not be granted him. I wish I could have inserted all Burton's Mormon anecdotes; for example, one person saying to another, "Sir, if you were Mr. Jesus Christ, or Mr. Joseph Smith himself sitting there, with your halo hanging above your head, I would pull your nose at any rate." But this, alas! the respectability of the *Edinburgh Review* would not allow.

With our best regards to Lady MacCarthy,

Yours ever,

R. M. M.

R. M. M. to George von Bunsen.

16, *Upper Brook Street, Feb. 6th*, 1862.

MY DEAR GEORGE,—I send you my article on the Mormons, and thank you much for your information. The editor did not wish me to go into the polygamic question as much as I should have liked to do. I cannot understand by what right the Rabbis undertook to alter the traditionary laws and customs of their people, though they may have reasonably thought monogamy expedient. I enclose you a letter from our friend MacCarthy, which you will be glad to receive. Parliament meets to-day, with no great prospect of change of any kind. The feeling about America is intensely Southern, and I, with my Northern sympathies, remain in greater isolation than ever. The manufacturing districts are behaving very well, doing nothing to urge the Government to break the blockade, feeling, I suspect, that it is by no means certain whether the further complications which would be induced might not make things still worse. There is a very true feeling of regret among all politicians for Prince Albert's death; it is they who will be the real sufferers. He was of inestimable value as an intermediary person between the Ministers and the Queen. . . . The work of English Ministers was hard enough before; it will now be most grievous. The Court are set on marrying the Prince of Wales as soon as possible. Do you know anything of this Danish princess? and how is it that the Princess Royal urges this marriage?

Mrs. Milnes and the children are well at Crewe, and do not come to town at present. Pray remember me to Brandis when you write.* I got quite fond of him, and hope he will not forget me. Lord Palmerston is very well at present, but he had a severe shock and warning. Please write about yourself; you know how I like your letters, however short.

Among the many minor services which Milnes was constantly asked to render men of letters, was the promotion of their candidature for various clubs to which he belonged, and more particularly the Athenæum. One of those whom he assisted in this matter was Mr. Browning.

Robert Browning to R. M. M.

October, 1861.

MY DEAR MILNES,—True thanks for your kindness and considerateness, and those of Mrs. Milnes. I wish I could profit by your invitation, but there must be no more travelling for me or the boy this year. I am wanting to get him into the steady way of life and work, which our unsettled habits of late have sadly disturbed. We "go no more a-roving," you are to know; and be sure that, if you care at all about seeing me from time to time, it will be a very pleasant thing for me to look on to, through the cold days coming or come.

By the way, I will mention a thing now to save trouble: on arriving here, friends (Twisleton for one) suggested that I should be introduced to the Athenæum by the expeditious method. "There will be no difficulty," he flatteringly says, proposing to second another man who is to put me forward—and then follows the committee's part. Looking over the names in it, among a few known to me, yours struck us both as the friendliest and

---

* Johannes Brandis, the Queen of Prussia's private secretary, and well known as a pioneer in Assyriology.

most efficacious. How do you say? Nothing that can vex me, certainly, though much that gratifies me always—witness your invitation, which again thanking you and Mrs. Milnes for, believe me   Yours faithfully ever,

ROBERT BROWNING.

Robert Browning to R. M. M.

February, 1862.

MY DEAR MILNES,—I want extremely to see you, to thank you for the prosperous issue of the Athenæum business, and for other kindnesses. Next Saturday, however, I am going to Paris (for just a week). If anything keeps me a day or two longer here, pray let me write a word on Friday, and so save the pleasure I must otherwise forego, or look forward to on some later occasion.   Ever yours faithfully,

ROBERT BROWNING.

Wilkie Collins to Mrs. Milnes.

12, *Harley Street, W., May* 17*th,* 1862.

DEAR MRS. MILNES,—I have always had a foreign tendency to believe in *Fate.* That tendency has now settled into a conviction. Fate sits on the doorstep at 16, Upper Brook Street, and allows all your guests the happiness of accepting your hospitality with the one miserable exception of the Doomed Man who writes this letter. When your kindness opened the door to me on the occasion of your "At Home," Fate closed it again, using as the instrument of exclusion a neuralgic attack in my head. Quinine and patience help me to get the better of this, and Mrs. Milnes (with an indulgence which I am penitently conscious of not having deserved) offers me a second chance. Fate, working with a postman for an instrument on this occasion, sends me a dinner invitation for Thursday, the 22nd, one day before I receive Mrs. Milnes's kind note. No guardian angel warns me to pause. I accept the invitation, and find myself engaged to dine on the

22nd, *not* in London, for I might then have asked permission to come to Brook Street in the evening, but at Richmond, where there is no help for me.

I think this "plain statement" really makes out my case. I have not the audacity to ask you to accept my apologies. My aspirations are limited to presenting myself as a fit object for your compassion. The ancients, in any emergency, were accustomed to mollify Fate by a sacrifice. I am quite ready to try the experiment. If I presented myself on the doorstep of your house with a portable altar, a toga, a live sheep, and a sacrificial knife, would it be convenient? I fear not. A crowd might collect; the Animals' Protection Society might interfere at the moment of divination, and Mr. Milnes might be subjected to annoying inquiries in the House of Commons. My only resource left is to ask you to exercise the Christian privilege of forgiveness, and to assure you that I deserve it, by being really, and not as a figure of speech, very sorry.

Believe me, very truly yours,
WILKIE COLLINS.

Charles Dickens to Mrs. Milnes.

Gad's Hill Place, Higham-by-Rochester, Kent,
Friday, 18th July, 1862.

MY DEAR MRS. MILNES,—I think the photograph of your charming labour of love proves the Cricket comes out exceedingly well, though it does not render full justice to the beauty and delicacy of your design. It is highly interesting to me to have it, and I thank you for it heartily.

Pray convey my kind regards to Milnes. I am exceedingly sorry to hear of his being ill.

I am glad you liked "Copperfield." It is far more interesting to me than any of the other Readings, and I am half-ashamed to confess, even to you, what a tenderness I have for it.

Believe me, always,
Faithfully yours,
CHARLES DICKENS.

During the summer of this year, 1862, Milnes suffered from a severe illness, which at one time caused serious anxiety to his family and friends. For some time he was quite unable to keep up his correspondence with his friends; but a sojourn at Buxton in the autumn did him good, and he again took up his pen.

R. M. M. to his Sister.
Stanley in Peak, Bakewell, Aug. 21st, 1862.

DEAREST HARRIETTE,—When Annabel was well at Crewe I became my own master, and ran away here, and am all the better for the change. T. drives me about all day, and Mrs. T. quite reminds me of her mother. The place is 750 feet above the level of the sea, only 200 lower than Buxton. Mrs. T. says she is a walking mausoleum—so many families end in her, the Milneses of Derbyshire among them. I return to Buxton on Monday. I left Alfred Tennyson in our rooms at the hotel; he is strictly *incognito*, and known by everybody except T., who asked him if he was a Southerner, assuming that he was an American. I don't want to stay above another fortnight at Buxton; they won't let me drink, and I don't think the baths have done more than clean me outside.

Your affectionate
R. M. M.

Buxton, Aug. 27, 1862.
To his Elder Daughter.

DEAREST AMY,— . . . I was none the worse for my visit to Mr. Thornbill's—not your Thornhill's, but people who have no children, and make up for it by having a quantity of dogs and other pets instead. There was one little dog which could lie in a finger-glass after dinner. I dined downstairs after seven o'clock like a gentleman, but was obliged to refuse the champagne, which looked very nice and creamy, and was not, I believe, at all unwholesome. There is no objection to your going to church, except that you may give your cough to both the congregation and the clergyman, as I fancy you are now just as much in quarantine (find out what that is) as ever, and it would disturb the order of things if he was to set up a whoop in the pulpit. I am glad you have left off your supper. Perhaps Aunt Jane will give up her five o'clock tea next. I am all for people eating only twice a day—at noon and at sunset. These are the natural times for food; the old Romans, all the Eastern peoples, and, indeed, most of the European ones except the English, live this way.

Mr. Palgrave has been here for a third time with Mr. Tennyson, who did not like to be known, as people stared at him so much, which was no wonder, as he wore an immense broad hat and a beard.

Your affectionate
R. M. M.

Lady Palmerston to R. M. M.

Piccadilly, Sept. 7th, 1862.

DEAR MR. MILNES,—I was delighted to receive your letter, and to hear that you are better. I would have answered directly; but your letter found me on a tour of hard labour, something like the treadmill, and I was so fatigued every day, with talking and walking, inspecting farms and fields and mines, making the agreeable, and listening to all the various conflicting reports on the same subject, that I was quite worn out. You should know that I had not looked over these Scotland estates for nine years, so you may believe how much I had to do and to settle of my private affairs, beside all the glorification and popularity of Palmerston, which burst out on every opportunity, and added very much to our labours. However, the fourteen days' work being over, we have returned now, to be quiet a few days in London, and feel very much pleased at all we have settled and done. Next Saturday we settle at Broadlands, and shall be very happy to see you and Mrs. Milnes whenever you can come to us; but don't hurry away from Buxton as long as you find that the waters are doing you good, for health is the first object, and you must look on a Bath residence as a necessary evil to be endured.

Lord Dufferin's marriage is announced with a Miss Hamilton, a neighbour of his in Ireland—a pleasant girl, who came to town for a short time last year. The Prince of Wales's marriage seems also to be in a fair train, and everybody says she is charming. I like the idea of a Danish connection; we have had too much of Germany, and Berlin, and Coburgs, and this is returning to our old friends and a few honest people. There are but few aristocracy in town, and P. and I go to the Exhibition constantly. However, we have foreigners everywhere; Olizaga dines with us to-day, and Ricasoli to-morrow. We are all sorry for Garibaldi, but he has no sense or judgment.

E. PALMERSTON.

R. M. M. to C. J. MacCarthy.

Leighhurst, Sept. 17th, 1862.

DEAR FRIEND,—I now write with sufficient ease to give you a letter with my own hand, and, I believe, not more illegible than when I write with facility. The gout still hangs about me; the fire is quenched, but I have the ashes in both arms and legs, impeding exercise, and necessitating physic. The baths at Buxton did not, I think, do me material good; but five weeks of high pure air and temperate life have been of decided use to me. I am now paying some visits, to get out of the pleasant habits of invalid life and recognised idleness. I go to London next week, to have ten days of the Exhibition before I settle in the country. I was the head of a jury before I was ill, and thus saw nothing but an uninteresting department. The whole thing is inferior in every way to the Exhibition of 1851, and you need little regret not having seen it. After London, I settle in Yorkshire for some quiet months, and get through the cold winter as well as I may. This is Mr. Nightingale's house in Derbyshire. The dear heroine is very ill, and will never see these fair hillsides and terraced gardens again.* Your short

---

* A prediction most happily falsified by the event.

notice of your own illness made me tremble; it is quite wonderful to see that, with your plethoric habit, and your small prudence, and your disrespect for medicine, you are still alive in a hot climate. The Americans told ——, " Sir, we are a recuperative people" (they need it now, poor fellows!); so one looks on you as a recuperative friend and governor. Mrs. Milnes has to thank Lady MacCarthy for an amusing letter, for which she returns all thanks. You tell me you are to have your railroad; but I had always looked on you as the opponent of the said rail, and the demonstrator of its infallible bankruptcy. I had heard before of your favour at the Colonial Office, and don't doubt you may become the sweetest of modern insects, if you desire it. With Layard's assistance, I have got a very fair reform of the Diplomatic Service, the regulations of which you will see in the *Gazette*. Lord Russell did not take much interest in it. As to general politics, you know as much as I do. The Garibaldi folly has ended very well; and the Italians are showing that unenthusiastic, ungrateful, practical sense which renders them so capable of politics and fit for freedom. They have all something of the great Florentine about them. Lord Palmerston's digestion is excellent, and thus England is comfortable in the midst of the cotton famine, which only starves a few thousand operatives, who are patiently passing away. . . .

I remain yours affectionately,

R. M. M.

Mrs. Procter to R. M. M.

10, *Adelaide Crescent, Brighton, Sept. 20th*, 1862.

MY DEAR MR. MILNES,—I rejoice to see your handwriting once more. It was very kind of you to write to me. Having once begun, you may perhaps write a book, and your walking powers may enable you to join the Alpine Club. Adelaide* sends us better accounts of herself; and, whilst reading her letters, a bath appears the pleasant thing, and to be packed—

* Adelaide Anne Procter, the gifted poetess, at this time staying at Malvern.

Elysium. She is at Holyrood—the ladies' house. Hume, the conjurer (?) or cheat (?), is on a visit with Dr. Gully—very poorly, and having, for the present, lost his power. I should like to come to Fryston very much indeed; we stay here until the middle of October. Perhaps between that time and the 1st of December I shall hear from you and Mrs. Milnes what time will suit you. Mrs. Fanny Kemble is here. Should you encounter her, do not speak of America; she cried so terribly on Thursday, upon my husband speaking of the subject. She says the women are working during the night at the harvest, the men all gone as soldiers, and the heat being too great to work during the day. My love to Mrs. Milnes.

Yours,

ANNE B. PROCTER.

R. M. M. to C. J. MacCarthy.

Fryston, Oct. 24th, 1862.

DEAR FRIEND,—I am getting better slowly, but am not yet returned to my former activity. Illness is a charming excuser of business and busy pleasure. If I were my own master, I would throw myself into the railway, and not stop until I got to Colombo; but I am not ill enough for that, though I may be perhaps next year. Your Hindoo barrister has called often in Upper Brook Street, but has never left any address. I should have liked of all things to have had him in the country, and shown him something of British home-life; but he has left no indication by which I can trace him. We are going on very well domestically, the children recovering fast from the whooping-cough, and in good progress of mind and body. The second little girl has developed into a verse-writer of a very curious ability. She began theologically and wrote hymns, which I soon checked on observing that she put together words and sentences out of the sacred verse she knew; and set her to write about things she saw and observed. What she now produces is very like the verse of William Blake, and containing many images that she could never have read of. She cannot write, but she dictates them to her elder sister, who is astonished at the phenomenon. We, of course, do not let her see that it is anything surprising; and the chances are that it goes off as she gets older and knows more. The lyrical faculty in men and nations seems to belong to a childish condition of mind, and to disappear with experience and knowledge. The distress in the cotton districts is frightful, and is a sad example of the want of prevision in the wealth-makers of England. Even now I don't understand why British capital has not run off with all the Indian cotton, and left the Hindoos naked. The deficiency in carriage is no answer, for there so much is carried on men's backs, it only wants money to get more brought down to the sea. The manufacturers, for their part, have no notion of being ruined, as well as their artisans. They have made their own wealth, not inherited it; and have no notion of looking on it as a trust, but as their own, which they can do what they like with. It will thus require very fine language indeed to get much out of their pockets, and I doubt whether even Gladstone could do it. For my part, I see no gleam of good in anything American. The lower civilisation, as represented by the South, is much braver and cunninger and daringer than the cultivated shopkeeper of the North. It is just as if the younger sons of the Irish and Scotch nobility were turned loose against the *bourgeoisie* of Leeds. They would kill the men, and run away with the women, and fire the houses before the respectables knew where they were, or had learned the goose-step. And then the rebels will found such a jolly republic, with little work, and plenty of quadroons, and everything pleasant. I shall not be surprised to see the slave-trade going briskly before you and I retire. It is quite curious to see how the old Clarksonian feeling has weakened in England among all the genteel classes. I hear that the Colonial Office intend making you an example of a self-supporting dependency. If you do this, it must be understood that you are to be rewarded for the unenviable distinction.

Yours affectionately,

R. M. M.

The Hindoo barrister to whom reference was made in the foregoing letter was Mr. Coomara Samy, a member of the Legislative Council of Ceylon, of good family, broad education, and great intelligence. He was at this time on a visit to England. Milnes received him, as he had received so many other strangers and visitors from a distance; and he was, for some time, an honoured guest at Fryston. Milnes's son and daughters still retain the pleasantest recollections of the accomplished Hindoo who was their father's guest in their early days. It happened that during his first visit to Yorkshire Mr. Coomara Samy suffered from a very serious illness, which at one time threatened his life, and through which he was assiduously nursed by the family at Fryston. A lively recollection is still retained of the anxiety which Milnes showed at the time when Mr. Coomara Samy was at the worst. He had given his guest a promise that if the illness from which he was suffering ended fatally he should not be buried in the English fashion, but should be cremated. Those who knew Lord Houghton will understand how, having given that promise, he was eager to prepare for its fulfilment should the necessity unhappily arise; and a legend is still extant of the way in which he wandered about the broad domains and the umbrageous woods at Fryston, until he had at last fixed upon a spot which was, in his opinion, entirely suited to what would have been the first cremation on English soil in modern times. Fortunately for the object of these delicate attentions the good nursing at Fryston proved effectual, saving him from the fate to which he had been dedicated. No one, it need hardly be said, rejoiced more heartily than Milnes at the recovery of his interesting friend, but mingled with his rejoicing was a droll sense of disappointment at the thought of the distinction which had been lost to Fryston for ever.

Mr. Coomara Samy to R. M. M.

London, Dec. 12th, 1862.

MY DEAR SIR,—Since I wrote to Mrs. Milnes yesterday I have received your note. Many thanks for your kind inquiries. I would have written earlier, but I thought I had better wait till I got quite well. I am quite recovered now. Tender, please, my thanks to those friends whom I met at your home, and who were kind enough to inquire of me. I hope to have the opportunity of seeing some of them in London, where I shall remain for some time yet. The weather has been bright and glorious for the last few days—at least, in this part of London. You showed me all the attention you could have possibly shown me; you could not have given me strength and health, and I was unlucky in having lost them just when I wanted them most. It is not the cold either of your country that affected me, for I never felt the cold in your house; but it was the fearful exertion (fearful to me, who lead a very easy life) which I had to go through in knocking about London to see this Bencher and that Bencher of Lincoln's Inn, that began to tell upon me when I visited you. Complete rest—not the Nirwana—and a little quinine have restored my spirits and my health. In my anxiety to combine the *utile* with the *dulce* (as the Venetian bard suggests it) during my trip to Europe, I fear I had overdone myself. I intend to take things more easily, and await the issue of events more philosophically. But I fear I fatigue you with irrelevant matter.

I am yours very truly,
M. COOMARA SAMY.

The Same to the Same.

The Grand Hotel, Paris, Aug. 19*th*, 1864.

I am now here on my way to the East, and I think it my duty, before I travel further from the shores of England, to write and thank you for the great kindness which you showed me during my sojourn in your country. I say, in all sincerity, that, but for my having had the rare fortune to know you, and, through you, other kind friends, my stay in England, which I had originally intended to last only six months, would not have extended to upwards of two years, as it has. I now long for the day when I can revisit it, and see you all again

Yours sincerely,
M. COOMARA SAMY.

Mr. Coomara Samy went back to Ceylon, eventually attained high rank in the service of the Government in that island, receiving the honour of knighthood, and died at Colombo in 1879. In the interval between his first sojourn and his death he visited England on several occasions, always to be received with hospitality by Milnes, who derived from his friendship a new pleasure, finding in him a link between the Western world, with which he was so familiar, and the thought and feeling of the far East, which he had hitherto known only through books.

R. M. M. to C. J. MacCarthy.

Crewe Hall, Jan. 23*rd*, 1863.

DEAR FRIEND,—You will see, by this mail, the report that I am likely to be turned into a lord. Nothing is decided; but it is not impossible the offer will be made to me on the occasion of the Prince's marriage; and though it connects itself closely with ideas of superannuation and exile after my long residence and work in the House of Commons, yet, I suppose, for what people call family reasons, I shall accept it. In this lord-loving country, one ought not to decline anything that helps to make other people listen to one. But, on the whole, I look on it as the token of a half-success in life—a second-class in politics. We have been much interested in your friend Coomara Samy. He came to Fryston to stay some time, but his visit was cut short by illness. There was nothing serious about it, though I did think of the embarrassment of his dying in the house, and of the difficulty of burying him. He was so sorry for himself that it made every one sorry for him; and there was the continual danger that the servants might surreptitiously substitute the abomination of beef-tea for the mutton-broth on which, with port-wine, he mainly lived. He recovered soon after his return to London, and afterwards went to Serlby, which he enjoyed very much, to the extent of going out with the hounds and dancing a quadrille. There seems, too, a good hope of his getting his admission to the English Bar, the meaning of which I take to be a seat on the Bench at Ceylon. We all liked him. We are all well here. The gout still hampers and cripples me, to the extent of not letting me do much of anything, which is odious to a hater of mediocrity. I should have gone to Nice with Lord Ashburton; but he was taken ill at Paris, and for the last three months has been battling for dear life. How do you like your new Bishop? I pressed on the Duke the importance of giving you a pleasant playfellow.

Yours affectionately,
R. M. M.

CHAPTER XIV

THE PEERAGE.

Rumours of the Peerage—Marriage of Prince of Wales—Illness of Lord Ashburton—Mrs. Carlyle—Milnes raised to the Peerage—Comments of the Press—Speech to his Constituents—Congratulations—Landor's Last Letter Thackeray—His Affection for Milnes—His Death—Carlyle's Last Sight of Thackeray—"A Literary Squabble."

THE elevation of Mr. Milnes to the peerage did not take place quite so soon as he had anticipated in the letter to MacCarthy, with which the preceding chapter closes. The offer of a barony came to him spontaneously from Lord Palmerston, who had always been his friend, and had been quite willing, at the time of Mr. Pemberton Milnes's refusal of the honour, to transfer it to the son. But for various reasons Milnes's actual elevation did not take place until the summer of 1863. The rumour of his coming dignity had, however, got into print, and he was naturally the recipient of many letters, congratulatory and otherwise, upon the subject.

Extracts from Letters to his Wife.

January, 1863.

I enclose you two anonymous letters, the one respecting the name, I suspect, from the ——'s. It is clearly from some one who knows nothing personally about me, or that the Monckton name comes from the Galways. The rumour now is, that someone told the Queen the promotions and honours on the Prince's marriage should not be of a party or political character, as the effect of it would be to identify him with their politics. With my usual fairness, I see something in this. There is to be a black drawing-room in February, held by the Princess of Prussia, and a *demi-deuil* one after the marriage. The Queen sent Sir Henry Holland yesterday the Prince's speeches, "from his broken-hearted widow," in her own hand. I went last night to Cardinal Wiseman's lecture at the Royal Institution. It was deplorable—an hour and three-quarters of verbiage, without a fresh thought of any kind. As I heard him lecture twenty-eight years ago, I am a tolerable judge of his style. I go to Mentmore this afternoon.

Mentmore, Leighton Buzzard, Feb. 1st.

Alas, Lord Lansdowne !* Streleczki was walking with him when he fell, and picked him up, but did not think him seriously hurt. I pay the penalty of having lived with those much older than myself, in seeing them drop around me. Robin won't know one of his father's friends. The Baroness [Rothschild] has had a sharp attack of sore throat, but is getting better; so I return to-morrow, and come back next Saturday to meet the Dudley Carletons. Where has this wonderful piece of wit been lying since I said it to J. five years ago? [Enclosure, a newspaper cutting.]

"Shortly after the annexation of Nice and Savoy a member of the French Embassy, on his way to the refreshment-room at Apsley House, said, 'Je vais prendre quelque chose' ('I am going to take something'), to which a political and literary friend, said to be Monckton Milnes, tartly rejoined, 'It is a custom of your country.'"

February 12th.

. . . I met the Dudley Carletons at Mentmore. In conversation, I mentioned a house (Sir B. Heywood's) where the

---

* Lord Lansdowne, whose seizure is referred to by Milnes, lived until 1866.

adies always got up by candlelight in the winter "What a delightful house!" said Mrs. D. C.; "how I should like to know them!" She thought it was the candlelight in the afternoon.

"I begin to think Palmerston is quite right, and that I was never meant to be a statesman," is the lament which Milnes utters, in acknowledging to his wife that he had not been altogether successful in organising a family expedition to witness the landing of the Princess Alexandra in this country, on the eve of her marriage to the Prince of Wales; but he consoles himself somewhat later with the reflection that, after all, his wife had not suffered so severely as another distinguished lady had done, who, when riding beside her husband on the night of the illuminations, had her dress set on fire by a light thrown into the carriage by someone in the crowd. The husband was one of the most distinguished of English prelates, and Milnes suggested that the perpetrator of the deed must have been an African bishop.

Immediately after the Royal marriage festivities, Milnes went to Paris to pay a visit to Lord Ashburton. Unfortunately, he arrived just as Lord Ashburton was seized with a very serious illness, and the pleasure of his visit was, consequently, greatly diminished; but, as usual, he found something to do, and something kind. His old friend Rio was, he learned, in some distress, owing to the withdrawal of the pension he had hitherto received from the Government; and he immediately set himself to work to secure its restoration, using his influence with Prince Napoleon for that purpose, although he felt compelled to hold aloof from the Emperor, whose share in the *coup d'état* he could not forget.

It had been his wish to entertain the Carlyles, Thackeray, and Spedding at Fryston during the Easter recess. The two latter came, this being the last occasion on which Thackeray stayed under the roof of his old friend. But Carlyle was deep in his "Frederick," and sternly withstood the temptation which was held out to him.

Mrs. Carlyle to R. M. M.

Cheyne Row, March 19*th.*

MY DEAR MR. MILNES,—It is no go! I was a fool to hope that anything so pleasant could get carried out, and the ghost of that old Prussian despot still unlaid. I have introduced the subject at every least inauspicious moment presenting itself since the night you were here, but every time with more determined ill-success.

"It is such a distance!" "Well, what of an hour or two longer on the road when we are once started?" "Oh! very easy for *you* to say that, who rather like railway travelling; but for me, who hate it, a-bo-minate it, am driven *perfectly mad* by it, etc., etc., etc." And, in short, he thinks to give a week of his time at Easter, for the good of his health and the assuagement of his soul, would be a sort of schoolboy truant-playing unworthy of a historian! And so God help him! And God particularly help *me!* For (in the words of an Annandale poet not sufficiently known to fame)

"I'm a poor luckless cretur;
And if I were *ded*,
And a stone at my *hed*,
I think it would be *beter.*"

Yours affectionately anyhow,
JANE W. CARLYLE.

R. M. M. to C. J. MacCarthy.

London, April 25*th,* 1863.

DEAR FRIEND,—As your boy wrote to you by the last mail, I reserved myself for this. I have been so much in the country for the last month that of public matters I have little to say. I ran over to Paris to see Lord Ashburton, who gives some hope of recovery, but was still in a dangerous way. I found all my Orleanist friends discontented, as usual; but had a pleasant dinner at Prince Napoleon's, who always is agreeable, and who suggests to me very much the sort of half-ruffianly charm which the old Napoleon seems to have exercised. . . . You will be anxious to hear about Richard, and I can say that he is as gentlemanlike in his manners, and amiable in his temper as ever. Yours ever,

R. M. M.

The Same to the Same.

16, *Upper Brook Street, June* 25*th,* 1863.

MY DEAR FRIEND,—Lady MacCarthy's interesting and cordial letter gave us much pleasure, and if I were my own master it is indisputable that you would see me at Ceylon this winter; and I went so far as to take my doctor's opinion on the subject. He reported decidedly against the project. I should never pay the least regard to this result, but unfortunately he told Mrs. M——, and she is in open opposition—at least, at present. Another year I have a project of taking the whole family abroad, and planting them somewhere on the Continent while I run over to you. This at present seems the only hopeful prospect of our meeting. It has been a dull and disagreeable season and Session. The great obstacle to social comfort are their Royal Highnesses, the Prince and Princess of Wales. They crowd the streets to look at her; they go to exclusive parties, making the uninvited sick with envy and wounded pride; they take away any notable you happen to have asked to dinner two days before the party was to have come off. . My own health is certainly improved. I find the use of the so-called

Turkish—and really Roman—baths very beneficial. They are a kind of artificial exercise without the bore of perpetual motion. I doubt their succeeding as a general practice in this country, from the length of time they take; and an Englishman does not think that he can spend two hours in this way, but wishes to misuse his time in some more busy idleness. Coomara Samy makes himself so pleasant, and is so fresh in his notions of things, that he will be quite a loss to us; he interests everybody about him. If his health allowed him to remain here, and plead in Indian cases before the Privy Council, he might make a real success. My children are all well, and the little boy becoming very amusing. He is quick to learn, and will not be a dunce, whatever else he may turn out. The Duke of Newcastle reigns quietly over his Office, and is buying estates and building houses as if he were as rich as Lord Overstone. . We are having scandalous trials in plenty to make up for the want of political excitement. My friend Christie again has got into great trouble at Rio, and is likely to be shelved altogether, more, I think, by Lord Russell's fault than his own. Reprisals seem to me a very foolish proceeding from a strong power to a weak one. It is like knocking down a child. The American affair gets worse, the French strongly pressing recognition of the South. I shall oppose it to the last, whether brought forward by this or any other Government. Poland also looks serious : the weakness of Russia is most tempting to France; a French army landed at Riga would march to Warsaw without a blow. The real difficulty is with the Poles themselves, who are as Oriental a people as the Russians, and cannot, I believe, ever act homogeneously with European nations. The only noticeable books are on Biblical criticism, a subject which you treat with profound contempt, but which pleases my captious intellect.

Yours affectionately,
R. M. M.

At the close of July the step which had long been in contemplation was taken, and Milnes was raised to the peerage under the title of Baron Houghton of Great Houghton. Great Houghton Hall, which is still in the possession of the family, was the old house of the Rodes's, through whom Milnes was able to trace his descent from one of the companions of the Conqueror. The reader has seen from a letter to MacCarthy, in which mention was made of his approaching elevation to the peerage, in what light Milnes regarded that event. He took it as the visible token of a "half success" in politics—a second-class in the school of life. But, with his keen perception of the conditions and factors of English society, he was well aware that the honour which he had attained would be regarded differently by others, and that many who had never cared to trouble themselves about the opinions of Monckton Milnes would listen to the utterances of Lord Houghton. We are a lord-loving country, as Milnes himself remarked to MacCarthy; and the cheery, warm-hearted cynic, whose philosophy had been founded upon the hard lessons of experience, was not at all indisposed to derive as much benefit as he could from our national weakness. Yet it must have been with a pang of real regret that Milnes left the House of Commons for the calmer atmosphere of the House of Lords. He had long since learned that in the stormy popular arena success could never fall to the lot of one with his special gifts and special failings. Perhaps in the Upper Chamber there would be more room for that kind of personal independence which was so dear to him, and which had always prevented him from being the mere tool of a party. But, conscious as he was of his own great powers, it must have been with deep sadness that he recognised the fact that the ambitions with which he had started on his public life had been disappointed, and that the path which he had sought to tread, and in which not a few who intellectually were vastly inferior to him had attained brilliant success, was closed to him for ever. It was only, however, in his own heart, or to his most intimate friends, that he made any revelation of his real feelings. The outer world saw him accept the dignity offered to him by the Queen with cheerfulness and alacrity. And those who knew him only on the surface would have been amazed if they had suspected, however dimly, that he took his peerage with any other feeling than one of self-complacency and self-satisfaction.

Among the many stories current in society regarding his sayings and doings, there is one which deserves to be repeated here. It was on the very morrow of the announcement of his elevation that, walking in Piccadilly, he met an old friend who was himself a commoner of high social distinction. The friend greeted Milnes under his new title, and jokingly asked what it felt like to be a lord. Milnes's eyes twinkled with irrepressible humour, as he made answer, "I never knew until to-day how immeasurable is the gulf which divides the humblest member of the peerage from the most exalted commoner in England." I venture to tell this story in spite of the warning given to me by one of the earliest and greatest of Milnes's friends. "If you tell that," said Lord Tennyson, "every fool will think that Milnes meant it." No one who really knew the man will fall into such a mistake, or will confound one of the most amusing examples of his love of paradox with his real sentiments.

The announcement that the Queen had called him to the House of Lords brought to the feet of Milnes a host of pleasant congratulations from old friends and comrades, as well as from many who knew him only through the little deeds of kindness which formed, as it were, the background of his career. It may not be amiss to quote the words of the *Times* in commenting upon the honour:—

The elevation of Mr. Monckton Milnes to the peerage, by the title of Baron Houghton [said that journal], will take no one by surprise. His name has more than once been designated for this honour by rumours of that kind which are officially called premature, and has been favourably received by the public. Few people would agree beforehand as to the precise theory upon which the ranks of our hereditary nobility should be recruited; but there is a sort of tacit understanding in high quarters, to which the country is more or less privy, which generally excludes unfit candidates, if it does not always secure the promotion of the worthiest. The popular text-books of our constitution inform us that the grand prize of hereditary nobility is reserved for the greatest ornaments of the House of Commons, the heads of the legal profession, and officers who have earned it by eminent achievements by land or sea. Practically we know that it is not so, and that individuals who have none of these titles in a transcendent degree sometimes find their way into the Upper House, and, what is more, prove very useful members of it. Here, as elsewhere, it is a combination of qualities which is in request; and the fortunate possessor of this combination not only wins favour and success, but frequently justifies it. This is exactly Mr. Monckton Milnes's case. To a high social position and sufficient wealth he unites an honourable literary reputation, a long political experience, and a good deal of that prestige which is the general result of recognised ability and character. In what may be called the secondary questions of politics, and in those political questions which are better discussed outside the House of Commons than within its walls, he has taken a very active and influential part. Until lately, there were few persons in England who felt so warm an interest in Continental politics, or who had anything like the same acquaintance with them; and very few indeed who had thought and written so much about such matters as national education, sanitary reform, and the treatment of criminals. These merits and accomplishments are not the elements of Parliamentary fame; but they are of great value in themselves, and certainly contribute to adorn a seat in the House of Lords. Mr. Milnes does not belong to the highest rank of poets or statesmen, or philanthropists or economists; but he is enrolled as a working member in all of these classes, and has done a greater amount of good service for the public than many more conspicuous men. To this, rather than to any claims upon the gratitude of the Liberal party, we must attribute the choice of the Premier. It has no political significance whatever. Mr. Monckton Milnes's temperament is not that of a partisan, and his seat has been too secure to make it necessary for him to profess uncompromising adhesion to any political leader. Perhaps his career has been as nearly independent as that of any of his contemporaries that can be named, and the difficulty of counting on his vote must have given successive whippers-in on both sides a good deal of trouble. When he was called a Liberal-Conservative, he never conformed to the traditional policy of Conservatism; and when he became a Conservative-Liberal, he was constantly rebelling against party discipline, and taking up some line of his own. When there was an open breach in the Liberal camp between the followers of Lord Russell and those of Lord Palmerston, Mr. Milnes sided with the latter; but when a fresh issue was raised on the Conspiracy Bill, he was found both speaking and voting against his late chief. In his subsequent conduct he has shown a similar insubordination, especially on the famous measure for the abolition of the East India Company. Opinions may well differ as to the wisdom of this course of action; but Mr. Milnes is at least entitled to the credit of it, as a proof that he does not owe his peerage to political subserviency. If he cannot be said to deserve it as Wellington or Brougham deserved it, he deserves it far better than most of the country gentlemen who have been ennobled by virtue of territorial influence.

It will, I think, strike most persons that the foregoing comments do not err on the side of extravagance. The remarks of the *Daily Telegraph* have a little more of warmth and colour:—

The last act of the Ministers [said that paper] before taking their Parliamentary holiday was to create two peers. One of them, Monckton Milnes, must not be passed over in silence, for he has long been one of the most generally popular men in England. He was one of the heroes of Young England in Disraeli's novel of "Coningsby;" few who now see him trotting along Birdcage Walk on his fat, iron-gray roan cob, would believe that he was ever one of the exquisites of the White Waistcoat party. But it is not his politics that have earned Lord Houghton his enviable position—nor his poetry, although he has written some songs everywhere popular—nor his wealth, which is sufficient—nor his taste in art and literature, which is far above the average; but it is the combination of all these with the most extraordinary geniality. Monckton Milnes had— perhaps, if the gout will let him, may have still—a kind word for every one, and a taste for everything. He has travelled everywhere, and fraternised with every nation; been up in a balloon, and down in a diving-bell; has seen everybody and everything extraordinary—Chartist orators, Carlist refugees, euphuistic poets, astonishing working-men; every one who had ever done anything, or written anything, or said anything extraordinary, was to be found at least once at his hospitable table. Nor was his kindness confined to words: artists and literary men of all countries always found him a real friend in need. We think, therefore, we can congratulate the peerage on its gain in a poet and a philosopher of the best kind.

This, rather than the estimate of the *Times*, was a correct representation of the popular conception of Milnes. Neither view, as the reader by this time probably understands, was wholly correct. There was both more and less in Milnes than the critics of the day believed. It was the fashion to exaggerate his eccentricities as well as his wealth, whilst it was no less distinctly the fashion to under-estimate his talents, and to ignore that vein of serious feeling which, as we have seen, ran steadily through all his actions.

In taking leave of the constituents he had so long represented in the House of Commons, he spoke with a gravity which certainly showed that he had never made light of his political duties and position.

I have been [he said], in more than a conventional sense, the representative of all of you, without distinction of political parties; and I have endeavoured, by moderation in my views, and by discretion in my public conduct, to express what I believe to be the sound convictions of the large majority of my constituents and the general opinion of the inhabitants of your district.

He went on to express his strong sense of gratitude for the manner in which his constituents had allowed him a personal independence rarely enjoyed by a member of Parliament. The old system of pocket boroughs—and in those days Pontefract was, to a certain extent, a borough of that kind—had the great advantage of enabling men like Milnes to hold their own in Parliament without committing themselves absolutely to any party tie. The old system, with its picturesqueness, its easy-going relations between member and constituency, and its freedom from the restraints of party organisation, has disappeared, never to be restored. We live under a more virtuous and a more rigorous *régime*. But even those who rejoice most in the triumph of the reforms which have changed the face of Parliament, may pay a tribute of regret to methods which, however indefensible in theory, were in practice productive of such admirable results.

Lord Houghton did not allow his connection with his old constituency to close with a formal written farewell. Later in the year he spoke at a dinner in the borough, and said some things which cannot be omitted from this record of his life.

Every man [he said] who comes to the time of life at which I have arrived must know pretty well what his own character is. I know, so far as mine is concerned, that I do not possess those gifts and talents which would, in the bustling career of public life as connected with large constituencies, have greatly recommended me to their favour. I have none of those natural gifts which enable a man to sway crowds to his command, and to hold dominion over the minds of multitudes. At the same time I am conscious of an inability (it may be a matter of praise in some people's minds and of dispraise in others) which, I think, would have very much injured me if I had represented a large constituency; I mean, the difficulty I have always had in believing my own side to be entirely in the right and other people entirely in the wrong. It has been said of some lawyers, of Lord Denman and Lord Thurlow, that for a fee of a few pounds they really did bring themselves to think that their side was absolutely right and the other side absolutely wrong. I never had that faculty, and, whatever may be the advantage to myself or my friends, I have never been able to throw myself into that full party spirit which, in a country like ours, is perhaps almost necessary for the prominent success of any public man. I remember Sir Thomas Freemantle, our whipper-in, in the House of Commons coming to me and saying, "Now, do try for once in your life to make a speech in which you are not going to be candid." I am not sure whether I succeeded, but at any rate I am perfectly conscious that this peculiarity of my mind, the inability to throw myself utterly and completely into any cause whatever, unfitted me for representing any constituency moved by large waves of popular passion, and excited into a condition of absolute confidence in themselves and absolute hatred of anyone else. I am very thankful that the condition of this borough has been such as to enable me to act with so much independence. That private independence even here has carried with it some advantages. I cannot forget that there was a period in our political history in which a change of the opinions of the leaders of my party—Sir Robert Peel's party—threw the whole of his followers into a position in which they were compelled to determine whether they would remain in an order and condition of thought which was then considered rather as a going backwards than otherwise, or whether they would join themselves to men who had hitherto been considered their political opponents. After due consideration I determined to take the latter course. I have never regretted that I did so, because I believe that politically it was the right course; but I am also conscious that there were circumstances connected with the course of events at that time which threw an aspect, I will not say of bad faith, but at least of dubious conduct, over a large portion of Sir Robert Peel's party.

After referring to the stand he had taken on the question of the Maynooth Grant, and the fact that it had led many of his constituents to withdraw their support from him, and after alluding to the growing dislike of country gentlemen to take their place in the House of Commons, Milnes continued—

In looking back, it is impossible for me not to remember the many forms of intelligence, youth, power, and strength with which I was familiar in my early days in Parliament, but which in the course of this time, though my own contemporaries, have passed away from among us, though not entirely from our memories. I cannot forget that the men whom I should have expected to meet in the House of Lords, to which the favour of Her Majesty has called me, would have been Lord Herbert, Lord Canning, Lord Dalhousie, Lord Elgin—men who have fallen in the service of their country as surely as if they had been shot down by the enemy's cannon in the battle-field. I also would not forget the name of one who is suffering at this moment under what I fear may be a mortal malady, the Duke of Newcastle, a statesman to whose ability, good sense, and judgment this country looked forward as likely to produce a great statesman in future times, when those old ones we now have shall have passed away.

Finally, the new peer offered to his old constituents a confession of his political faith for the future, of which it is only necessary to say that it was more advanced in its Liberalism than any which had previously fallen from his lips. No one who heard it could doubt that his transfer from the popular to the aristocratic House had strengthened rather than weakened his sympathies with the democratic element in society. Upon some subjects on which he touched he had long "thought apart." He had, for instance, been the consistent opponent of capital punishment; he had, in the face of ridicule and opposition of no ordinary kind, long advocated a reform in the treatment of juvenile offenders; whilst far in advance of his party he had urged the establishment of a really national system of education.

In 1846 I brought in a Bill (for the establishment of Reformatories) respecting which a very sensible member of Parliament said to me, "I think this is the most foolish Bill ever proposed." But that gentleman told me the other day he had completely changed his mind; and well he might, for almost every provision in that Bill is now the law of the land. Reformatories have been established in almost all the counties of this kingdom, and their effect has been utterly to break up those gangs of young thieves in the great towns, which were breeding, as it were, whole preserves of felons, and thus gradually to diminish the adult criminals of the country.

Milnes evidently felt, and with ample justification, that, after all, however barren of personal success his political career in the House of Commons might have been, it could not be regarded as a failure, seeing that he had been enabled to take so large a part in that movement of social life which, even during his lifetime, resulted in so marked a diminution in the crime of our country, and so distinct an improvement in the condition of the classes by which in former days that crime was fed.

His speech attracted considerable attention—more

attention, in fact, than most speeches of his had received when he was plain Monckton Milnes. Already he was enabled to reap some of the advantages of being a lord in a lord-loving country.

It is a happy speech [wrote one of his newspaper critics]—happy in critical language simply as a speech, but still happier as expressing the thoughts of a happy speaker. It is as bright as a handful of apple-blossoms, and as fragrant as a sprig of sweet-briar. There is nothing harsh in it—not a drop of rancour, nor even a whiff of violent emotion. Lord Houghton is a very agreeable man, and takes a very agreeable view of things; he himself would waive the notion of any personal merit on this score, and would perhaps confess that it would be a shame if it were otherwise. When Nature made him, she was in a rhythmical mood, and she has been constant to the last.

The writer, who can hardly have had any personal knowledge of the man of whom he wrote, went on to laud the brilliant success which Milnes had achieved in the battle of life, and to offer incense at the shrine of one who was at once "a peer, a poet, and in receipt of £20,000 a year."

It is not necessary, however, that I should impose upon my readers any longer extracts from an article to which I have merely referred as an evidence of the effect which Milnes's elevation to the peerage seemed to have upon a large section of society. There were congratulations less rhetorical, but not less welcome, from some of his old friends. Mrs. Procter expressed her feelings in verse:—

>   He enters from the common air
>   Into that temple dim;

> He learns among those ermined peers
>   The diplomatic hymn.
> His peers? Alas! when will they learn
>   To grow up peers to him?

Mr. Gladstone to R. M. M.

11, *Carlton House Terrace, S.W., July* 28*th*, 1863.

MY DEAR MILNES,—I cannot sign the appointment to the Chiltern Hundreds, which has to-day reached me, without a word, even though I write it partially in the dark. It is only to express a sincere regret on the close of the long period—over a quarter of a century—since we were first Members of Parliament together. If you are about to be removed to "another place," I sincerely hope you may derive satisfaction from the transfer, which, I believe, would be regarded by the public as a just tribute to your character and powers. The superior beings among whom you would then go could not have more pleasure in receiving you than we, your humble companions, have regret in losing you.

Believe me

Always most sincerely yours,

W. E. GLADSTONE.

The Bishop of St. David's to R. M. M.

Carmarthen, July 31*st*, 1863.

MY DEAR MILNES,—It is rather melancholy to think that this is the last time I shall so address you. As you have accepted a seat in the House of Lords, it is the duty of your friends to wish you joy, without knowing how far it may contribute to your happiness. The *Times* has shown its characteristic good sense in its construction of your peerage; you come up as one of the representative peers—the smallest, and therefore the most distinguished, class—and in this class you are distinguished from all the rest, as representing not a specialty, such as law or literature, or political economy, or bishop-baiting, or Welsh nationality, but a range of interests as large as the circle of your friends. You will be the representative peer *par excellence*. The House of Lords would, as an institution, be imperfect without you. You will have an excellent position; and I hope that you will not let yourself be overcome with drowsiness by the air of the place, but will assert the universal character of your mission by frequently enlivening its discussions. I think it must be a healthier climate than the House of Commons, and will, I trust, promote both your happiness and your longevity.

Believe me yours ever truly,
C. St. David's.

From Mr. Delane to R. M. M.
July 27th, 1863.

MY DEAR LORD HOUGHTON,—I hope I may be at least one of the first to address you by the title which becomes you so well, and will be so willingly accorded to you by every member of the large and varied society you have adorned and delighted. I do not believe it will be possible to name a peerage the creation of which would give such widespread satisfaction as this. It forms the fitting complement of your career, and I trust it may be adorned by a long line of descendants, each conspicuous in politics or literature, and each, if it be possible, inheriting the kindly social qualities which have made the first Baron so widely known, and have won for him so much sincere affection.

With all good wishes,
I am ever
Very faithfully yours,
JOHN T. DELANE.

From Dean Stanley to R. M. M.

July 30*th,* 1863.

My dear Milnes,—For the last time let me call you by the old familiar name, to wish you joy of what gave me sincere pleasure when I saw it to-day in the papers, because I presume it is agreeable to you, and it certainly is to me. I cannot help regarding you as a *spiritual* peer without the temptations of Bishops—a rose without thorns. Pray keep a watch on your episcopal compeers, and help us through our difficulties. I am sure that you will be able to do good.

Ever yours truly,

A. P. Stanley.

It would weary the reader were I to prolong this chorus of congratulation from old friends and new friends alike, which proved that Milnes was at least well loved by his contemporaries; but one or two other letters must be given, rather because of the personal interest which they possess than because of the subject to which they refer. Hardly in the voluminous correspondence of Lord Houghton is a sadder letter to be found than the following, addressed to him by the friend of his early days in Italy, the great poet and brilliant man of letters, who was now slowly dragging out the remainder of his life in a weary exile.

W. S. Landor to Lord Houghton.

(*undated*)

My dear Lord Houghton,—Your remembrance is very delightful to me. I did not congratulate you on your elevation to the peerage—it elevates others. Believe me, I am more gratified by the account you have given me of your domestic happiness. How different is yours from mine! Never should I have returned to Tuscany had my dear and wise sister Elizabeth not urged me. Probably Madame Gotscharf may have told you what she knew and saw in the villa at Fiesole; at last it became quite impossible I could remain there. . . . Nearly the whole of December I have been so helpless as to be unable to get into my bed without the laborious help of two persons. May you never be so tortured by rheumatism and sciatica! At the close of the present January I enter my 90th year. God grant that I may not live into the middle of it*; and that you may enjoy as many happy New Years as I have endured unhappy ones. Kiss the hand of your lady for me, telling her she partakes in the good wishes—she and her little family—so feebly and faintly expressed by old

WALTER LANDOR.

The following letter from Carlyle needs a word of introduction. The reader will hardly have forgotten that on the morning of Christmas Eve, 1863, Mr. Thackeray was found dead in his bed at Kensington. His death severed one of Milnes's lifelong friendships. He had known Thackeray from his University days, and had uniformly liked and admired him. At one period in Thackeray's life, when the difficulties of his position were greatest, Milnes made strenuous efforts to assist him; and later, when he was prosperous as well as famous, there was no one who rejoiced more heartily in his well-earned good fortune than Milnes did. Among the letters of the author of "Vanity Fair" which he addressed to Milnes is one mere scrap, bidding him good-bye on the eve of the writer's departure for America:—

* Landor died in the following September.

W. M. Thackeray to R. M. M.

Liverpool, October 29th.

MY DEAR MILNES,—A word and a God bless you and yours at parting. I was thinking of our acquaintance the other day, and how it has been marked on your part by constant kindnesses, along which I can trace it. Thank you for them, and let me shake your hand, and say *Vale* and *Salve*.

Yours,
W. M. THACKERAY.

Give £1 for me to Hood's Tomb, please.

On the fatal Christmas Eve on which the great writer passed away, the post brought, as usual at that season, to Fryston many cards and greetings of affection and goodwill, and there was one which Milnes valued more than any other. It was a simple sheet of notepaper, dated from Palace Green, Kensington, upon which no words were written, but which bore a little coloured sketch of a robin-redbreast perched upon the coronet of a baron. It was Thackeray's farewell greeting to his old friend on this last Christmas of his life. How Milnes returned this token of goodwill will be known to all who recall the exquisite lines from his pen which appeared in the first number of the *Cornhill Magazine* published after the death of its old editor and founder—lines which still remain the most perfect tribute paid by any English poet to the memory of the man to whom we owe "Esmond" and "Vanity Fair."

T. Carlyle to R. M. M.

Chelsea, Dec. 29th, 1863.

DEAR LORD HOUGHTON (*quocunque nomine care*),—I hoped to have made my congratulations on the new grace of Fortune last

time you wrote, but when I called at Brook Street you had gone
out. Speaking of it or not, it is a thing we are all glad of, and
wish well to. I will say only, May the noble British Peerage,
once one of the noblest things in all the world, and still a very
noble, find you an honour and possession tó it, and you *it* a
ditto, ditto, to you!

My poor wife is in great pain and distress; general neuralgia,
the doctors call it—pain of that hurt limb, all manner of latent
hurts and injuries, kindled into a flaming paroxysm by some fit
of influenza: such a tempest of misery, as fills us with pain even
to witness it; for about two weeks since the doctors, who were
all agreed, but could do no good whatever, gave up the opiate
abominations, and left matters alone. We have struggled to
hope, and do still hope there was an improvement; but it is
sadly slow—*sleep*, in particular, almost refusing to return as
yet, and the progress towards better hardly discernible amid
many interruptions. God help us, and send us better days
again! I can find no consolation, except in struggling to get a
little work done in spite of the dire element, which in every
atom of it is saying, "No, you shan't!" The doctors confidently call it a superficial "merely nervous" torment of pain,
and assert that, "except by failure of strength," it is not
dangerous—"except," indeed! But let us be silent—let us
hope in this place of hope.

Poor Thackeray! I saw him not ten days ago. I was
riding in the dusk, heavy of heart, along by the Serpentine and
Hyde Park, when some human brother from a chariot, with
a young lady in it, threw me a shower of salutations. I
looked up—it was Thackeray with his daughter: the last time
I was to see him in this world. He had many fine qualities,
no guile or malice against any mortal; a big mass of a soul,
but not strong in proportion; a beautiful vein of genius lay
struggling about in him. Nobody in our day wrote, I should
say, with such perfection of style. I predict of his books very
much as you do. Poor Thackeray!—adieu! adieu!

My unfortunate history has bulged into a sixth volume;

the fourth is coming out so soon as the engraver (Wilhelmina's portrait) has done. The sixth volume—a poor thing—is partly ready in the rough. The fifth and it cannot be out within eight months or ten. Alas! I, too, am getting weary.

The no blockhead, several blackguards kindred, was not the ———'s, but an obscurer Scotch kindred, whom also the definition fits. The Welshes of Druscore descended from John Welsh and a daughter of John Knox. I think it was my wife's grand-uncle (himself rather a black) who made use of the phrase.

Adieu, dear friend,
T. CARLYLE.

P.S.—Lady Ashburton (generous impetuous soul!) came running up one day, ran sick-nursing about till the evening train. Lord Ashburton is considered to be in a satisfactory state, slowly gathering strength; still weak, but cheerful, and mostly free from pain. I had a letter from him since the lady was here. "Come and see us," he said.

A good deal of doubt existed as to the manner in which the new name which Milnes had chosen for himself was pronounced, and so many different theories prevailed upon the subject, that Mr. J. R. Planché took the opportunity of penning the following lines, in order to set the matter at rest·—

A LITERARY SQUABBLE.

> The Alphabet rejoiced to hear
> That Monckton Milnes was made a peer;
> For in this present world of letters,
> But few, if any, are his betters.
> So an address, by acclamation,
> They voted of congratulation;
> And H O U G T and N
> Were chosen the address to pen.

Possessing each an interest vital
In the new peer's baronial title,
'Twas done in language terse and telling,
Perfect in grammar and in spelling;
But when 'twas read aloud—O mercy!—
There sprang up such a controversy
About the true pronunciation
Of said baronial appellation.
The vowels O and U averred
They were entitled to be heard.
The consonants denied the claim,
Insisting that they mute became.
Johnson and Walker were applied to,
Sheridan, Bailey, Webster, tried too;
But all in vain, for each picked out
A word that left the case in doubt.
O, looking round upon them all,
Cried, "If it be correct to call
T H R O U G H '*throo*,'
H O U G H must be '*Hoo;*'
Therefore there can be no dispute on
The question. We should say 'Lord *Hooton.*'"
U brought "bought," "sought," and "fought" to show
He should be doubled, and not O;
For, sure, if "ought" was *awt*, then "nought" on
Earth could the title be but *Hawton*.
"H, on the other hand," said he,
In 'cough' and 'trough' stood next to G,
And, like an F, was then looked oft on,
Which made him think it should be *Hof*ton."
But G corrected H, and drew
Attention other cases to:
"Tough," "rough," and "chough," more than "enough"
To prove O U G H spelt *uff;*

And growled out, in a sort of gruff tone,
"They must pronounce the title *Huff*ton."
N said, emphatically, "No!
There is D O U G H, 'doh!'
And, *though* (look there, again!) that stuff
At sea for fun they nicknamed 'duff,'
He should propose they took a vote on
The question—Should it not be *Ho*ton?
Besides, in French 'twould have such force—
A lord was of *haut ton*, of course."
Higher and higher contention rose,
From words they almost came to blows,
Till T, as yet who hadn't spoke,
And dearly loved a little joke,
Put in his word, and said, "Look there!
'*Plough*' in this *row* must have its *share*."
At this atrocious pun each page
Of Johnson whiter turned with rage;
Bailey looked desperately cut up,
And Sheridan completely shut up;
Webster, who is no idle talker,
Made a sign indicating "Walker!"
While Walker, who had been used badly,
Just shook his dirty dog's-ears sadly.
But as we find, in prose or rhyme,
A joke made happily in time,
However poor, will often tend
The hottest argument to end,
And smother anger in a laugh,
So T succeeded with his chaff
(Containing, as it did, some wheat),
In calming this fierce verbal heat.
Authorities were all conflicting,
And T there was no contradicting.
P L O U G H was *Plow;*
Even "enough" was called "enow;"

And no one who preferred "enough"
Would dream of saying " Speed the *pluff!* "
So they considered it more wise
With T to make a compromise;
And leave no loop to hang a doubt on,

By giving three cheers for Lord ⎧ How ⎫ ton!
⎩ Hough ⎭

J. R. P.

CHAPTER XV

FRIENDSHIPS OLD AND NEW.

Visit to Broadlands—Goes to the Riviera and Italy—Death of Lord Ashburton—"Essays and Reviews"—Houghton attacks Convocation—Lord Westbury's Memorable Speech—Death of Sir Charles MacCarthy—Houghton seconds Address in House of Lords—Mr. Swinburne—Houghton reviews "Atalanta in Calydon"—Letter from Swinburne—Charles Dickens—Houghton's Friendship for Henry Bright—John Bright—Carlyle's Lord Rectorship—Visit to Fryston—A Distinguished Party—Mrs. Carlyle's Last Letters—Death of Mrs. Carlyle.

THE Christmas of 1863 was not spent by Lord Houghton at home. He writes to his wife from Serlby Hall on December 26th as follows :—

It must have been a rather gloomy Christmas-tree for you, had it not been for the three lamps you keep always lighted (their three children). So Thackeray too has gone. I was not surprised, knowing how full of disease he was, and thereby accounting for much of the inequality and occasional perversity in his conduct. Tell Amy to impress on her mind as well as she can, by thinking over his visit to Fryston, the kind, tall, amusing, gray-haired man, so that she may tell other people a great many years hence that she knew the great writer Mr. Thackeray, and that he had been very friendly to her and her sister and brother. The robin on the cushion was the last communication we had with him. You must keep up with his poor girls in return for it. . . . Baron Bentinck will come on the 31st; he begs his best thanks "for the invitation with which he has been honoured." These diplomatists are vastly civil. I went over to Bawtry Hall and Church yesterday; the service, what with the Athanasian Creed and the Sacraments, lasted from 10.30 to 2 p.m. J. was so faint that she could hardly appreciate the cold rabbit pie with which the L.'s entertained us. Mrs. L. amuses herself in slowly killing the trees by moving them about, but it does the place no serious harm.

Your affectionate
H^N.

To his Wife.

Broadlands, Saturday (Jan., 1864), 7.30 p.m.

The Turkish baths made me feverish, but I got to sleep and was none the worse this morning. Tweed has given me a pill and a draught of the orthodox fashion. Lady Palmerston misinterpreted your note into meaning that I should be here yesterday, and they sent for me twice to the station (Tell —— that is how the Premier treats me), and I found her in the act of writing to you to ask if I was worse. She looks well, but has not been out of the house for three weeks. The Jocelyns, A. Cravens, and W. Cowpers are here. Lord Palmerston went to a Council, but returns to-morrow.

Broadlands, Monday.

I am still here, having got a telegram from Carleton recommending me to put off the visit to Tedworth till to-morrow. I was rather glad of it, having still much cold in my head. I saw the doctor here, who ordered me a tonic, and told me not to coddle any more. I have had a week of illness in society, which you know I do not dislike. If you are to be ill, anybody's house is better than your own. Lady Tankerville has been nearly dead of croup, and is still very ill. Lord Palmerston went out shooting to-day. They shot an immense number of pheasants and three boys; the latter only hit in the face, and not dangerously. Lady Jocelyn was so glad her boy, who is turning out very nice, was not there. Poor Mrs. Norton wrote yesterday that she was quite ill from not having been asked to Broadlands; and it is too late now, as they are all breaking up.

Tedworth House, Marlborough, Tuesday, 5 p.m.

Just arrived, found Lord Broughton very unwell with sciatica, but nothing serious. It affects his spirits, they say, but he is all the better for company. The party is deprived of its chief splendour by Lady W. Poulett becoming a duchess. If it had happened here, we should have crowned her with strawberry leaves. The Barringtons and Disraelis come to-morrow. The poor Duchess of Sutherland is ill again, and obliged to come to London. . . . I saw the Romsey doctor again this morning. He thought me getting better, but I have still much headache, especially when I read and write. I was talking about my coma, and the time it usually comes on, on which Lord Stanley remarked, "Then you will be generally insensible in the House of Lords between 5 and 7, and of great use to your party." I believe, however, he has been much nearer apoplexy than I have as yet. This is the best joke yet, but I think you could do something still better.

Tedworth House, Jan. 23rd.

I post this as I go through town. I cannot throw off the cold, or get up my strength, and must wait for better weather.

Disraeli was in the grand style, and not very pleasant. We have had low whist, which has suited my intelligence. Mrs. Carleton asked Dizzy what he would like to do to amuse himself. "Let me exist," he answered.

Unable to shake off the cold which had weighed upon him during the winter, Lord Houghton paid a visit to the Riviera in March, from which he derived great benefit. He visited his friend MacCarthy in Paris on his way.

To his Wife.

Hyères, March 24, 1864.

It is certainly strange finding oneself, in full summer, writing with shut blinds, and taking the precautions against the effect of the sun on the skin, to which I am so subject. I was almost blistered yesterday when we went down to the sea-shore and I saw once again the rich sapphire of the Mediterranean, with its bright white setting of foam against the rocks. This morning I have been sitting under the thick shade of the palm-trees on the terrace. There is, however, a sharpish wind to be careful of. Dr. ——'s account of MacCarthy was not very encouraging. I don't think he seemed quite to understand him, and I shall recommend his seeing someone else, either in Paris or in London. He is in a frightful state of debility, but bright and cheerful in mind. Swinburne came in to tea, and his recitations so excited MacCarthy that he had quite a bad night. He thought them wonderful, and they quite haunted him. I saw nobody else but Rio, who was in good force and on good terms with the Government. He was only anxious about his remaining girl, who has shown consumptive tendencies. I propose to go to Cannes on the 30th, and to Nice on the 2nd April; so you will judge about letters. . . . The ——s complain a great deal of the dulness of this place, but they don't seem to have looked out for acquaintances. Queen Christina of Spain has been here the whole winter, and must have had some pleasant people about her, if they had only known how to look after them. The place is, in fact, much larger and more frequented than I thought.

Cannes, 29th.

The stormy weather (the mistral at Hyères nearly blew me out of bed) has only increased the beauty of this coast, making the water still bluer, the light more varied, and giving you a snow-line in the upper distance. I came here to the hotel, but Lord Brougham seems to wish me to go to his house, so I do so until Saturday, when I shall drive to Nice. He is very old and benign. I came in for his week's reception last night; a party ending in a dance, some pleasant French people, but nothing eminent in English. . . . Merimée and Cousin are just gone, but Odilon Barrot is still here. From what I see of this place it would only be agreeable for people who have all their resources about them, and have not to look for them elsewhere. The villas seem very pretty and commodious.

Cannes, April 2nd.

This is assuredly a very beautiful place, but the almost continual wind is a great objection to me. The two subjects of conversation are lungs and anemones—whether the former are really injured, and whether one lady has found some variety of the latter which the other has not got. They go out on regular anemone hunts under the olive groves, and are tremendously fond of a double orange or a treble pink. The scent of the air in the drives is very peculiar. You have a gust of lavender or a puff of jonquils or the mild incense of fir-cones. The fields of roses are, however, not out, and the year is so backward that even the nightingales do not gush out as usual. . . . Poor old Brougham himself is scarcely conscious of what goes on, but was roused by a note from Florence Yelverton, appealing to his old memorable defence of the Queen, and asking him to take up her defence in the same way, and stating that she had come to Cannes on purpose. She called yesterday, but he would not see her, and wrote to her, very properly, that he was in fact to be one of the judges of her case in the House of Lords, and therefore could not prejudge the case by an *ex-parte* statement.

It was whilst staying at Hyères that Lord Houghton received news of the death of Lord Ashburton. Writing to his wife he says—

So the "Grange" has gone from me and mine. Taken with its personages, it fills a large place in my memories. I had much in common with him, mainly the failure in public life, which he bore with a dignity and manliness I have never assumed, but which he felt quite as acutely: indeed, in the comparison between himself and other men I think there was more of contempt and self-depreciation than goes with my nature. Robin [the present Lord Houghton] will have to make all his own friends. I shall have none left to give him.

Lord Houghton to George von Bunsen.

Cannes, April 1st, 1864.

My dear George,—I have been long balanced between my intentions of writing to you and my expectations of hearing from you. I have sometimes thought that if you wanted to talk to me on the subjects uppermost in your mind, you would do it, and that your silence meant that you would rather not. I have not been very well this winter, but have nothing seriously to complain of, and am here only on an excursion, and to see some friends who are invalids in body, and poor Lord Brougham, with whom I am staying, whose mind is gradually declining. One cannot wish that he should last much longer.

I am thankful I went to see Lord Ashburton before he died. I came away without any hope. Altogether he was the noblest and purest-minded man I have ever known. If he had had powers and facilities of expression, he would have been a great one. He had no *eigenen Gesang*, though he had the *liebe Frauen*. This reminds me of the little book of "Two Visits to Goethe" which you were to send me from Berlin, and did not. I should like to see a good report of your speech on the Danish treaty. What a pity your dear father (whom this place still well remembers) signed that fatuous document! Even now the history of it—the secret history, I mean—is unintelligible. Nobody, not even the Czar, can have thought that it secured the peaceable succession of the Danish Crown, and without that things might just as well have been left to chance. I have nothing to find fault with in Lord Russell's management of the business. Considering the dynastic connection and the public sentiment, he has acted with singular moderation and good sense. I am afraid you must make up your mind to see the thing patched up for the present, and keep the question as a preserve for future revolutions.

This is a beautiful coast, but it is haunted by odious winds, the mistral to-day, the bise to-morrow. I go on to Genoa on Monday, never having yet set foot in free Italy. Turin would have great attractions for me if Cavour was still there, but I hardly care to go now. But I perhaps shall find myself there, and hope to find your brother Charles. You may tell him to be on the look-out for me. I hope before this you will have found out that Lady H. and the *kleine Comtesse* are in Upper Brook Street, and very glad to see you and Madame Bunsen. My wife declares that the good living you gave me on the Rhine destroyed all the advantages of Carlsbad. Somehow or other I have never been able to walk five miles since I was there, and think the waters over-drenched my blood. I do hope you will be still in England when I return about the 20th.

From Cannes Lord Houghton went on to Turin.

To his Wife.

Turin, Wednesday.

I have yours of the 10th, so you see we are not very far asunder. This place is new to me and not easily got at again, and the personages amusing, so I have settled to stay here till the end of the week, and cut Paris short. I shall not be there before Sunday or Monday, so write to Meurice's. You would like this climate very much, a sky continually bright, and a fresh air. I think it keeps me rather "tender" and nervous. I am afraid I shall be at Stoneleigh* on the 23rd, and you must write up to Stanley, who, however, I believe you may say, agrees with me that there never was such a man as the lamented Shakespeare. I am glad you go to Stafford House, as I wrote to the Duke of Sutherland from Genoa about Garibaldi. . . . If Ricciotti is still in London, you could ask him to luncheon. . . . Everybody here, from the king downwards, is angry at the reception of Garibaldi,† and they have ordered Azeglio not to attend any festival in his honour. It is the same thing as if Bright was to receive an ovation in Paris, and our Government were told it was a compliment to them. Mr. Elliot [English

---

* Lord Leigh had asked him to stay at Stoneleigh on the occasion of the Shakespeare celebration at Stratford.

† Garibaldi was at this time paying his famous visit to England.

Minister at the Sardinian Court] has a hard game to play, but, it seems to me, does it very well, taking the thing very good-humouredly. I dined with him yesterday, and met Countess Teleki and some of the Ministers. The Prefect of Turin gives me a dinner to-morrow; the king is in the country with his mistress and her family, and rarely comes to town, so I may not see him. Your account of the children is charming. I am quite unhappy about S———. Are none but the stupid and ignorant permitted to live? If you are writing to Harriette [Lady Galway], tell her I have seen Count Spada, who is a senator here, and who asked a great deal about the beautiful tall girl he remembered so well. He has lost his wife, and four out of five children. The editor of the chief paper here was to call on me this morning, but I have just learnt that he has fought a duel instead, and wounded his adversary, a nephew of Cavour's.

Lord Houghton evidently received a good deal of attention during this pleasant spring visit to Italy. A letter from one of her friends, then staying at Genoa, to Lady Houghton says:—

I cannot tell you how pleasant your husband has been. We could do little for him; but he is so willing to make the best of everything and everybody, and he enjoys seeing as no one now does, though the cold has been too great to do much in that way. Yesterday evening a dinner was given him by a rich banker here; we went to tea, and I found him the cynosure of seven or eight pairs of eyes that make up the English colony in Genoa. To-day he is off for Turin, where he seems to have many notable people to see.

Coming back to town, Lord Houghton spent the Session in the usual engagements, social and political; busy with the Newspaper Press Fund, of which from its foundation he had been the most zealous friend;

with dinners and breakfast-parties, where his old friends gathered round him, and new ones made their appearance upon the scene; and with the House of Lords, where he spoke once or twice, finding himself strangely nervous in the unaccustomed place. In the various dinner-lists of his guests I find, among other names, that of his friend Sir Charles MacCarthy, whose life was now drawing to a close. It was a pleasure to Milnes to have near him one with whom he had maintained almost from boyhood so close and unbroken a friendship; but MacCarthy's health, to which reference has been made in one of the letters just quoted, worried him greatly, and he was anxious to see him sent abroad to one of the foreign Baths, in hope of an improvement. The health of Lady Houghton was also very seriously impaired at this time, and added much to his anxieties.

Lord Houghton to George von Bunsen.

16, *Upper Brook Street, July* 13*th,* 1864.

My dear George,—When you saw my wife, you spoke of coming to England in the month of July. Can you arrange to come with Mrs. Bunsen and your family to Fryston from the 6th to the 20th of August? My wife has been so poorly that we shall have no large party—nothing beyond a few pleasant men; so you need not have any compunction if you come with the caravan of a sheikh. The children will find grass, and croquet, and ponies.

It was very curious to hear all this Dano-German talk on a false issue; the one fact that coloured and distorted everything— the Danish Marriage—was never alluded to. How could one speak one's mind about the Treaty, and the conduct of either party, with the Princess of Wales sitting opposite? Hirsch-

mann's speech expressed a good deal of my mind on the subject. The Bernstorffs [Prussian Ambassador] now creep a little out of their shell, in which they have been hid all the spring. It will be agreeable to you to know that Lord Clarendon said that nobody was the better for the Conference except Bismarck. I shall go to Vichy for three weeks after the 20th of August, which is the reason for limiting your visit to that date. Hoping to see you all,
I am yours affectionately,

HOUGHTON.

My wife is at the seaside getting strength to receive you.

On the 8th of August Mr. Bunsen visited Fryston, where he found, among other guests, Dr. Smith (of the dictionaries), Mr. Venables, Mr. Spedding, Mr. W. B. Donne, and Mr. Wilkie Collins.

T. Carlyle to Lord Houghton.

Chelsea, August 11*th,* 1864.

DEAR LORD HOUGHTON,—I fear you over-rate any improvement there is in my poor wife's situation. She is still almost continually in very great suffering, though I think the prospect does clear now up a little to myself (and also to her, which is still more important) by the better insight one now has of what the real element is—want of sleep, want of sleep, which has been going on, gradually on the increase, for many years back, and has now reached some crisis or consummation. That is the root of all the mischief, the one thing wrong, and for that it is now evident enough (even to herself) that medicine in any form or degree can do nothing, though carefully-studied regimen with the aid of time and Nature perhaps still may. The accounts from Scotland are changeful and fitful, oftenest extremely miserable to me, but they do rather improve than otherwise. God be merciful!

As to myself, night and day, every moment of my time (for her sake as my own) is religiously devoted to getting that frightful millstone of a book shot off the neck of me in some not dishonest way, and in the universe there is nothing but working at it that can be any consolation to me in present circumstances.

May the waters of Vichy do you good! May you be happy and merry, dear old friend, for many years to come! I still hope to see Fryston under good omens, were these black tornadoes done. My kind regards to Venables, *after* not before, my lady and the little ones.

Yours ever,

T. CARLYLE.

The closing scenes of the great struggle in the United States, in which Lord Houghton's sympathies had been so strongly excited, were now engaging the attention of the world; but of even nearer interest to Englishmen was the struggle in Denmark, referred to in the foregoing letters, which was to be the starting-point of so many and such momentous changes in the state of Europe. Houghton's most important appearance in the House of Lords during the year had no reference, however, to either of these burning questions, but was concerned with a subject which, if possible, came nearer home to him than either—the vindication of freedom of opinion and the liberties of literature, which, in his opinion, had been seriously threatened by the action of Convocation in pronouncing a formal condemnation of the well-known volume called "Essays and Reviews." Houghton warmly espoused the cause of the writers of that volume; and on the 15th of July he addressed a question to the Lord Chancellor as to whether the Government had taken the opinion of the officers of the Crown as to the powers of Convocation to pass a synodical judgment on books written either by clergymen or laymen. His speech entered into no theological controversy, but was marked by all the speaker's sympathy with that freedom of opinion of which through his life he had been the advocate. It was marked also by that tenderness of sympathy for men who were at the moment suffering from a storm of obloquy and unpopularity which was no less striking a characteristic of his nature. The distinguished prelates who had seen fit to pass a formal condemnation of "Essays and Reviews" had disclaimed any intention of doing more than liberating their own minds, and had protested against the idea that they were inflicting any punishment upon those whom they condemned. Lord Houghton exposed the fallacious character of these pretences.

It is intended [he said] when a censure is passed that it should be injurious to the person censured, and it is regarded as a punishment. Let me take the case of the first author whose name appears in this volume of "Essays and Reviews"—the Rev. Dr. Temple, a most distinguished man, the Master of Rugby School, of the excellence of which the late Royal Commission spoke in such high terms. It seems to me that it may be very well argued that Dr. Temple's interests in that school are seriously injured by the decision which has been pronounced by Convocation. It may be that it may have the effect of preventing parents from sending their boys to the school, or of inducing them to remove them from it, and thereby inflict an injury on Dr. Temple in his *status* and emoluments. Then there is the case of the last author whose name appears in this book—Mr. Jowett, a professor of Oxford, who has been treated with such signal injustice as to excite even the strongly expressed feeling of your Lordships' House. Can anyone say that Professor Jowett may not have suffered injury in his future career from the censure to which I am referring?

The Lord Chancellor of that day was the famous Lord Westbury, and his reply to Lord Houghton's speech was one of the most characteristic of his many remarkable utterances. He pointed out that any attempt on the part of Convocation to pronounce any sentence or execute any law or ordinance, without the previous licence and authority of the Crown, would expose the members of Convocation to the penalties of a *præmunire*.

I am afraid my noble friend has not considered what the pains and penalties of a *præmunire* are, or his gentle heart would have melted at the prospect. The most reverend Primate and the Bishops would have to appear at this bar, not in the solemn state in which we see them here, but as penitents in sackcloth and ashes; and what would be the sentence? I observe that the most reverend Primate gave two votes—his original vote and a casting vote. I will take the measure of his sentence from the sentence passed by the Bishop on one of these authors—a year's deprivation of his benefice. For two years, therefore, the most reverend Primate might be condemned to have all the revenues of his high position sequestrated. I have not ventured—I say it seriously—I have not ventured to present this question to Her Majesty's Government; for, my lords, only imagine what a temptation it would be for my right honourable friend, the Chancellor of the Exchequer, to spread his net, and in one haul take in £30,000 from the highest dignitary, not to speak of the *hoi polloi*—the bishops, deacons, archdeacons, canons, vicars—all included in one common crime, all subject to one common penalty.

Lord Westbury went on, in memorable phrase, to state that if the report of the judgment which he had read was a correct one, he was happy to be able to tell Lord Houghton that what was called a synodical judgment was a "well-lubricated set of words, a sentence so oily and saponaceous that no one can grasp it; like an eel it slips through your fingers." There was no doubt as to the meaning of this phrase or its personal application, and it is not surprising that both the Archbishop of Canterbury and the Bishop of Oxford hotly resented the Lord Chancellor's tone, though making no complaint of that of Lord Houghton. Short as the debate was, it was in many respects memorable, and deserves to be mentioned as one of the most notable occasions on which Lord Houghton spoke, in the Chamber of which he was now a member.

Writing on the following day to his wife, he says:—

You will see what an animated debate we had last night; a peer said to me, "You have run the best fox of the season." The Chancellor and Bishop quite took the wind out of my sails, and made the debate themselves, which perhaps, all considered, was quite as well for me. I spoke better than I had hitherto done in the Lords, but a great deal below what I mean to speak some day. The town is mourning (in its gay way) the pretty Miss Errington, who acted in a tableau at Lady Rokeby's last week, caught cold, diphtheria came on, and she died in forty-eight hours. The Philobiblon breakfast went off well.

The Duc d'Aumale just arrived from Switzerland. I dine at Twickenham to-day, sleep at Richmond, go to the Camp at Wimbledon to-morrow morning to hear the Archbishop of York preach to the Volunteers, and then rail to Lord [illegible] to dinner, returning on Monday.

The heavy loss which Lord Houghton had been anticipating for some months occurred in August. On the 14th of that month Sir Charles MacCarthy died at Spa. Writing to Lady Houghton after seeing MacCarthy for the last time, some weeks before his death, Houghton said, "MacCarthy has gone back to the appearance of his youth, and I could almost see him as the robed student in Wiseman's garden in the English College at Rome." The death of so old a friend was a severe blow to a man of Houghton's sympathetic temperament. It closed a long chapter in his life; henceforward there were to be no long letters of gossip from Ceylon or from the other distant stations where MacCarthy was serving his country with distinction and success. From this point forward also Houghton's biographer is deprived of one of the chief sources of information regarding his movements and opinions—the letters which for a period of thirty years he had been in the habit of writing to his friend. Justice cannot be done in these pages to the warmth of the affection which Milnes had always shown from his early days in Rome to the young student whom he had constantly watched and helped, and whom he had seen rise to a position of dignity and usefulness. Yet, if the story of that friendship could be written in full, the reader would perhaps know more of the true nature of the man than he could do if he had met Milnes at a hundred dinner-tables. It was a friendship which brought to view the best side of his character, which had in it no touch or hint of selfishness, and which, when at last death severed the tie between them, was transferred to the dead man's widow and children.

It was very soon after MacCarthy's death that Milnes, who was himself out of health, went to Vichy.

Extracts from Letters to his Wife.
Hôtel de Prince, Bains de Vichy,
August 28th, 1864.

I gave up my through passage, and stopped Friday night at Paris, coming on here leisurely yesterday. I had written for rooms, and have both bedroom and sitting-room on the ground floor—that is, above the offices. The place looks much thinner than when I was last here, but still there are a great many people. There were about seventy English at church this morning, only one of whom, a Scotch lawyer, I knew by sight. I afterwards paid my court to H.S.H. the Duchess of Sutherland, whom I found in a lovely châlet surrounded with flowers, Tennyson on the table, and very cheerful, though she has a cataract over one eye, and very little sight in the other. She has her youngest son with her. I saw the same doctor I had ten years ago. He has only set me drinking a little at present, and will see about the baths. The weather to-day is delicious, quite a fresh air with a most brilliant sky; if it remains so, it will answer all my purpose. . . . I hope you liked my short "In Memoriam" [in the *Times*, of Sir Charles MacCarthy]. I did not venture to make all I wished, for fear of Lord Torrington's preventing Delane from sending it.

Vichy, August 30th.

One of the letters you sent was from a madman whose letters I never open; he writes on the outside to make me do so. I send you the cover, that you may not send me any more of them.

I dined yesterday with H.S.H. The only peculiarity was that a courier carried a large single rose before her, and placed it on the table opposite her plate. She gives a gloomy account of Lord Carlisle. He is at Castle Howard, with all the Sisterhood about him. He has sent in his resignation; she says he is in a very placid state of mind.

Vichy, September 13*th*.

About this time last year I remember thinking that after the peerage there was not much more for me to do socially and politically, but that I had two objects to look after—your health, and my few remaining friends; and now you have been very ill, and I have lost the oldest friend I had—so go human intentions.

September 19*th*.

I went on Saturday to Bourges, at the invitation of Prince Latour d'Auvergne, to dine with his brother the Archbishop, and see the Cathedral. Monseigneur is the youngest Archbishop of Christendom, I suppose even including Ebor. He was consecrated at thirty-three years of age, and is now only thirty-five. It was a family gathering, and the mother seemed very happy with her prosperous family—the ambassador, the Archbishop, another high in the army, and the ambassador's son, a charming boy of twelve, who inherits a large fortune from his deceased mother. —— herself would have envied the magnificence of the Palace and the service, which was in the best possible style. I found Sa Grandeur very agreeable and tolerant. He showed me from his windows a village where Calvin preached, and left a congregation that still subsists. He was about to proceed on a tour of fifty-six confirmations, two *per diem*, each accompanied by a dinner at the presbytère, to say nothing of the neighbouring châteaux, so that he said it was very difficult to be civil and not make himself ill. The Cathedral is the grandest specimen of architecture I have ever seen in a Gothic edifice, not excepting Cologne. I was thinking of going to see an old friend of mine, the Abbé Gerbet, Bishop of Perpignan, when in the first paper I took up here I read his death. What a curious irony of fate is the death of poor Speke [the African explorer], like a clumsy gamekeeper's after his myriad dangers! It is worth knowing that you can have a safeguard on any gun for £1 10s. which renders such an accident impossible. I shall be at Arlès Dufour's at Oullins on Wednesday evening. The trains on these lines are all terribly slow, but else the railways are well managed. Coming back last night from Bourges I found Sir Alexander Cockburn on his way here, and brought him to my hotel. He remains his three weeks, and does not seem to mind the prospect of solitary confinement. How admirable are Lady MacCarthy's letters! She would, by-the-bye, have never lost her husband had I gone to Ceylon last November, as I desired to do, and brought him back with me, just as David Gray would not have died had I bought him a great-coat, just as, &c. &c. &c.

Somewhat unexpectedly, and owing to a bereavement in the family of the Duke of Cleveland, Lord Houghton was asked to second the address in reply to the Queen's Speech at the opening of the Session of 1865. The notice he received was very short, but he was able to discharge his task with some satisfaction to himself.

To his Wife.
The Athenæum, Monday, February 4th, 1865.

There is a west wind here, which has prevented, I hope, my catching cold from the double operation of having my hair cut and my photograph taken. I heard Vaughan at the Chapel Royal yesterday—a remarkable sermon in the customary form of Liberal divines, making all kinds of admissions, and then gobbling them up with some dogmatic assertions at the end. I found Lord and Lady Palmerston quite Darby and Joan on Saturday evening. He went over the speech with me.

February 8th.

"Got over the speech very well," Lord Clarendon said to me. "Excellent—young man!" I replied, "I accept the latter part of the compliment." The hits at Lord Amberley and the Chancellor were well taken. You do not see me till Monday, as I dine on Saturday with the Comte de Paris. I expect to meet General Maclellan, who is in the House of Lords. The Duchess of Sutherland is very unwell again, and obliged to give up Torquay. Lord —— maintained to me yesterday that the Bishop of Chester was the best on the Bench. By never reading anybody's letters, he never gets into any controversy, and it is the only diocese in which you never hear of theology.

During the summer Lord Houghton found time to devote himself to some literary work of importance, including an article on "Atalanta in Calydon" in the *Edinburgh Review*, which did so much to make Swinburne known to the world at large. Mention has already been made of the fact that Houghton had been one of the first to recognise the genius of the young poet. For a time indeed he inclined to the belief that he was destined to eclipse the illustrious man who had been his own companion at college and his friend throughout his life; but though before he died Lord Houghton made full acknowledgment of the absolute supremacy of Tennyson among living poets, he continued to the end to be a warm admirer of the genius of Swinburne. In connection with the review of "Atalanta in Calydon" he had an interesting correspondence with the Bishop of St. David's. Mr. Swinburne had been indebted to Lord Houghton for a personal introduction to Landor, a fact to which he refers in the letter I am allowed to print here.

A. C. Swinburne to Lord Houghton.

Albergo della Gran Bretagna.
March 31*st*, 1864.

MY DEAR LORD HOUGHTON,—I meant to write you a word or two days since, and a sufficiently delirious epistle you would have had, but luckily an equivocal and occasionally beneficent Providence intervened. With much labour I hunted out the most ancient of the demi-gods at 93, Via della Chiesa, but (although knockdown blows were not, as you anticipated, his mode of salutation) I found him, owing, I suppose, to the violent cold, too much weakened and confused to realise the fact of the introduction without distress. In effect he seemed so feeble and uncomfortable that I came away in a grievous state of disappointment and depression myself, fearing I was really too late. But taking heart of grace, I wrote him a note of apology and explanation, saying why and how I had made up my mind to call upon him after you had furnished me with an introduction; that is, expressing as far as was expressible my immense admiration and reverence in the plainest and sincerest way I could manage. To which missive of mine came a note of invitation, which I answered by setting off again for his lodging. After losing myself for an hour in the accursed Borgo San Frediano, I found it at last, and found him as alert, brilliant, and altogether delicious as I suppose others may have found him twenty years since. I cannot thank you enough for procuring me this great pleasure and exquisite satisfaction. I am seriously more obliged for this than for anything that could have been done for me. I have got the one thing I wanted with all my heart. If both or either of us die to-morrow, at least to-day he has told me that my presence here has made him happy. He said more than that—things for which of course I take no credit to myself, but which are not the less pleasant to hear from such a man. There is no other man living from whom I should so much have prized any expression of acceptance or good-will in return for my homage, for all other men as great are so much younger that in his case one sort of reverence serves as the lining for another. My grandfather was upon the whole *mieux conservé*, but he had written no Hellenics. In answer to something that Mr. Landor said to-day of his own age, I reminded him of his equals and precursors, Sophocles and Titian. He said he should not live up to the age of Sophocles, not see ninety. I do not see why he should not if he has people about him who care for him as he should be cared for. I told him, as we were talking of poems and such things, that his poems had first given me inexplicable pleasure when I was a small fellow of twelve at Eton. My first recollection of them is the song of the Hours in the *Iphigenia*.

If I let myself loose, I shall go on giving you indirect thanks for bringing me acquainted with Landor, till time and paper fail me, and patience fails you. Even if I did so, I could hardly tell you what pleasure I have had to-day in a half-hour's intercourse with him, nor what delicious things he said in recognition of my half-expressed gratitude to him. It is comfortable when one does once in a way go in for a complete quiet bit of hero-worship, and an honest interlude of belief, to find it taken up instead of thrown away; and the chance of this I owe to you, and you must simply take my thanks for granted. It is better than a public to me. What more can a *rimailleur inédit* possibly say?

A. C. SWINBURNE.

The "Atalanta in Calydon" includes a tribute of veneration to the memory of Walter Savage Landor in two compositions of Greek elegiac verse. The first is a dedication addressed to Landor while living, in the form of a valediction on the occasion of his last return to Italy; the second, much the longer of the two, an elegy on his death. It was in connection with these Greek verses, and the criticism of them in the *Edinburgh Review*, that Houghton received the following letters from Bishop Thirlwall.

Abergwili Palace, Carmarthen, April 21*st*, 1865.

MY DEAR HOUGHTON,—I am glad that you are going to review the Atalanta. It has, perhaps, not yet been reviewed by a poet, who alone is qualified for the task; but I cannot think that the interest of your review would be increased by any little criticism of the Greek verses which to ninety-nine out of one hundred of your readers would be unintelligible, and to the rest needless and useless. Of the conceits, which are certainly curious, in many respects you are far better qualified to speak than I am. What would be really desirable would be a poetical translation, which your acquaintance with the author would enable you to make perfect. I must own that there are some lines which are obscure to me; but if English was to become as dead as Greek, perhaps many parts of the tragedy would exercise learned annotators quite as much as the Greek.

Yours ever faithfully,
C. St. David's.

The Same to the Same.
Abergwili Palace, April 24th, 1865.

My dear Houghton,—I shall be happy to dine with you next Sunday, and between this and then will think more about the Greek verses. No one who can read them would deny that they are quite the reverse of bad—indeed, of a very high order of merit and both in their strength and weakness worthy of the poem itself, as here and there they seem to reflect some of the peculiarities of its diction, though there are also a few lines which I believe for other reasons a Greek would not have written. I should like to know a little about the author. He must be a young man, but it would be psychically interesting to ascertain until what time of life such a man can continue to regard Landor as by far the greatest of all poet—past, present, and to come. I am still more curious to know to what kind of reactionary school the author belongs. Somehow I cannot fancy him a stiff Churchman or an obscurantine Romanist; still less as an intolerant Puritan; and yet he takes the side of the old, now pretty nearly antiquated, orthodoxy which thought itself in peril if it admitted that there was anything good and holy, or in fact not diabolical, in the Pagan religion, but even goes back beyond that standing-point, and charges the Greeks with a dogma which would have made Æschylus stare, and Sophocles shudder. If it had been put in the mouth of one of the characters in the drama, it might have simply heightened the tragic effect; but it is enunciated by the chorus, and therefore must be the poet's last word and his way of expressing the national sentiment. Both as a Philhellene and as a liberal theologian I repudiate this imputation. . . . Even from the purely poetical point of view it seems to me a mistake. The tragic action, as it seems to me, is not brought out in stronger relief, but rather effaced by the intense unbroken murkiness of the background.

Yours ever truly,
C. ST. DAVID'S.

The result of the dinner to which the Bishop refers was that he undertook to interpolate in Houghton's review of "Atalanta in Calydon" a couple of paragraphs commenting upon the Greek verse.

Charles Dickens to Lord Houghton.
16, Somers Place, Hyde Park,
Thursday, March 23rd, 1865.

MY DEAR LORD HOUGHTON,—I am disabled from accepting your kind invitation by a cause almost as odd as disagreeable. From much walking in the snow at Gad's Hill I got laid up with a frostbitten foot a month ago, like an Arctic sailor. On Tuesday last the tortures came on afresh (invited by the east wind, it is supposed), and have kept me in bed until to-day, engendering the weakest submission to my doctor. In the van of his prescriptions is this one, "Do not go out this season; and whenever you do not want to be at your desk, rush to the sea-air." So between work and flight I expect to pass my time—if I can be helped, out of pain—until I go back to Cannes in June. It is something to know that Lady Houghton has even made the progress you describe. I beg to send her my kindest regards.

Believe me always faithfully yours,
CHARLES DICKENS.

Parliament was dissolved in 1865, and Houghton looked on as a mere spectator at a scene in which he had so long played an active part.

A new friendship, practically the last great friendship of his mature life, had been formed shortly before this by Lord Houghton. The object of it was Mr. Henry Bright, a young Liverpool merchant, whose commercial pursuits in no way interfered with a real love of letters, or even with regular literary work. Mr. Bright, who was the friend of Nathaniel Hawthorne during his stay in Liverpool as American Consul, is known widely by his book entitled "A Year in a Lancashire Garden," as well as by his critical contributions to the *Pall Mall Gazette*, the *Athenæum*, and other journals. Lord Houghton's friendship with him began long before he had achieved literary distinction, and was due simply to a common liking and common tastes. As time passed this friendship developed on both sides into a warm and true affection, and Bright became one of the very small number of men with whom Houghton regularly corresponded.

To Henry Bright.
July 14th, 1865.

The result of the elections is not altogether agreeable. There is certainly no Conservative reaction, but there is great Liberal apathy. After Mill's and Hughes' success, one had the right to expect something much better. I lose a great number of Yorkshire representatives—old, dear familiar faces in the House of Commons—Ramsden, Smyth of Hull, Leatham, Thompson of Kirby, &c. &c. &c.; and no new ones that I care about have taken their places.

We are just going to drive to Oxford, to see how Gladstone is going on. The belief of the best men is that he will be a little behind Hardy for the first *three* days, and that then many men who did not intend to vote at all will rush to the rescue.

Lord Houghton to Comte de Montalembert.

16, *Upper Brook Street, July* 15*th*, 1865.

MY DEAR MONTALEMBERT,—I thank you heartily for your admirable pamphlet. I can account for the great sympathy with the South on the part of the upper and middle classes here from motives, as you state, not very creditable to themselves; but I cannot explain the absence of prevision, on the part of so many sagacious politicians and acute men of business, as to the probable success of the rebellion. The long persistence of the South was in itself a most melancholy event to me, for I clearly foresaw it was leading them on to the desolation and hopelessness in which they are now placed "Sir, we are a recuperative people," said an American to Mr. Trollope, and some ten years hence it is quite possible that even the South will be prosperous. The elections here are going on without Conservative reaction and without Liberal enthusiasm. The Radicals, on the whole, are the losers, which I am not glad of, as I foresee a danger in our *bourgeoisie* becoming too exclusively an aristocracy (without much peculiar personal merit), and thus forming the *pays légal* inside the nation which was so fatal to you in '48. I hope your health has been better, and that you suffer less from your old enemy. Mine—the gout—has much benefited by Vichy. I hope to do this year without going abroad, and drink my waters at home. The House of Lords suits me very well; the business there is in a very few hands, and there is a fair recognition of anyone who takes a prominent part in public and private affairs. But, of course, a new member of any assembly must take time to get his place there, and I am still the Benjamin of the family.

You will be glad to see that Sir John Acton is elected, and I hope Sir John Simeon will also win.

I am yours very truly,

HOUGHTON.

Mr. Bright to Lord Houghton.

Rochdale, July 30*th*, 1865.

DEAR LORD HOUGHTON,—I should have had particular pleasure in coming to see you, but unluckily I am engaged to go down into Wales on Tuesday next, and cannot be home before Saturday, if indeed before Monday; and the engagement being on a matter of importance in which others are concerned, I cannot escape from it or postpone it. America is going "all well." There will be some difficulties, but they will be easily surmounted. Here the elections show there is no Conservative reaction since 1859. That article has been only discoverable in the Cabinet, but I think it cannot long take shelter even there. I am afraid you are not happy in the serene atmosphere to which you have betaken yourself. I don't wonder at it. I am sorry I cannot come and discuss both the States and England with you. I hope to get down into Scotland for two or three weeks after I get back from Wales. Many thanks for your kind invitation.

Always sincerely yours,

JOHN BRIGHT.

The Same to the Same.

Rochdale, August 10*th*, 1865.

DEAR LORD HOUGHTON,—The Fates are sorely against me and I cannot leave home on pleasure just now. I am writing two other letters of a like character to this, and you will see that my difficulty is a real one. I am not revolutionary, except in a Conservative sense, as all I have done, or been concerned in doing, in the past will clearly show. As to your House of Lords, the remedies you suggest are not likely to be adopted by a Tory majority among the peers, and the House of Commons could not insist upon them except in a time of revolution. There is no real remedy for anything of moment but in the admission of a million more electors, and in the growth of opinion through the discussions of the press. I am sorry I cannot come, but your kind good nature will forgive me.

Mr. Carlyle had been elected this year Lord Rector of the University of Edinburgh, and his address to the students on the occasion of his assuming office was looked forward to with profound interest. Among those upon whom it was proposed to confer an honorary degree at the time of Mr. Carlyle's visit to Edinburgh was Lord Houghton. He could not at that time accept the invitation of the University, but he invited Carlyle on his way north once more to break his journey at Fryston.

T. Carlyle to Lord Houghton.

Chelsea, November 23rd, 1865.

DEAR OLD FRIEND,—I will see Fryston again one day, and bring my wife, unless Fate itself have forbidden, but for the present all the indications are that it actually will not do. We are both as weak as possible (I, you would almost say, the weaker—sleepless, catarrhal, &c. &c.) ; nor is this the sole consideration, though I think it really might be the sufficient one ; but the truth withal is, ever since I saw you I have been endeavouring to combine a visit to Fryston with that "inaugural" journey to Edinburgh (which it does appear I am bound, to my sorrow, on) ; and for that latter the choice hangs for ten days past "between the week before Christmas" just coming, and the "first week of April next," which, I believe, will be Easter-time, when Fryston may again be alive with your presence. Easter, I find, for many reasons will probably suit me best, and, though the decision is not yet quite irrevocable, I believe it will fall that way, and Edinburgh in a day or two hear that it is so. Edinburgh is sorrowfully *indistinct* hitherto, talks of early in January and other dates; but I must settle it myself, and on strict survey cannot well otherwise than above. Pity me! Do not be angry at me, and fancy I care nothing for you—hardly ever in the world were you more mistaken.

Yours sincerely, as of old,
T. CARLYLE.

The April date was that finally selected, and the reader has already been told of the party which met at Fryston when Carlyle passed through on his way to the North—a party which included Professor Tyndall, Professor Huxley, Mr. J. F. Maclennan, M. de Circourt, and the present Sir James Kitson. Mrs. Carlyle had been asked to accompany her husband, but the following letters explain her failure to do so. They are among the last she ever wrote.

Mrs. Carlyle to Lord Houghton.
5, *Cheyne Row* (? *March*, 1866).

MY DEAR, KIND LORD HOUGHTON,—I have been out in far worse winds than yesterday's since I came to depend on my drives for *sleep!* And I am not afraid of the *journey* to Fryston, nor of *bodily* fatigue generally. For, you see, I am what is pleasantly called "*a living miracle!*" meaning—a woman who, according to Nature, should have been dead and buried away two years ago, and is here still, going about in society alive and well.

(To be sure, both the aliveness and the wellness "*may be strongly doubted*," as they say in Edinburgh.)

What I *am* afraid of, and what has determined me against accompanying Mr. C—— on this "accursed adventure" (I don't mean the Fryston part of it), is the agitation that was getting hold of me about *his* agitation. I had visions of his breaking down in his *address!* of his lying ill with fuss and *dinners!* of his going to wreck and ruin in every possible way! And *I* unable to do anything, *now*, for his furtherance, but just to take the terrible *pain in my back* which assails me under all violent emotion. In intervals of good sense I perceived that my only chance of escaping an illness was to cut myself loose from him till the "accursed affair" was over.

"What the eye sees not,
The heart grieves not."

When he is gone out of my sight I shall calm down. But if I should *prolong* the nervousness of these days, going with him and the others to Fryston, I should get no good of Fryston, and risk a spell of illness. I want to go to Fryston (it would be the first time, remember) in a state of mind that would not interfere with my enjoyment of it. Mr. C—— says he "cannot give me any advice; will not take the responsibility of my going; but if I don't think it wise to go with him now, I may say that I will come in the summer weather *if you like*, and bring *him* along with me." Will you let me come later? And will you believe how much I should like it in my normal state, and how much I like *you?* Lady Houghton, too, has written to me so kindly.

Affectionately yours,

JANE CARLYLE.

Mrs. Carlyle to Lady Houghton.

5, *Cheyne Row* (? *March*, 1866).

DEAR LADY HOUGHTON,—You are kind to write me a letter "all to myself" (as the children say), about coming with

Mr. C—— to Fryston—more than *kind*; it strikes me as almost *heroic* to take graciously to the Bore of an extraneous individual in one's house, when one has just had a bad illness, and is still feeling ill.

I am afraid, however, that all in admiring your sweet nature, I should not have been unselfish enough to keep away, in the fear of being tiresome, had not other quite selfish fears decided me to stay at home while my husband is away seeking —*not* a golden fleece (it is to be feared).

I leave it to Lord Houghton to explain my ridiculous reasons, and also to convey to you my hope that you will ask me another time—when we are all better !

Sincerely yours,

JANE W. CARLYLE.

The story of Carlyle's journey to the North, with its wonderful triumph and its disastrous close in the sudden death of Mrs. Carlyle, has been told by his companion, Professor Tyndall, nor does it lie within the scope of this narrative to dwell upon it; yet so far as the break in the journey at Fryston is concerned, the reader must necessarily be interested in it. It was Carlyle's last visit to the house in which he had first been received as a guest twenty-three years before.

In these years he had ceased to be the struggling genius, recognised only by the few, and had become the undisputed ruler in the republic of letters. He had at the same time attained a social position which has seldom fallen to a literary man, and doubtless he would have smiled had he recalled the impression which the first sight of Fryston made upon his untrained imagination. But, as the letters I have just quoted show, whatever other changes had occurred, there had been no change in the affection with which he regarded Milnes. This last memorable visit to his old friend was by no means the least satisfactory to both. It began somewhat unfortunately, owing to Carlyle's inability to sleep—an inability which made him restless and irritable. One of his fellow-guests still recalls the almost ferocious way in which, turning upon him as though he were the incarnation of the guilt of which he had to complain, Carlyle said, "They tell me, sir, that the people of Leeds have set up a roaring blast furnace in the middle of the ruins of Kirkstall Abbey; is that so, or is it not?" Even the assurance that the outrage of which he spoke had not been committed hardly sufficed to calm his temper, and that first evening at Fryston was one of somewhat mingled experiences. But a good night's rest made Carlyle a different creature. Next morning he was tolerant, amiable, and good-natured to everybody. The evening was spent, as so many evenings were in those days at Fryston, in the brightest interchange of thought and wit among the little party of distinguished men, of whom the host himself was by no means the least distinguished. The scene is one upon which all who knew Fryston must love to dwell. Happily, many years of life still remained before Lord Houghton himself, and whilst he lived the glory of Fryston never entirely departed; but with the death of Thackeray, and that breakdown in the health of Carlyle which followed his wife's sudden end, a change came over the place which seemed to prove to those who knew it that as one of the great centres of the intellectual life of England its brightest days were past.

Extracts from Letters to his Wife.

House of Lords, April 23rd, 1866.

Caroline Bromley called on me late on Saturday evening, and left the sad news of Mrs. Carlyle's death. I enclose Miss Jewsbury's letter. He was getting quite over his Rectorial troubles, and expecting to return home to her next week. It would be best that she should be buried in Scotland, and that he should not come back to his vacant home.

10*th* (? *June*, 1866).

I have just returned from lunching with the Aumales, whom I had not seen since the death of the queen. I had an Italian gossip with the Duchess, who becomes quite Neapolitan in her native language. Carlyle let me in yesterday, and talked about her (Mrs. Carlyle) for near an hour. How I wish I could have taken down what he said word for word! "She wrapped me round like a cloak, to keep all the hard and cold world off me." "When I came home, sick with mankind, there she was on the sofa, always with a cheerful story of something or somebody, and I never knew that she, poor darling! had been fighting with bitter pains all day." "To think that little dog should have been the instrument to take the light of life away from me." "What would it be for me now to have the fame of Trismegistus, without her to be glad at it?" "She had never a mean thought or word from the day I first saw her looking like a flower out of the window of her mother's old brick house, my Jeanie, my queen;" and so on.

CHAPTER XVI.

THE FRENCH EXHIBITION.

Politics in 1866—Houghton's genuine Liberalism—Correspondence with Mr. Gladstone—Houghton at Vichy—Count de Montalembert—Biarritz—The Imperial Family—The Cambridge Union—Houghton opens the New Rooms—His Speech—The French Exhibition—Houghton accepts Presidency of Group of Liberal Arts—His Stay in Paris—Distinguished Acquaintances—A Pleasant Dinner—The Sultan in England—Female Suffrage—Letters from Mr. Mill—The Great Review at Paris—Meeting with the Queen of Holland—Speech on the Roman Question—Goes to Rome—Longfellow in England—A Catholic Breakfast-Party and a Narrow Escape—The Queen and Carlyle—Lord Houghton visits the Queen of Holland—Attends the Opening of the Suez Canal—The Ecumenical Council.

THE year 1866 was notable in English politics; it witnessed the abortive attempt of the Liberal Government, of which, since the death of Lord Palmerston in October, 1865, Lord Russell had been the head, to introduce a Reform Bill; the opposition of the Whig section, under the brilliant leadership of Mr. Lowe; the formation of the Cave of Adullam; the fall of the Government; the reinstallation of Lord Derby as Prime Minister; and the great agitation throughout the country on behalf of an extended franchise, in which Mr. Bright took a leading part. Houghton held strongly to the Liberal side throughout the movement, and again afforded proof of the fact that his elevation to the House of Lords had strengthened, rather than weakened, his faith in the people and in popular institutions. Early in April he presided at one of the great popular meetings in favour of Reform. It was held when Lord Russell was still in office, and was intended to strengthen his and Mr. Gladstone's hands in carrying the measure which they had laid before Parliament. The scene of the meeting was the Cloth Hall at Leeds—a spot famous in the political history of the West Riding—and Lord Houghton's speech was as advanced in tone as the most thorough-going Reformer could have wished it to be. He was, indeed, one of the very few peers who took an open and pronounced part in the agitation of the year. Throughout the Session political events in London were of great interest, and we get glimpses of them from his correspondence with his wife.

Extracts from Letters to his Wife.

House of Lords, February 28*th*, 1866.

A bitter Oriental wind, varied by yellow fog—such is the climate you are avoiding. . . . Half the company never came to the Downshire's. Lady D. thought she had asked them for the wrong day. There was a good party at Mrs. Procter's, Lady Strangford wearing the Order of the Holy Sepulchre, given her by the Patriarch as a descendant of the Beaufort of the Crusades; Minnie Thackeray and her tall lover who smiles silently on her. . . . The meeting at Gladstone's seems to have been a real success, both Bright and Lord Grosvenor having been well received, and Lord Russell having virtually abdicated into Gladstone's hands.

(*Undated.*)

I heard Lowe with interest and admiration. When he had done, some one said, "This goes against 1831, not 1866." I answered, "It is against 1688, and is all for a wise despotism." I had a long talk with Mrs. Gladstone, and consoled her by saying it would have been just the same whatever Gladstone had done. All the fellows who are going to lose their places are very savage with him.

(Undated.)

The party seemed very lively at Lady Russell's last night, and seemed to be confident of a fair majority. He thanked me for my Leeds speech. I dined with Trollope and the *Fortnightly* writers. Huxley and Tyndall were there, and gave a good account of Carlyle. He is still in Scotland. You should see him in this week's *Punch*.

(Undated.)

Party spirit is running very high, and the Grosvenors and Argylls are said not to speak. B. positively goes against the Government; Peel is still doubtful. The Rothschilds are in great anxiety at the state of things on the Continent. If a war broke out they would lose as much as they did in 1848. I sat by Gladstone at the Delamere's. He was very much excited, not only about politics, but cattle plague, China, and everything else. It is indeed a contrast to Palmerston's ha—ha and *laissez faire*.

April 30th.

The only objection to the Government's remaining in office is that the party may show its anti-Reform tendencies still more strongly than they have done, and result in a general break-up.

Lord Houghton to Mr. Gladstone.

16, *Upper Brook Street, March 20th*, 1866.

MY DEAR GLADSTONE,—As you are hardly accessible for conversation, I should be glad of a line from you as to what you advise respecting the agitation for the Reform Bill during the recess. This combination of the houses of Grosvenor and Stanley affords a favourable standpoint for those who would defend the Franchise as an advantage in itself (which is my main care in the matter), and who resent the notion that an additional popular element is a diminished national security. I am sure we could get up an enthusiastic county meeting in Yorkshire, with Lord Fitzwilliam in the chair, if it is well worked. I judge from the Leeds meeting at which I presided just before the beginning of the Session. The only danger is that the Reformers might exhibit dissension of object and distraction of purpose, which would do more harm than good to the cause. Some of our friends whom I have spoken to are evidently afraid of this, but it will hardly do to give the sanction and pretence of the popular silence to doubtful or hesitating voters.

I am yours very truly,

HOUGHTON.

Mr. Gladstone to Lord Houghton.

11, *Carlton House Terrace, S.W., March* 21*st,* 1866.

MY DEAR HOUGHTON,—If you have occasion to call, I shall be most happy to see you on the subject about which you have written to me. You are one of those who are in earnest about the business—I believe an increasing band. I think that all public demonstrations on behalf of the Bill are likely to be useful—one from Yorkshire would be pre-eminently so; of course it must be referred to the judgment of those who are acquainted with the local circumstances and feelings, to judge in each case whether there is any risk in the experiment.

Believe me

Very sincerely yours,

W. E. GLADSTONE.

It is likely that I shall myself attend a large meeting at Liverpool in Easter week.

Lord Houghton to G. von Bunsen.

16, *Upper Brook Street, July* 13*th,* 1866.

MY DEAR GEORGE,—I wish I had seen you on your way through town to the sea, but I trust I shall not miss you again. I am here all next week, and shall be very glad if you can dine here on Friday, the 20th. You would meet our new Foreign Minister, Lord Stanley, whom you might like to talk with. I go to the country on Saturday the 21st, and, with the exception of the middle of the day on Monday, shall be absent till the Friday following. Out of town again for two days on the 30th, and off for France and Vichy on the 4th.

These public matters are too great to write about. I have been ostracised in society for my Prussian *velléités*, and I am the only public man who has dared to have Bernstorff to dinner. I am also thankful the Austrians are out of Venetia anyhow; but at the same time the act of the French Emperor in accepting the mediation, and at the same time letting loose the army of Italy on Austria, is quite a new form of diplomatic wickedness.

I should think the best thing the Liberal party could do would be to look on the present condition of things as a temporary dictatorship, and reserve your forces till the crisis is over. It seems to me quite on the cards that Bismarck will have to fall back on the extreme Liberal party, and go in for a monarchical republic.

My wife is a good deal better, but not well, or up to much exertion; the doctor thinks that Vichy will suit her as well as me. The change of Ministry has passed over very quietly. It was a real collapse, and inevitable by human skill. Gladstone showed a real fervour of conviction, which has won him the attachment of 300 men, and the horror of the rest of the House of Commons. He will be all the better for a year or two's opposition.

Our children keep quite well, and will be very glad to see you again. Pray tell your wife not to drop us, but to look us up whenever she can.

Yours affectionately,

HOUGHTON.

In August Lord Houghton went abroad to Vichy, Bordeaux, and Biarritz, passing through Paris on his way.

Lord Houghton to George von Bunsen.

Vichy, Aug. 14*th,* 1866.

MY DEAR GEORGE BUNSEN,—I heard of your family sorrow; after what you told us it could be hardly a surprise, but perhaps none the better for that. We should be glad to hear of your wife.

We have been here some days, of continual rain; if the air were as full of alkali as the earth, we should only want a *Luft-bad*. Lady Houghton is already better for the change. We are in a little châlet with our own servants, and comfortable enough. I saw Drouyn de l'Huys and Prince Napoleon as I went through Paris—the latter very indignant about Italy, and, I think, with justice. Prussia ought to have taken care that the Italian Question should be settled once for all; it is the only justification of the Alliance, beyond the most mercenary motives. If the 200,000 Italians are left to groan and rebel under German rule in the Tyrol, it is Venice over again, and there will be another row. The Buonapartes are the only friends that Italy has in France; they are real *Buona*-partes to her. I believe, too, that the said dynasty is a good deal more friendly to you than the people. The official people I saw were in the worst temper possible. Please write me a good long letter in any language you please; perhaps English is the safest. I enclose an article I wrote in the *Pall Mall,* and which may amuse you. I saw in the *Débats* a furious article by John Lemoinne on the extravagance of the sympathy of England for Bismarck and Prussia. Did you find it so? I think you have got off fairly well with your royal speech; you may think yourselves very lucky if you get off with the loss of Saarbruck.

Anthony Trollope to Lord Houghton.

Waltham House, Waltham Cross (1866).

MY DEAR LORD HOUGHTON,—I send you a copy of "The Warden," which Wm. Longman assures me is the last of the First Edit. There were, I think, only 750 printed, and they have been over ten years in hand. But I regard the book with affection, as I made £9 2s. 6d. by the first year's sale, having previously written and published for ten years without any such golden results. Since then, I have improved even upon that.

Yours always faithfully,
ANTHONY TROLLOPE.

Count de Montalembert to Lord Houghton.

Paris, August 20*th*, 1866.

MY DEAR LORD HOUGHTON,—From your letter of *to-day*, the 20th, received *yesterday*, the 19th, I conclude that you never got a letter from my daughter addressed to Meurice's Hotel, in which she informed you that if you prolonged your stay in Paris, or came back through here, I should be most happy to see you. This I now repeat, in case you should have some hours' leisure on your return back to England; but I am in a very sad state, having been confined to my bed for the last four months, and only being able to see one or two persons at the close of the day, between 4 and 6. Mind, therefore, not to attempt to crush me by your boisterous Prussian and Italian sympathies, for I am quite unable to fight the battle of Sadowa over again with you. Mrs. Craven is now in Italy, after having passed the winter in Paris to publish her book. She would be delighted to hear from you, particularly if you take the trouble to read her book, "Récit d'une Sœur," the second edition of which has just come out, and which contains all the history of her family at Rome and Naples from 1830 to 1836. I am sure it will greatly interest you. Hoping to see you soon again,

I remain
Ever yours most sincerely,
CHARLES MONTALEMBERT.

Lord Houghton to Lady Galway.

Biarritz, Oct. 5*th*, 1866.

The sun is now looking in at the "winder" (as the English young ladies say) direct, for the first time since we came here. As it must, however, be drier here than elsewhere, with the full Biscayan Sea, and the absence of vegetation, I shall not move till Annabel is pretty well again. It is thought a dull season here, but I have found it lively after Vichy, and have seen some rather notable people. But there is neither a personage nor a locality to bring them together, and, except for the afternoon promenade, when a poor band of the line performs, anybody, however important—M. Bismarck himself—might be here without being generally noticed. The château* sees nobody. I go there and talk with Merimée, and the great people are civil when one sees them about, but I keep out of their way. *She* (the Empress) talks to Amy, who thinks her very goodnatured, but not at all pretty. She is getting too stout for the character of her face. They neither of them make any concealment about his suffering a good deal, and they call it rheumatism. . . . . I went into Spain for a night, to see the monastery of Loyola, where St. Ignatius was born, and luckily had fine weather. It is an interesting place in sad decay. One of the few monks left said to me, with evident delight, of the Spanish Government, "After having stolen everything from us, they are poorer than ever." During the constant rain one of the bathing-men said to a priest, "Es vrai, Mounsr l'Abbé, que lou Boun Diu es parti pour l'Amerique?"

From Biarritz, Lord Houghton and his wife and daughter went to Val Richer, to visit M. Guizot and his family. In November a Reform Banquet was held in the Free Trade Hall, Manchester, at which Mr. Bright was the principal speaker. Lord Houghton attended it, and made a speech, which was not very well reported in the *Times*, and brought down upon him the rebukes of some of his friends whose faith in Liberalism was not so robust as his own.

* Seaside residence of the Emperor and Empress.

To his Wife.

Tatton Park, Knutsford, November 21*st,* 1866.

There is such a stupid and untrue report in the *Times* of what I said at Manchester last night that I send you the Manchester paper with a better, though even that is not accurate. The sight very, very fine, and the speaking on the whole good. I never heard Bright so amusing; he was really better than a play; and Forster spoke with much effect. The resolution was not extreme, and one of the ladies said to me, "Oh! why don't those foolish men let Lord Russell's Bill pass? It would be such a comfort to cease being a Radical!" Mr. Potter entertained me magnificently; he has had his house done up by Crace, with all the luxury becoming "one of the people." The ladies at the banquet came out with great effect, most of them in scarlet burnouses.

Lord Houghton to Henry Bright.

November 27*th,* 1866.

What a beautiful thing that Free Trade Hall, when full, is! For once the reporters, who generally are very good to me, made me talk hideous nonsense, and I quite agreed with the *Standard* on the subject. It happens that what I said was better than usual, and was well taken—though not quite agreeable to the audience. You see, I am on the Neutrality Commission; I suppose we shall visit Messrs. Laird's yards in the course of our inquiry, and examine into the facilities for piratical picnics.

G. S. Venables to Lord Houghton.

26, *Cavendish Place, Eastbourne, November* 23*rd,* 1866.

. . . . I am depressed, and almost alarmed, about public affairs. Bright's agitation seems to me the most formidable and dangerous of our time; he has taught, or is teaching, the horse that it can kick the rider off, as it certainly can—and it follows that it probably will. I no more believe that political democracy in England will be compatible with social aristocracy than I do that Colenso is compatible with Christianity. Perhaps an American England may produce a larger average of happiness than the existing system, but it would not be a country for a gentleman, and I for one should be quite strange in it. Besides, I believe the happiness of America consists chiefly in having plenty of land, which cannot be created in England. The happiness in France is compounded of land in insufficient quantities, a tolerably warm climate, and dealing as the man in the story, though he was Italian, dealt with *la tua madre*. I have no doubt that freeholders are much happier than tenants, but a world of freehold farmers does not interest me. Another thing I am disturbed about is our lapse from the rank of a Great Power, which cannot be recovered without a conscription, and that is far off, though with a democratic reform it may come in time. If Dizzy can keep his head straight, and if the Ministers are prepared to eat everything they have ever said, I have no doubt the great majority of the Liberal party in the House of Commons will give them every support, being with reason more opposed to Bright than to the Tories. I expect, and fear, mobs every night to intimidate Parliament. I was very much gratified with your kindly mention of my name at Cambridge. I hear that your address there was a great success

Yours sincerely,
G. S. VENABLES.

The allusion in the foregoing letter to the Cambridge speech refers to an engagement in which Lord Houghton had taken part that had nothing to do with politics. This was the opening of the new rooms of the Union Society in his old University. Houghton was asked to deliver the Inaugural Address, and the speech he made was not the least felicitous of his efforts in this line.

When I accepted your kind invitation to appear here to-day, and say a few words in inauguration of your new hall of debate, it would have been well if I had recollected an anecdote which I have read somewhere about Goethe, the great German poet. When he was in his maturity, a young man came to him and asked him to explain the meaning of a passage in "Faust." Goethe replied, "Why do you come to me? You with your youth are ten times more likely to understand what I meant than I am in my maturity."

And thus, gentlemen, if you do not inspire me with something of your ardour—it may be, with something of your youthful audacity—I do not know how I can justify your choice or express my gratitude. For now, after the distance of time, and in this dissimilitude of circumstances, it is impossible for me to appeal to the power of association. The *genius loci* entirely fails me. This is not my Cambridge Union.

My Cambridge Union was a low, ill-ventilated, ill-lit apartment, at the back of the Red Lion Inn—cavernous, tavernous—something between a commercial room and a district branch meeting-house. How can I compare it with this superb building, these commodious apartments, these perhaps over-luxurious applications of architecture which you will have to enjoy? But I remember that those old and humble walls had, at the time I first entered them, just ceased to echo voices which England will not willingly let die. The strange irony of destiny, which so often strikes exactly those whose long life we should imagine most needed for the welfare of mankind, has already taken away from us Macaulay, a great historical orator and oratorical historian; Praed, that perfect master of light and social verse; Charles Buller, whose young statesmanship you will see recorded in Westminster Abbey, but whose charm of character and talent belong to the domain of personal regard; and John Sterling, whose tumultuous spirit and lofty character still live, and will long live, in the biographies of Hare and Carlyle. My lot was cast with a somewhat later generation, and I must beg you to pardon the affection and the prejudice with which I am inclined to believe that the members of that generation were for the wealth of their promise—a promise in most cases perfectly fulfilled—a rare body of men, such as this University has seldom contained. I speak not here of eminence in the especial studies of the place, in classics or mathematics, though I cannot omit the name of our respected Chancellor, the Duke of Devonshire, but you will permit me to recall some names dear to myself, and many of them familiar to you all. There was Tennyson, the Laureate, whose goodly bay-tree decorates our language and our land; Arthur, the younger Hallam, the subject of "In Memoriam," the poet and his friend passing, linked hand-in-hand, together down the slopes of fame. There was Trench, the present Archbishop of Dublin, and Alford, Dean of Canterbury, both profound Scriptural philologists who have not disdained the secular muse. There was Spedding, who has, by a philosophical affinity, devoted the whole of his valuable life to the rehabilitation of the character of Lord Bacon; and there was Merivale, who—I hope by some attraction of repulsion—has devoted so much learning to the vindication of the Cæsars. There were Kemble and Kinglake, the historian of our earliest civilisation and of our latest war—Kemble, as interesting an individual as ever was portrayed by the dramatic genius of his own race; Kinglake, as bold a man-at-arms in literature as ever confronted public opinion. There was Venables, whose admirable writings, unfortunately anonymous, we are reading every day, without knowing to whom to attribute them; and there was Blakesley, honorary Canon of Canterbury, the "Hertfordshire Incumbent" of the *Times*. There were sons of families which seemed to have an hereditary right to, a sort of habit of, academic distinction, like the Heaths and the Lushingtons. But I must check this throng of advancing memories, and I will pass from this point with the mention of two names which you would not let me omit—one of them, that of your Professor of Greek, whom it is the honour of Her Majesty's late Government to have made Master of Trinity; and the other, that of your latest Professor, Mr. F. Maurice, in whom you will all soon recognise the true enthusiasm of humanity, and upon whom this University has conferred a far greater favour than any that honours or emoluments can give—an expanded sphere of usefulness, and the extension of moral sympathies.

Of these men, all, I believe, were members of the Cambridge Union Society, and most of them active participants in its debates, and I would ask you to draw from this the moral that it is well that the purposes of this society should not be confined merely to its own immediate objects, but that it should be regarded as an addition and succedaneum to the ordinary studies of the University. The majority of these men won your highest honours, and at the same time were the best speakers in the Union. There was one exception. There was one man—the greatest speaker, I think, I ever heard—a man with the strongest oratorical gift, a man of the name of Sunderland, who only lives in the memory of his own generation, and for this reason—that he was only known at the Union at Cambridge. Perhaps the sole record of him is the prize declamation which he delivered in Trinity Chapel in the year that I performed the same function. I remember now with a certain shame a kind of hope that I entertained that the first prize, which was so undoubtedly due to his rare oratorical faculty, would be lost to him on account of the extreme violence of the politics and the curious heretical nature of his essay; but somehow or other the college forgot all the moral demerits in the intellectual excellence of that production, and I came off only second-best. It was in company with Mr. Sunderland and Arthur Hallam that I formed part of a deputation sent from the Union of Cambridge to the Union of Oxford; and what do you think we went about? Why, we went to assert the right of Mr. Shelley to be considered a greater poet than Lord Byron. At that time we at Cambridge were all very full of Mr. Shelley. We had printed the "Adonais" for the first time in England, and a friend of ours suggested that as Shelley had been expelled from Oxford, and greatly ill-treated, it would be a very grand thing for us to go to Oxford and raise a debate upon his character and powers. So, with full permission of the authorities, we went to Oxford—in those days a long post-chaise journey of ten hours—and we were hospitably entertained by a young student of the name of Gladstone—who, by-the-bye, has himself since been expelled. We had a very interesting debate, one of the principal speakers in which, who reminded me of the circumstance, is now an Archbishop of the Roman Catholic Church; but we were very much shocked, and our vanity was not a little wounded, to find that nobody at Oxford knew anything about Mr. Shelley. In fact, a considerable number of our auditors believed that it was Shenstone, and said that they only knew one poem of his, beginning, "My banks are all furnished with bees."

We hoped, however, that our apostolate was of some good, and I have no doubt that the excellent President of the Union at Oxford will now tell you that the poetry of Shelley is just as much and widely appreciated at Oxford as at Cambridge. The reference to the interest which we took in this literary question reminds me that on looking over the late records of this society I do not find the mention of a single literary debate. You seem so absorbed in politics that you have no time for literature. Will you permit me humbly to suggest that you may combine the two, and that it will be well for you, and will afford an agreeable variety, if some of your debates are of a literary character? In my time we were certainly much more forced upon these subjects than you are, because by a limitation—I do not know whether of our own imposing or required by the authorities—we were not allowed to discuss any political subjects later than the beginning of the present century; so we got fervent upon the character of Lord North, and fierce upon the policy of Cardinal Richelieu. Although you no doubt think this very barbarous, it had its advantages. It forced us to read about these things, and kept us more in connection with history than with newspapers. It combined the circumstances of the society with the general education, and was, I am bound to say, attended with many advantageous results. Of course, you could not now go back to that state of things; but I believe that the character of these debates very much diminished the weight of the objections which are frequently brought against societies of this kind.

To one or two of them you will perhaps allow me to allude. One is, that debating societies of this nature tend to encourage volubility of speech where there is abundance neither of knowledge nor of idea. No doubt in some cases that may be so, but both our national character and our national language conspire to render those cases rare. Our national character is certainly not garrulous; our defects are all on the other side. Garrulity is not the sin of the English youth. We find every day, both here and in the world, young men who have seen a great deal and know a great deal, but who, for want of ready and accurate speech, hide a great deal of their light under a bushel; and I think that these societies have a very great advantage by developing the powers of speech and remedying these defects.

Nor is our language one that lends itself to frequent and ready speech. I have attended public debates in France, Spain, and other foreign countries, and I never witnessed abroad anything like the hesitation, the haggling, and the difficulty of finding words which prevail in our House of Commons.

Englishmen always seem to say what they must say, while Frenchmen seem to be able to say anything they choose. The truth is, that the composite nature of the English language produces in the mind of a speaker hesitation as to the best construction and the best word to employ; and thus some of our best public speakers hang, as it were, on a precipice for the choice of a word, and bring down the acclamations of their audience when they happen to hit upon a right one.

Therefore, from the constitution of our national character and our national language, I do not fear that the practice of public speaking will necessarily tend to make you too loquacious, but I think that it will give you that accurate and ready form of speech which is absolutely necessary for all political success, and is advantageous in every profession. Another more serious objection which is brought against institutions of this kind is, that they lead young men too early into the discussion of politics. For my own part, I do not see how any man, however young, or even any boy, can be brought to the serious study of history without at the same time awakening in his mind political associations, and to a certain degree conveying political ideas.

If history is to be nothing but a dry series of dates, a mere chronicle of events, a boy with a good memory will remember it, and a boy with a bad memory will forget it, and neither one nor the other will derive from it any considerable intellectual or moral advantage. But when a youth connects the history of the past with the political life of his own time, he is able to realise that past, and to apply it to the present. Then history becomes a living reality, and is no longer the dead body it would otherwise be. I cannot help feeling that in thus advising you I am recommending a study which may lead to conclusions somewhat different from my own opinions, because there can be no doubt whatever that political study, both at this University and at Oxford, has, I will not say from what cause, resulted in a remarkable prevalence of Conservative opinions. While the *étudiant* of Paris and the *Bursche* are, at best, considered as a very agitated element in society, and at the worst as the firebrand of revolution, the student of an English University is, generally speaking, a model of devotion to the Altar and the Throne. I am inhibited by circumstances from giving any reasons for this phenomenon. I simply recognise it as a fact, and I think there is something generous in the feeling which makes me say, notwithstanding this result, cultivate your politics. Cultivation may bring with it modification of opinion, and I do not know that you will eventually be worse critics or more sedulous reformers because you have, at one time of your lives, as I may think, too blindly reverenced or too affectionately loved what you may afterwards perceive requires alteration and improvement.

The moral advantages of such institutions as this have been dwelt upon with great ability by my noble friend, Lord Powis. It is impossible to over-estimate the advantage which any man gains by placing his own mind in clear and fair conflict with another mind. It is in such societies as this that you will learn the value of political forms—forms in themselves perhaps apparently frivolous and pedantic, but which you will find to be absolutely necessary for the government of these societies, and, in fact, of all societies of men. You will learn that while there is here an open field for all your ambitions, for the exhibition of all your powers, the great advantage that you gain is not in the expression of your own opinion, nor even in hearing the opinions of others; it is in the fair conflict of intellects; it is in the meeting of man and man.

Go on, then, as you have done. Make this noble room a worthy arena of your young ambitions, teaching you to respect one another, and to respect yourselves; teaching you to tolerate even the intolerant; place this edifice under the tutelary protection of Good Manners and Good Sense, and no one will ever find fault with the Cambridge Union Society.

I have ventured to quote this speech at length, chiefly because of its autobiographical character, but in part as an example of a kind of oratory in which Lord Houghton was most at home.

The proceedings attracted a great deal of notice from the press, and much was written about the Union and the days to which Houghton had referred. One of the most striking of the articles suggested by the occasion appeared in the *Daily News*, and was devoted to the story of Thomas Sunderland—a story the facts of which could then only be conjectured, though I have now laid them before my readers in the early portion of this narrative.

The year 1867 was almost as full of political interest and excitement as 1866 had been. All the world knows how the Session was devoted to the carrying of a great measure of Parliamentary reform—a measure which, after undergoing many changes, and passing through an extraordinary number of crises, eventually received the Royal Assent in the shape of a Bill establishing Household Suffrage in the towns. Another feature of the year had even a closer personal interest for Lord Houghton than the passing of the Reform Bill—this was the International Exhibition held in Paris under the auspices of the Emperor. Lord Houghton had been asked by the English Government to be one of the jurors, and the French Government emphasised the compliment by asking him to become President of the group of Liberal Arts, an invitation which he accepted. His duties required him to remain in Paris for several months during the year. Lady Houghton was, unfortunately, in very delicate health, and was unable to accompany him; but his sister, Lady Galway, took the head of his establishment in Paris, and assisted him in entertaining his friends.

To his Wife.

* *Hickleton, January,* 1867.

The party are Ebor [the Archbishop of York], the F. Cavendishes, the Thomsons of Kirby, Sir David Dundas, and the Vaughans to dinner. I am going this morning with Ebor to see the Barnsley disaster.† He was there yesterday, but wishes to go again. The accounts are very curious—one of them that when ———, the man saved as by a miracle, was taken home, his wife burst out in abuse of the people who brought him for not leaving him in the pit, saying he was such a blackguard, and she had hoped she was "shut" of him.

* The house of Lord Halifax.

† There had been an explosion of a very disastrous kind at the Oaks Colliery, Barnsley, a few weeks previously, causing the loss of some hundreds of lives.

His term of office in Paris was one of great enjoyment to Lord Houghton. The Empire was then at its zenith; the beautiful city had never in its long history been gayer or more beautiful; its streets were crowded with visitors from all parts of the world, and the Imperial Government lavished its money in making the spectacle as imposing and magnificent as possible. The Czar and other monarchs became the guests of the Emperor; distinguished statesmen entered Paris in their train. Hospitality was exercised not only by the Imperial Court, but by all associated with it, on the most lavish scale. The world had seldom seen a display of such magnificence. Lord Houghton enjoyed everything thoroughly. He enjoyed, according to his wont, the great fêtes which were given in honour of the royal and distinguished visitors; he enjoyed the banquets, at which he met most of the leading statesmen of Europe; but, above everything else, he enjoyed the opportunity of making the acquaintance of many of those distinguished men of letters whom he had hitherto known only by name. Flaubert, Edmond About, Daudet, Emile Zola, Tourgenieff, were among the new acquaintances whom in this *annus mirabilis* he added to his long list of friends. Many marks of distinguished attention were shown to him, not only by the Emperor, but by the leading Imperialists. For example, a special order was given under which he was allowed to make use of the President's box in the *Corps Législatif* whenever he wished to do so. But even now, under all the glamour of a success more dazzling than any which the latter-day world has seen, he remained true to his own convictions, and stood firmly by the friends of his youth, the men who were the real representatives of order and liberty in France. I bring together a number of his letters from Paris during the year.

To his Son.

April 3rd, 1867.

MY DEAREST ROBIN,—With the fine sunshine and warm air of to-day I fancy you riding about the woods and enjoying yourself extremely. I have sprained my ankle, and thus can only hobble along. It was very tiring, at the opening of the Exhibition, to stand or dawdle about for two or three hours. Both the Emperor and Empress looked rather *tristes*. They are said to be very unhappy about their little boy, whom Amy saw at Biarritz. He has had to have his leg cut open, and bore the operation with very great courage. I think Florey's verses on Ferry Bridge capital, but she is more patriotic than I am, for I think it a dreadful-looking place now.

To his Wife.

It was a roughish passage, and I went down-stairs. The consequence was, I was very poorly. I left London two inches deep in snow, and found here the warmth of spring. The change was quite comical. I went to Madame Mohl's in the evening, and found myself talking to Renan, &c., as if I had been in Paris a month. *Comme la vie est facile ici!* The *appartement* is only too comfortable.

March 30*th.*

. . . . I am unfortunate here in my friends. Among the popular men I have lost Drouyn de l'Huys, though I dined with him as a private guest on Monday, and now Walewski, who is all hospitality and civility, has sent in his resignation as Speaker. It was most convenient to me to have him in that place, as it secured me a place in the Chamber to hear the debates, and she was a charming hostess besides. He has been turned out for letting Thiers abuse the Empire and the "Deux Décembre" without calling him to order. I think he did quite right; for the little man was in such a fury that any opposition would have only irritated him and made him worse. I was with Thiers at the Opera last night. I dined yesterday with Madame Mohl—quite a crack intellectual party. Brookfield came in the evening. He is librarian to the British part of the Exposition, and is lodged and fed at the expense of the country. I took —— with me to the opening as Lady Houghton. Lord Orford is here, very agreeable, and Van de Weyer, but not many Londoners as yet. One of them was charged something immense at a café, and said, "Je suppose que ces sont les prix de l'Exposition?" Answer: "Monsieur a raison; nous les essayons dès aujourd'hui; monsieur est le premier qui les éprouve." I have only seen old Guizot once. M. and Madame Guillaume dined at Madame Mohl's. She seems rather liked at Paris. Montalembert is worse, and I have not yet seen him; but Rio is in great force, and I dine with him on Sunday.

April 9th.

There are very few English in Paris, and hardly anyone in the Exposition. The Americans swarm. We have alternate days of rain, which makes the fine ones very fine. The chestnuts are quite out. The political violence here is extreme, and you would fancy from the *talk* that they were going to war with Prussia to-morrow; but I think there is no chance of it. Our affairs do not look at all well, and I should not be surprised at a dissolution of Parliament, which is the only reason one is glad to be out of it, otherwise I hardly feel myself an Englishman out of Parliament.

April 18th.

I have been so much occupied with jury work that I have hardly seen the Exhibition at all thoroughly, and shall therefore stay a day or two longer than I proposed. . We had a beautiful ball at the Cowleys, on Friday, and a dull one at the Tuileries last night. I dined at Prince Napoleon's to meet our

Princes, who have made themselves much liked by their cheerfulness and simplicity. I saw Montalembert yesterday; he looks better, but said to someone, "I am a drowning man who feels the water rising higher and higher."

Saturday Evening.

The weather continues warm and pleasant, with sharp spring showers. I hope you have something like it, and can get out. I have already dispersed nearly all the cards you and Florey wrote me, but have not seen very many people. The Cowleys have told me to send in the morning whenever I have nowhere else to dine, which is civil, and I have dined there the last two days. I went to a private representation of the *Misanthrope* last night, by the very best actors of the Français, at Marshal Vaillant's, and a capital performance it was too, about one hundred people comfortably seated—rather different from Lady M.'s theatricals. It was amusing to hear the Marshal say to Lord Cowley, "Ce terrible Cole est arrivé." Strange that the energetic little man makes himself felt here as in London. The Emperor is said to be very anxious about the little prince, who has had the abscess in his thigh twice operated on. So very *parvenu* a family as the Buonapartes had really no right to the king's evil. I mounted up five stairs to Mrs. Greville yesterday, and found her on her couch with the faithful "Julie" at her feet. My friend Duvergier is gone to Cannes to see his sick son, and several notables are laid up. The wife of M. de Lavalette is dying; so though "the weather" is propitious, the health is not. I am going by appointment to see Prince Napoleon, so good-morning. It is a thousand pities he did not remain at the head of the Exhibition; there would have been none of the meanness and fraud there now has been.

To his Daughter.

Paris, May 10*th*, 1867.

MY DEAREST AMY,—Mrs. Symons has come in for the day, and is talking to me while I am writing to you. Aunt

Harriette has gone to look out for a smart gown to go in to Lady Cowley's to-morrow. This is the more necessary as there is a total change in costume, all the ladies being dressed like the picture of your grandmother in the breakfast-room, and nobody but cooks wearing crinolines. . The inside of the Exhibition is perhaps the coolest place in Paris. I meet the Prince of Wales at dinner at Lord Cowley's to-morrow, and Aunt Harriette comes in the evening. We dine to-day with M. Thiers, and go to the opera afterwards.

To Henry Bright.

Paris, May 12*th*, 1867.

I have been here for some time, and sit with *Conseil Supérieur*, making speeches utterly irrespective of tenses or genders. But, as one of the Chamiers said to me, "You are here to look after English interests, not French grammar." There has been a good deal of meanness in the whole administration of the affair, of which, I think, they are somewhat ashamed. The Exhibition itself is very amusing, and is a wonderful congeries of human labour and ingenuity.

His duties in connection with the Exhibition for the moment at an end, Lord Houghton returned to town to find the political situation still full of complications; the Tory Ministry gradually breaking up in the process of passing the Reform Bill.

Lord Houghton to Mr. Gladstone.

Athenæum Club, April 20*th*, 1867.

MY DEAR GLADSTONE,—If you go to Paris, do not forget to call on our old friend Rio, who lives at 22, Rue d'Oudinot. He is very susceptible of a little attention, and is as charming as ever.

A different person, Prince Napoleon, told me he much wished to see you. He is very interesting, and his resignation of the Presidency of the Exposition has caused it irreparable injury. The present management of it is very bad, and everybody is discontented; yet it is well worth seeing, and will be more so every day.

I am delighted at your last political move; it will give you some repose from responsibility, and will be an excellent discipline for the party, which will now reform itself in a natural way; as it is at present, it is certainly not fit to reform anyone else.

Yours very truly,

HOUGHTON.

Lord Houghton to George von Bunsen.

Fryston, April 23*rd,* 1867.

MY DEAR GEORGE,—I did not write to you from Paris because if I had anything to say of any value it would probably be opened and read. I wished to sum up my impressions of opinion there to the last. I left it on Saturday, and the feelings and expectations were so mutable as to be quite ridiculous. There was no supposition too extravagant, but the sum-total was no doubt a very positive resolution that you should not retain the garrison of Luxembourg. The thing heard from the family and *entourage* of the Emperor was that your great man had three times formally offered Luxembourg to the French as a minimum of compensation for the acquisitions of Prussia, and now, when it was convenient to them to take it, they would not be put off by any sham constitutional objections. If Bismarck made the pretence that it was necessary for the integrity of Belgium, they would say that he had offered France the undisturbed possession of that country if she would engage not to interfere with his German projects, and that therefore he would not make that pretence even. The French country is certainly very much excited, and Emile Girardin's ingenious device of the Prussian quadrilateral had immense success. At the same time, apart from the Luxembourg question, I do not think there is any desire of active hostility towards Germany, and it is most unfortunate that Bismarck ever made the suggestion to France to take it. You will have to give it up, as the Americans did Mason and Slidell—or, at least, to appear to do so, unless you choose it to be believed that Bismarck requires a war to unify Germany. However, I do not think a fair defensive war would be injurious to you; but an offensive war, such as your detention of Luxembourg and the continued occupation of Northern Schleswig would bring on, would be seriously criticised by future history. I cannot see how it would be *worth while*. You seem to believe that the Orleanists are preaching war because they think it will damage the Emperor. So far from it, Thiers and his friends believe that a victorious contest would only rivet their chains, and establish the despotism on a still firmer basis. Of course they make all the capital they can out of the Emperor's unpopularity.

I am here for ten days, and return to Paris on the 6th of May for a short time. I liked what I saw of Goltz; he seemed to me to have a capital mask of frankness, and a good deal of diplomatic ingenuity under it. The Exhibition is vulgar and speculative—a congeries of incongruous interests, of real industrial usefulness and the lowest form of gratified curiosity. You see Lord Shaftesbury haranguing between the Chinese dancing girls and the great guns. What it will be in the heat and confusion of summer is unimaginable. My wife is far from well, and I am afraid we shall have to go south for the winter. I am hesitating between Nice, Palermo, and Algiers.

I say nothing of our poor insular politics; Disraeli is triumphant, and the Christian hero Gladstone in the dust. *Resurgat!*

Yours affectionately,

HOUGHTON.

To his Wife.
London, May, 1867.

I met Gladstone at breakfast. He seems quite awed with the diabolical cleverness of Dizzy, who, he says, is gradually driving all ideas of political honour out of the House, and accustoming it to the most revolting cynicism. It seems he has most difficulty in keeping Hardy in the Cabinet. Delane says the extreme party for Reform are now the grandees, and that the dukes are quite ready to follow Beale into Hyde Park. Venables, Collins, and Kinglake, dined at the Procters', which was agreeable, as usual. I go to Paris to-morrow night.

Friday, 20th (? June), 2 a.m.
(<i>After a capital concert at Lord Dudley's</i>)</p>

The political position is so stretched that it is quite a comfort to get away from it anyhow. If one was fairly in it, that would be different; but one is not, and one must run away. There is a *mot* of James Lowther's going the round of the town, that he did not see how he could meet his constituents after having refused a moderate measure from a good Christian and taken an extreme measure from a bad Jew. Lady Russell asked Wentworth Beaumont yesterday whether he did not think Lord Russell's conduct *beautiful*. Lord Derby asked Lady Cranbourne (they call the new Cave, Cranbourne Alley) if she remained awake all night, like Cranbourne, calculating the effects of the Bill. "Yes," she said, "I was engaged in a sum of subtraction, and I found that if you took 3 from 12 (the number of the Cabinet), nothing remained.* We discussed the Cave to-day at dinner, and Lowe said he "always regretted having made any admissions, as he was sure that candour was the original sin."

Pascoe Grenfell is dead—a curious combination of an ironmaster and a dandy, impossible nowadays. Fancy me tossing sick in a bitter east wind to-day! It will do you good to compare it with your own comfortable boudoir. Such is mankind.

June 27th.

... Garrison† was very interesting this morning. He was the Wilberforce of America, with the difference that while the

---

* Lord Cranbourne, Lord Carnarvon, and General Peel, had resigned.
† William Lloyd Garrison, then on a visit to England.

one had a life of general affluence and was buried in Westminster Abbey, the other has lived a life of constant persecution, imprisonment, and danger of death, and has at last lived to see slavery abolished in America. He is of course fanatical, and told us that in a few years the blacks would be the sovereign race in the Southern States in wealth, intelligence, and power.

Tuesday, Midnight, July 2nd.

A pleasant dinner is enclosed.* I suppose the company thought so, as they are only just gone. Bright stayed to the last, talking very instructively of the past and future. Gladstone was talkative and gay; Gaskell silent. Lord Halifax was roughly pleasant; Julian Fane, full of his daughter, whose health we drank; Monteith, abstracted, but not absurd; and Mr. Winthrop asked much of you. Swinburne accepted, and never came, *more suo*, as Amy will translate to you. I met *Ecce Homo* at breakfast this morning at Sir H. Holland's. He is a delightful man, simple and dignified as his book, and humorous withal.

The Cottage, Milford, Godalming,
July 30*th*, 1867.

Our expedition to Tennyson's was a moral success, but a physical failure; for we had so bad a pair of posters that we regularly knocked up seven miles from this house, and should have had to walk there in the moonlight had we not met with a London cab returning from Goodwood. As I should have had to carry Mrs. Greville, you can imagine what we escaped. The bard was very agreeable, and his wife and son delightful. He has built himself a very handsome and commodious home in a most inaccessible site, with every comfort he can require, and every discomfort to all who approach him. What can be more poetical? The Gladstones and the Duke of Argyll were there last week.

* Viscount Halifax, Mr. Gladstone, Mr. R. C. Winthrop, Mr. Bright, Sir Bartle Frere, Mr. Albert Rutson, Mr. Frederic Harrison, Mr. Milnes Gaskell, M.P., Hon. Julian Fane, Sir Francis Goldschmidt, Mr. R. Monteith, M.P.

(*Undated.*)

Swinburne writes in good spirits: much amused at the doctors recommending him light reading and repose, "just as if," he says, "I ever read or did anything serious."*

The fête last night was not only magnificent, but beautiful altogether; the finest thing I have seen in England, and perhaps anywhere.† You will see in the papers the grim ending of the "Arabian Night." Madame Musurus attacked at the Sultan's supper-table. Dudley Carleton helped to carry her out, but she was never conscious again. She was a capital woman, and had been the making of her husband. He was a tutor in her family. Her children quite adored her. Harriette had shaken hands with her a few minutes before, and was quite affected. The Sultan kept us waiting above an hour, saying his nerves were quite overcome by this event. He went round the circle in the French way, Fuad Pasha saying to each, "Sa Majesté est charmé or enchanté or très heureux de faire votre connaissance." Kinglake was there and many grandees.

Lord Houghton to his Daughter.

July 19th, 1867.

DEAREST AMY,—I was just thinking of writing to you to-day instead of mamma when your letter arrived. You see by the enclosed that she was at the Guildhall last night, which perhaps you did not know. There was a tremendous crowd, and I had to get out by the kitchen, to get to dine at the India House, where we had a rehearsal of the dinner the Sultan is to have there to-day. As I was in uniform, the crowd chaffed a good deal when they saw me coming out the back way; and one said, "Here's a chap who has made himself sick already." And another, "He

---

* Mr. Swinburne had been seized with serious illness while breakfasting with Lord Houghton a few days previously.

† In honour of the Sultan, who was then visiting London.

has got a stick and a sword too;" but they were very good-natured. The Sultan is a fine-looking man, and has his little boy with him, about Robin's age, but shorter and a good deal graver. He looked quite solemnly round at the people; he will not be the heir to the throne, as in the East the succession goes to the representative of the eldest branch—thus the son of his eldest brother will inherit, a young man of about twenty, who looks very fierce. I am to see the Sultan to-morrow at Buckingham Palace. I enclose an article on Miss Coutts which mamma might like to see. I am going to her fête to-day; she dines 3,000 Belgians and others in tents. All the chickens are to be cut up and then tied together, so that nothing need be carved except string.

It was at this period that Lord Houghton joined an undertaking at that time very unpopular, but with which he was in full sympathy—the movement for securing the suffrage for women. He did so, as will be seen, at the invitation of Mr. Mill.

John Stuart Mill to Lord Houghton.

Blackheath Park, August 2nd, 1867.

DEAR LORD HOUGHTON,—A society is in course of formation to carry on the movement for admitting women to the suffrage, to which, I know, you are favourable, and it will be of great value to the society if you would give your adhesion to it by allowing me to add your name to the General Committee. Business will be conducted by the Executive Committee of ladies, and the members of the General Committee are responsible for nothing except approval of the object and an annual subscription of a guinea. My daughter and I are on the General Committee, and it would give me great pleasure to be allowed to enrol you on the list. Very truly yours,

J. S. MILL.

The Same to the Same.

DEAR LORD HOUGHTON,—I am very glad that you are willing to be on the General Committee of the Women's Suffrage Society. The grounds of justice and of principle for removing the disabilities of women cannot be better stated than in your words, and in those of Lady Houghton cited in your note. Would it be too much to ask the benefit of her name along with yours on the General Committee? I am not uneasy about the future fate of representation of minorities, for the working men do not share the indifference of the middle class to superior cultivation, and are much more willing than the middle class to give full and thoroughgoing effect to a principle. Hughes stated at the meeting on Wednesday that the question was debated at the Working Men's College, and after several discussions was at last decided in favour of representation of minorities. The only plan which fully and fairly carries out the democratic principle is Mr. Hare's, and that is now rapidly making way among thinking people.

Very truly yours,

J. S. MILL.

In August Lord Houghton joined his wife at Bonn, and went with her to Wildbad.

Lord Houghton to George von Bunsen.

Wildbad, August 22nd, 1867.

MY DEAR GEORGE,—I am glad on the whole that you did not come to Bonn, for I should have been fancying that you were losing some electoral chance; yet it would have been very pleasant to have seen you there, even for a few hours. The old place would have looked like itself again. We arrived here yesterday after a sweltering but not disagreeable journey, and shall be stationary I suppose for three weeks. Three doctors without consultation recommended these baths to my wife, and as I am always breaking my ankles they can do me no harm. After we leave here I have a thought of Switzerland, and Miss

Wynn gave me a hope that about that time you might be visiting your mother at Blouay. Write me whether there is a chance of it. I saw Dr. J. Brandis, Bernays, V. Sybel, and Roggenbach at Bonn, and passed two pleasant talkative evenings. The visit was to Lady MacCarthy, and full of sad memories it was. I have played Providence to some three or four remarkable men, and Nemesis has just come in when they were in their prime of work and strength, and carried them into the Infinite. I wonder always whether the Great Providence is treated the same way when He tries to do something good and great.

As I passed through Nassau the people were grinding their teeth at the Prussians having appropriated the family property of the old reigning family, including the Stein vineyards.

I don't understand why it is not the interest of Prussia to make the princely families into a wealthy aristocracy, which in a short time would look on themselves as ramparts of the throne. The other game is the same sort of unconscious democracy which Lord Derby is playing in England, and which must be dangerous, for it is fraudulent and short-sighted. Write me a long gossiping letter to beguile the time at this place, where I do not expect to find any reasonable playfellows. Do you happen to know anyone here, or likely to come?

With our best regards,
Yours ever,
HOUGHTON.

To his Younger Daughter.

Wildbad, August 23rd.

DEAREST FLORENCE,—We ascended to this lofty sanitarium the day before yesterday in a drive of three hours through hay-fields with their second crop, and fir forests with clear red stems. Mamma is already better for the baking we have had on the Rhine—especially, I think, for one long day on the river from Bonn to Bingen. It was a great pleasure to me to see Lady MacCarthy so cheerful and contented in her humble life at

Bonn, after the loss of all her wealth and grandeur, which she had so long as my dear friend was alive. She has a nice little boy, a year younger than Robin, who, now that he is a Highlander, you may call your Rob Roy. Amicia enjoyed Heidelberg very much, and was very full of all the sad adventures of the Queen of Bohemia, King James's daughter, from whom, you know, our Royal Family inherit the crown of England. Our acquaintance here is as yet limited to Sir Alexander and Lady Malet, and Mr. and Mrs. Godfrey Lushington. .

I hope you are making the most of your three governesses. I doubt whether any princess in Germany has more; and Amicia tries to nourish her mind on any crumbs of knowledge that fall from her parents' table. I hope you won't find her intelligence very thin when we all meet again. There is a lame German prince in our hotel with seven children, who occupies all the best rooms, so that we are not likely to have many new acquaintances. We cannot yet tell how the baths suit, but they are pleasant to take. Love to all.

Your affectionate

HOUGHTON.

Mrs. Procter to Lord Houghton.

Hampstead, Sept. 30th, 1867.

MY DEAR LORD HOUGHTON,—I want very much to hear tidings of you and my dear Lady Houghton. I have been thinking of you more than usual of late, for I have been rereading "Henrietta Temple." How charming it is! I know no man but you who would admire it. Most men have had all the tenderness and sentiment of their character rubbed off by the world. The old saying, "Tell me your company, and I shall know what you are," I read, "Tell me your books."

We have been here for three weeks, and go home on the 8th of October. We are at one side of the Heath, and have delicious walks round this neighbourhood. It has done my husband a great deal of good—the change and good air. We are close to the George Smiths.

I had a holiday for three weeks at Malvern Wells; since that I have been staying at Knebworth. It is charming there—the best thing life offers except Fryston. Lord Lytton is such good company, and so good to me! We had long walks and long talks. Mr. and Mrs. Lytton were there, Anthony Trollope and his wife, and Mr. Farrar ("Eric; or, Little by Little"). I found Trollope very pleasant.

Since that I have been here, and seen Wilkie Collins, who is working hard at a new book to appear in *All the Year Round* about January next. Mr. —— I met at dinner the other day, and he told me that by his brother's death he comes into £20,000. Some part of it he intends to spend in giving dinners—not a bad way; it is the only manner in which you and I shall benefit by the legacy. May he ask us soon, and let me sit next you! I ask no more. Pierce Butler is dead, and Mrs. Fanny Kemble sailed—or, rather, steamed—for America the very week the news came. You will see that Mr. Lytton announces two new books; and, oh! happy that we are, the author of "Only Dare" has a book in the press. Mr. Venables having reviewed it and praised it in the *Saturday* no doubt has been the cause of this second attempt. I cannot tell you how he has degraded himself in my opinion by doing this. His praise or blame are now quite worthless. I never could write a book, and one strong reason for not doing so was the idea of some few seeing how poor it was. Venables was one of the few; I need not say that you were one and Kinglake.

Pray let me hear from you; take a little time from some friend or acquaintance, and give it to your affectionate and grateful old friend

ANNE B. PROCTER.

P.S.—B. C. sends his love to Lady Houghton, and kisses her hand, appointing Robin his substitute. I have been reading Maria Edgeworth's memoirs; Lady Strangford lent them me. They will amuse you and Lady Houghton; so much about people you have heard of, and some you have known. Miss Edgeworth praises too much; she calls Abbotsford a *magnificent castle*. How Sir Walter must have flattered her! I found also some mention of a Madame Belloc who translated Miss Edgeworth's books into French. M. Belloc, her son, married Bessie Parkes. I and Edith went to her wedding. The mother was there, and is, I believe, known to Madame Mohl. I hear that Miss Wynn goes on the 16th of October to the South of France. Oh! for the good old days when people stayed at home, and the world was at war!

It was decided that Lady Houghton should spend the winter at Cannes, her delicate health making a sojourn in a warmer climate than that of Yorkshire necessary. Lord Houghton travelled through Switzerland with her by easy stages from Wildbad to the South of France, and then returned to Paris to resume his duties in connection with the Exhibition. One of the incidents of the brilliant year of dissipation in Paris was the review of the French troops held in honour of the visit of the Emperor of Austria. It took place whilst Houghton was in Paris, and he saw as much of it as possible.

A beautiful sight [says one of the newspapers], that glorious day in the bright sunshine, the anniversary of Balaclava, where French and English fought together. It could be seen that the Emperor Francis Joseph rode on the left of the Emperor Napoleon and next the troops. The Emperor Napoleon was on his favourite chestnut, and wore over his uniform the broad riband of the Austrian Order of St. Stephen. Marshals, generals, and officers—French, Austrian, and Italian—and great personages followed the line behind Prince Napoleon, and the Archdukes Charles and Louis Victor. There was one red coat in the midst of the gay cavalcade—a red coat with silver epaulettes and buttons, surmounted by a cocked hat with white plumes, and supplemented by blue trousers with silver stripe; and it might be said of Lord Houghton as he sat his steed among the press of knights, all radiant with stars and crosses and orders, in that plain, unadorned, and peaceful attire of a Deputy-Lieutenant of an English county, "*Ma foi! il est bien distingué!*"

Whilst he was still in Paris the politics of Europe were disturbed by the announcement of the determination of the Emperor of the French to occupy Rome with his troops.

To his Wife.

28, *Avenue des Champs Élysées, October* 19*th*, 1867.

Arrived about an hour ago, and drove from the station in an open carriage with a bright morning moon. Am going to meet the Stanleys at breakfast at Madame Mohl's at 10.30. Just missed the dinner to the Queen of Holland, which came off last night. Found my Radical friends at Lyons in great excitement about a fresh intervention in Rome, which they looked on as certain, saying it was all the doing of *l'Espagnole*, who they only wished had been drowned the other day at St. Jean de Luz, and who would come to the same end as *l'Autrichienne* if she did not take care. . . . Anxious to hear how you are, and how Cannes looks.

Tuesday, 10 *a.m.*

No letter from Cannes yet arrived, so you will judge what time it takes for a letter to get here. . . . I had an interesting breakfast with M. Négrier. He read me the despatches just received. The King of Italy gives way to the threats and power of France, who would else have certainly taken Genoa, from which it would have been difficult to dislodge her. Nobody knows where Garibaldi has gone to. I wish he was safe at Chiswick. The Queen of Holland was very agreeable yesterday, and seems to be enjoying herself much here. I found Charles Villiers sitting with her. The weather here is very bright and pleasant. I am going to drive this morning to St. Cloud to write my name for the Emperor. The Granvilles have been here for two months, and their own horses and establishment, and only return for the meeting of Parliament.

Paris, Oct. 27th.

It is quite possible that you saw from your windows yesterday morning the French fleet on their way to Italy. The news fell like a thunderbolt on the world here, everyone having looked on the affair as being well settled—at least, for a short time. Now everyone asks, What next? and the agitation is extreme. This is indeed a delightful place to live in, always some confusion and excitement going on; in fact, these people could not live without it. The banquet yesterday was very magnificent and uncomfortable, as these things usually are. I sat by the wife of a Deputy, who told me they had a villa at Nice which they had not time to occupy above a month in the year. I said she had better let it to me. She said no, but she would lend it to me with pleasure. I wonder whether she meant me to take her at her word. The Emperors are gone to the Races at Vincennes, and I am going to a meeting of the "Société de Protection des Apprentis," presided over by the Empress. . . . I still intend to leave this on Friday, so let me know whether you would like *Galignani* continued or the *Times*. Delane, by-the-bye, is here in great force. I took him to the Queen of Holland. She asked him (rather an awkward question), "Combien d'abonnés il pourrait avoir?" He said, "Un million, madame." She called him to someone in his presence, "Le quatrième pouvoir de l'état Britannique." He seemed much amused. Granville began his speech yesterday with a little accent; but as he went on you would not have known it was not a Frenchman. It could not have been better done. You will read the report to-morrow. M. Rouher's political oration was in very bad taste, with some Italians present.

There was an autumn session of Parliament, and Lord Houghton came to town to attend it.

To his Wife.

Travellers' Club, November 11*th,* 1867.

With this yellow fog and your blue atmosphere combined, an artist like yourself would rub up a fine green colour.

I dined at the Guildhall yesterday, the new Lord Mayor being a bookseller and an old acquaintance of mine. I sat very much where we did two years ago, and in your absence I had Lady John Manners for my companion. She and her Minister have been over to Paris to learn the French dodges about planting and sewering and street-making, and so we may expect some results. The thing that struck them most was the way in which each tree in the Boulevards receives air to its roots from an open grating, and water through a pipe that runs round its roots. He says he should like to make a boulevard of Regent Street. I do not see the use of trees as long as our smoke blackens everything. . . . I stay over to-morrow for an Abyssinian meeting of the Geographical Society: it ought to be interesting. The speaking last night at Guildhall was supremely dull. I actually went into a state of coma while Dizzy was orating. Lord Derby was laid up with the gout, and the story now is—which I do not believe—that he is likely to resign, and will recommend the Queen to make Dizzy Premier.*

16, *Upper Brook Street, November* 20*th.*

You will see I came out on the Roman question in the House of Lords,† and I should like to know whether you see the *Times,* as I could send you any number of particular interest.

---

* Lord Derby resigned in the following February, and was succeeded by Mr. Disraeli.

† Lord Houghton spoke at length during the debate. He was charged in the papers at the time with having assumed to speak as the representative of Louis Napoleon and the exponent of his policy. The charge was of course absurd; but there was no doubt that during his stay in Paris, in his frequent conversations with the leading statesmen of that capital, he had gained a more intimate knowledge of the intentions of the Emperor than most Englishmen possessed.

I saw Lady Palmerston yesterday, much saddened by her granddaughter's condition, which is most painful. . . . The Bishop of Oxford at Grillion's yesterday told me the Bishopric of Lichfield had been offered to, and refused by, the Bishop of New Zealand. I am not sorry for the refusal, Selwyn having come out very strong in the Synod against the Bishop of London. I dine with the Procters to-day to celebrate his 78th birthday, and go to Fryston to-morrow, returning on Wednesday for the Neutrality Commission, which has begun to sit weekly.

There seems some little hope of Mrs. Disraeli to-day: the scene in the House of Commons was very striking, Dizzy quite unable to restrain his tears.* I think Cannes will do very well for you, or for you and the children, but I do not think I should like it, and I hope you may not dislike going somewhere else in the beginning of the next year.

Sunday Evening, December 15*th*, 1867.

I have heard nothing from Fryston in this subterranean city, but shall keep this open for to-morrow's bulletin. I have just come from the scene of the Fenian Gunpowder Plot.† I do not believe such havoc could have been wrought by one barrel of gunpowder, and think it must have been filled with some still more explosive material. Some of the houses were literally blown away, and are nothing but a heap of bricks. It is hoped that the poor little wretched children, some twenty of them, will not survive—they are so frightfully injured. Two looking out

---

* When Parliament met, Mrs. Disraeli was lying dangerously ill, and Mr. Gladstone, in the opening sentence of his speech on the Address, gave public expression to the sympathy of all parties in the House with her husband. It was then that Disraeli was overcome, as Lord Houghton describes.

† On the previous Friday, December 13th, an attempt was made by a party of Fenians to blow up the House of Detention at Clerkenwell, where one of the Fenian leaders was confined. Twelve deaths in all resulted from this outrage. The principal perpetrator, Barrett, was convicted, and hanged at the Old Bailey.

of the window with curiosity, to see what the men were doing with the barrel, had their faces blown off. There would be more indignation at the sacrifice of these poor innocents than if half a dozen Lords had been murdered; and the American Minister said to me, "You will be having some lynching here soon." My friend Sir Richard Mayne is blamed for not having a larger police force present, for they had full warning of the attempt by an anonymous letter. Tell —— there is great discussion of Dr. Kenealy's conduct in throwing up the brief for the defence. There can be no reasonable doubt that his clients are implicated in the plot of rescue, but as yet there is no legal proof. It is the most Irish part of the matter that had the Fenians been in the yard, as the conspirators expected, in all probability they would have been killed by the concussion, as well as a large number of other prisoners.

In the beginning of 1868 Lord Houghton accompanied his wife to Rome, where they spent some time. His children were with him, and he was able to introduce them to scenes with which he had long been familiar.

To Miss Jane Milnes.

Rome, April 18*th,* 1868.

MY DEAREST JANE,—Whether it be the cold weather here— quite exceptional for the season—or some constitutional recurrence of the disorder, I do not know, but Annabel has been very poorly again. I have, therefore, given up going to Florence as I intended, and remain here until I start for England by the direct boat to Marseilles on Friday next. I hope thus to find myself in England on Monday, the 27th. I have taken the house on here till the 8th of May, to the great delight of the children, who cannot have enough of Rome, and to whom it has certainly been very useful. By that time the row in Florence contingent on the Royal Marriage will be over, and they will be able to spend a week there on their way to Wildbad. Mary von Orlich is quite cross that I do not send them there for the fêtes; but it would increase Annabel's trouble, and they have seen wonders enough here for the present. . . . The elder Peers are thinning off fast, and I shall meet a dozen younger colleagues on my return. . The Pope's voice is the most curious thing in the ceremonies, all which he goes through as a perfect actor. I have not been to see him, but have had some interesting conversations with Cardinal Antonelli, who is remarkable. Of course, they are pleased here at the Irish Church affair, but would, I think, have preferred the endowment of their own Church, as I should. They also look on Gladstone as a revolutionist, and take everything doubtfully from his hands.

Extracts from Letters to his Wife.

16, *Upper Brook Street, Saturday, May* 2*nd.*

It has been a week of strong political excitement, beginning with Lord Derby very improperly interfering, like a schoolmaster addressing his young friends, and begging them not to resign. Gladstone is the great triumph; but as he owns that he has to drive a four-in-hand, consisting of English Liberals, English Dissenters, Scotch Presbyterians, and Irish Catholics, he requires all his courage to look his difficulties in the face, and trust to surmount them. I was in hopes I could have told you the result of Dizzy's visit to Osborne; but nothing has yet transpired, and to-morrow will be left to the plenitude of rumours in which a London Sunday delights to indulge. The Duke of Northumberland has refused both the Lord-Lieutenancy of Middlesex and the Garter, evidently not wishing to take anything from the present men. The Duke of Wellington has the former, and Lord Bath is likely to have the latter. I have seen Lady Palmerston, in great vivacity, full of stories of Dizzy, his talking to the Queen as "two authors," and Mrs. Dizzy's new carriage and two footmen.

16, *Upper Brook Street, May* 27*th*.

The weather is so genial here that I hope it may be so in your lofty valley [Wildbad], where the fresh green must be delightful under the dark firs. I dined yesterday with Dean Stanley, and sat by Princess Christian. The party consisted of the Grotes, Lyells, Milmans, Stanley, and Maurice. The Dean and I talked a good deal across the Princess, and she seemed much amused. Mrs. Bruce came in the evening, full of inquiries about you all, and vivacious as ever. . . . There was a purely political party at Strawberry Hill—Forster, Goschen, the Childers, and the Gladstones. It was very agreeable, though Gladstone is in a terribly worried state of mind. It is almost comical to see him in antagonism to the whole English Church. He professes not to be disappointed; but I hardly think he counted the cost when he proclaimed his policy.*

Lady Houghton remained abroad until July. In the spring of that year an Exhibition of Fine Arts was opened at Leeds, in a large building just erected from the designs of Sir Gilbert Scott as an Infirmary for the West Riding. Lord Houghton had taken much interest in the undertaking, and, besides assisting it in other ways, contributed several of the family portraits to the temporary gallery which was opened by the Prince of Wales. During the summer many visitors of distinction who went to Yorkshire to see the Leeds Exhibition were entertained at Fryston. One of these, whose name must be mentioned here because of his long friendship with Lord Houghton, was Mr. Walkiss Lloyd.

* Disestablishment of the Irish Church.

To his Wife.

Fryston, May 30*th.*

I write alone in the big house, haunted too with your smile and the children's laughter; but the united efforts of Mrs. Eliza and Mary Davy have given me such a good dinner that I have no right to be sentimental, especially as I indulged in a bottle of very old claret, just to try it. The Prince's visit to Yorkshire was a success, though he had a bad cold. At Mr. Denison's we had the beautiful Lady Dudley, whom her husband decorates with the most magnificent jewels. It was trying work for an old gentleman like me, not in bed till 4 a.m. each morning. You will, I think, enjoy the Exhibition in a quiet way. Lady Milnes was conspicuously admired. I made the only joke of the period. Somebody said at lunch,* " What room is this to be?" "The dissecting-room of course; will you take a leg?" I was asked to dine at Temple Newsam, but declined, being very well where I was. The long gallery at Temple Newsam was entirely lit up with candles, and looked very handsome. The Prince said he was hot; so they instantly smashed the windows which would not open easily. Curious the different nature of England from the Continent. This modest place, with its lush and various greens, and the air heavy with white and red may, and the songs of the innumerable birds, had a quiet charm even after Italy; not more or less, but one of its own. Considering how things have been left to themselves, they have done very well. The garden and houses promise abundantly (a great apple-year), and —— only laments that to please the farmers he shall have no rabbit-pies for you.

Political affairs are most interesting. On the eve of a change of Government the Queen goes off to Balmoral, for which Delane taps her rather hardly. Pomfret had a near escape on Monday, Rainald Knightley having moved to take away one member, but Mr. Baxter's motion to disfranchise the smallest boroughs was carried. I do not see how the Government can stay in with any dignity or comfort. At the only

* In the Infirmary.

ball I have been to in London, I found the waltz going on to the tune of "Strangers Yet," and Mrs. Sainton Dolby has set what I call your poem, "Recollections," charmingly.

To his Wife.
June 13*th*, 1868.

Though we do not make much of anniversaries when together, yet at this distance I must tell you how dearly I think of you to-day, and how full of you all the world is for me wherever I go.* I had some people to lunch, and I was doubtful whether I should ask them to drink your health; but somehow or other I felt your own disinclination about it, and drank it secretly myself.

The party was Monseigneur Talbot, who dresses like a High-Church parson, and looks puffy and prelatic, and less gentleman-like than in his robes. I had perverts enough to meet him to send Aunt Lulu into fits—Monteiths, Procters, Gaisfords, Mrs. Montgomery, A. de Vere, then Mrs. Bruce as a hyphen to join on Harriette and the Arthur Russells. We had a really miraculous escape at lunch—not from fire, at least of a physical nature, but from an explosion. As I went out of the dining-room, Day said a young gentleman had called, and he had asked him into the dining-room; but he would not come in, and would call another day, and had left his card:

R. GARIBALDI!

No human being but would have believed that I had asked him to meet Talbot; and what a confirmation it would have been of the wildest stories of my parties! I dined yesterday with Mrs. Denison, in the same room in which I remember dining with the Bishop at his first dinner after his marriage with Miss Ker-Seymer.

"And we the painted shadows on the wall."

---

* Lady Houghton's birthday. She was at this time abroad, owing to the state of her health.

The Queen gives a breakfast to six hundred people in the gardens of Buckingham Palace. The Tories have not asked us once to Court this year.

During the summer of 1868 Mr. Longfellow paid a visit to England, and renewed his acquaintance with Lord Houghton. The latter was his conductor on a visit to the House of Lords, and, together with Lord Stanhope, arranged for a dinner in his honour at the Athenæum Club.

Lord Houghton to Mr. Henry Bright.

June 16*th*, 1868.

You should see London in its state of political anarchy. I quite go with Robertson Gladstone about the calumnies against the great man, coming, as they do, from the Church of which he has been the faithful and eminent servitor for the whole of his life. Does it ever strike you that nothing shocks pious people so much as any immediate and practical application of the character and life of Christ? On the question itself, I do not go with him, valuing most highly the connection of any Church with the *State,* which really means with the governing laity.

I am to review "The Spanish Gypsy" for the *Edinburgh,* and should much like your impression of it. She* has gone abroad to get out of the way of criticism.

I hope Longfellow will come straight to me, as I have some invitations for him.

To his Wife.

London, June 23*rd*, 1868.

I was delighted to get the quadruple letter; it was quite what our ancestors would have called a posy. The weather has been so sultry that I have been divided between wishes and

* George Eliot.

regrets for you. Your room here has been 70° every night with the passsage-window open; but then the Rhine may be still hotter, and your room may not be so comfortable. The effects of the drought on farming have been very disastrous: the wheat and turnips have both suffered considerably. There is a little better prospect to-day, the sky being overclouded with frequent showers. Mr. Markham, fresh from Magdala, breakfasted with me yesterday, and left us all Theodorians. The whole career of King Theodore is like a bit of Biblical history, ending with his "dying in the gate." He shot himself, believing that the English had betrayed him. . . . Julian Fane has left the profession altogether, telling some one he meant to retire to the country and lead a pastoral life. What is more surprising is that Odo Russell has refused the post at Paris, which both his mother and Lord Clarendon thought just the thing for him, as Lady Mary would have made a capital Ambassadress for the bachelor Lord Lyons. There is a great rush for dinners this and next week, and nothing much after; so you will find London going out of town. Henry Bright comes up to me to-day to stay till the end of the week. I shall take him to breakfast with Gladstone, and tea with Lord Stanley. Gustave Doré has just been here, looking over my Blakes; he is a charming man.

(? June 30th, 1868.)

I hope Longfellow will not be gone when you come. I took him to the House of Lords yesterday, where they treated him with great distinction, and gave him a place under the throne. Longfellow breakfasts here on Friday, and we give him a dinner at the Athenæum on Monday. I met Rassam at breakfast this morning, and he tells many curious stories of Theodore.* The little boy is seven years old, and the king told him to consider Rassam as his father. So when Rassam asked him to sit down and eat with him, he said, "How can I do that? am I not your son? Shall a son dare to sit down and eat in his father's presence?" You see what good family rule there is in Abyssinia.

* King of Abyssinia.

The Athenæum dinner was a distinct success, though the arrangements were not completed without the usual amount of friction caused by the difficulty of including in the party all who thought they had a right to join it; and Houghton's correspondence of this period bears testimony to the fact that he was not successful in avoiding all personal offence in the arrangements, for which he was chiefly responsible. Honour was, however, done to the distinguished American poet, and that, after all, was the chief object at which the promoters of the dinner aimed.

In the autumn of this year Lord Houghton enjoyed the distinction of being elected a Fellow of the Royal Society—a compliment which was all the greater because he received it in virtue not of his scientific but his literary and social eminence.

At the last meeting of the Royal Society [writes Sir Roderick Murchison, November 29th, 1868] General Sabine proposed from the chair that you should at a subsequent meeting be elected F.R.S. He asked me to be the seconder, which I became with the greatest pleasure, and said a few words in honour of your acquirements in geographical science, as well as in praise of your well-known position among men of letters; but why, my dear friend, did you not ask your old president to propose you? If I had had any notion of your wish to be F.R.S., I should have done the thing long ago.

Towards the close of the year Lord Houghton visited the Duke of Wellington at Strathfieldsaye.

To his Wife.

Strathfieldsaye House, Hants, December 1st.

The party here, technically speaking, is a failure—health and weather! Our two princesses have failed! The Viscountess

Beaconsfield has also failed. Dizzy says, because his brother is dying, which nobody believes. It would have been great fun if they had both been here, but it is as good as other parties. My old college friend, the Dean of Windsor, John Hay, and the Beauchamps—the Lady Mary Stanhope. The Dean told me that Oxford would have had London but that Dizzy strongly opposed, and that Dizzy's candidate for Canterbury was ——, the foolishest creature on the Bench. He told us the sharpest Bishopmaking the Queen ever had was when she rejected Waldegrave for York, and Lord Palmerston told her she knew nothing about it, and she answered, "No more do you," and she named your Ebor. . The merit of this place is in the trees, which are very fine; but the house is a ramshackling old place, without a fine room in it. A small beam fell on the Duchess in the library this afternoon, and knocked her down, without, however, hurting her much. A couple of inches nearer would have smashed her beautiful head. It has rained all day, and I have only walked to the monument which the Duke has put up to his father—not more satisfactory than these things in general. Young Wellesley, the heir, is here—a very pleasing, cheery youth.

Strathfieldsaye House, Wednesday.

We are in great political excitement, expecting every moment to hear that Dizzy has resigned.* It is curious that everybody now says that it is the best thing he can do, whereas nobody before has ever suggested it. It would no doubt have many advantages for his party, as he and it would remain entirely unpledged, and might abolish the English as well as the Irish Establishment. If this resignation takes place, it will go far to break up the Winter Session; there must be something said and done, but all the charm of the prize fight will be over.

Lady Houghton's health gave him much anxiety during the winter and spring, and to some extent inter-

---

* The elections to the new Parliament had resulted in a great Liberal majority.

fered with his social engagements in London. His aunt, Miss Caroline Milnes, died in April, and he felt severely the loss of one who had been as a sister to him. Still, he was able to entertain many friends at breakfast and luncheon in Upper Brook Street, and in the autumn of 1869 he paid a visit of unusual interest to the Queen of Holland, whose acquaintance he had formed in Paris in the Exhibition year, and who had learned to entertain a warm regard for him "You can't think how the Queen of Holland praised you up last night, and said you were her kindest friend. Don't be proud, or lose your taste for simpler pleasures," wrote one of his friends. The fact was that the Queen, whose intellectual gifts are well known, took delight in his conversation, and was eager to entertain him as a guest under her own roof. He had written offering himself in the spring.

The Queen of Holland to Lord Houghton.
The Hague, May 4th, 1869.

DEAR LORD HOUGHTON,—I wont lose one instant answering your very kind letter. I am, alas! in the necessity of leaving the Hague Monday, the 17th. If you could come before the 17th, it would give me the greatest pleasure. Whitsuntide being the 16th, I have a faint hope your coming here might be possible. I cannot delay my journey, as it concerns my second son, whom I am going to join in the Vosges, where he is taking a cold-water cure. The Hague is just now in its brightest colour with the first shade of foliage, and I venture to ask you to come a few days before the 17th.

Hoping soon to receive a favourable answer,
I remain, dear Lord Houghton,
Very sincerely yours,
SOPHIA.

From the letters of the year I make the following extracts:—

R. M. M. to his Daughter.

February, 1869.

DEAREST AMY,—I am afraid you must be very cold in the "Modern Athens," as they call it. There has been a dreadful wind here, with showers of sleet, bringing back all the bronchitises that had been getting well. There are some *tableaux* going on at Lady Edward Howard's, which I have not seen; but I met Lady Sebright at dinner in her costume—a Louis XIV. dress, made out of the pink and yellow one she wore at Fryston, and her hair powdered. She has to be mounted up on a swing in a Watteau picture. Lady Di Beauclerk was to do a water-nymph, standing with bare feet on a glass to do for water. This is all for the distressed Irish.

I heard Gladstone for near five hours; he spoke so pleasantly that nobody was tired. He proposes to give all the property of the Irish Church to charitable institutions. Your friend the Archbishop says the English Church will soon follow, and that he expects to see Bishopthorpe turned into an idiot asylum.

Your affectionate
HOUGHTON.

To Henry Bright.

February 17*th,* 1869.

"I don't think our friend Temple is in his usual condition of eighteenth-century common-sense-edness. It is no new discovery that the Rubric is the law of the land, and Charles Buller used to regret that immediately after the Apostles' Creed the words "as is by statute appointed and provided" were not inserted. The Privy Council has only decided that such and such things are illegal, not being parts of the Rubric—a plain matter of fact. I do not expect that there will be a large secession—only occasional droppings into the great Papal saucepan.

It is curious to see how more and more anti-national—more and more Anglo-Fenian—the Ritualists are becoming. . . . The Yorkshire Radicals are very malcontent. One of them said to me lately, " If Gladstone does not lay down principles that will disestablish the Church of England, we will have a Radical Cave of a hundred in a month."

The following letter, written to his kinsman Mr. Milnes Gaskell, on the occasion of the death of the wife of the latter, deserves to be printed.

Lord Houghton to J. Milnes Gaskell.

16, *Upper Brook Street, May 6th*, 1869.

MY DEAR MILNES GASKELL,—I found, too late for me to change my plans, that the motion in the House of Lords, on which I had an amendment, was put off, and that I might have been with you to-day.

This distresses me, although to me it would have been a dreary satisfaction, and to you a mere recognition of what you know already, my deep esteem and earnest appreciation of her great qualities of mind and heart. The sympathy of other men, especially of those for whom we entertain kindly feelings, has no doubt a large effect in mitigating the pains of life; but in the great calamities of a man's career, the turning-points of his existence, he must face his disaster as best he can alone. The best that he can get from others is the acknowledgment of his right to sorrow. I hope you will still remember the worth of those near relations who are left you, and of some sincere friends, among whom you may count

Yours most sincerely,

HOUGHTON.

The double loss of such friends has perceptibly affected my wife's health; time alone will relieve her.

To his Wife.

The 6th (? May, 1869).

The talk of the town is Dean Stanley's five o'clock tea on Thursday to the Queen, Princess Louise, Mr. and Mrs. Grote, Sir Charles and Lady Lyell, Carlyle, and Browning. Carlyle sat opposite Her Majesty, and prophesied to her for a quarter of an hour, telling her, among other truths, that there were no poor in Scotland, which she contradicted. She pleased Browning, by telling him that she had much enjoyed some of his wife's poems. She gave me a very kindly smile at the Levée yesterday, where there was a dreadful crush. One poor man tumbled over in kissing her hand, and she leant down and picked him up.

June 2nd.

Mrs. Greville recited one of my poems to the Queen of Holland the other night. Dickens told someone that what struck him the most about *our* Queen was her innocence and girlishness. When he got up to go away, she seemed much embarrassed, and said she was going to take a liberty with him, and at last asked him to take a copy of her book.

Lord Houghton to Mr. Gladstone.

16, Upper Brook Street, July 12th, 1869.

I was looking the other day at a letter of yours written to me at the time of the Maynooth Grant agitation, in kind recognition of and assent to my pamphlet on religious equality in Ireland. I think you had then no difficulty about raising the *status* of the Roman Catholic clergy in Ireland. What we then did with regard to Maynooth has undisputably had a depressing effect. From all evidence, they are a lower and less intellectual body of men than they were even then. Why so? I confess I don't understand.

The visit to Holland was paid in the early part of September.

To his Wife.

House in the Wood, Saturday Evening.

The Queen had a great dinner to-day with the King. She asked me to put off my visit till this evening, which, of course, I agreed to do. It suited me very well; for I was able to come yesterday to Admiral Harris's, our Minister here, and attend the meeting of the Statistical Congress last evening and to-day. The passage to Antwerp was worse for the cold than anything else. I stood on deck till 2 a.m., and was quite driven down. I was not ill, but only discomfortable. The pleasant country scene set me right. The oddity of being in a place one knew so well from pictures, without ever having seen the reality, is surprising. When the steamer came in sight of Dort, I knew exactly what to expect, from Turner's picture at the Fawkeses at Farnley; and the moment I got into the streets, there came Van der Heydts and Teniers all about one. The estuaries are Cuyps all over; and one is always looking out for the white horse of Wouvermanns. I have drunk tea with the Queen and her younger son, and she laid herself out to be charming. I have, of course, an *appartement*, overdone with decoration, but comfortable enough. The meetings have been agreeable enough of the Congress; and the Dutch pronounce French so ill that I am less shy in speaking it. It was, however, trying to be called upon for a French speech quite extempore, to return thanks to the Ministers for our reception.

To his Daughter.

The House in the Wood, Sunday Evening.

DEAREST AMY,—A real house in the wood, and a fine wood too, with beautiful walks all up from the town. You have not seen so many Dutch as Italian pictures, or you would feel, as I do, the oddity of knowing the country quite well without ever having seen it. When the steamer came in front of Dort, there was my old friend the Tower over the dining-room chimney-piece at Farnley. Then there are on every side the clean little dapper houses, and the bright lights and their shadows of the Dutch painters. Everything is fresh and clean, with a curious neatness and friendly comfort. Then it is all so quiet and contented, as if it only asked to be let alone. I went with the Queen this morning to the first Chapel established here by the French Calvinists after they escaped from the persecutions of Louis XIV. It is quite a simple little place, with an eloquent and earnest pastor, who preached for an hour in Aunt Lulu's ways of thought, and ended with a very pathetic prayer for the Queen. The peculiarity of the service was that the men only stood during the prayers, and the women sat all through. I have four rooms looking into the garden, and a carriage when I go out. We drove out this afternoon, in great state, to a sea place near the Hague, which I should not dislike to come to if at any time the family insist on marine pursuits. The Prince of Orange and Prince Frederick of Schleswig-Holstein dined to-day—nobody else. To-morrow there are more people, and on Tuesday I dine with one of the Ministers. I had to make an extempore speech in French on Friday at a large meeting, but I was consoled by finding how badly the Dutch speak French. If you see Miss Coutts, tell her the Queen asked much about her, and said how much she was obliged by the offer of the house at Torquay. The Queen admires the place so much, she is very likely to go there again. This is an old red house, not unlike the Bishop's Palace at Fulham.

Your affectionate

HOUGHTON.

To his Son.

Maison dans le Bois, the Hague,
September 10*th*, 1869.

MY DEAREST ROBIN,—As I have not often the opportunity of writing to you from a Royal Palace, I do not delay to thank you for yours. This place amuses me very much, both because the Queen does everything to make it agreeable to me, and because it is very pretty and interesting in itself. It now strikes me as very curious that though I have been in Egypt and Turkey,

I never came to a country, within a few hours' steam, full of natural interest and historical association. I suppose this is owing to what a distinguished poet whom you know has remarked—

> "A man's best things lie nearest him,
> Lie close about his feet;
> It is the distant and the dim
> That we are sick to greet."

The wood in which this house stands is the finest as a whole, without large single trees, that I have ever seen; the house consists of a *corps de logis* with an immense hall painted all over with the victories of the House of Orange, and the wings, in one of which I live, and in the other the ladies of the household. The Queen has with her one son, near eighteen, but whom she looks after and sends to his lessons, and tells to go to bed at 10 o'clock, more exactly than your mamma does with you. His name is Alexander, but he was born on St. Louis' Day, and she wanted to call him Louis, but could not do so, so she makes up for it by giving him the *petit nom* Loulou; and there is a parrot in the hall which keeps screaming out "Loulou!" so like the Queen that he never knows which is calling him; the sound takes me quite back to Torquay. We had a beautiful illumination of the wood one night, and I drove about with the Queen, who was immensely cheered. I gave her health at a great dinner yesterday at Scheveningen, the place from which King William III. embarked for Britain. Love to all.

Your affectionate

HOUGHTON.

To his Wife.

Hotel Amstel, Amsterdam, Wednesday Evening.

The wild winds of this country are worse than the South of France, and the windmills rush round and round like maniacs. I much enjoyed the quiet old University of Leyden, and thought of Oliver Goldsmith walking into the town with the intention of making his living by teaching English, forgetting that he did not understand Dutch. This is a very handsome town, but not so interesting as the others, so I do not care to stay beyond a day or two. I shall follow up my principle of leaving something to be seen next time. *Auf Wiedersehen!*

The Queen of Holland to Lord Houghton.

House in the Wood, Sept. 26th, 1869.

DEAR LORD HOUGHTON,—Nearly a fortnight has passed since you left me, and I have not heard from you. As you have probably left Homburg or Wildbad, I direct this to Brook Street, from where it must always reach you. I long to know how you feel after your stay in Holland in fine and in bad weather, in sunshine and storm.

Our Congress has passed unobserved and unnoticed. Can you account why the *Times* has not deigned to mention it? Have we undergone the bad will of Mr. Delane? Why? And in what manner? Pray tell me if you can discover it. I had a kind visit from Lady Cowley, who has just left me to return to England. Your letter to Prince Napoleon has reached him. I added your direction to Homburg; I hope his answer has not missed you. About the 6th October I mean to go for one week to Germany to see my family, but will be home before the 20th. Lady Palmerston's end must have struck you; you had just left her young and active; but her death has been singularly lucky, as her life had been.

Believe me, dear Lord Houghton,

Very sincerely yours,

SOPHIA.

In October, after his return to England, Lord Houghton performed a congenial task in unveiling the monument erected to the memory of Leigh Hunt in Kensal Green Cemetery. Although comparatively few traces of his friendship with the genial poet and essayist are to be found in his correspondence, he had known him for many years, and was not one of those who allowed his foibles of taste and his eccentricities of life to prevent a full recognition of his genuine worth.

A gentleman still living remembers Hunt calling one day on Milnes in his rooms in Pall Mall. The talk turned upon Byron and upon Leigh Hunt's recollections of him. "Do you really think Byron *never* was in earnest?" Hunt was asked. He thought for a moment, and then said slowly, "No; never." "Not even at Missolonghi?" "Decidedly not at Missolonghi," responded Leigh Hunt promptly. "There was no doubt whatever in my mind that Byron was all the time strutting about as on a stage."

The opening of the Suez Canal took place at the close of the year, and was made the occasion of a great international demonstration of interest in the vast undertaking. Various English societies sent represen tatives in response to the invitations of the Khedive, and amongst these was Lord Houghton, who went at the request of the Council of the Royal Geographical Society, and at the urgent solicitation of his friend Sir Roderick Murchison.

Sir Roderick Murchison to Lord Houghton.

Travellers' Club, Oct. 9th, 1869.

MY DEAR HOUGHTON,—I hope you got the same tempting official invitation which was sent to me, and that you will not be scared from the grand scene of the epoch by any sinister reports. You are just the man to take a part in the great Inter-Oceanic opening, and I am sure the Geographers will be well represented if you go. . . .

Yours sincerely,
RODERICK MURCHISON.

It need hardly be said that the invitation was one which had many attractions for Lord Houghton, but it was with some hesitation, chiefly owing to the state of his wife's health, that he accepted it. There was another historic event, fixed also for the close of the year, which he was just as anxious to witness as the Suez Canal. This was the Œcumenical Council summoned by Pope Pius IX. at Rome. He found that it would be possible to combine a visit to Egypt for the opening of the Canal with attendance in Rome at the time of the meeting of the Council, and this led him to decide upon being present at both events.

Lord Houghton to Henry Bright.

Oct. 15th, 1869.

The Khedive of Egypt has asked me to the opening of the Canal, paying my expenses both ways, and giving me a house and carriage at Cairo; but the uncertainty of Lady Hn.'s health has so prevented me from making arrangements that I fear it is now too late, and that all the passages in the early November packets are taken. It will be a great cosmopolitan spectacle, and I am sorry to miss it. If I had gone, I should have taken the Roman Council on my way home, thus combining two enterprises, both probably destined to be damned—the one *up*, the other *down*.

Lord Houghton to his Son.

London, October 20th, 1869.

MY DEAREST ROBIN,—I send you a copy of the *Daily News* of to-day, which gives the best report of my speech yesterday at the monument of Mr. Leigh Hunt. It was very cold work, or there would have been more people. You will like to hear that the Pasha of Egypt has invited me to go to Cairo

THE FRENCH EXHIBITION. 207

for the opening of the Suez Canal next month. I have accepted the invitation, and shall start from Fryston on the 4th of November. I expect I shall be away about a month. It will be a curious feeling to steam for the first time from the Mediterranean into the Red Sea. Even Alexander the Great could not do that, though he did make a canal across the isthmus, which very soon filled and silted up.

Your affectionate
H^N.

The expedition to Egypt was not wholly a success. Houghton enjoyed it, as he enjoyed every stirring spectacle, but the fatigue and discomfort to which he was subjected were greater than he had anticipated. The Empress Eugénie and the Emperor of Austria were the most distinguished guests entertained on the occasion by the Khedive, but there were many others already known to Lord Houghton, and some whose friendship he now acquired for the first time. It is needless to say that in all that motley throng of visitors from the West to the scene of the great engineering achievement in the land of the Pyramids, there was none with a more thorough appreciation of the quaint contrast which the opening of the canal presented to the ordinary background of Egyptian history than Lord Houghton, nor was there one who contributed more largely to the social enjoyment of the visitors of all nations.

To his Wife.

Mediterranean, Lat. 35, *Long.* 20, *Nov. 9th.*

No wonder I wrote May with this sun and air so fresh and warm about one. We had a rush to Marseilles, but plenty of time to stay on board. The *Delta* is not one of the largest

P. and O. boats—indeed, is rather looked down upon as an obsolete paddler instead of a screw; but on that account she is much more agreeable, making no noise and having none of the continual shiver. We are some sixty passengers on board, not above half the complement, so we have abundance of room. I have a large cabin to myself, and but for the habitual shelf instead of bed should be as well as in my own dressing-room. On Sunday afternoon we went through the Straits of Bonifacio in perfect calm, and moved in and out of the islands, on one of which Garibaldi lives. We were fully in sight of his house for some time, and should probably have paid him a visit had there not been some passengers on board going to India, and the Captain did not think himself justified in running any risk of delaying them. Yesterday we went through the Lipari group at sunset. Stromboli looked beautiful, smoking though not flaming. Our only *contretemps* has been that we passed between Scylla and Charybdis in the dark, with a low crescent moon, so that we could not even trace Etna, still less Taormina. The party is very varied—Lord Dudley, most amiable, and one of Lyttelton's sons with him; Pender, the great Manchesterian; some pleasant officers; the Governor of Aden; representatives of the Royal Society, Chambers of Commerce, Trinity House, &c.; correspondents of the *Mercantile Gazette, Illustrated Times*, New York and Boston newspapers; Gregory and Edwards, M.P.'s; Bateman and Hawkshaw, engineers. Our party you know. We expect to reach Alexandria on Thursday evening, and no one, from Lord Dudley downwards, has a notion what is to become of us. I am afraid I shall not be able to tell you before the post leaves.

Port Saïd, November 17th, 1869.

I hope you got the telegram all right, and that you are as well as when you wrote. I told you the passage was pleasant, and at Alexandria we were well entertained at the Viceroy's cost, including the opera, where the chief incident was the appearance of Ricciotti Garibaldi, and the patriotic hymn was played, and everybody rose and cheered. When we left Alexandria the small troubles of the journey began. I was put on board a magnificent yacht, and was told that nobody but *persone di distinzione* would be on board. This no doubt was the original idea; but the issue was that all the riff-raff not otherwise provided for were put on her. The living was so bad that it made me quite uncomfortable, and they ended by stealing my watch with A. H. M. and R. M. M. on the back, and which has gone through the adventures of eighteen years. (N.B.—That knowing Tom Bruce always takes an "expedition" watch worth £2, and an iron chain, on his travels.) I left the ship in disgust, and after other adventures got on board the *Hawk*, Mr. Pender's Telegraph Ship, in which I hope to start in an hour's time to go up the Canal. Already the royal ships have started, the Empress leading the way in the *Aigle*. Now for the bright side of the story. The weather is charming, not over-hot, and the sky pellucid. I went on board our Ambassador's yacht to lunch, and then with him to the *Aigle*, where the Empress received me with much amiability. I found an old friend of mine with her, so we had a pleasant visit. The Empress said she only regretted not being able to go on to India, which had been the dream of her life. "Ah! how can your Queen have such a delightful dominion, and not go there? If it was ours, I should be there over and over again." She said she had expected the Sutherlands and Manchesters, and was quite disappointed at finding so few friends. We then went to the religious ceremony of the benediction of the work. There was a large stand, in front of which sat the Khedive, the Empress, the Emperor of Austria, the Crown Prince of Prussia, and a dozen small royalties, and behind the Empress stood—guess who? *Abdul Kader!* In his burnouse covered with decorations, a most striking figure. Lesseps came up to me and said, "Vous étiez de nos amis quand les amis étaient rares." Opposite the stand were two others—one with a Moslem pulpit turned towards Mecca, and the other with a Catholic altar. The Moslem began the prayers, every one remaining covered; and when he had done, there was a Catholic service to bare heads, and a French discourse from Monseigneur Bauer, a converted Jew, *aumônier* to the Empress, big and florid; the only pretty turn, "Notre enterprise n'a que deux ennemis, le sable et l'espace." The compliments of course were fulsome.

3 p.m.

We are fairly in the Canal which is to join two worlds. The boat, the motion, everything, reminds me of my Nile of twenty-seven years ago. The Empress led the way, as I told you, and we follow at some four hours' distance, but hope to reach Ismailia in the evening. The effect from the fact of the vessels seeming to enter the desert was very solemn.

18th, Ismailia.

Here we are safely anchored, the guns saluting enough to break the drums of one's ears. There is a great fête with fireworks in the evening, and we start for Suez to-morrow. The Khedive has brought an immense number of Arab sheikhs, who are tented all round. As my telegram may not have been intelligible, I repeat that I start from Alexandria on the 29th, which should take me to Messina on the 3rd, to Naples on the 4th, and to Rome on the 5th. I shall ask for letters at all places. I was very near going to Jerusalem next week, but the plan broke down.

Cairo, November 22nd, 1869.

This goes by a private opportunity, so I do not enter into any details. We came successfully through the Canal on Friday and Saturday, and got here last night. It is a rough kind of democratic fête given by Egypt to Europe, and thus one has to put up with a good deal of inconvenience; but all the necessities are well provided for. I travel mostly with Mr. Hawkshaw, a very agreeable and amiable companion. The great fête at Ismailia, where you saw the Royalties of Europe in the midst of 100,000 Arabs, was a most curious spectacle. Nothing could have been better than the climate; not one hot or cold day. I fear you will not get my Port Saïd letter till after this. . I am glad to have seen these beautiful lights and shades and the glorious Nile verdure once again. The organisation of everything here is bad, but the profusion like a fairy tale. We have every night had fireworks that cost thousands, and the fête at Ismailia cannot have cost less than £200,000. But the Viceroy has six or seven millions sterling of income, so he can stand it.

Farewell and *au revoir*.

To his Son.

Cairo, November 26th, 1869.

MY DEAREST ROBERT,—This is just a line to tell you I am safe here, and start for Rome on Monday, to stay a few days with Mr. and Mrs. Payne. I am afraid you will have got my letter from the Canal a week later than you ought to have done, from my not putting "*viâ* Marseilles" on it. We got successfully into the Red Sea, passing over the great Bitter Lake, which Mr. Hawkshaw, who was with us, had rode over as dry ground only a year ago. It was there the waters of the Red Sea and the Mediterranean met; their respective fishes must have been rather astonished to make acquaintance. It is supposed that the Red Sea extended to the Bitter Lakes in the old time, and that it was there that the Israelites crossed it. You never saw anything like the row of the journey from Suez and at the hotel here; if it had not been for the kindness of my fellow-travellers I should have been very uncomfortable. There were races here one day, in which the English horses beat the Arabs; and there was a trotting race of dromedaries, which went quite twenty-five miles an hour. I was at the Pyramids yesterday, and rather proud, with my gouty knees, of climbing to the top. A Scotch gamekeeper of Lord Dudley's walked up it like a hill in the Highlands. In the evening they were lit up with coloured lights. Sir Samuel Baker starts next week, to remain in the interior for four years. Your affectionate H^N.

To his Wife.

Rome, December 8th, 1869.

Severn has just sent me yours, Amy's, and Louisa's of the 25th. On the whole I am glad I did not know you had caught cold; it would have worried me very much. You will wonder that I am writing to you while the Holy Father is opening the Council; but the truth is that neither Mr. Payne nor I had the courage to confront the crowd this morning in a pelting rain, and we are going to drive to St. Peter's about 12 o'clock for the chance of getting our noses in and saying we have been there. We were told last night that the Piazza was full of *contadini*, sleeping there to be ready for the opening of the doors. There are no reserved places or entrances. Even the Roman princesses had to ballot for entrance into a little "patio," and the diplomatists cannot take their ladies. . . . The Paynes have a dinner of Liberal Catholics to-morrow for Lord Acton, who is *très mal vu* here. I hope to hear from somebody every other day while I am here. The cannon began at 5 this morning, and the *Osservatore* says it is the most eventful day in the history of the world.

To his Son.

Rome, December 9th, 1869.

DEAREST ROBERT,—I am sorry I shall not be at Fryston to receive you on the 18th, as I came here later than I expected. I trust, however, that we shall begin the New Year together. I came from Alexandria to Brindisi in a vessel which had been lightened of its ballast to pass the Suez Canal. When, therefore, it got into a heavy sea, it rolled about like a tub, and I spent three days quite as much on my head as on my heels. I was not sick, but it deranged me a good deal. I had been at Brindisi thirty years ago, when I travelled with Wordsworth, the present Bishop of Lincoln. It is curious to be at the place where certainly Horace took a trip to from Rome, and where Virgil died. They pretend to show you the actual house. I am staying here with those good people Mr. and Mrs. Payne. Mrs. Bruce, the Monks, and others have asked after you, and I am glad I can give so good a report. The great Council began yesterday in St. Peter's. It was a very bad, rainy, dark day, which did harm to the spectacle. It was still, however, very fine to see the seven hundred bishops and patriarchs sitting in seven rows, with the Pope in the middle. They were all in white and gold, except the Eastern patriarchs, who were in wonderful costumes. Some of them were quite dark brown. The Pope's voice is quite as loud and clear as when you heard it. He chanted some of the Litanies and the *Veni Creator*, by himself, and quite filled the Church.

Your affectionate
H^N.

To the Same.

Rome, December 23rd, 1869.

MY DEAREST ROBIN,—This, I expect, will be my last letter from the great old city, as I mean to go to Florence on Sunday night. I shall stay there a day or two, and then to Bologna, where I shall hear whether the road over Mont Cenis is passable. I shall go to Meurice's, Rue de Rivoli, at Paris. I thought of sending you a telegram on Christmas Day, wishing you a happy Christmas, but, on reflection, have invested the sum required (and something more) in a Roman pin for you at Castellari's. The rain continues persistently, damaging the look of the old place considerably. A Roman prince said to me, "You expect dark weather at London, but you have a right to the sun at Rome" Your old friend the Pope is very vigorous, and in great spirits. He said to a knight of Malta the other day, "You knights used to fight against the Turks; ah! the blessed Turks are not my enemies nowadays; I wish I had no worse." He sings away like a whole choir in himself. Mrs. Bruce and the Monks are still here, but not so many English as when we were here. I have seen one of the Maxwells, who is a Zouave, and says he likes the service very much, and ——, who says that he has not cleverness enough to be a priest, and who is going to travel in the Holy Land. Best love and plenty of sleep to dear mamma, and all Christmas salutations *à ces aimables demoiselles,*

Tout à vous,
H^N.

After his return to England Lord Houghton, as the Envoy of the Royal Geographical Society at the opening of the Canal, had to discharge an official duty by reading a report of his visit at a meeting of the Society. The story of the Canal is ancient history now, and future generations will perhaps look with surprise upon the records of the enthusiasm which its completion excited throughout Europe. It is needless to follow Lord Houghton in his account of the circumstances under which the project of the Canal was launched and carried out. But one or two passages from his personal narrative may be given to supplement his letters to his family. After explaining that England was somewhat sparsely represented at the ceremony, mainly by the representatives of important societies and newspaper correspondents, he continued :—

But the French and the Germans came in large bodies, and we English were merged in the multitude; in fact, it was a great excursion train from Europe to Africa. That is the only fair description which can be given of it, and in an excursion train, you know, it is very difficult to distinguish anybody; so that, on the whole, I am rather glad that our excellent President did not go himself, but made me his substitute, for what with that lovely and enterprising lady the Empress of the French, with the Emperor of Austria, who charmed everybody by the simplicity of his demeanour, and the intelligent interest he took in all matters connected with the Canal, with our own connection the Crown Prince of Prussia, and a great many other Royalties, I could not help feeling that even our illustrious President might have been submitted to the ordinary confusion and discomforts of a crowd. Now there was the best intention on the part of the Egyptian Government; the magnificent entertainments, and the amount of money that was spent was something fabulous; and whatever failed, everybody felt that any inconvenience they were put to really came from the accidents, the inevitable circumstances, and in no way whatever from the complicity of the Government by which they were entertained. There was one unfortunate event, of which I have no difficulty in speaking, because it was one of which Nubar Pasha, Foreign Minister to the Khedive, a most gracious and intelligent gentleman, for whom everybody, who is acquainted with him, has the greatest esteem, went to the extravagant length of saying, " You may forgive me for this blunder, but I can never forgive myself." It seems to me that he was not in the least guilty. The circumstance was this:—I mentioned that I went to Alexandria under the guidance of the Peninsular and Oriental Co., but at Alexandria the guests were placed in large and luxurious Egyptian steamers, many of them the private yachts of the Khedive, and conveyed to Port Saïd for the purpose of being taken through the Suez Canal at Port Saïd. The ceremonies connected with the opening were of the greatest interest. On the evening of that day M. de Lesseps came to Nubar Pasha, and told him that, to his great grief, he had come to the conclusion that none of the large Egyptian vessels could securely pass through the Canal. Now these large Egyptian vessels contained all the guests of the Pasha, and therefore what was to become of them? Such as could find any private refuge did so; the rest were put into smaller vessels and taken to Ismailia, where they were placed in tents, and taken care of until their return to Cairo. I have never been able to explain to myself why this resolution was taken so late. As it was, that was the one great inconvenience to which the guests of the Pasha were subjected. When they were at Ismailia, they found comfort—almost luxury. For my own part, and on the part of those who were with me, I can only say that we found perfect hospitality in the English vessels which were there. Lord Dudley and his party went on board Mr. Talbot's yacht, the *Lynx*, and I was kindly received by Mr. Elliott and Mr. Pender in the *Hawk*, in which I had the very great advantage of going through the Canal in the company of Mr. Hawkshaw and Mr. Bateman, the two illustrious engineers.

At Port Saïd I saw M. de Lesseps, and was somewhat flattered when he came up to me and said, "I remember you; you were one of our English friends when our friends were few." I then recalled to mind that at the time M. de Lesseps had come here, and had been somewhat ill received by the commercial classes and the political opinion of this country, I expressed to him my full belief that he would succeed in his enterprise. . .

I first met M. de Lesseps at Lord Palmerston's house, and at a time when a great ill-will was excited in certain circles in France by the notion that Lord Palmerston had exercised an almost undue political influence in opposing the Suez Canal. But there is a point which I should be very glad to see put upon record, which is—that the project which Lord Palmerston opposed was not the project which has now been carried out. The project to which Lord Palmerston gave his political opposition was the arrangement between M. de Lesseps and Saïd Pasha, the effect of which would have been to transfer to a French Company, and through that Company at any time to the French Government, the possession of a large province of Egypt, which was to be irrigated by a French Water Company in conjunction with that across the Isthmus. Lord Palmerston took the ground that it was not necessary for the purposes of the Ship Canal, nor in any degree a necessary part of the commercial enterprise, that a French Company should possess a whole province of Egypt.

Well, so we started from Port Saïd. A striking moment it was, and to my mind, on looking back to my impressions, it is the grandest of the whole. I see here persons who were present with me at that moment, and I think I might appeal to them whether the entrance of that quiet and solemn procession of ships into the desert, on that bright, beautiful Egyptian morning, was not a spectacle they can hardly forget. . . . And so the whole of that day we traversed the silent desert. I don't know whether it was done on purpose, with that sense of art which the French so curiously exemplify in all their great manifestations, but every sign of life seemed to be withdrawn from the banks. There was not a dwelling, there was hardly a wandering Arab. In this place, which had been the sepulchre of so many lives—which had been the hive of humanity for the last ten years—there was a perfect, desolate stillness. On went the vessels through the marsh, through the sand—as it were, new animals invading that solitude—until we arrived at Lake Timseh. When Mr. Hawkshaw landed at Port Saïd, M. de Lesseps took him by the hand, and presented him to the engineers who were about him, and said, " This is the gentleman to whom I owe the Canal." And it was literally true. At the time when the reputation of the Canal was at its worst, when public opinion in Europe was growing against it, when money was the hardest to get, the Khedive asked for an English engineer who would give him a final opinion as to the practicability of the Canal. He selected Mr. Hawkshaw, a man not only high in his profession, but of the most singular independence and simplicity of character. The Khedive told Mr. Hawkshaw that if he would report to him confidentially that the Canal was impracticable, he would take care that the works were brought to an end without injury to anybody. You have had before you the report of Mr. Hawkshaw. He reported that the Canal was not only feasible, not only practicable, but that, to his mind, the main engineering difficulties which had been raised were not such, in any degree, as would authorise its abandonment; that he believed the Canal could be made, and could be maintained at a moderate and reasonable expense; and therefore, when M. de Lesseps presented Mr. Hawkshaw, as I saw him do, to the persons present at Port Saïd, he was thoroughly justified in saying, " It is to him that I mainly owe the accomplishment of this great enterprise."

You ask me, sir, to state something with regard to my presentation to the Khedive. I saw His Highness the first time at Ismailia, on board his own steam yacht. I was introduced to him by our Ambassador, and I presented to him the compliments of this distinguished Society. His Highness was pleased to express his gratification and his thanks. At that moment he was in a state of great excitement, because he had achieved, as he considered, a very great work, and he told us what it was. He said, " Last night I had rather a hard time of it. I was very anxious of course that the *Aigle,* on board of which was the Empress of the French, should have a perfectly free course, and so I sent a ship called the *Latiff* to clear the way. The *Latiff* a very short time after having got into the Canal ran against the side of the Canal, stopping it up altogether. The captain of the *Latiff* sent to Port Saïd, and awoke me up between eleven and twelve o'clock at night, upon which I got into my own little vessel and took 300 men with me, *je faisais un peu le capitaine moi-même,* so that by six o'clock in the morning I had got the *Latiff* off, and seen her shunted at one of the stations, and went on in my yacht, so as to have the course clear for the *Aigle,* which was to start at seven o'clock in the morning." There seemed to me something very practical and interesting in the sovereign of the country himself not only leading but clearing the way through his own country. He told another person that if he could not have got the *Latiff* off, he should certainly have blown her up, so that the *Aigle* might have got on clear. I am not quite sure that the feat would have been successful, but, at any rate, it shows the Viceroy's energy.

It is only fair to Lord Houghton to say that this address was given extempore, and that the passage I have quoted above is taken from a report of his speech.

CHAPTER XVII.

" MONOGRAPHS: PERSONAL AND SOCIAL."

The War of 1870—Letter from the Queen of Holland—A Minister without Disguise—Dinner to Tennyson—Landor and Blake—"Lothair"—A Literary Dispute—Letters of Anthony Trollope—Death of Charles Dickens—His Funeral—The War Feeling in Germany—Besieged Paris—Letter to Mr. Gladstone—An Autumn in the Highlands—Dunrobin—"The Complaint of Glenquoich"—Guests at Fryston—Carlyle and W. E. Forster—Mr. Edmund Yates and Lord Houghton—The Alabama Arbitration—Visit to Venice—Publication of the "Monographs"—Presides over Social Science Congress.

EVENTFUL as it was in the history of Europe, the year 1870 was not marked by any incident of importance in Lord Houghton's life. The raging of the great war on the Continent prevented his taking his usual journey abroad, and in common with the majority of his fellow-countrymen he was compelled to spend the autumn at home; Fryston being in consequence more than usually full of guests during the months in which the plains of Lorraine were covered with wounded and dying men, and Paris was entering upon the long agony of the siege. Houghton, like other men, was greatly moved by the exciting incidents of the struggle between France and Germany, and his emotional nature having been deeply stirred, he found relief in literary work. His pen had never been quite laid aside, as the numerous articles which he contributed to the leading Reviews, and latterly to the *Pall Mall Gazette,* testified; but during

1870 there was a revival of literary effort on his part, and he wrote much in the *Edinburgh* and other Reviews, besides writing a preface to the collected edition of Peacock's works, and making speeches on various occasions. Unable to visit the Continent, he made a short tour in Scotland, staying at Dunrobin with the Duke and Duchess of Sutherland, at Glenquoich with Mr. Ellice, and finally at Loch Luichart with Lady Ashburton.

The Queen of Holland to Lord Houghton.

The Hague, January 11*th*, 1870.

MY DEAR LORD HOUGHTON,—If I delayed so long answering your very kind and interesting letter from Cairo, it was because you announced your departure for Rome and the Council without intimating the length of time you were to remain there, and as Italian, especially Roman, posts are proverbially faithless, and I have a horror of lost letters, I forbore and only heard of your return to London three days ago. I was very thankful for your kind remembrance from so far. You must have enjoyed both Egypt and Rome at such moments of historical importance. My life has been one of silence and sadness. My boy is gone; and since he left, all the sunshine of my existence has gone. I hoped to come to England now. Circumstances have put it off, and I now hope to come after the 20th of February; but till now, alas! it is but a hope. My health is not good, and renders travelling less easy than it generally appears to me. Great changes have taken place in France. I hope they may prove happy ones. The Emperor wrote me cheerfully, which I find a good omen; but there is so little reliance to put upon public opinion in France that some uneasiness is allowable. May I trouble you with an errand? When Lord W—— died in October, I wrote to Lady W——, whom I have known all my life. To this hour I never got an answer, and I know she answered letters from other persons in my family. My letter must have been lost. Would you kindly inquire whether it ever reached her? God bless and keep you, dear Lord Houghton.

Believe me
Very sincerely yours,
SOPHIA.

Lord Houghton to Lady Galway.

I met Forster in the bath, a Minister without disguise for once. He asked about George's candidature; said he (Forster) was in the unhappy position of being the only Minister that the Tories did not abuse. A deputation told him they loved him politically, but ecclesiastically abhorred him.

Lord Houghton to his Aunts.

London, March 27th, 1870.

DEAR LADIES,—I have the great honour of entertaining Tennyson at dinner to-morrow. He insists on dining at 7, and on having some old port. I have brought some from Fryston which my father called "the Alderman," which is, I suppose, from the year when that horse won the St. Leger, which I don't doubt you will remember.

Lord Houghton's correspondence still continued to extend to all sorts and conditions of men, and occasionally he received letters which, although they have comparatively little bearing on his life, are too full of interest to be omitted from this narrative. One of the results of an article in the *Edinburgh Review* on Landor was the following communication from a friend not only of Landor's but of Blake's.

Seymour Kirkup to Lord Houghton.

Florence, 2, Ponte Vecchio, March 25th, 1870.

MY DEAR LORD,—I have had a misfortune. Your article in the *Edinburgh Review* on Landor, which you were so kind as to give me, has been spoiled and almost destroyed by the fault of a servant—or, rather, my own, for leaving it out instead of locking it up. If you have others, I would ask you to send me one by the book-post; and pray renew the inscription to me which you gave the former one. If ever you write again of Landor, I will send you some anecdotes, of which I was witness, to put into any form which you think best. Another person with whom I was intimate long ago is one in whom I know that your lordship has taken great interest, and has collected a great number of most valuable works of his genius—W. Blake. I was much with him from 1810 to 1816, when I came abroad, and have remained in Italy ever since. I might have learned much from him. I was then a student of the Royal Academy, in the antique school, where I gained a medal, and thought more of form than anything else. I was by nature a lover of colour, and my *beau ideal* was the union of Phidias and Titian. Blake was the determined enemy of colourists, and his drawing was not very academical. His high qualities I did not prize at that time; besides, I thought him mad. I do not think so now. I never suspected him of imposture. His manner was too honest for that. He was very kind to me, though very positive in his opinion, with which I never agreed. His excellent old wife was a sincere believer in all his visions. She told me seriously one day, "I have very little of Mr. Blake's company; he is always in Paradise." She prepared his colours, and was as good as a servant. He had no other. It was Mr. Butts who introduced me to him. I was a schoolfellow of his son's, whom he sent to Blake to learn engraving, which was his original art. Let me tell you now of a large picture he painted in my time. I thought it his best work—a battle from the Welsh Triads. The three last men who remained of Arthur's army, and who defeated the enemy—the strongest man, the handsomest man, and the ugliest man. As he was an enemy to oil painting, which he said was the ruin of painting, he invented a method of applying fresco to canvas, and this life-size picture was the result. It made so great an impression on me that I made a drawing of it fifty years afterwards, which I gave to Swinburne. You can see it. It (the picture) must have been about 14 feet by 10. In texture it was rather mealy, as we call it, and was too red; the sun seemed setting in blood. It was not Greek in character. Though the figures reminded one of Hercules, Apollo, and Pan, they were naked Britons. If you should ever hear of it, it is worth seeking. There is more power and drawing in it than in any of his works that I have known, even in Blair's grave, respecting which he was enraged against Schiavonetti for correcting some defects. In general, engravers fail to do justice, and the most precious works have been etched by the painters themselves.

Your lordship's faithful servant,
SEYMOUR KIRKUP.

"Lothair" was one of the books of the season. Everybody was eager to know whether a novelist who had been Prime Minister had preserved his art in spite of his greatness. Writing to his friend Henry Bright, Lord Houghton said—

There is immense and most malevolent curiosity about Disraeli's novel. His wisest friends think that it must be a mistake, and his enemies hope it will be his ruin. He told Longman he believed he was the first ex-Premier who had ventured on a work of fiction. If he had said this to me, I should have suggested M. Guizot's "Meditations Religieuses."

Lord Houghton reviewed the book in the *Edinburgh*. Among the topics which its appearance suggested was that of the price paid to its illustrious author by the publisher, and Houghton became involved in an amusing dispute with Mr. Anthony Trollope on the subject. The exact sum which had been offered to Mr. Disraeli happened to be known to Lord Houghton, a fact which did not prevent Mr. Trollope from insisting that it was impossible that any such sum could have been paid. Finally Mr. Trollope bet Lord Houghton £10 that the sum of £10,000 never had been offered to an author for a novel. Lord Houghton produced evidence showing that Mr. Disraeli had received an offer of this very sum, and Mr. Trollope paid his bet. His letters on the subject have an interest of their own.

Anthony Trollope to Lord Houghton.

Waltham House, Waltham Cross, April 22nd, 1870.

MY DEAR LORD HOUGHTON,—I hardly gather from your letter whether you meant that an offer made in 1848 (if the fact of the offer be genuine, and the offer ever was) supplies an answer to the question that was in dispute between us. Were we not discussing an affair of the day? But I was clearly wrong in this, that I did not limit my assertion by any stipulation as to the solvency of the offerer. I might offer you half a million for Fryston, and you would thereby be justified in saying that so much money had been offered for that property; but if you were thinking of selling Fryston, my offer would have no weight with you, because you would know that the half-million was not forthcoming. Twelve years ago—not to talk of twenty-two —novels were worth almost double what they are now; but I think that no novel has ever been sold for £10,000, and no novel would be worth it, except by Dickens, whose prices, by-the-bye, are much more moderate. However, if you think I have lost my bet, I will pay it with a happy heart. I hope you will dine with me on May 4th.

Yours always,
ANTHONY TROLLOPE.

The Same to the Same.
Waltham House, Waltham Cross, May 19th, 1870.

MY DEAR LORD HOUGHTON,—We will have no compromise and as I do not in the least doubt the truth of every word you say, I enclose a cheque for £10. But my conviction is not in the least altered; and I look upon the offer—which, it seems, was made two years ago, not for "Lothair," but for some other novel not then known to be written—to be of the same worth as would be an offer from me to you of half a million for your property at Fryston. Whether you might wish to sell Fryston or not, you would discard the offer, coming from a man who clearly could not pay the sum offered. Two years ago Dallas was editing the paper called *Once a Week;* and, as it happened, I sold a novel through him to the proprietors of that paper, just at that time for publication in the paper. My price was not exorbitant—that is, it was exactly at the rate I was being paid for the article from other sources. I found that he was running amuck among novelists, offering to buy this and that—buying, indeed, this and that; and in the meanwhile the paper had to be disposed of as worthless. It was sold, I believe, for all but nothing. My bargain had been made *bonâ fide* with the proprietors, and my novel was written for them; but I was obliged to assent to another mode of publication, and to abate my price. Therefore I regard an offer made by Dallas as no genuine offer, even though his offer were for "Lothair;" and, again, I know fully well the value of these articles in the market, and I think that I know that no novel would be worth £10,000 to a publisher by any author: no house could afford to give such a sum. Dickens's last novel (which, I do not hesitate to say, is worth three times the value of "Lothair" in a simply pecuniary view) has been sold for a considerably less sum—not indeed the entire copyright, but the immediate publication, and half-copyright afterwards. I have heard you quote as to other works sums reputed to be paid, but which were fabulous. For a novel published as "Lothair" is published, and sure of a large circulation, a publisher could offer to give an author about 10s. a copy for all copies sold by him at the cost price, nominally 31s. 6d., for which he gets about 17s. 6d. The other 7s. 6d. would pay the cost, the advertising, and give the publisher a small profit. —— told me the other day that 6,000 copies had been sold— that would make £3,000 for the author; and the market has been so glutted with the work, that the publisher cannot hope to sell above another thousand. Where could he possibly recoup himself in an expenditure of £10,000?

I do, however, believe that Dallas made the offer two years since.

Yours' always,

ANTHONY TROLLOPE.

Lord Houghton to his Wife.

Wednesday, 11 a.m. (? *May*, 1870).

Bright's illness is serious—the old affection of the head. He can do no business, and is ordered to Scotland for a month to divert himself with fishing—pleasant in this weather. London, with its usual coolness, thinks this event rather advantageous to the Government than otherwise, and recommends the favourite of the hour to Bright's place in the Cabinet. That favourite—Forster—told me nothing in his political life had given him so much pleasure as my speech at Bradford. Granville and Clarendon are both very poorly with influenza, and Gladstone looks gaunt to a degree. Julian Fane has been all but dead, and there is only a gleam of hope for him.

There was one incident of the year which moved the English-speaking peoples all over the world deeply—

this was the sudden death of Charles Dickens, on the 9th of June. Houghton had been the friend of the illustrious writer from his early days. There was, however, a still older tie uniting the family at Fryston with the author of the "Pickwick Papers." When Lady Houghton was a girl at Crewe, the person who filled the responsible office of housekeeper at Crewe Hall was a Mrs. Dickens, the grandmother of Charles. Lady Houghton used to tell that, when she was a child, the greatest treat that could be given to herself and her brother and sister was an afternoon in the housekeeper's room at Crewe; for Mrs. Dickens was an inimitable storyteller, and she loved to have the children round her, and to beguile them, not only with fairy tales, but with reminiscences of her own, and stories from the page of history. It was natural therefore that when, after her marriage, Lady Houghton became personally acquainted with Charles Dickens, she should feel a peculiar interest in him. Not very long before Dickens's death a dinner was arranged at Lord Houghton's town-house, chiefly for the purpose of enabling the Prince of Wales and the King of the Belgians to make the acquaintance of the great writer. Dickens was at the time disabled by rheumatic gout, and he remained in the dining-room until the party had assembled, the introduction to the Prince of Wales taking place at the dinner-table. It was the last occasion on which he was the guest of his old friend. The letters I have to quote will show something of the part Lord Houghton took at the time of his death.

The Dean of Westminster to Lord Houghton.

The Deanery, Westminster, June 13*th,* 1870.

MY DEAR LORD HOUGHTON,—On hearing of the news of the death of Charles Dickens, I communicated with his family, through F. Locker, that I should be ready to receive any proposal for his burial in the Abbey. I have had no intimation of any kind, and it is possible that they have determined against it. The usual course in these cases (and the most suitable for obvious reasons) is that friends and distinguished persons should present the case to the dean, and ask for his approval, and I am unwilling to depart from this precedent, because, if the dean were to take the initiative, a funeral of this kind would be regarded as an expression of his individual feeling rather than of the public sentiment. But I am unwilling that a tribute of this nature, if desired by the public and the friends, should miscarry through any misunderstanding, and hence this note. Will you kindly act as you think best?

Yours sincerely,

A. P. STANLEY.

Dickens, it will be remembered, had given stringent directions as to his funeral, and his family were anxious to comply with his wishes. On the other hand the sentiment of the nation in favour of his interment in Westminster Abbey was universal. There was an almost passionate outcry from all classes of the community for this last tribute of honour to one to whom the whole race felt grateful. It was in these circumstances that Dean Stanley, not unmindful perhaps of those lines written by Houghton on the death of Thackeray, in which he commented on the fact that no dean had offered a grave in Westminster to the author of "Vanity Fair," turned to his friend for help. The result, as everybody knows, was that Dickens's family yielded to the national desire, only imposing as an absolute condition that the funeral should be private, and conducted without any trace of the pomp and ceremony which usually attend sepulture in the great English shrine. Their wishes were respected, and as a consequence Dickens's honoured dust has found a resting-place in Poets' Corner.

Lady Augusta Stanley to Lord Houghton.

Deanery, Westminster, June 14th, 6 p.m.

DEAR LORD HOUGHTON,—I was to have written a letter to you earlier in the day to say that all had gone off to a wish this morning, and exactly in accordance with the directions of Mr. C. Dickens in his will, and that with the sanction of the executor and family the grave has remained open to-day, and will only be closed quite late to-night. Arthur thought you might like to look down upon it before this, and has written to you at the House of Lords; but as you were not there, I write a duplicate, which I am sending to your house. If you will come to the deanery any time this evening before eleven, our butler will take you into the Abbey to show you the spot, though we shall be out.

Yours sincerely,

A. STANLEY.

Lord Houghton to his Son.

Fryston, June 18th, 1870.

MY DEAREST ROBIN,—You may like a letter from this date. I came here on Thursday, having been very poorly with a bilious attack, owing partly to the great heat in London. I was thinking of you running about and liable to catch a *coup de soleil*,

I was obliged to put off a large dinner I was going to give to my Yorkshire neighbours here in London. . . . I fear you never saw Charles Dickens. When he dined with us to meet the Prince of Wales, he pressed us to visit Gadshill any day, and we might have been there at the time of his seizure. He has died happily, in the zenith of his fame.

On July 15th war was declared between France and Germany. Lord Houghton had so many friends in both countries that his sympathies would naturally have been balanced somewhat evenly between the two great combatants. He was, however, strongly pro-Prussian in his feeling. On one point, indeed, he never wavered in his own mind. He detested the origin and the vices of the Second Empire, and whilst he could not but feel a certain measure of personal sympathy for his old friend Napoleon III., he looked with relief to the downfall of a system of government which was odious to him. Many letters reached him on the outbreak of hostilities from men of eminence in both countries, and the following from Mr. George Bunsen may be given here:—

George von Bunsen to Lord Houghton.

Maienstrasse, Berlin, July 20th, 1870.

MY DEAR LORD HOUGHTON,—I wish you were here, as in 1844, to study the character of the revolution we are passing through. We are surprised at ourselves. We had not thought to be one, although we knew we must be one. A Schleswig-Holstein "particularist" M.P. resented as an insult my words of praise for the attitude taken by his countrymen. You know that, for example, *all* students of the University of Kiel (200) have enlisted as volunteers. A good many Catholic priests in Baden are reported to have tried an agitation against the German war. They were silenced one and all by their flocks, who declined, remembering well enough what Napoleonic invasions mean. "In the Prussian Rhine provinces there is not enthusiasm, but fury," said an M.P. on my asking him. The authorities have not taken the trouble of sending individual summonses, but merely publish in the newspaper the places of rendezvous, and the turnpike roads are crowded. Unfortunately (in my opinion, but not in that of anybody else) the King of —— seems to join us. Unfortunately; but yet I hope there will be an opportunity given him, by the entry of French troops, to show his real colours—a better event, I humbly believe, than the dissimulation to which public opinion seems to have driven him.

For us Anglo-maniacs in Berlin, it is sad and painful to observe how utterly the attitude of England is regarded with mistrustful alienation. "England is truly an Asiatic power." "England is ludicrously afraid of a French invasion." "There is no man in England whom the prestige of Napoleon III., or his skill, do not seem to overshadow." "The English are keeping neutral their very hearts, waiting until victory may have decided one way or another." "They mistake neutrality to mean impartiality—or, worse still, there is a malignant hope among the English that our half-dozen men-of-war may be destroyed without trouble to themselves, and the Baltic made a Russian lake." Such are the expressions—or, rather, the unexpressed sentiments —regarding your country. There was many a half-suppressed laugh to-day when mention was made (in a very becoming manner) by Count Bismarck of a note by Lord A. Loftus in favour of conciliation. I need not explain this to you, who know that Continentals continue to believe the *Times* to express English sentiment. *Vide* the *Times*' first leader a few days ago. Having inherited a warm affection for England, and the belief that she is the flower of the universe, I feel this estrangement intensely, and should wish it to be removed by open acts of condemnation and commination performed by England *before*, not after, we have occasion to fight. Public opinion in this country believes that we may meet with disasters at first because of the *utter surprise*. (I am credibly assured that Bismarck thought on the 14th evening that he would return to Varzin the next day.) But I don't meet with doubts anywhere as to the final issue. We imagine there is more to fall back upon materially and morally in this country. This, however, will be a mistake.

It will be a great disappointment if the King refuses Vogel von Falkenstein a great command. This strange man is too comet-like for His Majesty; but his prestige among the South Germans, whose armies he defeated in 1866, is so great that throughout Bavaria the announcement of his appointment to the chief command under our Crown Prince in the South was *received with enthusiasm!* My witness is a very Radical M.P., who traversed the country from the Brenner northward on his way hitherward. Thinking you might be interested by it, I enclose a photograph of General Falkenstein, and also one of Moltke. Prim has sold himself to Napoleon, body and soul, if we are well informed here. There is much apprehension in military quarters lest Andrassy may have already been drawn into the nets of that wily Beust. *La diplomatie ne s'improvise pas* would be confirmed by such a fiasco of Hungarian sagacity May I ask for a word from you? With devoted regards to Lady Houghton,

Yours very truly,

G. v. BUNSEN.

Lord Houghton to Henry Bright.
August 1st.

I *was* going in the middle of September, after depositing my boy at Harrow, to Ammergau, to see the Miracle Play; but the chief person is taken off to serve in the artillery, with Judas Iscariot as his superior officer. Nor am I sure that I can come to the Association, and should not like you to keep a room for me. I certainly should not go to any public ceremonial where I had to speak. . What is called society here is wholly French, on account of the Cumberlands and other dispossessed relatives. I am Prussian to the backbone, which is a pure homage to principle, as they are the least agreeable people in the world. I think Parliament ought to be adjourned, not prorogued; but so many M.P.'s think the grouse more important than the war, that it will not be done. Gladstone looks very ill and careworn. He made an excellent speech last night, especially on coal, which is a burning question.

Coal was a question that threatened to give rise to serious trouble—the right of a neutral to supply it to a combatant having been called in question, and much bitter feeling excited against England by the fact that she continued freely to supply either combatant with this necessary article.

To his Daughter

Serlby, August 7th, 1870.

DEAREST AMY, This atrocious invasion of Germany by the French seems likely to meet with its appropriate punishment. I wish it only fell on its iniquitous authors, and not on the comparatively innocent French people. If you live to a long life, you will to the last, I believe, hear it spoken of as the most unjustifiable war in history. You know what my estimate of the French Emperor has always been, and how I have believed him capable of committing as great crimes as his uncle, without the excuses the latter may have had in his revolutionary training, and in the temptations of his consummate genius.

To the Same.

The Athenæum Club, September 10*th.*

DEAREST AMY,— . . . You will have seen in the papers of the disaster of the great iron ship.* It is too true that

---

* The *Captain*, turret-ship designed by Captain Cowper Coles, who was on board when she foundered in a gale in the Bay of Biscay.

Mr. Childers' second son is lost, as well as Lady Herbert's and Lord Northbrook's. There were, besides, a very fine set of officers, and the inventor himself of the ship. I dined with Count Bernstorff yesterday. They are much obliged for your things, and will send them off to-day. Col. Lindsay's fund have great difficulty in getting their stores to the seat of war. They begged to have no more nurses. They want candles instead, the poor people dying by thousands in the dark. It seems pretty certain that the poor Empress arrived without any servants, but with M. Lesseps and a friend, at Ryde in the middle of the night, having crossed from Trouville in a little sailing vessel. . . .

I am your affectionate
HOUGHTON.

Travellers' Club, September 15*th,* 1870.

I have been with M. and Madame Thiers this morning; all very sad. They are going to Russia from Hull on Monday. They had not a notion where Hull was, and thought it close to London.

Lord Houghton to Lady Galway.
Aug. 28*th,* 1870.

Prescott Hewitt has been to Metz to see the Emperor, and does not expect him to live more than a very few weeks. He wrote to the Queen of Holland last week in a tone of despair, saying the position was irretrievable, and that he had been deceived by everybody. Circourt writes in terror of a "*rouge*" outbreak in Paris, and says the fickle Parisians are now beginning to abuse and distrust Trochu.

The Same to the Same.
Thursday (Aug., 1870).

You will understand that the question is not one of judgment of events, but of alternatives. If the French were not now punished for their wilful vanity, they would be murdering and pillaging the quiet inoffensive Germans in Germany, who never thought of touching a hair on a Frenchman's head. Which was the first cry, "A Berlin!" or "Zu Paris"?

To his Wife.

The Athenæum Club, September 9th, 1870.

I went to the Rothschilds' after dinner. They were more cheerful than I expected. Madame Alphonse was there, not very fearful of the state of Paris. The Orleanist Princes were in Paris for twelve hours *incognito;* but Trochu persuaded them they could only do harm, so they are returned. Madame Walewski is at Brown's Hotel; Princess Metternich in Half-Moon Street. I shall call on them to-morrow. To-day I lunched with Madame ——, who is very angry because the Sick and Wounded Committee won't employ her and the people she designates. I dine at the Bernstorffs'.

September 10*th,* 1870.

You will have seen the disaster of the great iron ship. Among the midshipmen lost are Childers' second son, whom Pauncefort just now said was "so much of a man, though quite a youth;" Lady Herbert's, whom she went this spring to Lisbon to nurse; Lord Northbrook's supposed heir, a brother of Lord Huntley's; and as fine a set of superior officers as there are in the Navy. It was the crack ship, and cost £300,000. Childers is still abroad, not known where, that letters may not be sent to him. His private secretary started last night with the sad news.

The Empress came over from Trouville, in a small sailing vessel, with a lady and M. Lesseps, and without a maid. She was wet through, and had difficulty in getting into a hotel at Ryde. I dined with the Bernstorffs' yesterday; much obliged for your contribution, which will be sent off to-night. There was an officer just arrived from Sedan; he told us there was a large *ambulance de la reine d'Angleterre* there doing much good. Sir Henry Havelock was the chief manager of it. The Prussians believe that the Parisians will make no serious resistance. It must have been hard for the Orleanist princes to return after twelve hours at the Hôtel Bristol. I dine with the Rothschilds to-day, and at Holland House to-morrow, where I shall probably meet some French refugees. I am going to call on Princess Metternich this afternoon. I think I must go to Liverpool on Saturday for the British Association. Tyndall gives a lecture on the connection of science and imagination.

Boodle's, Monday (undated).

Lord Ronald Gower arrived at Holland House to dinner yesterday. He was one of the last travellers that left Paris. The bridge at Creil (you remember the station) was to be blown up in twenty-four hours. He saw the whole of the Bois de Boulogne cut down, and turned into a cattle and sheep market. There is also an order to destroy the forests of Compiègne and Fontainebleau. He said the abuse of the Emperor and of the superior officers by the French army, even before Sedan, was most surprising. The Empress was very much knocked up, and has only seen some few French people who have gone down from London. I have called on some, but have not seen any. The Prince Imperial only heard at Dover of the Emperor's surrender. He ran into a room and locked the door, and they had difficulty in getting him out. A gentleman has just been here to say he had quite given up all hopes of his nephew, a midshipman in the *Captain*, and he has just heard he was invalided in the hospital at Lisbon; but, alas! alone.

Riddelsworth, Thetford, Tuesday, 11 p.m.

Just opened yours of Monday. Dearest, I quite know you are and have been very ill. Do not ever think I do not know how ill you are, and how much I value your fight for life, for others more than yourself. Please remember this, and when we think of the multitudes in France dying in lonely agony or miserable tumult, there may be thankfulness even for quiet sorrow, and for suffering alleviated if possible by science and sympathy.

London is swarming with foreigners. One of the Orleanist princes said a Buonapartist flight was the only thing wanting to make the emigration complete, and they have got it. The Duc de Persigny abused the Emperor and Empress so brutally at the Rothschilds' that they turned him out of the room. The whole tone of the French here is most degrading. They are furious with Paris for resisting. The Queen has written to the Empress. If —— wants the last views of her friends, she had best write for *La Situation*, edited by M. Paul de Cassagnac, a daily penny paper, and which her newsvendor would send her. I saw Madame Mohl yesterday, very poorly. She said she believed her house in Paris was barricaded against the Rouges.

About this time Lord Houghton had some correspondence with Mr. Gladstone on the public aspect of the war.

Lord Houghton to Mr. Gladstone.

Serlby Hall, Bawtry, August 14th, 1870.

MY DEAR GLADSTONE,—I daresay your eye has caught an article in the *Times* of Saturday upon the 12th of August in England and on the Rhine. It seems to me very solemnly true, and I had it in my mind when there passed in the House of Lords what seemed to me a hasty and unnecessary prorogation of Parliament. The Foreign Enlistment Bill, in the concoction of which, through the Neutrality Commission, I took my part, was forced through the House of Lords without any fair discussion, and I was snubbed by my friend Charles Wood, *more suo*, in trying to raise one.

You also abandoned several useful Bills, as if there was some necessity for getting rid of Parliament before a certain day.

Remembering how severe you were on Lord Palmerston for letting the Indian Government have a short contest with Persia without the presence of Parliament, I do not think you likely to take Lord Redesdale's view of the advantage of its absence in critical times; but what I, who am of so little use to my country myself, could not say to those who are still less so, was that the dispersion of the aristocracy for a mere purpose of amusement at this juncture of the world's history had to me something repulsive and disgusting about it. I would have done anything to keep the whole State—Queen, Government, and Parliament—at least apparently close to their duties for the next month. I do hope you will be able to prevent any persons over whom you have authority being gazetted as engaged in the "pleasures of the season," both for their own sakes and for that of the Government. I also trust that you will allow no regard for the convenience of the idle classes to stand in the way of calling Parliament together at any moment. Our principles of public Government are well worth the risk of inane grumblings and even foolish speeches. This armament of the fortifications of Paris recalls to my recollection the interesting debate at which I was present in 1840. Messieurs Guizot and Thiers supported the construction on the ground that they would secure Paris from the insane panics and violences of 1792 and 1793, and from the facile submission of 1814. The Duc de Broglie, on the other hand, opposed them, as being likely to tempt France into an unjust and imprudent war; and said, "When she once had got such a costume ready, her vanity would always be urging her to try how well she looked in it." The improvement in artillery must doubtless much diminish the efficacy of the *enceinte*. If the detached forts are once taken, I do not see how resistance would be possible.

I have written this letter for my own satisfaction, and with no notion of an answer from you, even though refreshed by the Channel breezes.

Yours very truly,
Houghton.

Mr. Gladstone in his reply hardly admitted the justice of the strictures passed by Lord Houghton upon the Ministry and Parliament. The House, he declared, was only anxious to be prorogued, and the Bills dropped had been abandoned merely because they were threatened with formidable opposition. He declared, however, that no mercy would be shown to the idlers, if any occasion arose for calling Parliament together.

Lord Houghton to Mr. Gladstone.

Crewe Hall, Oct. 22nd, 1870.

MY DEAR GLADSTONE,—I have been this last week in a country house with the Duc Persigny, and though he told me nothing but what you probably know already, there was something curious and interesting in the freedom with which he stated the hopes and projects of the French Imperialists. He expressed great indignation at the Empress's refusal to sign any preliminaries of peace when M. Regnier brought over General Bourbaki, the scheme being that she and the Emperor should abdicate after the final arrangements, and the Prince should govern with a Council of Regency, which would in fact be a *République honnête*. There was meaning in his notion that an irresponsible child would alone hold the throne after a disgraceful peace; but I much doubt any such personal combinations being possible in such a crisis of events. He went off suddenly on Thursday—he said, to meet a Prussian agent. I have seen two letters from persons of authority in France anticipating civil war as inevitable. I hope the sale of arms from this country to France is not going on in any large proportions, for we may come at any moment to a time when that commerce is the only means of the prolongation of the war—by no means an agreeable responsibility. Bernstorff's last remonstrance has shown the incorrectness of the positive assertions made to me the last day of the Session by Lords Halifax, Cairns, and Hatherley, as to the legal inability of the Government to prohibit partially the export of munitions of war. These great authorities seem never to have consulted the Orders in Council during the Crimean War. But even without these precedents I cannot see on what principle such an inability could rest. Assuredly the larger power must include the smaller. The question of policy of course remains entirely separate from that of legality. I now deeply regret that I did not make a separate report, which I believe would have been supported by some of the best members of the Commission.

You will come and see this fine house some day. It is certainly a most successful restoration, and does infinite credit to Ayrton's victim, Edward Barry. He did not propose the health of Her Majesty's Ministers at the *déjeûner*.

Yours very truly,

HOUGHTON.

Mr. Gladstone to Lord Houghton.

11, *Carlton House Terrace, Oct 26th*, 1870.

MY DEAR HOUGHTON,—Thanks for your letter. Persigny, I find, is open-mouthed everywhere, but yours was the first account. In the *Daily News* of to-day there is a curious document purporting to come from Chislehurst; if it be accurate, the Empress has not *renounced* her Regency as far as her own intention is concerned.

With regard to the sale of arms, as far as I know, it has been far larger from the United States than from this country; but this, I see it stated, is never mentioned in any German paper. Halifax does not admit the failure of his doctrine regarding partial concession. Stephen Glynn brought us most interesting accounts of the entire function at Crewe. I have the following anecdote:—A horse-dealer, hearing him mentioned, said, " They may talk about Lord Crewe, but I know it is very hard to come round him about a horse." Stephen says his speech was excellent, like everything else.

Yours sincerely,

W. E. GLADSTONE.

We have no fresh news; the armistice can only be adjusted if both parties have a real desire for it, which remains to be proved.

In the autumn Houghton spent some time in Scotland. Among other places he visited was Invergarry, the Highland home of Mr. Ellice. It was whilst staying there, on this occasion, that he penned the following lines :—

THE COMPLAINT OF GLENQUOICH.

Far from the factions of the field of life,
    The veteran statesman fixed his autumn rest;
And of his friends or rivals in the strife
    There was not one but strove to be his guest.

Thus, where the shrouded hills for ages past
    Had known no voices save the storms and streams,
Scandal and gossip now profane the blast,
    And daily posts disturb the poet's dreams.

Where the lone eagle swept the vacant air,
    Fashion's gay creatures now distract the sight;
Wild birds of paradox flit here and there,
    And owls of politics infest the night;

"Parritch" scarce lingers on the breakfast scene,
    "Toddy" still dribbles, but the claret flows,
And the rich incense of the French cuisine
    Smothers the haggis and the hardy brose.

What thinks this nature, turbulent and stern,
    Of sportsmen who like sheep preserve their deer,
Of rulers who the very sky would turn
    Into blue books, were blue its colour here?

> Oh! worthy veteran, still so hale and blithe,
>   Ask, as you saunter down the heathery glade,
> How long that other veteran, with the scythe,
>   Would take to make the changes you have made.

Towards the close of the year Lord Houghton was at Fryston, entertaining many guests. The following letter from his friend Henry Bright is of interest because it touches upon the last days of one whom Lord Houghton greatly admired, and with whom, during his stay in England, he had been somewhat intimate—Nathaniel Hawthorne. Mr. Bright had been the intimate friend of Hawthorne during the stay of the latter in Liverpool:—

Henry Bright to Lord Houghton.

Ashfield, Liverpool, November 18*th.*

I have seen Mrs. Hawthorne. She lives out at Kensington with her two singularly pre-Raphaelite daughters. She told me much about poor Hawthorne's last weeks of life; how the war pressed upon him more and more; how he felt that, when the soldiers returned, the quiet rural life of the New England villages would be spoiled and coarsened; how he detested the Northern abuse of Lee and the best Southerners; how at last he would see no newspaper at all, and growing more and more miserable died apparently of no complaint beyond his own melancholy depression and hopeless forebodings. He was intending to write a story, besides the fragment "Pansy," with all his English experiences in it; he had indeed begun, but nothing can be made out, except that a young Englishman exiled to America and with a secret, returns to trace out the birthplace and graves of his ancestors. Mrs. Hawthorne greatly regrets that she allowed passages to remain in the Note-book which are far better away. She wants me to revise the second edition for her, but I fear it is too late to make the alterations now.

Lord Houghton to his Wife.

The Athenæum, December 6th, 1870.

I had a pleasant dinner yesterday, sitting by the Dean of Canterbury, who is on the Committee for revising the New Testament. He said they had found themselves compelled to make many more alterations than they had expected. This morning I met Père Hyacinthe at breakfast at Dean Stanley's. He is staying there, and made himself very pleasant, without being at all obtrusive of personal topics. The Dean and Lady Augusta come to Fryston on the 26th, unless peace is made, and then they mean to go to Paris instead. Doyle wrote to compliment Palgrave on those fine lines in the *Spectator*, but, alas! they were not his, but by my unappreciated young friend Pollock.

Robert Browning to Lord Houghton.

December 5th, 1870.

MY DEAR HOUGHTON,—I suppose this must be the third or fourth time that you have invited me to Fryston. If you do not understand that I am very sincerely grateful for this and much beside that has happened during what I shall venture to call our long friendship, it would be strange indeed. This autumn, since my return in October, I have not left London, spite of many pleasant requests from kind people; and I hardly ought to pick and choose at the end of all, and go to you in defiance of my own repeated excuses, which were valid enough, however. I am sure you may believe that I feel more than simply sorry that I can only thank you exceedingly for the gratification of your proposal while foregoing it, as I am forced to do; but—shall I be bold and add something? You extend your invitation to my son; he is now with a tutor in the country, but will come up for Christmas. If it would suit you to receive him by himself, few circumstances would delight me more. I begin to mistrust my own notions about him; the matter is too interesting to me, and I stand too close. The time is at hand when I must make up my mind as to what is to be done with him, and your opinion, or even fancy, of what the chances in his favour may seem, would be of such advantage to me that I take this nearest way to it. Should there be any inconvenience of any kind in his visit, you will, of course, say so with the frankness I think I deserve; nor will there prove the least disappointment to him, who is not only away, but (as it occurs to me) may have had other engagements of his own. So extend your habitual good nature to the consideration of what I suggest rather than propose, and determine my proceeding on it, or otherwise, by one word to

Yours very truly,
ROBERT BROWNING.

All thanks and best regards to Lady Houghton, if you please.

Mr. Robert Barrett Browning visited Fryston at Christmas.

Robert Browning to Lord Houghton.

Old Year's Day.

DEAR HOUGHTON,—I expected you and your family would be kind to Robert, but you have been miraculously kind, he says. Your reward must be in his thorough sense of it. He is a grateful and loyal boy, and sure to remember you all gratefully through life. Best New Year's wishes to Lady Houghton and Fryston generally. One may even bring in France, trusting with Horace, *Nil desperandum auspice Ducrot.*

Ever truly yours,
ROBERT BROWNING.

The author of "Friends in Council" was one of those whom Lord Houghton had asked to join the guests at Fryston towards the close of the year. Sir Arthur Helps was unable to accept the invitation for reasons detailed in the following pleasant letter.

Sir A. Helps to Lord Houghton.

Privy Council Office, Nov. 29th, 1870.

MY DEAR HOUGHTON,—I wish I could accept your kind invitation for my daughter and myself. I should think, without any flattery, that yours must be one of the pleasantest houses to go to in the world. But my married son and daughter are both of them coming to me with their conjugal appendages about the time you mention. By the way, I am not so very fond of being called " Grandpa," for I never felt so young as I do now. What a stupid thing of you it is to have been born a Yorkshireman! I daresay you are proud of it; most people are of the things they should be least proud of: and now if you had had the sense to have been born a Kentish man, and if Frognal had been Fryston, as it ought to have been, it would have been the centre of the intellectual universe, and you would have been plagued to death with A. H.'s visitations, whom now you secretly think to be a surly, uncompaniable, unapostolic sort of fellow. Ask Lady Houghton to be kind enough to accept a little book * which I am sending by this day's post.

Yours always,

ARTHUR HELPS.

The allusion to Fryston as "one of the pleasantest houses to go to in the world" enables the writer to introduce a personal experience of his own; for it was in December, 1870, that I first had the pleasure of staying as a guest with Lord Houghton. Enough has already been said to enable the reader to understand something of the peculiar features of Fryston, and of the atmosphere in which its inhabitants lived; but it would be difficult to do full justice to the hospitality, real and yet unobtrusive, which made the visitor to the house

* "Brevia," London, 1871.

feel at home in it the moment he crossed its threshold. The manner of life was that which is common to our country houses, though there was, perhaps, less formality, less of ordered ceremonial, about it than is usually the case. In those days, when Lady Houghton was still at the head of the household, lending an additional charm to her husband's hospitalities, breakfast was commonly partaken of in the sunny morning-room, which has now been converted into a drawing-room. Here several small tables were laid for the meal, and the guests took their place at any which chanced to suit their fancy, though those were envied who found themselves occupying a place beside the master of the house. Lord Houghton, as has already been told, was an early riser, but he often did not make his appearance in the morning-room until breakfast had begun, and then he dropped into any seat which happened to be vacant, always with a bright smile upon his face and a happy saying or a good story on his lips. Over breakfast, indeed, all were anxious to linger so long as he was in the room. The meal concluded, there were various occupations for all. Lord Houghton himself would by-and-by turn to his letters, but seldom until there had been an animated discussion, in which he took the leading part, on some topic of the day. A new book had arrived, or a letter had been received, telling of the movements of some writer or politician of fame. It mattered little who or what the subject of discussion was, Houghton invariably had something to tell his guests regarding it which they did not know for themselves. It was amazing, indeed, to observe the vastness and the universality of his knowledge; and dull indeed must have been the man who in that after-breakfast talk with the master of Fryston did not learn something of interest or of value.

As I look back upon many such talks, that which strikes me as most noteworthy in Lord Houghton's knowledge was the unequalled extent of his information about persons of interest. Not in vain had that passionate curiosity which was one of his distinguishing characteristics possessed him during a long life spent in the best European society. He could tell his interlocutors something about every man and woman of note whose name cropped up in the course of conversation—something which could not be learned from books, but which Houghton had acquired for himself in the course of his life of study and observation. By-and-by he would retire to his own room and to a book—for to the last he was an omnivorous reader; but if, as often happened to be the case, some favoured guest was in the room with him, he delighted to lay the book aside for a moment and discuss some point which it had raised in his mind.

Walks or drives in the spacious park or to the neighbouring town of Pomfret, whose old castle he delighted to show to his friends, would occupy the afternoon, until the gathering twilight found the party assembled once more in the drawing-room, again to indulge in talk very different from that which is heard in the average country house. At the dinner-table, again, there was the brightest and most cheerful of conversation; and after dinner, if a game of whist, of which he was fond, were not proposed, he would bring forth some of the treasures of his library, rare books or rarer autographs, and delight everybody by the charm of his manner and the abundance of his memories as he talked about book or paper. Never was he more delightful, however, than when he was dealing with some question which concerned the happiness or the well-being of some one in whom he was interested. It would be impossible to exaggerate the amount of pains, the earnest effort of which he was capable, in trying to serve any deserving person on whose behalf an appeal had been made to him. Here is a letter which furnishes a case in point.

Lord Houghton to Mr. Gladstone.

Fryston Hall, Christmas, 1873.

MY DEAR GLADSTONE,—I asked you some time ago for a pension for Mrs. Moxon, the adopted daughter Isola of Charles and Mary Lamb, who has been ruined. I thought that public opinion would recognise a certain claim in anyone so closely connected by association and family life with "Elia." You did not, and may have been right. There is now a subscription being raised to help her, and a donation from the Civil Fund would be very acceptable. Thomas Baring, to whom I never appealed in vain in a case of literary distress (how strange for so rich a man!) sent me £50 for her a few days before his death. I was very sorry for Winterbotham's death. Besides the rare position of a cultivated Dissenter, he had the courage of his opinions without the bravado of singularity. I am told he was discourteous in his office, but that, it seems, is the habit of the time. I see a good deal of Childers, and much regret his having left office. In the coarse public apprehension of character it goes hard with a man who twice gives up office, for any cause whatever, however imperative.

With all the best wishes of the time,

I am yours sincerely,

HOUGHTON.

I have already given a letter from Mr. Seymour Kirkup relating to Landor and Blake; another of this period is worth reproduction :—

Seymour Kirkup to Lord Houghton.
Florence, Dec. 18th, 1870.

MY DEAR LORD,—I have had an inflammation in my right eye, which has prevented my writing or reading. It is now so much better that I can send you a short line to say that Leader tells me that anything about Landor may be of use. I could send you some anecdotes, but they might be made use of against him, for he had many enemies, though his character was raised, in my humble opinion, by his good-humour and reasonableness—I may almost say, his docility. I do not remember if I told your lordship, or if it was Mr. Browning, of his challenging a Frenchman, and the way he was prevented fighting. Another curious story was his treatment of his landlord, who had a very bad name. It was a curious scene and ridiculous, from the garrulity of old Wallace the painter, whom I think you knew. Landor liked him for gossiping about pictures. I do not know Mr. Forster, but I sent to his friend Browning above fifty letters, odes in Latin and English, dialogues, scraps of newspapers, &c., for his use, at B.'s request, when he was writing the life of Landor. F. promised to return them, but he never has. And as the book is finished, he ought to send them to me. If they could be of any use to you, as you think of adding to your essay, you are quite welcome to ask F. for them in my name, and make any use of them; but most likely he has picked all the plums out of the pudding, if there were any, for I have never seen his book. I asked lately a friend of Landor's who Mr. Forster was, and he said "a vulgar swell;" and others said that Landor had cut him latterly. Your essay makes me think better of him. If you get these documents, keep them as long as you like; I am in no hurry for them. . . .

>Believe me
>>Always your faithful servant,
>>>SEYMOUR KIRKUP.

Lord Houghton was not well during the early part of 1871, and he was still worse later in the year, when he had to spend some time at Buxton, trying to get rid of a severe attack of the gout, which was now beginning to trouble him much.

To his Wife.

Travellers' Club, Feb. 5th, 1871.

I have seen a number of people to-day, beginning with the Prophet of Chelsea, and ending with the Duc d'Aumale. I went to the former's with Forster (W. E.), and it was touching to hear him tell the old man that if he ever did or became anything useful or notable, he owed it to the influence of his writings. I am sorry to say the Prophet cursed and swore a great deal, saying the Government might drag the nation down to hell, but he was not going with them, or with any Ministry that left the country with six guns, one torpedo, and a Cardwell.

House of Lords, Feb. 20th.

I dined with General Fox yesterday, and he asked me to come and stay in Addison Road; so my town lodgings are increasing. The Government have put me on the Admiralty Commission, and I have telegraphed to Childers to Lisbon to know whether he thinks I can be of any use to him. If he thinks I can, I must do it. He is a little better, but suffers much in his head, which is worse than anything. . . . It is not true that there is any question of M. Guizot coming here as ambassador. It will probably be the Duc de Broglie, whom I know very well, and whom I remember Lady —— calling "Le jeune homme le plus disgracieux de la France."

Broadlands, March 10*th.*

It is pathetic to be at this old place again. I see the pleasant lady's face in every corner. The shrubs are grown, and the park enlarged, but nothing much altered. We had a drive to Embly to-day—a beautiful one. Mr. Nightingale was away; Florence and her mother—both ghostly and invisible—were there. The Bishop of Oxford is here. He confirms and preaches to-morrow. Lady Ashburton was here yesterday, but went to London this morning. I enclose Vaughan's letter about the wife's sister; it is very striking. We shall probably get the Bill before the Lords next week; the prospects are very hopeful.

Lord Houghton had become the recognised leader of the movement for obtaining the legalisation of marriage with a deceased wife's sister, and for many years after this his most frequent appearances as a speaker in the House of Lords were in connection with this measure, with which he sympathised entirely.

To Henry Bright.

April 5*th.*

I left Lady William Russell very poorly. The east wind has penetrated even her catacomb, and she is torn by a terrible cough. Her *mot* to the Duc de Broglie—who said he had never believed till now that we were a nation of shopkeepers, that she had always believed till now that the French were a nation of soldiers—had a great success. I think the Government are gaining by the heavy and important measures they have introduced; and I should hope that this will be as practical a Session as the others of Gladstone's have been unpractical and poetical. There are a very large number of foreigners, even English and German, in the rebel force at Paris, so that all the world will gain by their defeat, which seems imminent.* But they are capable of any enormity in their desperation, and may burn down the city. I remember a saying of one of the roughs in 1848, "Nous aussi voulons tâter la Chair blanche;" but they do not seem much inclined to that amusement now. A French professor came to see me yesterday, and, when I asked him to have some breakfast, said that from the siege "il avait perdu le goût de manger." But that did not prevent him from making a very good one.

To his Wife.
July 1st, 1871.

The Buccleughs' was rather a fine fête than a good ball. The dancing was in two rooms, and —— lost some partners this way. The last sight was the little H. sitting in green tarlatan on the balustrade in the morning light, and with some smart young man. The Prince of Wales said to me, "So you and M. Thiers have settled all the affairs of Europe." "Yes, sir, it is all right." I had to speak and vote against my friend Forster last night.

Lord Houghton to Mr. Gladstone.

Luichart Lodge, Dingwall, N.B., Sept. 10*th,* 1871.

MY DEAR GLADSTONE,—I wish I could have been with you at Thornes, as Gaskell kindly proposed,† especially as I should have heard your answer to my Yorkshire friends with pleasure and sympathy. I cannot say as much of your Whitby speech, for it confirmed my feeling that on the "high mountain" where you

---

* The Communist rising had now taken place.

† Mr. Gladstone had just visited Yorkshire, where he had been the guest of Mr. Milnes Gaskell, M.P., at Thornes House, Wakefield. He had delivered speeches at Wakefield and Whitby.

stand there is a demon, not of demagoguism, but of demophilism, that is tempting you sorely. I am no alarmist, but it is undeniable that a new and thoroughly false conception of the relations of work and wealth is invading European society, and of which the Paris Commune is the last expression. Therefore any word from such a man as you implying that you look on individual wealth as anything else than a reserve of public wealth, and that there can be any antagonism between them, seems to me infinitely dangerous. I have hitherto rested in security on the rude but sound political economy which I believe the working classes of our towns possess, and which taught them that if all the accumulated wealth was dispersed among them to-morrow, they would in a month be all the worse off for its dispersion; but a certain encouragement is now given by some thoughtful men, not only to the envy of the superior material well-being of others, which is bad enough, but to a jealousy of intellectual eminence, and a dislike of culture itself. Surely it is the business of the Government first to satisfy the mind of the nation and then the body, and not to appeal to the body when he happens not to be in momentary accord with the mind. I am sure you can do both if you do not content yourself with the lower and easier function.

I am

Yours very truly,

HOUGHTON.

Mr. Gladstone replied with his usual frankness and friendliness to the remonstrances of his old friend, " whose criticisms are marked by the kindly tone which is habitual with you, though I do not agree in everything you say about property." He feared Lord Houghton must have been misled by some abstract or inaccurate report of his speech, especially on the subject of property.

To his Wife.

Dunrobin Castle, September 23rd, 1871.

A curious day . . . . A pleasant visit at the Bishop's; a row in the train, and I asserting that the Duke kept a carriage for Dunrobin, on which entered a sweet-looking old lady, whom I soon found out to be Miss Marsh ("Hedley Vickars," "English Hearts," &c.). Amy went with the C——'s as far as Dingwall, then came into our carriage, and we had Miss Marsh most interesting on the death of a wild man I had known as a boy; so much so as to set me crying (it might have been gout). The Duke met us at the station, and after dressing we have had a good dinner. At the present moment Amy is listening to Lady John Scott (who wrote "Annie Laurie") singing charmingly. Lord D—— is talking to Miss Marsh as if he were Hedley Vickars. By me are the chief financial adviser of the Khedive; a young French officer, late at Metz, who looks on the Emperor with horror, and Bazaine as an infamous traitor; the great engineer Sir Henry Jones; Lord Ronald Gower; a pleasant Mrs. Coke, lady-in-waiting to the Princess of Wales, and two or three other relatives. More guests are expected on Tuesday, and there is talk of a ball somewhere.

To his Son.

Dunrobin Castle, Sutherland, September 26th, 1871.

DEAREST ROBIN,—Your letter was of course very agreeable to me, and the fact, I doubt not, agreeable to yourself. I care a good deal about your place in the school this time, as it may affect the comfort of your position in your house. It is as well that you should begin that crack-jaw German at school, as I suspect the difficulty I have had in mastering it (though I went to the University of Bonn when I left Cambridge) comes from my never having been well grounded in its detestable grammar and absurd constructions. This is a gorgeous castle built over the sea, and you look on the Northern Ocean from long terraces as rich with flowers as a London villa. The Duchess is very kind to Amy, who, however, has had two shocks this morning—one, being close to a white rat which the little girl of the house was playing with at breakfast; and the other, seeing her dear Archbishop called a "loose fish" in one of the papers.

Lord Houghton during the autumn had been discussing a question which had engaged his attention more than once—that of the transaction of business in the House of Lords. A letter which he had written to the editor of the *Times* was not inserted, but the accident was explained by Mr. Delane.

Mr. Delane to Lord Houghton.
10, *Serjeants' Inn, Oct. 26th,* 1871.

MY DEAR LORD HOUGHTON,—On my return from Paris last night I found your letter of the 17th upon the transaction of business by the House of Lords, which had not been opened during my absence. I fear the opportuneness of its publication has now passed; but I send it to you in the hope that you may yet be able to make it available. I left Paris in anxious expectation of a Buonapartist restoration, upon which that ingenious and self respecting people will, I presume, replace all the N.'s and other Imperial emblems they have so assiduously defaced. Thiers is as lively as ever, and has very pleasant little parties at the Préfecture at Versailles, where the recollection of its late occupant never seems to recur to either host or guests. I have been also at Sedan and Metz, and through the Department still in German occupation. To the stranger it seems strange to see the Germans in possession of the railway, the post, and all the other offices and duties which a native Government ordinarily performs; but to the native the only thing strange seems to be that the stranger should think it strange at all.

The Duc d'Aumale has taken a fine house, and means to entertain largely. The Comte de Paris is also somewhere in the city from which he takes his name; but no one seems to know where.

Ever faithfully yours,
JOHN T. DELANE.

Mrs. Procter to Lord Houghton.

32, *Weymouth Street, Portland Place, W.,*
Nov. 17*th,* 1871.

MY DEAR LORD HOUGHTON,—I hear that you are still at Buxton, and better for the quiet and the baths. Although I do not often hear from you, the newspapers keep the world aware of your movements. Here we are indulging in cheap operas and pleasant little dinners. Last Sunday I met at dinner Mr. and Mrs. Bancroft—so very agreeable, quiet, and simple. I saw Browning on Sunday; he never fails me. He had dined with Knowles to meet Tennyson, who read his new poem to them. Browning has also written a new poem. How hard we have to work, we readers! You, Tennyson, and Browning, who write, only read your own works. You will perhaps have seen the *Atlantic Magazine,* containing some letters of Dickens's—letters alluding to old jokes between the writer and reader, but not suitable for the public. I am very much gratified by my Adelaide's verses being translated into German. I have had a charming letter from Herr Brinckmann, who has done the work. . . . Do read "Nobody's Fortune," by Yates. The scene is close to Pencarrell; but do not be deterred by the fear of rural life; the actors are all from London—convicts; the least objectionable person is a wicked old attorney. . How terribly you will lament that you cannot have Sir Charles Dilke at Fryston! *
Do make haste and get well, and have Voysey also. . . .

Your affectionate old friend,

ANNE B. PROCTER.

The mention of Mr. Edmund Yates in Mrs. Procter's letter recalls the friendship of that well-known journalist with Lord Houghton, and a characteristic anecdote

* Sir Charles Dilke was at this time attracting much public notice in consequence of his speeches on the subject of royalty and the expenses of the Court.

of the manner in which it began, which I am able to give in Mr. Yates's own words.

For many years [writes Mr. Yates] I enjoyed a tolerably close acquaintance with the late Lord Houghton, who showed great kindness in inviting me to his house, and in occasionally writing to me on the subjects of the day which had been touched upon in the *World*. I recollect, too, his coming to the Office to talk to me about some French puzzles which we were publishing at the time, and in which, as he averred, he was much interested. It is very pleasant, also, for me to remember that he was foremost among those friends by whom I was entertained at a public dinner in May, 1885, and that he made a most kindly and excellent speech on that occasion. It is the more pleasant to me to remember all this kindly feeling because my acquaintance with Lord Houghton had a somewhat inauspicious commencement. When quite a young man I had, at some public meeting at the Freemasons' Tavern, apologised for my own nervousness, saying, in the words of the noble lord, who was present, "the beating of my own heart was the only sound I heard." I understood afterwards, from a common friend, that Lord Houghton had taken these remarks in great dudgeon, imagining that I was "chaffing" him; but I thought no more of it. A few weeks afterwards, in November, 1867, the Freemasons' Hall was the scene of the farewell banquet to Charles Dickens, previous to his sailing on his second visit to America, over which Lord Lytton presided, and the arrangements of which had been entrusted to a small committee of three—Mr. Edward Lawson, Mr. Charles Kent, and myself. While the banquet was in progress Mr. Lawson came to me in great perturbation, informing me that Sir James Emerson Tennant, to whom an important toast had been assigned, had been suddenly taken ill, and had gone home. Some *remplaçant* must be found at once. We discussed various people, and finally settled on Lord Houghton, I undertaking, very much against my will, to approach him upon the subject. I went to Lord Houghton, who was seated near the chairman, and, explaining the circumstances, made my appeal to him to propose the toast. In a very curt manner he refused. "I will not, sir." I was a little astonished, and again pressed my suit. "The toast was an important one," I said, "and required an adequate proposer." "I will not do it, sir," he repeated; then, turning round and glaring angrily at me, "Why don't you do it yourself, sir? I heard you make a very pungent speech in this room some little time ago—a very pungent speech indeed, sir," and with that he turned his back upon me, and the interview was at an end. He never alluded to it in after-life, and our intercourse was of the pleasantest."

It was probably not so much any feeling of resentment against Mr. Yates that prompted the refusal to speak on this occasion, as Lord Houghton's great horror of having to make a speech without having prepared for it. There might, too, have been a feeling in his mind, neither unnatural nor unjustifiable, of surprise at the fact that so old a friend of Charles Dickens should only have been asked to speak on this occasion as a substitute for another.

A controversy had somehow or other arisen in the month of December, 1871, on the subject of the authorship of "Home, sweet Home;" and Lord Houghton, writing to the *Athenæum*, December 14th, was able to tell an anecdote of interest bearing upon his own early life in Milan:—

I was residing [he wrote] at Milan with my family at the time of the production of the opera of *Anna Bolena*. We were very intimate with Madame Pasta. I well remember her calling one day, and telling us she was very much discontented with her share in the partition of the last scene of the opera; and she added, "You English have so many beautiful airs which you sing among yourselves that I am sure you could help me." My mother, who was a very fine musician, mentioned " Home, sweet Home " as a song which its own air and words, and Miss Paton's singing, had made very popular in England. She sang it; and Madame Pasta, sitting down at the pianoforte, said, "It will do—I am sure it will do." Donizetti adopted it accordingly, and thanked us for having got him out of his difficulty. As to the authorship, not having any musical books about me, I can only express a vague remembrance that it appeared first in a collection of foreign songs with English words. The music, I believe, was arranged by Bishop, and the words were either by Baily or Thomas Moore. The air was Sicilian; and I particularly remember saying to Madame Pasta that it was curious that an Italian air should get back to its home through an English medium.

The illness which had troubled Lord Houghton so much in 1871 had not left him in the following year. It did not, however, prevent him from entertaining friends at Fryston, from taking some part in public life in London, and from paying two visits to the Continent, one of which was to Brussels, where he had an interview with the King. In January he went to Torquay to visit his aunts, with whom he delighted to keep up a constant intercourse.

To Henry Bright.

Jan. 3rd, 1872.

. . . I quite sympathise with you about T——; it is my experience of my best friends. Office is a terrible friend-killer. I have now quite lost W. E. Forster, and Childers came over to see me yesterday, simply because he is *out;* and yet one is foolish enough to give time and money to keep them *in.* You'll see, the Irish Bishops will have their own way; and when they've got it, their flocks will probably throw them over. . . .

To his Wife.

Torquay, Jan. 22nd, 1872.

I found the elderly—not old—ladies in good case, both very cheerful and pleasant. Tell Florey I shall be quite content if I see her like Aunt Louisa at the same time of life. . . . I had a pleasant hour of chat with Lord Lytton yesterday; he has a very pretty house, and congratulated me on being here with women, saying, "When one is ill, there is nothing like women." (*Vide* W. Scott.)

To his Son.

Fryston Lodge, Torquay, Jan. 30*th.*

DEAREST ROBERT,—I dined with Lord Lytton last week, and he talked all the time himself; but as he talked well, and the subjects were interesting, I was very glad to listen. The Baroness Coutts is very hospitable, and I dine with her to-day to meet the Bishop of Exeter, who has come to preside at a meeting about cruelty to animals. I declined attending, not wishing, I said, to censure my brother-in-law, who is Master of Hounds.

To his Wife.

Fryston Lodge, Saturday.

This place certainly suits me very well; it only tempts me to do too much, and I have once or twice tired myself with walking. It is worrying to be able to do so little. I am, however, none the worse this morning for an agreeable dinner at Lord Lytton's, where I took Jane. He perorated most eloquently on politics and literature, entertaining Mr. Toogood, the doctor, with an elaborate *éloge* on Corneille, and several young ladies with anecdotes of Disraeli. . . . I have declined Granville's full-dress dinner on the 5th, being inclined to linger in the South a little longer.

Fryston Lodge, Feb. 8th.

I am quite grieved with this American matter. At the time I was *blessé* that Gladstone had entirely passed me over when my name would, no doubt, have been very effective with the Americans; and now I don't know but that I might have been taken in like the others, and might have repented, even if I had got you made Viscountess Madeley.

The question at issue with America at this time was that of the indirect claims so unexpectedly raised by the United States Government after the agreement to submit the Alabama question to arbitration. Lord Houghton had, as his letter shows, felt somewhat aggrieved at being passed over when the Commission, of which Lord Ripon was the chief, was sent to Washington; and as he had long been known as one of the warmest friends of the North, his dissatisfaction was not without some justification. In connection with this question of the indirect claims, his old friend Mr. Hayward wrote to him as follows:—

St. James's Street, February 5th, 1872.

MY DEAR HOUGHTON,—You won't be wanted for the Collier business; the American affair dwarfs other subjects. I dined with Lord Granville on Saturday, and he told me he had no fear. The Government have told the United States practically that unless they give up the indirect damages they cannot go on with the arbitration; but they will meet Parliament with a simple assurance that the affair is under consideration, and try to maintain diplomatic reserve in the debate. Whether they can keep to this depends upon the temper of the House. . . . I hope you are getting well; no man is more missed in London.

Ever faithfully yours,
A. HAYWARD.

Lord Houghton's health improved in the spring, and he resumed his place in London society. He had given up the house in Brook Street, where he had lived since his marriage, and from this time forward he had no fixed residence in London, but took a house for the season, or rooms at Almond's Hotel in Clifford Street, as happened to be most convenient. During this spring, besides paying a flying visit to Brussels, he spoke at several dinners, his speech at the dinner of the Literary Fund being a special success. It was during this spring also that he received the Order of the Rose of Brazil from the Emperor, whose acquaintance he had made some time previously.

Dean Stanley to Lord Houghton.

Deanery, Westminster, April 1st, 1872.

MY DEAR LORD HOUGHTON,—You have been so kind to Père Hyacinthe that he wishes you to know—if possible, before you see it in the papers—what is to befall him on Tuesday. After long struggles and much agitation—not the cause, but in great part the consequence and accompaniment, of his rupture with the Roman Church—he has determined on the grave step of marriage. It is to an American lady, whose husband died when she was young. She has no fortune; she is a very remarkable person, full of a union of grace and energy such as you find in the best American women. It is a romantic story—too long to tell, but highly creditable to both parties. She, like himself, is a " Liberal Catholic," and they neither of them mean to leave the Roman Catholic Church. The difficulties of the French law compel them to be married in England. The wish to avoid the appearance of being Protestants compels them to be married before the registrar. On Wednesday morning will probably appear a document from himself, setting forth the grounds of his act. He is fully aware of what will be said of the act in France and elsewhere, and the prospects are no doubt sufficiently anxious. I had hoped that it might have been deferred till some more general movement in that direction took place; but this seemed indefinitely remote, and he felt anxious to take the step before the meeting at Cologne at the end of this month, in order to prevent misconstructions. They remain in England for about a fortnight, and thence probably go to Cologne, and thence to Paris, where he will take up his abode. It has been a heavy burden to me ever since I knew it; the contemplation of two human beings launched on such a sea of troubles is distracting; but I hope the best, and have worked for this to the best of my judgment, and trust to his other friends to do the same.

Ever yours truly,
A. P. STANLEY.

Edward Fitzgerald, the author of "Omar Khayam," had long been one of his correspondents, and in his later days Fitzgerald's letters took the place of those of some earlier friends who had passed away. From time to time I shall quote from his correspondence.

Edward Fitzgerald to Lord Houghton.

Market Hall, Woodbridge, April 8th, 1872.

DEAR LORD HOUGHTON,—It is rather hard to ask you to write about trifles—you have so much to write and do; but you have always been very obliging to me, and so here goes with my little business. I have just been reading your "Life and Letters of Keats" for the second time, edition 1867, and I want to know who was the lady he died in love with, or if I may not know her name, whether she was single or married. Was she the "Charmian" Miss of p. 192?—not the lady who said he looked "quite the little poet," to be sure; and, by-the-bye, how tall was he?—above five feet surely; which he talks of in one place?

I wonder Messrs. Browning, Morris, Rossetti, &c., can read Keats's hastiest doggerel and not be ashamed at being trumpeted as great poets in the *Athenæum* and elsewhere. Only to mention Tennyson alone, to compare themselves with; who *used not* to think himself equal to Keats at all. I don't know what he thinks now after so much worship has been offered him. To Keats he is not equal in invention and strength of continued flight, at any rate; but certainly farther above Browning & Co. than below his predecessor. I admire greatly the delicate way you have treated of the "Cockney School," which was the right word in the main; and one can scarce blame the reviewers for at first confusing Keats with the company he came out with. But I think *that Quarterly* should be printed along with this life of Keats, as a warning to reviewers. I think you will excuse my troubling you. A very few words will answer me; and do not answer if not proper or agreeable.

Yours sincerely,

E. FITZGERALD.

The Same to the Same.

Woodbridge, April 12*th*, 1872.

DEAR LORD HOUGHTON,—I must answer by return of post. Pray do send me Keats's first Hyperion, and so thank you for it and for your swift and very kind reply to my letter. I used to tell Tennyson thirty years ago that he should be a dragoon, or in some active employment that would keep his soul stirring, instead of revolving in its own idleness and tobacco-smoke; and now he is sunk in coterie worship, and (I tremble to say it) in the sympathy of his most lady-like, gentle wife. I can care nothing for his poems since his two volumes in 1842, except for the dramatic element in "Maud," and a few little bits in it; but I am told this is because I have shut up my mind, &c. So it may be. But surely he has became more artist than poet ever since; and if the artist have not the wherewithal to work on? I mourn over him as once a great man lost—that is, not risen to the greatness that was in him, for he has done enough to outlast all others of his time, I think, up to 1842. As to the princesses, king's idylls, &c., they seem to me to fail utterly in the one thing wanted—invention; to make a new and better thing of old legends, which without it are best left alone. I know no more of Mr. Swinburne than the *Athenæum* has quoted for me. I saw enough to prove to me that he has more of the right thing than Browning & Co., but a fiery, unquiet spirit. I thought that I did not care to make further acquaintance with " déjà," but I shall get " Atalanta."

Thank you again and again for the Hyperion that is forthcoming. I write so soon, partly to catch you in the country— where you are not so busy, I suppose.

And I am yours sincerely and much obliged,

EDWARD FITZGERALD.

" Napoleon in exile " was one of the familiar objects of London life at this particular epoch. It is true that the ex-Emperor's health did not permit him to take any large part in the gaieties of the London season, but he was sufficiently well to be able to renew his acquaintance with those old friends whom he had known in bygone days when he was the " Pretender " of Gore House. Lord Houghton, who had purposely seen so little of him during his reign as Emperor, now again became his friend, and did what in him lay to smooth the rough path of the fallen Emperor. After the ex-Emperor's death he saw something of the Prince Imperial, and tried to interest him among other things in the Newspaper Press Fund. He was successful, as the following letter shows, in inducing him to attend one of the annual dinners.

The Prince Imperial to Lord Houghton.

SIR,—I have received the letter you so kindly wrote to me from Paris, and I seize with pleasure this opportunity of thanking you for the invitation I owe to your most amiable regards. I have learned during my long stay in England to esteem the English press. My conviction is, that one needs only to read through an English newspaper to understand the greatness of that noble country, and I am therefore extremely glad to be able, when called upon, to answer to the toast to the visitors to give a public proof of my admiration for the English press.

Believe me, Sir,

Yours very truly,

NAPOLEON.

Towards the close of July Lord Houghton went to Paris, accompanied by his younger daughter. One object with which he went there was to accept an invitation he had received from M. Thiers, who was now President of the Republic. The visit was a very interesting one both for himself and his daughter. The attention paid to them by the President and his family was very great.

To his Wife.

Hotel Meurice, Rue de Rivoli, Saturday, July 27th.

A rainy night, which has cooled the air, but deprived me of the open-air siesta I contemplated. The boat was very full, it happening to be the day of the Indian mail by Brindisi. . . . I have a letter from M. Thiers, asking me to bring Florence to dine with them to-morrow, which of course I shall do. You were hardly out of sight when I read the news that will sadden all my Paris visit—the death of the Duc d'Aumale's only son. I looked forward with so much pleasure to seeing the Duke, and was sure to find him either here or at his château close to Vichy.

He has written to M. Thiers to say he must give up public life altogether. ———— thought the boy was studying too hard, but you know I don't believe in such causes and effects.

Saturday Evening.

Just returned from M. de Rothschild's superb villa in the Bois de Boulogne. . . . . There was great talk of St. Moritz, and the greatest difference of opinion. " C'est charmant!" "C'est détestable!" "Quel air!" "Quel froid!" "Quelle nourriture!" "Quel paysage!" Each taking it as they found it.* . . . You may tell ———— that the best joke is that Thiers is so full of the duty on *matières premières* (raw material) that he calls his wife " ma Thiers première."

Tuesday.

We had an interesting debate in the Assembly yesterday— we three in the State Box, and Lord Pollington, whom I took there. I met Mr. Stanley the discoverer at breakfast at ————'s yesterday—a really interesting man, something of the Burton type. We are now going to breakfast with Rio. I take Flo to dine at the Embassy to-morrow, as there is no party. . . . Madame Thiers thought her very distinguished, and quite insisted on her dining there again, though I made many difficulties.

Wednesday.

No particular news, except that I do not leave this till Saturday evening; so that you can send both Thursday's and Friday's letters here. Rio is quite *touchant* in his friendship for Florence, which she seems to reciprocate. We called afterwards (for a contrast) on M. Renan, and Florence was quite struck with his brilliant talk   Somehow or other ———— wants gaiety, which is the best element of happiness in life, and which has brought the French people through calamities that would have crushed England ten times over. How should we look with Ireland lost and a double debt? Yet there is a

* Lady Houghton was going to St. Moritz.

diminution of it even here; the streets are more still, and the gabble less continuous.

It may be permissible to introduce here an extract from a letter of his daughter to her mother, describing this visit to Paris, when they were entertained so hospitably by the head of the State.

It is delightful having papa here. I think he looks well; but of course he is out of spirits about the Duc de Guise. It was a dreadfully sad thing; he was the poor Duc d'Aumale's eighth and last child. Since papa came I have had several great pleasures. On Sunday an especial one, as he took me to Versailles to dine with M. Thiers. It was delightful, and it interested me extremely to hear him talk. I sat by him at dinner; and afterwards he was so kind, and promised to give me his photograph. We dine there on Thursday again. We were fourteen at dinner; but no ladies except Madame Thiers, her aunt, and sister. There were several officers—among others the General Ducrot, who was celebrated at Sedan. A good many gentlemen came in the evening. The house is beautiful, and guarded by soldiers in quite a royal manner. Yesterday M. Thiers lent us his *loge* in the Assembly, and it was delightful, as there was a tremendous row. It would be impossible to imagine the rage into which some of the deputies got; they looked as if they only longed to fight each other. Gambetta spoke.

From Paris Lord Houghton went to Vichy and, subsequently, to Venice.

To his Sister.

Hotel des Ambassadeurs, Vichy, August 6th.

DEAREST HARRIETTE,—I find hardly any English here, and the only two Frenchmen I know—Marshal Canrobert and General Fleury—keep themselves entirely out of the way. I came in a *coupé* with the latter, very depressed, as is not unnatural, and fancying that the gendarmes on the road were always looking after him, as he in his time had looked after others. The whole society seems very *bourgeoise,* and is certainly rather quieter than it used to be. There is a good theatre, as usual. Annabel leaves Paris on the 12th, goes for a day or two to Ragatz, and climbs to St. Moritz on the 19th, where she has rooms in the village. Florey enjoyed her first outing (dining thrice with Thiers, with Lord Lyons, and the Rothschilds), and behaved with great simplicity and *convenance.*

I am getting troubled about the social state of things in England [he wrote, while still abroad, to his friend Henry Bright]; we seem losing our sound political economy, which I value as our intellectual religion. The French Communism of 1848 was too ideal for us, but that of 1872 is fast invading us. It will not take the Gallic form of the suicide of society; but it may inflict immense social danger, and seriously distort the national moral sense.

To his Wife.

Pension Suisse, Venice, Sept. 21*st,* 1872.

I hope this letter will find you at the Villa d'Este, but I am by no means certain, on account of the fête on Thursday; but you will have lodged yourself somewhere, and I shall know to-day or to-morrow by telegram. I hope you will have got over your little journey without much trouble. We have done our trip very well, sleeping the first night at Parma (passing through Milan without stopping), the next at Ravenna, the next at Bologna, and here yesterday. This place, too, is very full. There was a fête last night to commemorate the entry of the Italians into Rome (no great good that, by-the-bye). The piazza was lit up with large gas candelabra, and made exactly the "great saloon" I have put into verse. . . . Here is everything nearly unchanged since eight-and-thirty years ago. Harriette said philosophically, "We have had bad and good days since, but more good than bad on the whole; and we should be thankful for that."

To his Son.
Venice, Sept. 22nd, 1872.

DEAREST ROBERT,—As you know this place sufficiently well through Canaletti's pictures and my verses, I have nothing topographical to say. Your aunt Harriette and I have been revisiting the scenes of our youth, and trying to get out of the motions of a gondola the emotions of thirty-six years ago. I have only found one old friend here, and he is totally blind; he said he should have known me by my voice. The novelty of this tour to me has been Ravenna, which I was very curious to see, as it is a kind of link between the fall of Rome and the rise of Venice. It fills up Italian history from about Anno Domini 400 to 800; and from the accident of the use of mosaic, which is as fresh as the day it was put together, you see exactly what the Eastern Emperors were like, and the sort of places they lived in. I hope to meet Mamma and Amy at Milan on Tuesday. There is a regular break-up of the weather, and I should think it likely they will have snow at Campfer in their descent on Italy. .

Your affectionate
H^N.

From this pleasant tour, in which he had renewed the memories of his youth, Houghton, after rejoining his wife on the Italian lakes, returned to England much benefited. The winter was spent at Fryston.

Lord Houghton to Mr. Gladstone.
Trentham, Stoke-upon-Trent, Dec. 31st, 1872.

MY DEAR GLADSTONE,—Mr. Murray was with us at Fryston when you wrote to him to announce your forthcoming lecture, so

I suppose we shall soon have it in an authorised form, and I wish you could enlarge it somewhat, so as to make it more clear why you consider the constructive efforts of the non-Christian party more dangerous than the old negative infidelity of the eighteenth century. Surely these builders of non-Christian Babels have failed enough, without your notice. There are not enough Comtists in England, France, and Germany to fill a village church, and Strauss has never got beyond an academic fame except (as your Liverpool audiences probably believed) when confounded with the popular musician. The vulgar, ribald atheism of our educated artisans has nothing constructive about it; I wish it had. John Bright paid us a visit last week; apparently very well, and determined to try a moderate amount of Parliament.

Many happy returns of your birthday. Many good wishes for the coming year, public and private. I should be thankful if it constructed something. As we get older, destruction becomes less agreeable.

Yours faithfully,

HOUGHTON.

Lord Houghton had been moved to write the foregoing letter to Mr. Gladstone by one which he had received from Mr. Henry Bright describing Mr. Gladstone's lecture. An extract from it may be given.

H. A. Bright to Lord Houghton.

Ashfield, Knotty Ash, Liverpool,
December 24*th,* 1872.

MY DEAR LORD HOUGHTON,—Many happy Christmases to you and all at Fryston, and many thanks for the lines you sent me. You have not answered my question as to writing a pamphlet for our atrocities. I feel a little tempted to do it. Shall I write to Shaw-Lefevre, or have you written? I am busy reviewing for the *Athenæum* Mr. Page's "Life of Hawthorne"—the most despicable book I ever opened. I only hope I shall be able to find words hot and strong enough to speak of it as it deserves, without exposing myself to an action for libel. Saturday I heard Mr. Gladstone at the Liverpool College. It was on all accounts a most interesting meeting. Tories and Liberals, Churchmen and Dissenters were all there, and all delighted; some because an orthodox Churchman was speaking, some because the Liberal chief was before them in the flesh. He read from a MS.; but this was hardly noticeable, his voice was so finely modulated, his action so easy and impressive. Butler very happily quoted after it was over,

"The guests were spell-bound in the dusky hall;"

and so it was. Only ——, who sat next me, whispered, "How certain it is that some enterprising publisher will now translate Strauss, and what an enormous circulation this attack will give the book!

Ever yours,

HENRY A. BRIGHT.

Lord Houghton to Henry Bright.

Fryston, Dec. 31st, 1872.

Thanks for your excellent description of Gladstone's lecture. Mr. ——'s remark was most appropriate. W. E. G. does not know that Strauss is by far the most innocent of the Neologists, and has never got beyond an academic circulation. I have written to him to that effect. I hope you will press the American cruelty case; it is just the sort of thing the House of Lords would take up. I could bring it forward, either by moving for some papers, or by calling attention to the subject. The main point is that I should be prepared with *some* practical remedy; it does not matter whether it is the best; we should thus get the Government pledged to interfere, or else to start some independent measure.

The Same to the Same.

Have you any copies of your pamphlet which might be given to persons taking interest in the matter? Would you advise me to communicate with General Schenk before bringing it on? The American Secretary is an excellent man, and would, I doubt not, interest himself in the affair.

The foregoing letter refers to a pamphlet which Mr. Bright had just published, under the title of "Unpunished Cruelties on the High Seas"—a reprint of a letter to Mr. Samuel Whitebread in 1859, and now inscribed to Lord Houghton. It dealt with the anomalous state of international law with regard to crime on shipboard, especially with a view to the prevention or punishment of acts of cruelty on the part of captains towards their men. Lord Houghton was eager to take up the question, which was one that would have enlisted his sympathies even if it had not been brought to his notice by a friend so much esteemed as Mr. Bright; and he did what he could, both in Parliament and elsewhere, to bring about the reform which Mr. Bright advocated.

In the spring of 1873 Lord Houghton again came before the world as an author. As the reader knows, he was a regular and frequent contributor to the leading Reviews, and he had found in the *Pall Mall Gazette* an organ through which he was able to address the world on many topics hardly suited for treatment in the graver quarterlies. Now, however, he came forward, not as an anonymous critic, but in his own proper person, with the delightful volume of "Monographs," which must take its place among the standard works of the kind. The book was a review of some of the more interesting friendships he had made during his long life, and it must always be of value because of the vivid light in which it places some men and women of whom the world will long be anxious to know. The publication achieved an immediate and distinct success, and it afforded the world at large an opportunity of learning something of the extent and the varied character of the society in which the author had moved. One result of the publication of the "Monographs" was that from that time forward Lord Houghton was constantly being importuned by publishers to write a supplementary volume, or to pen his own memoirs and reminiscences. How it was that he did not respond to this invitation must always remain a mystery, for to his friends and the members of his own family he always spoke as though he had some work of the kind either in contemplation or in actual progress. It was not until after his death, and after a careful examination of his papers, that it was found he had done nothing in this direction. Anyone who reads a chapter of the "Monographs" will understand how much has thus been lost to the world by this failure. Indeed, when we read that fascinating volume in conjunction with the correspondence which is to be found in the present work, the regret that Lord Houghton himself never put on paper the record of his life must be all the keener, for nowhere can be found the materials out of which a record can be framed comparable with that which he himself would have penned. The letters from which

I have quoted so freely, and the anecdotes with which I have sought to fill up the gaps left by the correspondence, are a poor substitute—are, indeed, hardly a substitute at all—for that complete and continuous narrative which Lord Houghton himself might have penned. In it we should have heard the true version of a thousand stories long current about him in London society—stories many of which were on the face of them so impossible, and many more of which were so ill-natured, that they have been carefully excluded from these pages. No biographer could indeed have given them without creating an entirely false impression of Lord Houghton's character in the mind of the reader; for it was an imaginary Houghton about whom the wits and gossips who only knew him slightly, if at all, chattered and made free; and by far the greater part of those stories which were current in society about him were purely mythical, the invention of those who saw a certain oddity in his manner, and could not associate it with the originality of his mind; who heard without understanding some of his most brilliant paradoxes, and forthwith believed that there was nothing too extraordinary or absurd for him to say. All this material, which, when thoroughly sifted, might have been so valuable to the biographer and so interesting to the reader, it has been necessary resolutely to put on one side, in the course of this narrative, owing to the simple fact that the sifting process is no longer possible. But if Houghton himself had responded to the many invitations he received, and had written his own memoirs, we should have known the truth, and, judging by the "Monographs," English literature would have been the richer by a unique and fascinating work.

His health, however, was now permanently impaired —the illness from which he suffered in 1871 and 1872 having left its marks upon a constitution which had never been very vigorous. Work, especially literary work, was becoming increasingly distasteful to him, and although the freshness of his spirit, the intellectual energy which distinguished him still, kept him always busy, he no longer found himself able to engage in serious literary labour. Thus it came to pass that at his death the only remains of a biographical kind which were discovered were the Commonplace Books, from which I have quoted so freely, and the last of which is dated in this year 1873.

Lord Houghton to Lady Galway.

Rawcliffe Hall, Serlby.

The main talk in town is of the Duke of Edinburgh's marriage. The Emperor gives the lady £50,000 per annum, and the Duke makes up £20,000. I walked with Gladstone on Tuesday, and when he left me a gentleman came up and said, "Might I ask if that was not Mr. Disraeli?" Such is fame!

Two points in the letters I am about to quote, from Lord Houghton to Mr. Gladstone, require passing notice. The first is the reference to Mr. Joaquin Miller, the American poet. When Mr. Miller came to England in 1873, one of the first to welcome him was Lord Houghton. He had heard of him through American friends, had been greatly struck by the originality of his writing, and made haste to receive him as a brother-poet and man of letters. He had shown the same attention to so many other visitors from abroad in his time that there was nothing specially noticeable about his reception of Joaquin Miller; but it resulted in a warm friendship between the two men, and many of Mr. Miller's letters afford proof of his gratitude towards one who did his best to make him feel at home in English society—a gratitude of which further evidence was afforded by the dedication of his completed poems to Lord Houghton.

The second point which deserves mention has reference to Houghton's wish to become one of the trustees of the British Museum. On every ground he was well fitted for the post of honour and responsibility which he coveted. His friends freely acknowledged this, and there is no doubt that he would long before 1873 have become one of the trustees, if it had not been for the personal differences which existed between himself and the chief librarian, Sir Antonio Panizzi. It is quite outside the scope of this narrative to enter into a discussion of these differences, which involved nothing discreditable to either man; but the fact that they existed must be mentioned, in order to explain the following letters, and to show how it was that Lord Houghton did not become a trustee of the British Museum until after the death of Panizzi.

Lord Houghton to Mr. Gladstone.

Travellers' Club, Pall Mall, August 5th, 1873.

MY DEAR GLADSTONE,—I had hoped politics were at peace with you for some months to come. Joaquin Miller is most interesting as poet and man. I have known and asked nothing as to his private life. I have made no canvass about the British Museum. I have told yourself, the Archbishop, Granville, and Stirling that I should like it, and would do the work. I shall speak of it to no one else. It is hardly a matter of claim; it is rather one of propriety. I am obliged to you for mentioning Panizzi; in my small life there are a few acts of public virtue as distinct from ordinary inclination, and this is one of them. I did think, and do think, that in the destitution of British men of letters it was wrong to give that place to a non-Englishman. This was the feeling in France and everywhere. *I* had the right to make the objection, being, like yourself, Italianissimo in politics and taste, and this being in its little way a matter of conscience. Of course I take its consequences without complaint or mention.

I trust you will have a quiet holiday after this discomfortable Session. You chose to raise that tertiary question of Irish University education in the first rank, and suffered for the disproportion much more than for the matter itself. I see a curious turn of opinion on all these educational matters. As long as they were boons to be accepted by a grateful people, public opinion thought them all right, and men were ready to make sacrifices; but it is a different thing when the only immediate result of the additional taxation is additional hatred and confusion, and when you are rated at once by your country and your class.

I have to preside at a Social Science Association, and wish I could say that we have proved more than we have done.

Yours very truly,

HOUGHTON.

The Same to the Same.

*Lancashire and Yorkshire Railway Board Room,
Manchester, August* 13*th,* 1873.

MY DEAR GLADSTONE,—Had I known anything of the pressure of your Ministerial arrangements, I should not have precipitately troubled you about the British Museum. You must not think this accidental date a protest against your distinction between men of letters and men of business, although I do seriously demur to its validity. It has done me too much harm in life for me to take it easily. I believe it to be practically untrue and psychologically wrong. The continuous industry and attention to detail implied in serious literary employment contrast, in my mind, favourably with the intellectual dawdle and slip-shod utterances of either House of Parliament; but the popular impression is with you. My shrewd father called every book of mine a nail in my political coffin, and I well remember Sir Robert Peel's annoyance at your literary productions. "With such a career before him," he said, "why should he write books?"

If at any time I became a trustee of the Musuem, I should write to Panizzi a respectful note, regretting the past and recognising his high services; but it would not do to open gratuitously a matter in which I still think he was wrong in taking personal offence. It would have been different if I had succeeded in limiting his career. With his multitude of patrons and friends he might have admitted one critic.

Believe me

Yours very truly,

HOUGHTON.

In the autumn of the year Lord Houghton was engaged with his important duties as President of the Social Science Congress at Norwich.

The meeting was unusually successful; many distinguished persons, friends of his own, giving him their support either by their presence or the contribution of papers. On the 1st of October he delivered his Presidential Address, a comprehensive survey of the history of the previous year, so far as social legislation was concerned. He took occasion in the course of it to refer to the work done by Mr. Henry Bright on behalf of our Merchant Marine, whilst he paid special attention to the question of reformatories and the treatment of juvenile offenders, which was under discussion. Not unnaturally, he recalled the fact that he himself had brought into the House of Commons the first Bill for the establishment of reformatories. Years afterwards, when he was lamenting his want of success in political life, in conversation with a friend, his face grew bright as he said, "There is one thing at least that I have done that has not helped me much, but has been of great help to others." He referred to the work he accomplished in Parliament on behalf of that forlorn section of our population which, until he took up its cause, may be said to have been consigned from the very cradle to the path of crime.

In this speech at Norwich he referred to another measure of social reform of which he had been the pioneer—this was the substitution of private for public executions. Years before that most desirable change in the mode of inflicting the penalty of death had been adopted by Parliament, he had urged on Sir James Graham, in the House of Commons, the wisdom of acceding to it, and he was entitled now, in surveying the course of social legislation in England, to congratulate himself upon the fact that a measure of which he had long been the advocate had at length been adopted.

His address concluded with a warm tribute to a woman whose name must always be associated with Norwich—Harriet Martineau.

To his Wife.

Ketteringham Park, Wymondham, Oct. 3rd, 1873.

I am none the worse for the work—indeed, in some things better. I kept up my voice for the hour and a half very well in the huge hall, and was fairly heard. The *Times*, you see, is sarcastically complimentary, and the *Daily News* very civil; the *Post* ignores me, and the *Standard* is ill-natured. . . . The papers and discussions have been good and animated. Miss Jex-Blake and Mrs. Grey both spoke capitally. Dear George Bunsen passed through Norwich yesterday on his way from Cromer to Tunbridge Wells, and sent me a message, saying he did not dare to see me.

To the Same.

Oct. 4th.

The whole meeting is much better than any other I have attended—principally, I think, owing to the absence of Lord Brougham.

Writing to Henry Bright a few days later, Lord Houghton bore similar testimony to the success of the meeting: "there being much less twaddle and newer subjects, and the women have come out remarkably well—much less exaggeration and one-sidedness."

George von Bunsen to Lord Houghton.

Cannon Street Hotel, London, Oct. 3rd, 1873.

MY DEAR LORD HOUGHTON,—I have read your address, and regret more vividly than before that I was unable to be present on your great day. Let me hope that you may live to see some results. The "sweat of the best" is not too high a price to pay for objects so all-important for the good of society. I should have wished to say something at your Congress on Schulze-Delitzsch's great co-operative movement, and on its twenty-three years' steadily-increasing magnitude and Conservative effects. Allow me to draw your attention to the writer of the article on "Savings of the People" in the July *Edinburgh*; his name is Frederick Seebohm. He is a banker, a logical thinker, and a hard-headed man, of a very shrinking temperament. You know his "Oxford Reformers." . .

Believe me
In aller Treue yours,
G. BUNSEN.

Lord Houghton had not forgotten to send a copy of his address to an old friend who would, he knew, be interested in it—Miss Martineau. In acknowledging its receipt, Miss Martineau declared that she found " the old charms of your prose (quite apart from those of your verse, however near akin), the richness of philosophic meaning, the glow of sympathy, the incomparable style. I need not say," she added, "that your closing words touched me, uttered in that old Hall where I used to go on the eve of 'Guild Day' to see the tables spread for the next day's dinner. Did anybody show you *Snap*, covered up with green baize ever since Municipal Reform days? I used to be ill with terror at Snap (St. George's dragon) wagging his abominable snaky head at us children, and snapping his jaws and chasing us. I am afraid he did not hunt you, but I hope you saw him."

Mrs. Procter to Lord Houghton.
32, *Weymouth Street, Portland Place, W.,*
Nov. 7th, 1873.

MY DEAR LORD HOUGHTON,—I did not receive your welcome letter until nine o'clock last night. . . . Chorley's novels—

for I have read them all—were good. Why the world would not have them, I do not know. One can truly say about books, "The race is not for the swift, nor the battle for the strong." Perhaps they are too imaginative; perhaps they suppose that the reader knows something—has read something. When I see the success of such a work as ———, I should, if a writer, put down my pen. A slight water-colour sketch!—is that to be mentioned in the same breath as George Eliot or Miss Brontë? To succeed now in literature you must have a tail. A party continually cry out, "Tennyson is our king: there is no other." People are so thankful to be spared the trouble of thinking. . .

Your affectionate old friend,
ANNE B. PROCTER.

During this autumn the struggle between Mr. Forster and the Birmingham League, on the subject of his educational policy, was at its height. Lord Houghton gave his warm sympathy and support to his old friend.

To Henry Bright.

Fryston, November 26*th,* 1873.

I should like to know the impression made by Forster's speech.* I am quite sorry that you should not have been well enough to hear it. It reads to me full of good sense and statesmanship; but it is hardly compatible with Bright's *quasi-*engagements at Birmingham. I was in the chair at a most interesting meeting at the Wakefield Asylum last night. It was, too, a curious sensation, sleeping under the same roof as 1,500 lunatics. I was kept awake by thoughts of *the kind of sleep* that was going on about me. . . . I made some preliminary remarks on the wide and desolate borderland of cerebral disturbance that lies between sleep and mania.

---

* At Liverpool, in vindication of the Education Act.

To the Same.

Fryston, December 21*st.*

A man the other day, who had rather disobliged me than not, asked me to do him a favour. I said I would, as a true Christian, " heap coals of fire on his head," utterly regardless of the present price *—rather like Elia. By-the-by, Charles Lamb's adopted daughter, Isola, Mrs. Moxon, is in great poverty. Would you be inclined to subscribe a tenner? Thomas Baring, just before he died, sent me £50 for her " in memory of the pleasure he had had from Charles Lamb." Is not that nice?

Lord Houghton to Mrs. Tennyson.

Fryston Hall, December 13*th,* 1873.

MY DEAR MRS. TENNYSON,—I shall not be in town to accept your kind invitation for the 18th. I take my daughter on Monday to Lord Brownlow's at Ashridge for a week. I am very sorry.

I am glad that Tennyson is making the experiment of London. When he has the use of it, I think he will appreciate its loneliness and independence. I think he would even like the Athenæum Club, where the few eagles and many bores live together, without encounter, and little recognition. I wonder whether your elder son [Mr. Hallam Tennyson] would like to pay us a visit in January. On the 20th of that month we shall have a party of young people that he may find agreeable.

Yours very truly,

HOUGHTON.

Lord Houghton to George von Bunsen.

Fryston Hall, Ferrybridge, December 22*nd,* 1873.

MY DEAR GEORGE BUNSEN,—I hear of you indirectly—which is something—from Arthur Russell at the Geographical Club,

* The price of coal during this winter rose to an almost unprecedented height.

where there was a chance of your dining, and from our country friends the Hills. The latter say that you soon migrate to Hastings. How are you about this Erastianism of Bismarck's?* I like it in theory, but the practice is disagreeable. It seems to me to want a gigantic figure like Henry VIII. to do it properly, and even Bismarck is not He. I cannot see what right the State has to interfere, except where salary is taken, either with religion or philosophy; and if it takes to limiting superstition, it will try to impose philosophy, as it did in Frederick William IV.'s time with Hegelianism. If not bad for you, please write me a letter on this subject.

Yours affectionately,
HOUGHTON.

George von Bunsen to Lord Houghton.

St. Catherine's Villa, St. Leonard's-on-Sea,
December 24th, 1873.

MY DEAR LORD HOUGHTON,—I am not aware that Prussia does more than enforce or resume those State-rights over the Roman priesthood which most Catholic countries, and Bavaria in particular, have never ceased exerting. Prussia, though traditionally more lenient than they, had taken her stand in the Landrecht (Frederick II. and his successor) upon certain principles considered necessary to secure the Liberal subject against the encroachments of an Established Church, to whose offices the State forces him to apply. These principles were abandoned *de facto* during thirty years since the accession of Frederick William IV., and many of them *de jure* also in the Prussian Constitution of 1848. You know the romanticism of the late King, the ancient love of Conservatism for the Church of Rome, and the influence which clerical popular leaders obtained in troublous times. The resumption was inevitable as soon as two conditions were fulfilled. Prussia had to overcome her Conservative pusillanimity, and South Germany

* The Kultur Kampf.

had to enter into political union with Prussia. Both conditions were fulfilled in 1871. It is a fact that South German statesmen and representatives of the Roman Catholic middle classes of South Germany were the originators of Bismarck's first decisive steps. It is unfortunate, perhaps, that the Bishops submitted to the Vaticanum; also that the clergy, who are mostly Gallican at heart, were precipitated by them into submission. Had matters been otherwise, there would have been a continuance of that good understanding between the hierarchy and our Government which some people think salutary. What Prussia now does is better, in my opinion, than Disestablishment would be. Who would have been more eager to disclaim the *Libera chiesa in libera stato* than the inventor of that mischievous sentence? There is, I apprehend, very little chance of an opinion analogous to mine just expressed spreading in England. In Switzerland, in Canada, in the United States it is fast gaining ground. Belgium and Holland begin to see that they are tottering on a precipice. If the same feeling should possess itself of English opinion, it will be, perhaps, on the ground of such conditions as the following:—You may remember, from your Roman experiences, the practice in the Propaganda of reading to the assembled pupils reports from various dioceses descriptive of the Roman or non-Roman tendencies fostered in each? It is known how many boys from Westphalia, from Upper Silesia, from the Rhine are sent to Rome, then drilled into D.D.'s, and then returned with the request to the Bishop to immediately appoint the extra-official spy to a parish. From the accounts thus obtained lists are made, which the Curia finds useful in the appointment of canons, bishops, &c. Does Bismarck know of this? If he did, he was right in insisting that priests should be educated in Germany and licensed by Government.

De te fabula narratur.

CHAPTER XVIII.

VISIT TO THE UNITED STATES.

Death of Lady Houghton—Goes to Vichy—Correspondence with his Children
Lady William Russell—Sir William Stirling Maxwell—Sir Richard Burton
—Lord Houghton Visits Canada and the United States—Extracts from
Diary—Goldwin Smith—Robert Collyer—General Sherman—An "Interviewer" at Work—A Speech "on Change"—Friends at Boston and
Cambridge—Longfellow and Emerson—"Uncle Sam"—Speech at the
Century Club.

IN February, 1874, a great blow—the heaviest from which he had yet suffered—fell upon Lord Houghton. The reader has seen something in previous chapters of the failing health of Lady Houghton, who had been compelled to withdraw largely from that social life she was so well qualified to adorn, and who for some years had spent a great part of her time in the search of health at different watering-places. It was owing to her illness that the house in Brook Street had been given up, and that her husband had ceased to be one of the chief entertainers in London society. When the year 1874 opened, she was not apparently worse than she had been for some time previously, and she took part in the first weeks of that year in entertaining parties of guests at Fryston. No one who saw her then imagined that the end was so near. The gentle charm which always distinguished her manner was felt as strongly as ever by those who had the privilege of meeting her, and almost to the very eve of her fatal illness she was able, within the limits prescribed by her physical weakness, to assist her husband, as she had so long done, in making Fryston the pleasantest of temporary homes for the guests who visited them. Her husband and family were quite unconscious of the impending stroke.

The sudden dissolution of Parliament by Mr. Gladstone startled the country in January.

The dissolution [wrote Lord Houghton to Henry Bright] is no *coup d'état*, but settled long ago—I suspect, after Stroud—and only delayed for the Premier to see his way clearer. What will Robertson Gladstone say to the abolition of the only form existing of direct taxation?

The General Election resulted in the decisive defeat of the Liberal party.

To his Son.

Fryston, February 8th, 1874.

DEAREST ROBERT,—Your sisters are such good correspondents that I have no gossip to tell you, but you will like to know something about politics. It was very interesting to do what one could for Childers, who had deserved so well of Pomfret. —— said, very nicely, "He is not quite my politics, but surely such a man must not be thrown;" and this feeling really showed itself in the election. No opponent treated him uncivilly, and there seemed a general relief when he was safe. The Counties contest will be sharp in all divisions. That of the North is most likely to return two Liberals. The others are very uncertain. Sir John Ramsden has come out at last, and does it very well, notwithstanding the fogs and a bad cold. We all went to hear him yesterday. "He speaks rarely, that he do," said a farmer. Lord Pollington took his defeat very good-naturedly, and wrote me a very nice letter. I am your affectionate

H^N.

A few days later there was a large party at Fryston, including several Yorkshire politicians who had been brought together to discuss the "Liberal *débâcle*," as Lord Houghton called it. Lady Houghton took the head of the table, as usual, and delighted her guests by her bright conversation, by the vividness of her reminiscences of bygone celebrities, and the sympathetic tact with which she brought persons of very opposite opinions and characteristics into friendly intercourse. In all these matters she had shown herself during her married life to be the worthy helpmeet of her husband.

It was on this occasion, I remember, that she told me of her acquaintance as a child with the grandmother of Charles Dickens, and carried the conversation down to the day—a week or two before his death—when Dickens, at her table, made the acquaintance of the Prince of Wales.

It was the last time that she sat at table with her family. On the following day a slight cold showed itself, congestion of the lungs was developed, and she rapidly sank, passing away on the 24th of February in the presence of her husband and daughters—her son, who had been hastily summoned by his father, being unable to reach the house whilst she still lived.

To Henry Bright.

February 24*th*, 1874.

MY DEAR BRIGHT,—You are so sympathetic for your friends that you will grieve to hear that my wife is dangerously ill.

She has had a severe attack of bronchitis and pneumonia, which, though in a great degree subdued, has left the action of the heart so weak that there is great fear that the system will not rally. She has little or no suffering. We have good medical advice from both Pomfret and Leeds, and every sedulous care. I have little hope myself, but try to keep up the girls. Mrs. Blackburn comes to-day, and Robert to-morrow.

Your affectionate
HOUGHTON.

P.S.—3 p.m. I had written this in the morning. She has just passed away without pain. She was a perfect woman. Pity us all!

Alfred Tennyson to Lord Houghton.

Farringford, Freshwater, Isle of Wight,
March 6th, 1874.

MY DEAR HOUGHTON,—I was the other day present at a funeral here, and one of the chief mourners reached me her hand silently almost over the grave, and I as silently gave her mine. No words were possible; and this little note, that can do really nothing to help you in your sorrow, is just such a reaching of the hand to you, my old college comrade of more than forty years' standing, to show you that I think of you. You have your children; she must live to you more or less in them, and to you and others in the memory and result of her good and charitable life, and I may say that I think I can see as far as one can see in this twilight that the nobler nature does not pass from its individuality when it passes out of this one life. If you could believe as much, it would be a comfort to you, and perhaps you do. I did not intend to say even so much as this, and will say no more, only that I am

Yours affectionately,
A. TENNYSON.

Robert Browning to Lord Houghton.

19, *Warwick Crescent, W., Feb. 28th*, 1874.

DEAR HOUGHTON,—I cannot help saying what all your friends must feel (and I am getting to be a very old friend now) how profoundly grieved I am at your loss, and in a due but very appreciable degree my own. It is a comfort to think you have always been one of the kindest of men, besides something more (or less), and that will console you as it ought. My son is abroad, but he forgets no favours done him, and he had much to remember after his visit to Fryston; I know how sorry he will be. Well, who is to go next? Let us hold hands in the meantime, and

Believe me, dear Houghton,

Ever yours affectionately,

ROBERT BROWNING.

I hope the young people comfort you, and are comforted by you, in this calamity.

For the remainder of his life, until in the fulness of time he was laid to rest by her side under the wall of the old church at Fryston, where they had so often worshipped together, Lord Houghton continued to cherish for his wife an abiding reverence and affection. Again and again, years afterwards, one noticed the softening of his tones, the break in his voice, when by any chance her name was mentioned. A man of his peculiarities of temperament—to say nothing of his intellectual endowments—was not one who could easily have found a wife suited to him in every respect; but such a wife had blessed his life during more than twenty years, had made him in all respects happier than he would have been without her, and had justified the opinion of his friends and of the world that in winning the affections of Miss Crewe, Monckton Milnes had been more fortunate than in all the other acts and incidents of his life—more fortunate indeed than most men are.

His health, as well as his spirits, suffered from his bereavement, and though he was not one to indulge in morbid introspection, always believing that the best diversion for a troubled mind was to be found in active employment or in social intercourse, he found it necessary in the early summer to go to Vichy.

To Henry Bright.
London, March 25th.

I have heard nothing of Isola's pension, where did you hear of it from? Have you read Hazlitt's book, " Charles and Mary Lamb "? It leaves one with the impression that all the family were habitually drunk when they were not mad; but it is very amusing, and not a *réchauffé*. Curious the letters I have had from old and young—the oldest from Mrs. Procter written much better than this. Curious, too, the few omissions, some of those with whom I thought myself closest.

To the Same.
May 13th, 1874.

I wish, if you are to go abroad, that you might go to Vichy, where I shall be next month. My dear girls go to Mrs. Blackburn at Chester for a few days, and then go to Torquay where their old aunts live. It is a great comfort to have that interest to occupy their minds.

Lord Houghton to John Morley.
Vichy, June 11th, 1874.

I saw only one side of politics the two days I was in Paris—the Left Centre—and missed the row between

Rouher and Gambetta in the Chamber which as near as possible came to blows. The audacity or impudence, or any quality you please, with which these seventeen Buonapartists confront the Assembly is almost comical. Where would have been their heads in '93? That is some gain on the road to Parliamentary freedom. M. Thiers looks well, though suffering from the heat. I notice that everybody still called him M. le Président. He said amusingly, in answer to my question whether they were still going to try for a Second Chamber, "No; as with the ancient Gauls the chief was buried with his arms and his dogs, so we have buried M. de Broglie and all his appurtenances." He said the real cause of his own resignation, with which he was often reproached, was that he would have been forced always towards a *coup d'état*, which the country would have approved, but which did not suit his principles.

Yours affectionately,

HOUGHTON.

To his Son.

Hôtel de Cherbourg, Vichy, June 13*th*, 1874.

DEAREST ROBERT,—You will like to know that I am arrived here after a very hot journey, and found this place hotter than I have ever known it before; but there is now a cool air, and it is very pleasant. I expected to find it fuller than it is; but the Assembly and doubtful aspect of political affairs still detain in Paris all persons who have to do with the great interests of the country. I did not leave cards on anyone in Paris, and only dined with M. Thiers in a small family party. The old gentleman was very talkative, and much pleased at the Duc de Broglie, who had put up Marshal MacMahon to take his place, being now bowled over in his turn. I noticed that the people who came in during the evening still called M. Thiers M. le Président; and if the new Assembly when it comes is Republican, as seems probable, and Marshal MacMahon gives up in disgust, I should not be surprised to see Thiers there for the rest of his life. As yet the waters have not done any good to the lameness of my feet. I often think I shall never take a good walk again, which is a disagreeable contemplation. Luckily we are not in the days of Priam, when a father had no vehicle but his son's shoulders.

I am your affectionate

HN.

To his Elder Daughter.

Hôtel de Cherbourg, June 13th, 1874.

DEAREST AMY,— . . . . The world is very small, and the inhabitants so few that everybody one meets knows somebody one knows, which is illustrated by the two old maids that arrived here with me, being the two Miss ———'s. The younger is very full of aunt Jane's kindness in writing to her. They are enterprising ladies, but the younger is now quite unable to walk for gout, which brings her here. We have talked over the Hares and Maurices. I have seen Lord Chesham and two or three other people, so that I shall not be at all lonely. At first, of course, this place is haunted, and the happiest recollections—such is the perversity of the human mind—are the worst. That little tour in the Cautel is a kind of closing epoch. She climbed half-way up the Puy de Dôme, and you and the young French poet all the way. The drive in the omnibus through that curious basaltic country from Riou, and she walking up the hills so well—never so well again! But why do I sadden you, darling? It is very selfish.

Your affectionate

HOUGHTON.

To his Son.

Vichy, June 25th, 1874.

DEAREST ROBERT,—It would be very unjust in me to be worried at your not getting prizes in competition with clever fellows, most of them above your own age. I am quite contented that you do your best. My poor father used to say I always bored him with repeating the sentiment

> "It is the battle, not the strife,
> That fills the warrior's heart with joy."

You did not enclose anything in your letter, but I shall be very pleased to see your Elegiacs. It would be a thrilling subject for a French novel. *Deux étudiants devoués l'un à l'autre,* till one carries off all the prizes from the other, *alors les mauvaises passions l'emportent,* and he puts small portions of strychnine in the bonbons—or, still better, something that reduces the competitor to idiocy. *Alors il emporte le prix.*

Your affectionate

H^N.

Mrs. Procter to Lord Houghton.

Home, *June* 20*th,* 1874.

MY DEAR FRIEND,—I always loved you and admired you, and now you are heir to a tender love I always felt for your dear wife. I hope you are already better for the change of scene, and being amongst strangers and pilgrims will be good for you. Here we are all complaining of cold east winds, and I have a fire. I saw Madame Mohl on Thursday. She is as bright as ever, and on a visit with Lady Augusta Stanley, who gave a great party in her honour. I am beaten by "Bothwell." I cannot read it, I am ashamed to say. I have no interest in the subject, and the length of the speeches is a great drawback; people in those days were better bred than in these; you would never have got through half a speech without being interrupted. We have tried to read Mrs. Bernal Osborne's book in vain. I was in hopes of finding her husband in it; but no, it is a book of travels. . . . I wish, my dear friend, I could have written you a more amusing letter—as tender as Madame de Sévigné, as witty as Horace Walpole; and see how my aspirations have failed! Your affectionate old friend,

ANNE B. PROCTER.

Lord Houghton returned from Vichy decidedly improved in health.

The name of Lady William Russell is a familiar one in society, but to the outer world it is almost entirely unknown. Born towards the close of the last century, she married Lord William Russell, who rose to a considerable position in the diplomatic service, and by him was the mother of the present Duke of Bedford, of the late Lord Ampthill, and of Lord Arthur Russell. Left a widow at a comparatively early age, she spent many years of her life in her home in South Audley Street. She had been crippled by a fall in Italy, and it was with great difficulty that, under the care of the late Lord Rosslyn, she was enabled to travel to England. When, at the end of her long journey, she was safely installed in her London home, she made a vow never again to leave it, and in South Audley Street she remained until the day of her death. Her habit was to receive her friends every evening during the year, and it was seldom that any one could enter her drawing-room without finding a group of interesting people in it. *Grande dame* to the tips of her fingers, she exercised a despotic sway over those who surrounded her. Though a very able woman, she was not attracted by mere literary fame or skill. Highly as she prized genius in itself, it was only when she encountered it in alliance with birth, political eminence, or brilliant social gifts, that she was able fully to appreciate its possessor. Her special inclination was towards the diplomatic service. She delighted to see herself surrounded by men of mark in that service, and, as Lord Houghton in one of his letters remarks, " would like to have died in the arms of an ambassador." As Monckton Milnes he had been a frequenter of her *salon*, and he continued not only to frequent it himself, but to introduce to it any men whom he believed Lady William would like to know, to the end of her days. Among those whom he thus brought into one of the most select "sets" in London society was his Liverpool friend Henry Bright.

Lord Houghton to Henry Bright.

London, July 15*th.*

I am come back from Vichy not very well, and shall be at Fryston the last week of the month. I think Lady William [Russell] is going at last. I took Robert to see her, but Jenner was with her, and would not let her see any one. However, she saw the Prince and Princess of Prussia the next day, to her great delight. I am just from Brookfield's funeral, and saddened by it.

To the Same.

Fryston, August 4*th,* 1874.

It was very comfortable to have you, even for so short a visit, as you really seemed better than I expected to find you. One often is told that a person has a valuable life, which always sounds to me like an expression on 'Change, and generally mean that they are making money. In this sense no doubt your life is "valuable," but I think it is so in quite another. It is valuable to me as that of one much younger than myself, and whom I look forward to to be the friend to my children that he has been to me.

His old friend Coomara Samy was in England on a visit at this time.

Coomara Samy to Lord Houghton.

National Club, August 10*th,* 1874.

MY DEAR LORD HOUGHTON,—I was sorry that I missed seeing you on your return from Vichy; I called at your hotel several times. I write to inform you that I had an audience of the Queen at Osborne last Thursday, when she conferred on me the honour of knighthood; and the Colonial Office wrote to me to say that this was done in recognition of my services in Ceylon. . . . On my way to Osborne I had a very interesting conversation with Disraeli. Remember me to your children, and to my friends at Serlby Hall.

I am yours very truly,

M. COOMARA SAMY.

Lord Houghton to Henry Bright.

Dalrannoch, Pitlochrie, N.B., Sept. 4*th.*

I am touring with Robert and Amicia, staying at a few houses where we know people well. He is getting some shooting (a puerile diversion becoming his age, but which I believe some poor incompetent persons carry on into mature life), and she is regaining health and spirits. I am still too lame to do more than poke about on a pony.

The Same to the Same.

Loch Luichart, N.B., Sept. 15*th.*

I cannot undertake to say which is the worst of your arguments. What earthly or heavenly right have you or I to find fault with a man who attaches himself to the faith held by nineteen-twentieths of the Christian world? And you especially, of whom Charles Lamb said in his cups that you "would take away two-thirds of his God"? All my friends who have embraced Popery have done better than those who have embraced wives. I am at a lovely place of Lady Ashburton's with Amicia, on my way to Glasgow on the 30th to give up the Chair of Social Science to Lord Rosebery, who came in second for the Derby.

The reference in the foregoing letter is to the conversion of Lord Ripon. Whatever other changes of opinion Lord Houghton had experienced, he had never faltered either in the tolerance which he showed to others on all questions of religious belief, or in the lurking tenderness he had felt for the Church of Rome when a young man.

We have had occasional glimpses in previous chapters of two friends of Lord Houghton's of whom some special mention should be made in the record of his life. The first to whom I would refer is Sir William Stirling Maxwell, who, alike as writer, as man of the world, and as a *dilettante* student of the arts, held a prominent place in the society to which Houghton himself belonged. The friendship between the two men was of long standing, and was close and sincere; it was heightened in later years by the marriage of Sir William Stirling Maxwell to Mrs. Norton, a woman for whom Houghton had always entertained a profound admiration, whose personal and intellectual gifts excited his enthusiasm, and with whom in all the vicissitudes of her remarkable life he had been on terms of affectionate intimacy. The identity of literary tastes was another bond of union between Lord Houghton and Sir William Stirling Maxwell; they had long worked together in the Philobiblon Society, and to the last they maintained a friendly intercourse.

The other man of distinction whose name I mention here is the well-known traveller Sir Richard Burton, of whom I must now also speak in the past tense. He, too, was one of Houghton's regular correspondents, and had been his guest on not a few occasions both at Fryston and in London. The man of action and adventure appealed as strongly to Houghton's sympathies as the man of thought and imagination. In the case of Sir Richard Burton both characters were blended, and it is not remarkable that he also inspired something like enthusiasm in the breast of his friend.

Sir William Stirling Maxwell to Lord Houghton.

Keir, Dunblane, N.B., September 7th, 1874.

My dear Houghton,—I received, and thank you for, the photograph [of Lady Houghton], which I shall keep as a relic of goodness and kindness that are gone, but not forgotten. The Motleys are here. He is a good deal better, and in good spirits. They go hence to Cortachy, and next to Invergarry. To-day, about 3.15 or a little earlier, we had a quarter of an hour or twenty minutes of darkness, which sent me to the almanac to see if there was an eclipse of the sun; but none is announced there. It was as dark as any eclipse at which I ever assisted; but it was only partial, for some visitors who came afterwards from four or five miles to the north, said they saw from a distance an immense black cloud brooding over us, but were not themselves in it. Ripon's conversion is one of the oddest news I have heard for long. There will be more rejoicing over that one repentant Robinson at Rome than over ninety-and-nine just Howards and Cliffords that went not astray. Monsignore Catesby* has certainly landed another big fish, but only to make the smaller fry more indignantly Protestant. It is as well to

* The name given to Monsignore Capel in "Lothair."

remember, however, that a little more or less of some unknown ingredient, which might appear or disappear in or from our blood or brain, and the same thing might happen to you or me. Meanwhile the newspapers must be pleasant reading at Studley.

Ever yours very truly,
WILLIAM STIRLING MAXWELL.

Lady Burton to Lord Houghton.

Trieste, August 12th, 1874.

MY DEAR LORD HOUGHTON,—I received your nice letter of March 25th, written in answer to mine of condolence on a sad occasion. I have now before me your official inquiry of July 17th, which, until this morning, I was unable to answer. This is what happened:—On the 14th of May, just ninety-one days ago, Richard was struck down by a sudden pain, which a few hours determined to be a tumour, in the groin, of a very severe nature. I sent at once for the best physician and the best surgeon in Trieste, who warned me that it would be a long and painful affair. So I telegraphed to London for water-bed, generous port, remedies, soups, &c., putting big iron rollers on the bed so as to move it easily; and, thus prepared, I took up my station by his pillow, which I never left for seventy-eight days and nights. He was in such pain; as weak as a child, and unable to turn in bed without assistance   In the midst of our worst our dear friend and travelling companion Drake died at Jerusalem of a typhoid fever, and this news caused the wound to open afresh; he loved Drake like a brother, and few know what a tender heart Richard has. On the 1st of August I obtained leave, with some difficulty, from the doctors to transfer him in a carriage, full length, and at foot's pace, to a rural inn an hour from and 1,200 feet above Trieste, where the view of sea and mountain is glorious, and the town is at our feet. Here the splendid air and perfect tranquillity, and the idea that he is free, are doing him so much good that now, after twelve days, we are rising at 5 o'clock, breakfasting and dining in the garden, taking little walks of ten minutes, and driving for two hours in a country caretta. . . . I do not like —— for neglecting you. He, and Richard and I, and many others I know, would have remained very much in the background if you had not taken us by the hand and pulled us into notice; and I abominate ingratitude. At any rate, please God, you will never find that with us.

Believe me,
Yours most sincerely,
ISABEL BURTON.

Lady Burton in the last lines of this letter hit upon an expression as happy as it was accurate regarding one of Lord Houghton's characteristics. Whatever might have been the case with a man of Sir Richard Burton's distinction, it is quite certain that there are many who would never have secured the attention of the public if Lord Houghton had not, as his correspondent puts it, "pulled them into notice." The man who was ready to force himself upon society might attract his attention, might amuse and interest him, but never moved his sympathy so strongly as did the man or woman whom he believed to have merit, but who had not the faculty of pushing themselves upon the world. These it was whom he delighted to take by the hand, and sometimes, almost against their will, to bring forward into positions for which he believed they were worthy.

In the winter of the year Lord Houghton busied himself with writing a preface to a collected edition of the works of Thomas Love Peacock, which was favourably received by the press and the public.

Lord Houghton to Henry Bright.

Fryston, January, 1875.

Are you my puffer in the *Athenæum?* I think so, for it is gracefully done. You will have seen Robert's glorification in the *Times.* I suppose Dr. Butler put it in. He owes it all to his dear mother, who knew Shakespeare by heart in all senses.

To the Same.

January 29*th,* 1875.

You made a mistake in not coming to Manchester. It was quite worth throwing over any duty, even any pleasure, to make the acquaintance of Lord and Lady Salisbury. I spoke with satisfaction for the first time to a Manchester audience. The *Guardian* was complimentary, and no paper said I was drunk.

To the Same.

February 5*th,* 1875.

You should get last week's *Academy* and this with my articles on Lord Russell. Lord Hartington* will do very well under the circumstances. How the future historians will chuckle over the defeat of Forster! The Nonconformist middle class had *one* chance of placing one of themselves in the Government of England, but preferred a trumpery squabble, which could be arranged by sensible men in ten minutes. It is enough to make any cultivated man a Churchman. Forster should get baptised immediately. I am going to breakfast with Sir Charles Dilke, to read Keats's love-letters to Miss Brown. I have seen some of them; very morbid and cross, and discomfortable.

* Lord Hartington had been chosen to succeed Mr. Gladstone as leader o the Liberal party.

To the Same.

Manchester, February 17*th.*

I am here for our half-yearly meeting [Yorkshire and Lincolnshire Railway], and return to Serlby this evening. I dined and slept at Agnew's, and had quite a literary and æsthetic party. He says Owen's College is immensely improving the tone of society here.

The Queen of Holland to Lord Houghton.

The Hague, February 17*th,* 1875.

MY DEAR LORD HOUGHTON,—I am very grateful for your kind letter, for the copy of the *Quarterly* of 1847, and for the promise of bringing your daughter, whom I shall be most happy to receive. The "last Stuarts" I meant were James and Charles Edward, and not those ambiguous gentlemen who, I believe, had no right whatever to the name they usurped. I believe I have found some publications about the events of 1715 and 1745, which are not generally known—"A Narrative of 1715 and 1745," by Robert Chambers; and "A History of Scotland, from 1688 to 1760," by Hill Burton. I have sent for them to communicate them to the author who has written an article for the *Revue de Deux Mondes;* but the *Revue* will not publish it without its being *accrochée* (I have no English word for it), hung behind some recent publication on the subject; and I hope by means of those books we may get into the *Revue.* I feel, nevertheless, very grateful for your kindness, and remain, dear Lord Houghton,

Very sincerely yours,

SOPHIE.

Henry Bright to Lord Houghton.

Ashfield, Knotty Ash, Liverpool, March 18*th,* 1875.

MY DEAR LORD HOUGHTON,—Here is my "Year in a Lancashire Garden." When you have looked at it, pray give it from me to one of your daughters. I don't think you care much about gardening; but this little book is almost as much about books as gardening. You will see I quote you at page 51, and allude to you at page 12; then, too, in the first page or two there is a hint I got from you when ·you came to us for a night, and I was planning these articles. I had then meant, when I had collected them all, to dedicate the book to Lady Houghton, as nowhere have I spent pleasanter hours than in the Fryston garden.

Ever yours,

HENRY A. BRIGHT.

To Henry Bright.

Trentham, March 26th.

I am staying here some days to look over the Duke's undertakings, which have almost the character of public works. He thinks no more of making a railroad than you or I should of an asphalt path. His son is a charming Lifeguardsman, who plays the piano to us all the evening. We went to Stoke yesterday, and I asked Minton if they were making a service for Dr. Kenealy. He said, " It is enough disgrace to be represented by him, without being his potter." Robert is getting over his accident.* . . . But Lord Galway has broken two ribs and other wise knocked himself about. He is going on well, but bones are not oleaginous enough to knit readily after 70.

A great pleasure brightened his life in the course of the summer. This was the success of his son at Cambridge in the competition for the prize poem, of which Lord Houghton had known nothing until the prize was won.

* His son had been suffering for some time from the effects of a severe fall.

To his Son.

Travellers' Club, Pall Mall, June 5th, 1875.

DEAREST ROBERT,—It was very discreet of you to keep your own counsel so completely as to the poem. Nobody can now say that I wrote it. I need not say that I am anxious to see it, and that any criticism or corrections are now quite legitimate before it is recited. I congratulate you on it most sincerely. The faculty of writing verse (quite apart from poetic genius) is the most delightful of literary accomplishments, and it almost always carries with it the more generally useful gift of writing good prose.

Your affectionate

H^N.

Talking one day to Sir Wilfrid Lawson, who had just produced a bright *jeu d'esprit,* and congratulating him upon it, Sir Wilfrid expressed his surprise that he should think anything of such slight performances; "it is only a jingle," he remarked apologetically. "Yes," replied Lord Houghton, "but good rhyme is always better than bad verse." He always, however, set the highest value upon the writing of poetry, even when the poetry itself might not be of a high class, as a preparation for the writing of prose. The latter art, he believed, was in great danger of dying out, amid the stress and the hurry of most prose writing of the day, and, himself the master of a delightful style, he was anxious at all times to inculcate upon others the virtue of writing with that distinction which style alone can give.

In the summer of 1875 Lord Houghton was enabled to realise a long-cherished dream, by visiting the United

States. The reader has seen how numerous and close were the friendships which bound him to distinguished Americans. He had been in early days the friend of Emerson, before Emerson's name was familiar to the English public. He had been the host of Longfellow, and the correspondent of Charles Sumner. Few distinguished men indeed, whether they were politicians or poets, or leaders of the national industry, had crossed the Atlantic on a visit to this country without making the acquaintance of Lord Houghton. The man who had spent no small portion of his youth in Italy, who knew Greece and Turkey and the Nile long before fashion prescribed a winter in Egypt or the Levant as a commonplace incident in one's life, was sufficiently catholic in his sentiments to feel as deep a sympathy with the growing nationalities of the West as with the time-worn races of the East. He had been one of the few Englishmen of position who had been true to the Great Republic in the crisis of its fate; and his faith in the future of the New World had never wavered even when few were found to share it with him. More than once in conversation before 1875 he had quoted the words, " See Naples, and die," and laughingly added that for him they meant, " See Niagara, and die." The delicate state of Lady Houghton's health had prevented his acceptance of the many invitations he had received from friends in the United States, but he was now free from that tender source of anxiety and care, and nothing stood in the way of his pilgrimage to the West. So eagerly did he look forward to the journey that when it was resolved upon, the resolution seemed to bring with it something like a renewal of youth. His insatiable eagerness to know and to see for himself made him delight in the prospect of a visit to that which in his case was literally a new world; and at the end of July, 1875, he sailed by the Allan Line for Quebec, accompanied by his son, with a heart as light, and anticipations as eager, as though he had still been a young man.

His sojourn in Canada and the United States, which extended over the months of August, September, October, and November, was a complete success. He travelled over a great extent of territory, and saw most of the natural wonders which in those days lay within reach of the traveller. Railway companies and public officials vied with each other in welcoming him and in giving him facilities for sight-seeing. The newspapers followed his footsteps everywhere, announced his arrival in the various cities of the States in words of glowing recognition, not only of his merits as a poet, but of his staunchness as a friend, and kept a watchful eye upon all his movements. Public bodies, clubs, associations, charitable institutions, joined in bidding him welcome. Every door seemed to fly open at the approach of one whose name had long been known to American men of letters, and whose attitude during the great war had done even more to secure the gratitude of the American people.

It is hardly necessary to say that the wonders of Nature were not those which had the greatest attraction for Lord Houghton. He was impressed by the awe-inspiring vision of Niagara; he marvelled at the greatness of Chicago and other cities which had sprung into existence within the term of his own life; but it was not colossal viaducts, newly-built towns, or vast manufactories which attracted him most. He went to America to make acquaintance with the Americans themselves, and he was singularly fortunate during his stay in forming friendships with a great number of men and women of worth and eminence.

Though he has unfortunately left no connected record of his tour, he often talked of it during the remainder of his life; dwelt upon it with evident pleasure and satisfaction, and was delighted to be able to make some return in this country to those from whom he had received kindness in America. The only record of his journey which he left is to be found in a small MS. volume entitled by him "Characteristics, August, 1875," from which some extracts of interest may be given. They are somewhat fragmentary:—

Sarmatian Steamer, August 5th to 15th.

Stopped 6th at Moville Harbour to take up Thursday's London mails. Old gentleman at Londonderry whose granduncle had helped to shut the gates. . . Proposed thanksgiving service on Friday evening for the unprecedented fine and quiet passage; but a fog came on in the afternoon, which set everybody in an antagonistic frame of mind, and detained us twenty-four hours. Icebergs much what I anticipated; huge one like a recumbent mastiff or sphinx; large square one quite clear in the sun; others in sunset looking like solemn statuary islands.

Quebec, 15th.

More like a modern French town than an old one—most of its characteristics improved away. Cheated out of five dols. to take selves and luggage from the quay to the hotel, St. Louis. Cabmen Irish at one stand, French at another; exacting and fraudulent, controlling the Municipality, which dared not keep them in order. . . . Policeman murdered by one of the cabmen a few days ago. Asking another what would be done to him, he replied, "He is apt to be hanged, but it is not very sure; it is thirteen years since they hanged any one; but he shot a man before, and got off."

Montreal, 18th.

Palace-boat on river; beautiful moonlight view. Curiously particular directions and precautions, in case of disaster, hanging up in each state-room, with life-belt for each passenger. (Boat, with 300 passengers, had been stranded a little above Montreal last week.) Town mostly built of fine grey stone from quarries close by. Statue of Nelson on a pillar in the large square. Why? Dined at the Club; drove to the new park just being made; noble view of the town—chief characteristic, the variety of colour. Thursday.—Drove with Mr. Redpath to the Lachine Rapids. Disappointed with the rapids, the breadth of the river making the descent insignificant. I dined with Mr. Redpath at the Club, and going away fell down the steps. The Mayor, who had been one of the guests, went home with me, and gave me a lotion.

Sept. 8th.

Park-like country from Hamilton to Niagara; dreary view of the stones of the lake. Came on Niagara in the 'bus from Clifton Station to the hotel. Noise much less than I expected. "Clifton Hotel" opposite the American fall, which thus looks entirely separate from the Horseshoe, and, being in a straight line, the water appears a gigantic millrace. The dividing line from this view is much larger than is usually seen. The whole is, therefore, not so imposing at first. Found Lady Howard De Walden and Charlotte Ellis in the hotel—come straight from San Francisco, Japan, Pekin, and Java. Interchange of London gossip and far-world impressions; her stories so agreeably interesting, as to make me think they were worth twenty months' wandering and discomfort. Bagdad, the Himalayas, and Japan what had pleased her most.

Sunday, 29th.

Hurlbert, of the *New York World,* arrived from New York by express *Herald* train that left New York at 2.35 a.m. and arrived at 2 p.m.; sent solely to distribute the paper to the betting and excursion world. This its last trip; Hurlbert delightful as ever. Took long drive along the rapids, the falls gaining every moment in the afternoon lights; rainbows broad and complete; the river above like a strip of tempestuous sea; the water at the brink rolling over with such soft regularity. . . .

30th.

To the other side. Dined at the "International." Prospect Park and Goat Island "got up" with too much exhibition; but the grandeur overpowers it. The scene of the inland sea grows upon you, and the rapids are a tempest under a calm blue sky.

31st.

Spent the day at Glencairn, on the Lower Niagara River; beautiful calm scene. View from Brock's Mountain of the same kind.

Buffalo, September 1st.

Most pretty town, though certainly no better than the ordinary English manufacturing place; but long streets of well designed villas stretching out in all directions. Mr. Fargo's (California Package Company) magnificent palace of wood; the noble decorations from top to bottom, including pantry and kitchen, all in tesselated woods, mostly Canadian; the general impression dull and monotonous, but undeniably handsome. Some good bronzes from the antique, and a most modern Italian marble of Charlotte Corday in her Normandy cap sitting on a chair; the furniture in French style, from New York. Small but pleasanter house of a Mr. ——, with capital theatre at the top of it, holding 300 people; he just making an arrangement with creditors, which accounted for the drawing-room not being furnished. Mr. Gray, editor of *Buffalo Courier*, bit of a poet, talking to me of David Gray.

These extracts are bare enough in all conscience, and they represent all that can be gleaned from his diary. His biographer is compelled, therefore, to fall back upon those scraps of correspondence which are left, and upon the record of his journeyings as it is told in the invitations which he received, and in the newspaper comments as he passed from town to town.

He landed at Quebec early in the month of August, and met with a hearty reception from the Governor of the province and the leading citizens. Mr. Goldwin Smith was one of the first to greet him on Canadian soil, and he spent some time with him at Toronto. From Toronto he went to Niagara, and thence to Buffalo; and, after visiting Springfield, proceeded west as far as Chicago, where he had old friends whom he was anxious to see—among them, Dr. Robert Collyer, the Yorkshire blacksmith, who had established his fame as one of the greatest of American preachers.

There was one special place of interest for him in Chicago—the New England Church, to the building of which he had contributed a stone from the old Meeting-House at Bawtry, where many of the leading Puritans met and worshipped before they started on their pilgrimage to the New World. At St. Louis, which he visited after Chicago, he was fortunate in being the guest of General Sherman, and here he was lionised in right royal style.

General Sherman to General Badeau, U.S. Minister, Brussels.

Head-Quarters Army, U.S., St. Louis, Mo.,
Sept. 24th, 1875.

DEAR BADEAU,—Lord Houghton and son, Mr. Milnes, were here last week, and presented your letter, which I was glad to receive. I showed his lordship all about the city, and entertained him and his son at dinner. The city authorities also took him in hand one day, introducing him at the Merchants' Exchange, and driving him to the parks and various places of interest; so that, on taking his departure for the East, he expressed himself well pleased. He is surely a gentleman of refinement and culture. You may safely send any of your friends to me here, and I will endeavour to redeem any promise you may make them. Generally strangers want to go out on the plains when an army acquaintance is indispensable.

Truly your friend,
W. T. SHERMAN.

Lord Houghton was not one of those who wished to "go out on the plains;" he greatly preferred remaining in the cities, and making acquaintance with men rather than with game. One St. Louis newspaper reports an interview with him which may be reproduced here :—

The Right Honourable Lord Houghton of England, perhaps better known in this country as Sir Monckton Milnes, arrived at the Lindell last night from Chicago *viá* the Illinois Central Railroad. A *Times* reporter sent up his card, and was most courteously received by the honourable gentleman.

"When did you arrive in America, Lord Houghton?" queried the reporter.

Lord H.: "On the 16th of August I landed at Quebec, and spent three weeks at Niagara Falls. This is my first visit to America, although I have all my life taken great interest in the country and desired to see it. I started over just as the war broke out, but postponed my visit in consequence of that occurrence."

Lord Houghton spent several days in Chicago, and will remain in St. Louis until Monday at least; he will then visit Cincinnati, Baltimore, and Washington, and will spend the fall in Massachusetts and New York. He has come over for the sole purpose of viewing America, and studying American institutions, of which he entertains a very high opinion; he may possibly visit the Southern States before his return. His son, the Honourable Robert Milnes, accompanied his father to America, and will arrive in St. Louis this morning, having lingered in Illinois for the purpose of engaging in a chicken hunt on the prairies. Lord Houghton has written a number of volumes, both in prose and poetry, which have won for him distinction in the literary world. His last work, that was republished in America, was entitled "Monograms," a work treating of society and its component parts. Upon his return he will probably give to the world a work on American manners and customs. He is a very pleasant and courteous gentleman. He has letters of introduction to Mayor Britton, Hon. Thomas Allen, William H. Benton, and other prominent citizens of St. Louis, who will no doubt show him all the interesting features of the city.

It was not at St. Louis, but at another town in the West, that Lord Houghton had an experience with an interviewer which he delighted afterwards to relate. He had retired to rest at an out-of-the-way place, fatigued after a long day's railway travelling, when his faithful English attendant Dey, the butler and house-steward of Fryston, who had accompanied him on the journey, entered his room to inform him that he could not get rid of a newspaper reporter who was bent upon seeing him, and who declined to regard the fact that he was in bed as any obstacle to the interview. Lord Houghton consented to see the importunate visitor, who forthwith asked his views regarding American institutions in general, and the American press in particular.

"What strikes me about your press," said he in reply to this modest request, "is the extreme violence of the language you use towards your political opponents. I see in one paper I read this morning that President Grant is described as a drunkard, a liar, and a thief. Now even supposing he were all these things—which I do not for a moment admit—do you not think that it would show more self-respect on the part of his opponents if they were to remember that he is at least the head of your nation, and its representative in the eyes of the world, and that consequently any attack made upon him is virtually an attack on the Republic itself?"

The next morning, when he opened the paper which contained an account of this interview, he found, after a graphic description of his own appearance in bed, the following statement:—

> Lord Houghton is not inclined to admit that President Grant is a drunkard and a thief, and he thinks that even if he is, the fact should not be published to the world in the newspapers.

After this it is perhaps unnecessary to say the

traveller was more wary in his interviews with the enterprising reporter. He was not allowed to escape from St. Louis without a speech. It was delivered on 'Change, and the reporters record his expression of astonishment at the fact that such a reception should have been given him, especially when he considered that he had come among the people in an unofficial capacity, having no claims upon them except that he looked upon Americans in the light of fellow-countrymen. He said that "as his life went on, and old age approached, a desire had entered his breast to turn his footsteps once towards the setting sun; he had made one or two of these footfalls, and now found himself in immense districts of rich agricultural lands, amid a large and sturdy population; he found magnificent buildings and structures, showing an appreciation of the arts truly commendable. He expressed his gratification at visiting a country where his own language was spoken, and where he found similar institutions of learning, progress, and public welfare to those of the country in which he had lived and moved and had his being—institutions which could not but be regarded as the foundations of liberty and civilisation."

It may be doubted whether this speech owes so much to Lord Houghton as it does to the reporter, who has at all events successfully preserved whatever was commonplace in the address, whilst with equal success suppressing anything characteristic of the style of the speaker. It was after delivering himself of this speech that he received a visit from the reporter of the St.

Louis *Republic*, who, in recording what passed, expresses his pleasure at having seen a live lord, and records his opinion that he was "as easy and plain as an old shoe."

Lord Houghton [says another journalistic critic] is the livest Englishman St. Louis has ever seen, and it is to be hoped our citizens will extend to him every facility for gaining information.

Naturally enough, it was in and around Boston and Cambridge that Lord Houghton met the greatest number of old friends. Longfellow, Lowell, Emerson, Joachim Miller, Julia Ward Howe, Charles Francis Adams, Mr. Bigelow (formerly United States Minister at Paris), Mr. Gurney (of Cambridge University), and others too numerous to be named, were among those with whom he enjoyed pleasant converse during the months of September and October. A few of the letters addressed to him by these distinguished Americans may be given.

H. W. Longfellow to Lord Houghton.

Cambridge, Sept. 23rd, 1875.

DEAR LORD HOUGHTON,—I should have written long ago to welcome you to America, but did not know where a letter would find you. I suppose you are at the Brevoort, and hasten to say how delighted I shall be to see you and your son on Saturday. You will find me in rather poor case and condition, but none the less glad on that account to have you under my roof.

Yours always faithfully,
HENRY W. LONGFELLOW.

Lord Houghton lunched with the poet, and met a distinguished party, including Mr. Lowell.

R. W. Emerson to Lord Houghton.

Concord, Mass., Oct. 4th, 1875.

DEAR LORD HOUGHTON,—Your note is a joyful surprise. I knew you were coming to us, but did not know that you had reached Massachusetts. Thursday shall be a welcome day to us. Take the train, Fitchbury Railroad, leaving Boston at 11 a.m., making sure your ticket and your train are for Concord, Massachusetts—for a train from the same depôt goes to Concord, New Hampshire—and we dine at two o'clock, and we will give you hearty welcome to our little town.

Always yours,

R. W. EMERSON.

Mr. Emerson followed up this invitation with a further one, begging Lord Houghton to remain as his guest for as many days as he could. He was not able to accept this extended invitation, but he had much pleasant talk with the distinguished writer over old days, and especially regarding Carlyle and their former relations.

Lord Houghton to Henry Bright.

Concord, October 5th.

I have been troubled with neuralgia ever since I have been in America, and it is little consolation to be told it is the malady of the nation. It has damped all my pleasure, and a week of medicine in New York has only made it worse. I like to write to you from here [from Emerson's house], and fresh from a walk to Hawthorne's "Old Manse" and grave. They have put up two good monuments—one to the thirty-six Concord men killed in the rebellion—another to the farmers who in 1775 were the first to fall in a contest with English troops. Emerson is very well, and easy to talk with, but, he says, unable to write. I had two charming days at Cambridge—Longfellow full of tenderness.

I am afraid he is ill, and so is Lowell. I dine to-morrow with Holmes, who is very sprightly, and like his books. On Monday I go to Albany and down the Hudson, intending to remain in New York till the end of the month. I am indeed sorry for Robertson Gladstone; I should think he was the best-loved of the family. The New England autumn colouring is all I expected, but it has come on too rapidly, and will be gone in a few days.

More than once Lord Houghton made a short stay in New York, leaving it for visits to Washington, Richmond, and other places of interest. In New York his old friend Hurlbert undertook the duties of chaperon, and enabled him to see the many persons with whom he was wishful to make acquaintance in the Empire City. He had another friend in the late Mr. Samuel Ward, so well-known to a wide social and political circle as "Uncle Sam," whose kindness did much to add to the pleasure of his visit to New York. His stay there was a round of social triumphs, the record of which is to be read in the papers of the time. The American newspapers were indeed full of Houghton and of his poetry whilst he remained in the United States, and the quotations I have already made from the Western newspapers might be multiplied indefinitely by the descriptions which appeared in the New York press of the distinguished visitor whom Americans delighted to honour. Some of the letters of Mr. Hurlbert to Lord Houghton before and during his stay in New York, and of Mr. Sam Ward to Lord Houghton's son, will convey better than any words of mine can do an idea of his surroundings during this very enjoyable trip.

W. H. Hurlbert to Lord Houghton.

Manhattan Club (? August 27th, 1875).

MY DEAR LORD HOUGHTON,—" And Satan also comes among them," as I by these presents notify you. This is from the *New York World* this morning—a sheet by no means so black as it is painted. I trust, however, you won't allow it to prevent you from accepting any invitations you may receive to go and be received by the leading lights of literature, society, negro minstrelsy, and the Cause (with a capital C) of Humanity (with a capital H). I never attended one of these things in my life, but I judge, from what I have heard of them, that they must be very edifying to the stranger in our midst. ——, I believe, judiciously got drunk before he submitted to the ordeal; Froude took it all in deadly earnest, and thought it portended a general uprising of the Anglo-Saxon element in America, to subdue and stamp out the accursed Catholic Celt. Forster threw his hosts into spasms of fury by appearing in a morning jacket and red cravat, while they were all point device in white chokers and patent pumps. .

Faithfully yours,
WILLIAM HENRY HURLBERT.

Mrs. Procter to Lord Houghton.

Beach House, Freshwater, October 3rd, 1875.

MY DEAR LORD HOUGHTON,—I am so far from the world that I have no news of you. Have you seen the Yankee proper? Have you delighted his eyes with the sight of a living Lord and the Honourable Mr. Milnes? Those whom you visited will never speak of 1875; it will be " the year when Lord Houghton was here." How you will be quoted! What wonderful sayings you will be said to have uttered! Here, we rejoice to know that the booksellers are ruined, so far as an American is ever ruined. We have been here nine weeks, and have liked the place more and more. I do not know if you have ever been here: a lovely little bay, fine downs, and pretty lanes with hedges redolent of sweetbriar and wild honeysuckle. The last week has brought Mr. Tennyson here, and we meet continually. He drops in at 11 in the morning, and sits gossiping; then we take walks together. It is a very great pleasure to me to be with him. His sons are very pleasant. We have had some friends staying at the hotel who came for the love of us—Miss Hampton, Madame Du Quaire, Hamilton Aïdé (who came looking for a house), Charles Hallé, and his sister. We have now in this house Mrs. Cornish. She wrote "Alcestes," a pretty novel.

On my way here I passed five golden days with my dear Adelaide Sartoris. Oh! what talks we had over old times during happy days that can return no more!

Since I have been here I have had two letters from A. C. Swinburne. I wrote to ask him for his autograph, and he sent me a little poem that has never been printed. I copy it for you, to make amends for this poor little note.

Your affectionate old friend,
ANNE B. PROCTER.

W. H. Hurlbert to Lord Houghton.

Tuesday, October 5th, 1875.

DEAR LORD HOUGHTON,—This is only to tell you that Stuart's dinner on the 19th is to include Beecher; Secretary Bristowe; Lester Wallack, the manager-actor; Burnside, who got the Union Army so handsomely whipped at Fredericsburg; Beauregard, the hero of Bullrun; John Kelly, the present King of Tamany; and, if he arrives in time, the Cardinal. Never was such a dinner planned since those wonderful days we passed together in Egypt. I thought you might like to have a week or so to prepare for such a gastronomic Armageddon. . . .

W. H. HURLBERT.

Mr. Sam Ward to the Hon. Robert Milnes.

Brevoort House, October 19*th*, 1875.

We have had your dear and lively old governor back here some five days, two of which *pars fui*. I do not conjecture to what extent this Ulysses of literature, poetry, and humanity, recounts his rambles, and as all about them must be honey to you, I proceed to say first that we all drank a bumper to your safe arrival; two, that Ulysses reached New York after a confused peregrination on Thursday, the 14th inst., as I was being scurried to Washington. He dined that night at the Manhattan Club with Hurlbert, Governor Tilden, Dorsheimer, Marble, Sidney Webster, and others. The next day, I still vaulting from car to car, he dined with Henry Ward Beecher, whom he enjoyed amazingly. The day after, Saturday, the 16th, he decorated the *déjeûner* of the Century Club as per enclosed report of festive proceedings. The same afternoon at 4 I escorted him, per steamboat, with Evarts, to Glen Cove, where Barlow entertained us feudally, and Ulysses behaved with all the attractive grace of a troubadour. . Yesterday morning we had a charming time of picturesque inspection, and at 11.30 Hurlbert arrived with Bret Harte. Bayard Taylor came over to get the Century speech for the *Tribune* of to-day, from which I enclose a complete version. . . . While writing the preceding, I heard the exasperating rap of Hurlbert's cane, and enter Ulysses, Evarts, and Hurlbert, from a dinner at Chief-Justice Shea's, to get seltzer in my den. To-day Ulysses dines at the Manhattan Club, and on Friday he will be entertained by Mr. Evarts.

The Same to the Same.

October 22*nd*, 1875.

Imprimis, the health of Ulysses is much better and steadier. Since his return from Barlow's he complains no more of neuralgia, and I have not seen Dr. Barker in the hotel since he came back from Boston. On the evening of the 19th we dined with W. Stuart at the Manhattan Club; twenty-two at table—Evarts,

Bayard Taylor, Lee, and no end of American notabilities. For so large a dinner it was a convivial and social success, and the Lord of Ithaca bore it extremely well, considering that he had spent the latter part of the day in revelry at the Harpers' book manufactory. He has been at Jay's in West Chester for the last three nights, and we dine this p.m. with Evarts *chez lui;* and so ends my chronicle, which would be incomplete did I neglect to add that his lovable popularity is daily on the increase. I hear on all sides reporters' praises of his heartiness, geniality, and bright intelligence. Had the British Government sent him here as plenipotentiary, with a salary of £24,000 per annum, to win the hearts of Jonathan Brothers, he could not do more than he has done, and is daily doing, to achieve that national purpose. Why did he not come on the high joint commission?

The Same to the Same.

Washington, October 27*th*, 1875.

The dinner of Evarts was a success. Governor Tilden and ex-Governor Morgan, both of New York, were there; this was Friday. Ulysses spent Saturday evening at the Century. Sunday he went to hear Beecher preach, with Mr. Evarts; paid the Duncans a visit at Staten Island; and dined with S. G. Ward, the agent of the Barings. Monday he visited the public schools, and gave a little dinner in his room to Beecher, Hurlbert, Stuart, and myself. It was very cosy, and they adjourned to see Booth play Hamlet. Yesterday he breakfasted with me, and lunched with Thurlow Weed. In the evening Mrs. General Sherwood gave him a reception, and I came hither. It is settled that he goes to Richmond, and then sojourns in my den from the 10th to the 15th November.

The Same to the Same.

Brevoort House, November 2*nd.*

Great dinner last evening by Bierstadt here; twenty guests and a charming time; photographs of Ulysses upon the bill of fare. This morning he gave a lovely breakfast to literary men in one of the parlours up-stairs. He goes to Philadelphia to-morrow, thence to Washington. Health improving.

The Same to the Same.

Washington, November 17*th,* 1875.

I enclose the latest news from our dear friend Ulysses, who after a series of ovations here, which culminated in my little festivity, started for Richmond on the 15th inst. He had intended making a visit to Lord and Lady Milton, near Covington, 250 miles west of Richmond, but received before leaving this place a regretful note from the latter, stating that her husband was too unwell to receive him suitably. To-morrow he dines with John Cadwallader, whom I was sorry to disappoint by being summoned to New York to-night. He leaves this Friday morning, the 19th, for New York, dines Saturday with the Lotos Club, Sunday with Mrs. Stephens, Monday has a grand function at Barlow's, Tuesday a reception at the Union League, and Wednesday he takes the *Bothnia* for home.

The Same to the Same.

Brevoort House, Nov. 20*th,* 1875.

Ulysses returned at 4 last evening enchanted with Richmond, which he found as different from New York as Florence is from Hull. He dined last evening with a railroad operator named John A. C. Gray, and to-day gives a lunch to Mr. and Mrs. Jennings, Mr. and Mrs. Webster, and others. In lieu of taking the *Bothnia* on Wednesday, he returns to Boston to spend a week at Plymouth, Massachusetts, where he will kiss the Plymouth Rock, the blarney stone of America, and look up reminiscences of his and your ancestors. This variation shows the wonderful energy of our wanderer. I write this in haste, to prepare you for the disappointment which this delay may cause at Fryston Hall.

These extracts from the letters of a genial member

of American society will convey a better idea of the whirl of hospitable entertainments in the midst of which Lord Houghton spent the greater part of his time in America than any words of mine could do. The American people treated him as one of themselves, and, from the President downwards, made him free of their homes. He had conquered the literary world before he set foot on American soil, for there were not many writing men in the United States whom he had not tried to help in the Old World; but he now took American society by storm, reviving thus, after the lapse of more than forty years, his early triumphs in society at home. President Grant, during his visit to Washington, showed him exceptional marks of attention, as did also the leading members of the Administration, the millionaires of New York, the great merchants of Philadelphia, and the *litterati* of Boston and Cambridge; and everywhere the leading members of society did what they could to make his time pass pleasantly. How thoroughly he enjoyed his visit is only known to those who, in later days, heard him dwell upon it in accents of lingering regret. One of the newspaper reporters in New York, describing him, had said that none could see him without feeling that he was " a chiel amang them taking notes." Those notes he never printed, never even committed to writing; but the newspaper reporter was not wrong. Few men ever visited America who made better use of their powers of observation than Lord Houghton did during his stay in the United States. Everything that was new interested him, and everything that was old; he was able to draw a thousand contrasts between society in New York or Washington, and society in London or Rome. He contrasted the spirit of the New World with that of the far East, with which he had made acquaintance in his youth. There was not a point in the social and political life of America which he failed to observe, or which he was unable to compare with an analogous feature of European life. He visited schools and prisons, and almshouses and public libraries. He dined impartially with the saint and the sinner, with the Republican and the Democrat, with the Northern Abolitionist and the slaveholder of the South; and everywhere he made his notes and brought them home, and used them in after-days to enliven many a happy evening at Fryston, or in the country houses he was visiting, and to illustrate his more serious talk on public affairs and institutions. It was a genuine pilgrimage which he made; and it was carried out in a manner which befitted his own character. This visit to America, indeed, might be regarded as an epitome of his whole life, seeing that it illustrated the breadth of his sympathies, the universality of his curiosity, his social gifts and his kindness of heart, the keenness of his interest in literature and men of letters, and the genuine attachment which he always felt to those social and political movements that promised to make for good in the world. One cannot but regret now that he was too much engrossed with his engagements from day to day to write at any length to his friends and family. Most of us would give not a little for a series of monographs such as Lord Houghton could have written on the chief features of social life in the United States in 1875.

Lord Houghton to Henry Bright.

British Legation, Washington, Nov. 14*th*, 1875.

I return by the *Bothnia*, which starts on the 24th. This tour of mine has had its difficulties, and I have never been quite well for a single day. I am perhaps better now, the weather being delightful—the real Indian summer. The President dined out yesterday to meet me, which, I am told, is a great honour. The Union League Club entertains me the night before my departure, which is a bore, as I cannot correct my speech. I dine with the Lotos Club next Saturday—rather a curious genus in the American flora. I go to Richmond to-morrow, to have a glimpse at the unhappy South; I should have no pleasure in going further.

To his Daughter.

Brevoort House, Fifth Avenue, Nov. 22*nd*, 1875.

DEAREST AMY,—You will not see me by this mail; you must have a short letter of explanation. I found that my Boston friends thought I had rather neglected them, and as there is now no pressing business at home, I thought it as well to go there from the 24th to the 29th, and to sail on the 1st by the *Abyssinia*. I thus hope to be with you about the 12th, allowing for a rest at Liverpool. The weather is clear and cold, and I am decidedly the better for it. . . . One of the Fitzwilliams appeared here Friday on his way to see Milton; I am very curious to know how he finds him. I asked Mrs. —— to invite him, "a son of Lord Fitzwilliam's." She understood me to say "my son-in-law Fitzwilliam," and she invited him accordingly, to our great amusement. He and Miles Stapleton return with me on the 1st. I suppose my speech of to-morrow will be in the *Times*. I am very nervous about it, as it is to be in a theatre and on a stage. . . . *Au revoir*.

Your affectionate,

H^N.

I must close this imperfect account of his visit with a few extracts from letters referring to it, and from newspaper reports of his speeches.

Sir George Bowen to the Dowager Viscountess Galway.

75, *Cadogan Square, S.W., July* 1*st*, 1889.

MY DEAR LADY GALWAY,—When I last had the pleasure of meeting you, you said that you would like me to send you some notes respecting my visit to Washington and Richmond in the United States in 1875 with your brother and my friend the late Lord Houghton.

I recollect that at a dinner at Washington, where President Grant was present, Lord Houghton talked humorously so much in favour of polygamy that the President said, grimly, " I really must appoint you to be the next Governor of Utah." Lord Houghton was received with the most flattering attention in America; for he combined in his own person two capacities which Americans like and admire—that of an English peer, and that of the distinguished man of letters. While at Richmond, in Virginia, we were driven by the Mayor over the famous battlefield where General Lee so long baffled the Northern armies. I was then on my return to Australia, where I was Governor of Victoria, from a short leave of absence in England. At Philadelphia I parted from your kind-hearted and accomplished brother, of whom I shall always cherish a very friendly remembrance. I afterwards received a letter from him, in which he wrote: " I shall never forget the party to which we were invited at Richmond by the Governor of Virginia, the former Confederate General, who had been wounded in battle; how much I was struck by a charming American lady suddenly striking up my own song, 'Strangers Yet'; and how, when the Governor apologised to us for retiring early because he had a ball in his back, you remarked to me that such an *arrière pensée* was a sufficient excuse—a *mot* which I often repeat in England as one of the most amusing I ever heard."

Yours very truly,
G. F. BOWEN.

At the entertainment at the Century Club Mr. Bryant, the President of the Club, presided, and made a genial speech, full of happy references to Lord Houghton's life and his literary work. The reply of Lord Houghton, as reported in the New York papers, may be given here.

MR. BRYANT AND GENTLEMEN,—In finding myself here now for the first time, I am agitated by conflicting emotions—by my pleasure in being among you, and by my regret at not having been here before.

In alluding to my poetic experience, Mr. Bryant mentioned that I had passed many years of my early life in Italy; and while he was so doing, there arose in my memory a little incident not inapplicable to my present position. I passed some time at Venice, and one summer evening, on the Piazza di San Marco, my attention was attracted by an old man, who walked up and down with a mingled air of wonder and delight, and who, after I had observed him for some moments, came and asked me, in the Venetian dialect, what streets he was to take towards a certain remote portion of the city. I said that I was a foreigner, and that he, being a native of the place, must know its geography better than I could do. He then told me that he was there for the first time. He had passed all his life in his own distant world, there earning his daily bread, and occupied by its little local interests. At last a friend had told him that he must see the Place and Church of San Marco before he died, and put him in a boat and landed him there ; and now he wanted to find his way home, charmed and contented.

Gentlemen, I am in the position of that Venetian veteran, and shall return to my country, happy that I have at last found my way to this great place and habitation of the *civitas* of English-speaking people.

Not that I have ever failed to regard this country, in many senses, as my own, from the time when I took moral comfort from the flight of Mr. Bryant's " Wild Fowl " across the ocean, and took in the best lesson of life from the Psalm of Longfellow. Since then I have ever been with you in all your intellectual progress, and in the necessarily chequered course of your constitutional history, and never more than in the late solemn years, in all the national difficulties which you have so energetically, so persistently, and so humanely surmounted. In looking back to my impressions at those times, I sometimes think that my sympathy with you was not wholly unselfish, but that I felt that, if I had ever written anything which has a chance of a prolonged existence, I should wish it to be read, not by any distracted and impotent communities of British race, but by America, one and indivisible. And, gentlemen, this is not unnatural; for, amid all the divisions or distractions of your history, your literature has ever been patriotic and national. Literature, in truth, has been to you a good and faithful emigrant, reproductive, not only of all intellectual growth, but of the sympathies—the largest sympathies—which bind together man to man. It has settled among you every classic writer of British origin ; and from the Continent it has brought to you Goethe, Schiller, and Heinrich Heine. It is also noticeable that by the side of these great colonisations of thought, you have not refused to receive, and to pass to your furthest territories, the humblest addition, the single volume of verse, the chance felicitous expression of combined thought and feeling ; even some accidental refrain of song that has pleasantly caught the ear and gone to the heart of man.

And this brings me to say to you one professional word

respecting that art and nature of poetry that you have been kind enough to connect with my name. The greater portion of the verses I have written were that product of the lyrical period of youth which is by no means uncommon among modern civilisation. It exhibits itself sometimes in the strangest manner, without connection with other culture, or even the most common intellectual opportunities. Of this I happen to have given to the world a signal instance in the volume I published of the poems of "David Gray," a Scotch weaver-boy, who, without one advantage beyond the common education of his class, described all the nature within his ken in the highest poetic perfection, and passed away, leaving a most pathetic record of a short life of imaginative sensibility. You can contrast this simple and wayside flower of a faculty with such rich and complete cultivation as it can assume in the efflorescence of Tennyson or Swinburne; but in whatever form you find it, do not the less value the faculty itself. Permit me to say that in no condition of society can it be encouraged and fertilised more usefully than among yourselves. For not only will it bring with it calm and comfort amid all the superabundant activities, ambitions, and confusions of daily life, but it has also the regulative power, teaching men to divide the sphere of the imagination from that of practical life, and thus obviating the dangers that so often arise from the want of this distinction. There is no better preservative than the exercise of the poetic faculty from religious hallucinations, from political delusions, and I would say even from financial extravagances. Therefore through the whole vast range of this New World be on the watch to look out for and to encourage this great gift to man. Do not be too hard with any imperfections or absence of refinement which may accompany its exhibition. Do not treat it too critically or with too much scholastic censure. Recognise also its value on another ground—the extension and the perpetuation of our great common language—an interest not less dear to every one of us here present than to the future welfare of mankind:

" Beyond the vague Atlantic deep,
   Far as the farthest prairies sweep,
   Where mountain wastes the sense appal,
   Where burns the radiant Western Fall,
     One duty lies on old and young—
   With filial piety to guard,
   As on its greenest native sward,
     The glory of the English tongue.

" That ample speech, that subtle speech,
   Apt for the need of all and each,
   Strong to endure, yet prompt to bend,
   Wherever human feeling tend,
     Preserve its force, expand its powers,
   And through the maze of civil life,
   In letters, commerce, e'en in strife,
     Remember, it is yours and ours."

At the Lotos Club, where he was entertained at dinner, the principal speech after his own was made by Mr. Bayard Taylor. The last entertainment in Houghton's honour in America was a reception at the Union League Club. There had been an intention on the part of his friends of different parties to organise a special demonstration in his honour of a most unique description in American life. The following circular explains the character of this entertainment :—

              New York, November 10*th*, 1875.

It is proposed to offer to Lord Houghton, on the eve of his return to England, a public testimonial of the respect and regard in which he is held in this country, not only as an accomplished and eminent man of letters, and as a conspicuous champion of

Liberal ideas in his own country, but as one of the very few Englishmen of rank, influence, and repute who steadfastly refused, during the darkest hours of our history, to despair of the American Republic.

Those who are most familiar with our diplomatic annals, best know how great a debt American freedom owes to such English statesmen as the Duke of Argyll, Lord Houghton, Mr. Bright, and Mr. Forster, who resolutely opposed and triumphantly defeated every attempt at bringing about, in any shape or under any pretext, an European intervention in the affairs of this country.

The undersigned, in behalf of a few gentlemen of this city, who feel with them the propriety of expressing in some informal and agreeable way the esteem which he has justly earned from all Americans, have the honour, therefore, to invite you to join them in a subscription dinner and concert, to be given to him at Delmonico's, in this city, on the 22nd instant.

The number of subscriptions will be limited to fifty, at one hundred dollars each, each subscriber having the privilege of inviting one lady. An equal number of invitations will be issued by the Committee, to include the members of the Government at Washington, and persons of eminence and authority throughout the country.

The favour of an immediate reply, to be addressed to any one of the undersigned, at Delmonico's, corner of Fourteenth Street and Fifth Avenue, New York, is requested by

Your very obedient servants,
SAMUEL J. TILDEN.
CHARLES O'CONNOR,
THURLOW WEED,
WM. M. EVARTS.

All sections of the political world in New York had joined in making arrangements for this banquet and reception, but it was abandoned in consequence of the action of the Union League Club, which had secured Lord Houghton's attendance on a later date than that fixed for the non-partisan gathering. At the Union League the speech in his honour was made by Mr. J. H. Choate, the President of the Club, and in his reply Lord Houghton said :—

I am asked often what I think of my experiences in this country, and I have no objection whatever in conversation to state my thoughts, but to such an audience as this I should be very careful of telling my experiences. You would at once see through them; you would see how imperfect—how foolishly imperfect—my deductions were; and you would say, " If he is a sensible man, he will go home and think of what he has seen, and read in books and newspapers, and will in his own due time form certain conclusions." Now that is just what I hope to do. When I come to individuals and to society which I have met, that is a totally different matter. I recognise that I have met in this country men whom I should have been glad to have met anywhere—men with whose familiarity I have been honoured; and I may say this, that if I were to compare the best men I have met here with the best men I have known in Europe, I should simply say this, that the men that I have found here seem to me as equal to the circumstances in which they are placed, as intelligent in all the relations of life, as noble in their innermost impulses, as just in their impressions, as any I have ever met in my intercourse in Europe. I have been received with great kindness by your intelligent and able President. I had the strange fortune the other day to sit by the death-bed of that amiable and honest man your Vice-President, in the Capitol in Washington, lying under the portrait of Washington. I have seen some of your able men with whom I have been intimate in Europe, and you will allow me to mention above all the man whose career I witnessed during that stormy time of your trouble, Charles Francis Adams.

It was a few days after making this speech that Lord Houghton's visit to America terminated, and he left it, leaving innumerable friends, with many of whom for the remainder of his life he kept up intimate relations.

CHAPTER XIX.

FAILING HEALTH.

Return to England—The Bulgarian Atrocities Agitation—Letters to Mr. Gladstone—Accident to the Hon. Robert Milnes—Fire at Fryston—Lord Houghton's "cheery stoicism"—Sympathy of Friends—Restoration of the Hall—Life at Fryston during the re-building—Unveiling of Burns' Memorial at Glasgow—The Home of Mr. and Mrs. Fox—Lord Houghton and the Prince of Wales—Meets with Accident—Death of Thiers—Failing Health—His Regard for Journalists—Appreciation of the Provincial Press—His Handwriting—Death of Stirling Maxwell—Lord Houghton succeeds him as Foreign Correspondence Secretary of Royal Academy—"George Eliot."

On his return to England Lord Houghton resumed his social life at Fryston and in London. His visit to the States made a great impression upon him. In spite of the unfavourable physical effects of the climate, he had benefited greatly, so far as mind and spirits were concerned, by actual contact with the people in the greatness of whose destinies he had always believed; and although direct observation of American life had made him acquainted with some of its less pleasing features and anomalies, it had in no degree slackened his enthusiasm for the Great Republic. Henceforward a new stream of visitors poured into Fryston. Americans of distinction had always been welcome there; but now came representatives of the many bodies from whom he had received acts of kindness during his stay in the States, and the friends whom he had made whilst there. In more than one of his speeches during the early part of 1876 he dwelt upon the lessons he had learned in America; and in the *Quarterly Review* he wrote an article on the social relations of England and America which drew from "Uncle Sam" the following acknowledgment.

Sam Ward to Lord Houghton.

United States Senate Chamber, Washington,
August 13*th*, 1876.

DEAR LORD HOUGHTON,—Many thanks for your admirable *aperçu* of your Yankee cousins, which I have read with pleasure and reflection. Your prose is as clear and pointed as your verses are graceful and dreamy, and the only thing one regrets is that you should not have had the spur of necessity to have driven more quills into the public mind. Bayard, now our most exalted public man, and by common consent our statesman of the future, expressed this regret while reading your *Quarterly* article, and said that I had promised him that you would send him a copy of the new edition of your poems with your autograph. Stewart was enchanted with his despatch-box. . . . Evarts I see as constantly as ever, and we often talk of you; but there is a tender theme of which I talk with no one, and that is my dear nephew, the heir-apparent, who has not confided to me of late his studies and aspirations. The United States are now waiting for the dissolution of their greatest living monarch, old Vanderbilt, who shares with Tilden and Hayes the honours of public attention. There is a story that Astor and Stewart have had a row with Charon about their ferryage, and that they have refused to submit to his exactions, because, say they, Vanderbilt will soon be there to put on an opposition ferry-boat. This is not a bad *jeu d'esprit*, as the old Commodore's fortune has been made by opposition, whereby in his early manhood he broke his own mother.

With affectionate wishes for your continued health and happiness,   Believe me
                    Faithfully yours,
                        UNCLE SAM.

In February of this year his brother-in-law and cousin, Viscount Galway, died. He was a man of fine character, whose real worth had long before been recognised by Carlyle. In habits and opinions no two men could well have been more dissimilar than Lord Houghton and Lord Galway; but from boyhood onwards they had been the best of friends, and the death of the latter was a severe blow to his kinsman. He had been member for the Bassetlaw division of Nottinghamshire for twenty-eight years, and had never been opposed.

Extracts from Letters to Henry Bright.

June 5th.

I give the King of the Belgians a literary soirée on the 30th—Herbert Spencer, G. H. Lewes, Robert Browning, Kinglake, Miss Broughton, &c. &c.

July 13th.

I hope you liked my American article in the *Quarterly;* that on Macaulay is by Gladstone, that on Ticknor by Hayward, and that on Croker by the devil.

March 31st.

Just returned from the *Academy* soirée. That wretched *Athenæum* never gives any, and I write to express my disgust with your letter. What will you have to say on the Judgment Day when you are called to account for all the pleasures you might have had, to God's glory? I met Mahaffy for the first time to-night. He has no scholarly look or manner, but looks like an Irish Dean. We talked over Greece and you, &c. Wedmore and others were there. They are to have an article on my poems next week, and I one on Macaulay a week after.

April 4th.

I spoke too late last night, and the House was eager for a division, but my argument was fresh. I like —— very much. I appreciate the attentions of young M.P.'s as an old coquette does those of the sons of her former lovers.

July 15th.

I gave the American Minister a dinner yesterday, including the three first personages in the realm, and the *Times, Quarterly,* and *Fortnightly* as well. I have also allied him in my article with the Duchess of Kingston; and if that is not a start for a Yankee in London, I don't know what is.

Vichy, St. Grouse's Day, August 12th.

I have finally settled to accept the Charlemonts' invitation for the 6th. I hope Mahaffy may be in Dublin some time whilst I am there, and may show me some of the lions, if there are any, literary or Papistical. That respectable Nonconformist, the titular Archbishop of Dublin, has broken both his knees, thus rendering him incapable of seeing his friends or praying to his Maker in the orthodox fashion. I am here bathing and drinking, and being bored. My only gaiety is dining with the Duc de Montpensier, where the other day I met the Princess who is to be the Queen of Spain. I am here till the 26th, and thirsting for news of all friends.

In the summer of this year, Lord Houghton was much gratified by his election as an Honorary Fellow of Trinity College, Cambridge. His old college friend, the Archbishop of Dublin, received a like honour at the same time.

The autumn of 1876 was a memorable one in the history of England. In the summer Mr. Disraeli had accepted a peerage, and retired from the House of Commons; and it seemed as if his retirement had been the signal for the fiercest political outbreak which the country had seen during many years. The publication in the *Daily News* of letters from Turkey describing the hideous atrocities committed by Bashi Bazouks upon the Christians in some of the chief towns of Bulgaria had stirred public indignation to the deepest depth. Mr. Gladstone, avowing that as a member of Lord Aberdeen's Ministry he had a certain degree of personal responsibility for the misgovernment of the Turk, placed himself at the head of that great part of the English people which clamoured for the repression of these cruelties. September, 1876, was a month which will long be remembered. At the time when, in ordinary circumstances, England is always wrapt in profound political repose, the country was ringing from one end to the other with the voice of indignant protest. Mr. Gladstone's pamphlet on the Bulgarian horrors fanned the flame, and Ministers suddenly found themselves confronted by an outcry resistance to which was hopeless.

Lord Houghton had not forgotten the lessons he had learned in the East as a young man. His hatred of cruelty and oppression, his genuine interest in the spread of Liberal institutions, did not blind him to the good qualities which he had found among the Mussulmans of Turkey nearly forty years before; and whilst he was compelled to recognise the inevitable tendency of events in the East, he was anxious for two things—that no injustice should be done to the Turks, and that, if possible, no help should be given to Russia, and to the ambitious designs which she was believed to cherish.

Lord Houghton to Mr. Gladstone.

Birr Castle, Sept. 21st, 1876.

MY DEAR GLADSTONE,—If you could lay your hand on my "Palm Leaves," published in 1844, and now republished in my collective works, you will find a poem entitled "The Turk at Constantinople," which might afford you some apposite quotations, and is really a fair bit of prophecy. I can understand the removal of the Turkish Government from Stamboul and its transference to any other power, but I cannot see any way to the administration of the provinces in which a large, if not the larger, proportion of the population is Moslem, under any other rule. The failure of the forty years of Greek independence is a most disappointing experience; in the language of the country I am visiting I do not see the conditions of Tenant Right or Home Rule in Bosnia or Bulgaria.

Mr. Gladstone to Lord Houghton.

Raby Castle, Darlington, Sept. 24th, 1876.

MY DEAR HOUGHTON,—When I get home I shall be among the "Palm Leaves," and glad to make the reference. I do not understand what people (a euphemism for you) mean when they talk of the failure of Greece. It is a gross failure as compared with the ideal Government, but its condition did not prevent 240,000 Cerfiotes round about from seeking ardently a union with it, of which they have never to my knowledge repented, though some Englishmen have been kind enough to repent for them. As compared with the prior Turkish State it is a signal success. It is not a disturbed or unhappy country, though it has bad laws and a bad upper class; and it has grown immensely in population, trade, wealth, and education, and Lord Palmerston and Lord Russell in 1862 wanted to get Albania and Thessaly added to it.

It may be that a little foreign nursing may be required before some of these provinces can manage themselves; but all the dangers or rather difficulties ahead are as nothing compared with the brutal degradation and the misery of the present state. I said in a speech yesterday I had now just one friend who did not see the need of decisive measures; I hope you do not make two.

Ever yours sincerely,

W. E. GLADSTONE.

Lord Houghton to Mr. Gladstone.

Shelburne Hotel, Dublin, Oct. 1st, 1876.

MY DEAR GLADSTONE,—What I mean by the failure of Greece is this: that if the Greeks had fulfilled the hopes of their champions in their faculties for order, administration, and enterprise, they would have been at this moment the solution of the now apparently insoluble question of the political destination of Eastern Europe. I wrote in 1843:—

> "And if to his old Asian seat,
> From this usurped unnatural throne,
> The Turk is driven; 'tis surely meet
> That we again should hold our own;
> Be but Byzantium's native sign
> Of Cross on Crescent once unfurled,
> And Greece shall guard by right divine
> The portals of the Eastern world."

Nor was this expectation unjust in the earlier portion of this century. For travellers found a polite, obese Turkish gentleman on an ottoman who was called the Pasha, but the Pashalik was really managed by a lithe, small-featured Greek secretary, who stood subservient behind him—a Tito in Romola, and now the Rallis, Ionides, etc., who are in high commerce in London, Manchester, and elsewhere, think no more of Athens than the Rothschilds of Jerusalem. King Louis Philippe said to me, "Mon beau-fils Leopold est prêt à se battre la téte contre la muraille, pour ne pas avoir accepté la trône de la Grèce; il dit toujours qu'il aurait été Empereur de l'Orient." I believe the real cause of his refusal was the diminution, it is said by the Duke of Wellington, of the extent of the kingdom. It was to have extended to the Pindus, and by some diplomatic jugglery the Porte retained Epirus and Thessaly.

I am a member of the Polish Association, and thus my prejudice against Russian occupation. I know her violation of engagements and "massacre" of mind. Material cruelty is short to suffer; semi-civilised political oppression is a lifelong torture; a century of Warsaw is worse than a week of Batak. In all else I am with you.

Yours very truly,
HOUGHTON.

Lord Houghton to George von Bunsen,

October 1*st*, 1876.

Looking over a last year's pocket-book I found the envelope in which this is enclosed. It must have been given me by some of your family, and it suggests to me that I should like to hear from yourself what I heard in London from others, as to your partial restoration to good health, and ability for active work. So please give me a line to Fryston, Ferrybridge, Yorkshire. I am now actually travelling about and making visits in Ireland, to the great amusement of my two girls, who examine it like a foreign country. I have another reason for wishing to hear from you. I am very curious as to the German views of this Oriental complication. The English change of front is very explicable. It was felt that the Crimean War had done nothing to improve the Turks; but still, they were thought honest in a commercial sense. In an ill-fated hour they did not pay their debts, or could not, which comes to the same thing. The mutation of opinion was unconscious, but not the less real. Then came the inhumanities of Bulgaria, and you know the rest. The Russian diplomacy is shameless as usual; they have Russianised the Servian Army, and insisted on peace. A defensive league between Germany and Austria to keep the mouths of the Danube free, seems to me the necessity of the hour, and this might be accompanied by a guarantee of all the Powers to keep open the Dardanelles. I do not fancy that at this moment anybody wants Stamboul, and the Turks are as well there as anybody else. Is it supposed that Prince Bismarck has any ideas about Turkey, or is he awaiting events? Count Munster's views of the facts of the case seem to me truer than Beust's. Gladstone with that one-idea-at-a-time (you Germans would make one word of it) faculty, which is his strength and his weakness, evidently looks on Servia as the Piedmont of Turkey, and would willingly make it a Slav State. Reasonable enough at first sight; but we do not sufficiently estimate the diversities of race and religion which the present despotism at least keeps down; that is my main difficulty.

My kindest remembrances to Mrs. de Bunsen and such of your children as remember us. Your affectionate friend,

HOUGHTON.

It was whilst the political controversy was still absorbing public attention that Houghton's mind was turned to other events nearer home. He was on a visit to Ireland when his son, who was also visiting in that country, met with a severe accident, which threatened serious consequences to his health, and Lord Houghton hastened to his bedside to assist in nursing him.

To Henry Bright.

Dublin, November 1st, 1876.

I am going to England to-morrow, straight to Keighley, to meet Lord Hartington, and return here on Saturday. Is not that patriotic or partyotic? I have to receive to-day the Lord Mayor and a great deputation on the subject of the Wife's Sisters Bill.

Lord Houghton and his son were staying in Dublin, at the Shelbourne Hotel, when on the 17th of November they received the news of another calamity. This was the burning of Fryston Hall. I have said in a previous chapter that Lord Houghton was not one of those men whose life is bound up with their country seat and estate. He preferred London as a place of residence to any other spot in England; but the reader has seen something of what Fryston Hall was, and within its walls at least its owner was happier than anywhere else. The house which had been the home of his fathers was now consecrated to himself by the memories of a happy married life, which had come to an end within its walls. It had been the scene of those many gatherings of friends from far and near, of which the reader has heard, and within its rooms were gathered together that great collection of books which Lord Houghton had devoted so large a part of his life, and no small portion of his fortune, to acquiring, and which he deemed not unjustly the most precious of all his earthly possessions. It is difficult to imagine a severer blow of the kind than that which fell upon him when he received the telegram announcing that Fryston Hall was on fire. Hour by hour during that sad day fresh telegrams came, announcing the progress of the flames. The first, which had been despatched at 6 o'clock in the morning, merely stated that a fire had broken out on the previous night, and was still burning. The last, which was sent off at 6 p.m., was as follows:—

Fire got out; all valuables saved except what was in tower; all front gone from roof to entrance-hall. We cannot account for the fire originating; it was first discovered in the tower at 10.30 p.m.

As soon as possible, Houghton set out for the scene of the disaster. Carlyle has made reference, in his "Reminiscences," to the "cheery stoicism" which distinguishes the better part of our English aristocracy. It is difficult to resist the belief that, when he penned those words, he had in mind the case of his old friend Milnes. Intensely sensitive as Lord Houghton was, and too subject to fits of severe depression, he had always possessed the power of meeting the ruder buffetings of fortune with a certain cheerful composure which surprised his friends, even while it won from them admiration for his fortitude. This cheery stoicism did not desert him now. He hurried to Fryston, leaving his son seriously ill in Dublin. He found, unhappily, that the reports of the great misfortune which had befallen him had not been exaggerated. All the front rooms of the old house—the rooms which included the hall, the drawing-room, and the morning-room, with the bedrooms above them—had been burnt out; many valuable papers stored in a part of the building known as the "Tower" had been lost. But even this did not represent the full extent of the calamity. When the news of the fire reached Pontefract, bands of willing workers hastened to the scene. They were men who had known Lord Houghton all his life, and who had learned to love him. These, with the few servants at the Hall, and the members of the Pontefract Fire Brigade, devoted themselves during the night, whilst the flames were still raging, to the task of saving the pictures and the books; and, thanks to their zealous efforts, hardly a volume was left in that part of the building which was burnt. But the Library, the orderly arrangement of which had once been the admiration of his friends, was now a mere heap of books flung together in apparently hopeless confusion. Nor was this all. When, after months of arduous labour, it was again reduced to some sort of order, Lord Houghton found, to his lasting sorrow, that many volumes were missing. He complained to the present writer, with a humorous smile, that his usual ill-luck had pursued him; for, in most cases, the missing books belonged to valuable sets of volumes, which thus became incomplete. How the books vanished, where they went, none could tell; though Lord Houghton himself, perhaps with a lively knowledge of the passion of the curiosity-hunter, jokingly held to the theory that they had been taken by friends of his own, who wished to possess a memento of the fire. All this lay in the future, however, on the November morning when he stood in front of the still smoking ruins of the pleasant house which had so long been his home. Even before he left Dublin he had thought of others in connection with the catastrophe, and had found time to write to his aunt, Miss Jane Milnes, whose earliest recollections were associated with Fryston, the following touching note:—

Lord Houghton to Miss Jane Milnes.

Shelburne Hotel, Nov. 17th.

DEAREST JANE,—I hope you will not have heard in any casual way the sad news of the fire at Fryston. The last telegram runs, "Fire now subdued; front and Tower all burnt;

pictures and books saved; no lives lost." Amy is so thankful that you and Louisa were not there. I go by the early train, and shall be there in the evening. It is a great misfortune that Dey was here looking after Robert; he would have known what to save and what not to mind. The fire began close to Amy's and Florence's rooms; and I fear all the little records and memorials of their short lives are gone, their mother's letters, and their friends' photographs. I will write on Sunday.

Your affectionate
HOUGHTON.

To his Son.

½ *Fryston Hall, Sunday, Nov.* 19*th*, 1876.

DEAREST ROBERT,—I did not get here till late, and found all as the telegrams told you. The Pomfret engine was not only short in the hose, but the hose was full of holes. If it had been right, the damage would have been a few hundreds. Briggs's Whitwood engine saved the Old Hall.* It is wonderful how much was done, for everything had to be recovered twice over. All the books and pictures were put in the back part of the house; and the Police Inspector said the whole house must go, and they had to be moved again into the brewhouse, stables, &c. Poor Hettie has worked herself ill: and Henry has hurt, not broken, his leg. Mrs. Hoff is considerably thinner. I have not seen Olly.† The foolish woman had £30 in banknotes, and some foreign bonds as well. The crowd was very amiable—at least to me; for they were heard saying they wished it had been ——'s house instead. There is a multitude of pleasure-seekers round the house now: it is an ill wind, &c.

Your affectionate
HOUGHTON.

* The part of the Hall burnt was that which had been erected in the previous century as an addition to the original building, which remained comparatively uninjured.

† Servants at Fryston.

It will be seen that his own misfortune rather served to stimulate than to suppress his interest in others. Referring, indeed, to one of the servants, who had lost part of her property during the fire and who was about to be married, he expressed the fear that her future husband would now get nothing with her. Cheery stoicism has seldom gone further than it did in the temper in which Lord Houghton viewed his own misfortune.

To Henry Bright.

½ *Fryston Hall, Nov. 20th.*

The morning room is open to the morning sun and the evening sky. *All* the front is gone—that is, all the best rooms. There is still left enough for selves and you or any other litterateur—a sort of lay parsonage. I dare not yet look over the books. Most are saved; but wetted, knocked about. The pictures little damaged. The people about worked night and day—quite a demonstration, intensified by the wish that somebody else's house had been burnt instead of mine. There is a *lovely* (American) article in the *Leeds Mercury* this morning. The loss would have been of hundreds, not thousands, had the Pomfret engine been effective; but it would not work, and the hose was as rotten as the ancient borough. My daughters have lost every scrap of property and every memorial of their past lives, their mother's jewellery, and their birthday presents. Florence had a journal from her childhood and her early poems; and Amicia, many curious books—all gone. But they have their lives before them. Robert, with the usual selfishness of manhood and youth, has lost nothing. He is getting well, but slowly.

Lord Houghton to C. Milnes Gaskell.

Crewe Hall, Nov. 29th, 1876.

MY DEAR GASKELL,—I was about to thank you for your kind inquiries. The whole front is gutted; a good many memories inside, but nothing else. I will take you at your word, and if I can think of any way of troubling you, I will do it. The signorine have lost every scrap of their little property, their mother's jewels and letters, their books from the author, their birthday gifts and keepsakes, their love letters if they have any, their photographs of dead and living. Their two ladies' maids had invested all their savings in despoiling the Egyptians, and are now despoiled in turn. Lord and Lady Portsmouth have offered me Hurstbourne after you leave it. I am thinking over the practicability of the offer, but do not require any thinking as to my gratitude for the kindness that prompted it. Please let them know this.

I am yours very sincerely,

HOUGHTON.

The sympathy which the disaster excited was not confined to Lord Houghton's numerous friends. In many papers besides the *Leeds Mercury* references were made to the fire at Fryston as though it were something in the nature of a public loss. The fame of the house as a great gathering place of men of letters was universally recognised, and sorrow was loudly expressed at the fact that such a misfortune had befallen the kind-hearted man who was its owner. Among the many letters which he received at this time I select for quotation one or two from men who knew what Fryston and its hospitalities were.

W. E. Forster to Lord Houghton.

Wharfside, Leeds, Nov. 20th.

MY DEAR HOUGHTON,—It is almost a shame to plague you just now with reading any letters, but I feel as if I must say how sincerely I, or rather we, feel for you in this calamity—how really grieved we are. For myself, I feel it as a personal loss.

I have spent so many happy hours in that dear old library, and I could have found my way to almost all the books. I feel as if I was knocked about when I think of their being thrown into the carts, though that saved them. Is there no way by which we can revenge ourselves on those Pomfret firemen with their broken hose? I most earnestly hope your son continues better. We go north to-morrow. How much better an address you would give to the Aberdeen youth than shall I.

Yours ever affectionately,
W. E. FORSTER.

Henry Bright to Lord Houghton.

Ashfield, Knotty Ash, Nov. 21st, 1876.

MY DEAR LORD HOUGHTON,—Thank you very much indeed for your kind letter. I know what a sad trouble, to say the very least, it must all be; and I only wish I could be as brave as you are. I do hope the books will not be much injured. I am so sorry, too, for your daughters. Shall you rebuild the house as it was, or change the front as I think Mr. Bennett once urged your doing? John Heywood and the Edwards-Mosses are asking after you, and I can now tell them.

Ever yours, dear Lord Houghton,
HENRY A. BRIGHT.

I have just got a *Leeds Mercury*. It is true, every word of it.

Mr. J. L. Motley to Lord Houghton.

5, Seamore Place, Mayfair, Nov. 23rd.

DEAR HOUGHTON,—I have been wishing to write a line to you ever since I read in the papers of the sad accident at Fryston, but I had no idea whither I could address a letter. Last evening the Duchess of Somerset told me where you were likely to be, and so I lose no time in telling you with what true sympathy, with how much deep regret, I read of the fire which has endangered, and I fear much injured, that delightful and most hospitable home of yours, which so many, many people of various stations and pursuits, highest and humbler, rich and poor, and of different countries—your thousands of friends, in short—have learned to regard with so much affection that the sense of the calamity will be a widespread one indeed. I trust that the accounts one gets in the papers may be exaggerated. If at any time you can find a leisure moment I shall be very glad if I might be informed by yourself that the damage is not irreparable. Although it is a good many years since I was at Fryston, I have very tender associations with it. I shall never forget the gentle kindness with which those dearest to me during my absence in America at the outbreak of our war were sheltered, and the glad welcome which I received in your old hall on my return. I will say no more, except to renew my hopes that the disaster is not as great as has been described, or as it might have been. I see so few people in this dead season of the year that it is impossible for me to learn particulars. I am glad also to know your address, as I have been for a few days desirous to communicate to you the fact of my daughter Lily's approaching marriage with William Harcourt. This matter gives me very great pleasure.

I am, dear Houghton,
Always sincerely yours,
J. L. MOTLEY.

These are but specimens of the many letters in which the peculiar claim of Fryston upon the affectionate remembrance of the writers was set forth. Keenly sensitive to sympathy as Lord Houghton was, there can be no doubt that the warm expressions of affectionate regret which now poured in upon him were regarded by him as a real compensation for the loss of so much of material possession, of physical comfort, and of tender association. The man of letters, whom Peel had once thought too little of a man of business to be admitted to the Ministry, showed on this occasion that he was full of the resourceful energy of the English character. Even whilst the smoke was still ascending from the ruined building, an architect from Leeds had been summoned to consult with its owner as to its restoration, and very quickly Lord Houghton set about the work of rebuilding. Within a couple of years from the date of the fire, Fryston Hall was restored in a new and improved form, in which, however, the leading features of the old house were tenderly preserved. The old drawing-room, sacred to so many memories, became Lord Houghton's sitting-room and library, whilst the original entrance hall was thrown into the old morning-room, which was converted into the present spacious drawing-room. But there was an interval during which Lord Houghton lived with his daughters in the main building as yet unrestored, and it was an interval very precious to his more intimate friends. For, as he had told Henry Bright, he had one room to spare, a kind of prophet's chamber, which was reserved for friends whose society he especially coveted. The visitors' book is silent as to the actual guests who stayed at the Hall during this period, but as one of them, I can testify to the pleasure which the favoured man, whoever he might be, derived from the undivided companionship of a host so richly gifted. Though no large party could be assembled in the little ante-chamber, which was the only apartment that could now be used as a dining-room, Houghton talked just as brightly and suggestively to his single guest as if he had been surrounded by wits and politicians. His temper, as his own letters indicate, was left quite unsoured by his misfortune, and he could joke philosophically over his very losses. In a speech made at Pomfret soon after the fire took place, he said that he was now "keeping open house" in a new sense of the word, and he never lost temper, or heart or hope, over a misfortune which would have sorely tried many a more pretentious philosopher. One of his first acts after the extinction of the fire should have been mentioned at an earlier point in this narrative. He made it his business to ascertain the names of all those neighbours at Pontefract who had taken any part in the work of saving his property, and having secured the list from an authoritative quarter, he presented to each of these humble assistants a handsome token of his gratitude. Some of the letters of thanks which he received from them were very touching, and afforded evidence of the esteem in which he was held by his immediate neighbours.

To H. A. Bright.

December 20th.

My best books will not turn up; they tell me they were saved, but I should like to see them. You must send me any *Athenæums* you wish me to read. I could not purchase that scurrilous print that compared me to Eliza Cook even at a bookstall. I quite go with you about Kingsley. He literally *rowed* himself to death, and everybody about him. How preferable was Newman's gentlemanlike falsehood to his strepitose fidgety truth.

To his Son.

Crewe Hall, Dec. 22*nd,* 1876.

DEAREST ROBERT,—We have a better and a brighter day, and I hope you are getting a pleasant drive. I have just finished "Harold" with great delight. There is a grand unity and local colour in the field of history about it that stamps it first-rate. I shall write and tell the Laureate I think so. Venables was telling us that his house in Bolton Row was the scene of the death of Frederick Maurice and of the reception of Manning into the Catholic Church. On which I improvised an inscription to put over the door which met with general applause:—

EX HAC DOMO
FREDERICUS MAURICE
AD SUPEROS,
HENRICUS MANNING
AD INFEROS,
TRANSIERUNT.

. I propose if you are pretty well that you should go back with me to Fryston on Saturday, to return to Serlby for Christmas, and to some discharge of your obligations to them.

Your affectionate

HOUGHTON.

One of Lord Houghton's engagements during the winter was at Glasgow, where he unveiled a statue of Robert Burns. The ceremony took place in January, on the poet's birthday, and the task entrusted to him was thoroughly congenial, though the weather was hardly suited to an out-door meeting. "An open-air demonstration in January," he observed in a letter, "is worthy of a people who wear no breeches." His speech on the occasion was happy, and the whole proceedings were decidedly successful.

To his Son.

3, *Park Terrace, Glasgow, Jan.* 23*rd*, 1877.

DEAREST ROBERT,—It will amuse you to have a slip of my morning speech on Thursday, but do not let it get into print. It is a comfort that I shall not have to deliver it in the garb of the Gael, but with three shirts on and extra underclothing. I only want a wig. . We shall probably go to Edinburgh on Friday, and home Saturday. The girls delighted in Lord Winmarleigh's old-world stories: his having been twice switched at Eton for attending two royal funerals without leave, and his having run a race with George IV. at Frogmore to meet Queen Charlotte. He was quite devoted to the late Lord Derby; the only creditable thing I know about that Homeric statesman. Gladstone's speech means mischief.*

Lord Houghton to Mr. Gladstone.

Fryston, Jan. 29*th*, 1877.

MY DEAR GLADSTONE,—I send you through Murray my last edition, that you may revive your recollection of my Oriental poems. They are quite as good prophecy as that of the Millenarians.

You were much regretted at Glasgow, and I applied to Burns and the lyric popular poetry of Scotland your fine image of vapour and flood, with great success. There were over one hundred thousand persons present.

Apropos of your article on the Prince Consort, I have always heard that Queen Anne was taken ill of the paroxysm of which she died in the Cabinet; that George I. presided over the first and second after his arrival, but not understanding the language, told Walpole to come and tell him afterwards what was done, so that the absence of the Sovereign is purely accidental.

You will have to tackle a question put to me the other day,

* On the Eastern question.

and which I could not answer: Is there in all history an example where foreign interference terminated or even mitigated the strife and violences of contending races and religions in the same country, without complete occupation and rule, such as ours in India? Hope to see you somewhere next week.

Yours very truly,
HOUGHTON.

Mrs. Procter to Lord Houghton.

Queen Anne's Mansion, Jan. 28th, 1877.

MY DEAR FRIEND,—It was very kind of you to recollect me. It must have been a fine sight, and I am glad your children were with you, and could hear you speak. For myself I always feel "too late!" It is much better that you should write to me, come and see me, than pronounce an eulogium upon me when dead. You and your generation are not to blame. James Perry, of the *Morning Chronicle*, offered him money and work, and this should not be forgotten. Your allusion to your father was charming. I remember saying once to Mr. Milnes, "How was it you did not make your son a Conservative?" "I made him something better—I made him a good man." I have had my share of good things in this world; but the greatest compliment I ever received was your father at dinner putting a £10 note on my plate, and saying that if I would stay another day I should have it. This is the only occasion upon which I had any chance of earning money. Be good and let me know when you come to London. Here I am at St. Leonard's-on-Sea until Thursday, when we go home. I suppose you are building. I have made the acquaintance of Mr. Rutson,* who is a friend and admirer of yours. Mr. Patmore and I are putting together a few papers left by my dear one. It will make a volume the size of Charles Lamb's life. My love to your daughters.

Your affectionate old friend,
ANNE B. PROCTER.

* The late Albert Oslif Rutson, Member of the London School Board.

Lord Houghton to Henry Bright.

St. Ann's Hill, Chertsey, Feb. 11*th.*

This is the place where Mr. and Mrs. Fox lived, and which was a place of pilgrimage to the English Whigs. I remember the old lady showing me a ramshackle summer-house where she and Mr. Fox used to dine off bacon and *greens*, not beans, as she said. It is now the most beautifully decorated villa in England.

I met the great Crusader (Mr. Gladstone) at dinner on Friday. He was in great force, and has a right to be so. Every Liberal feels himself twice as safe in his seat as he did six months ago. It will be amusing to see how the Parliamentary game goes on. Both parties want to fight—the Turkish party to show their majority, and the Russians to force the Government into some violence.

To his Son.

St. Ann's Hill, Chertsey, Feb. 20*th.*

DEAREST ROBERT,—I don't think you have seen this charming place. It is beautiful even without sunshine or greenery. The Prince of Wales was very affable on Saturday. He gave me a cigarette, remarking that he thought I had not got that vice. I told him I only did it out of respect for his presence. He spoke excellently; in fact, after your relative, he is the best after-dinner speaker in the country. I am to see him at Marlborough House about the D.W.S. (Deceased Wife's Sister) after the *levée* on Saturday.

Your affectionate
HOUGHTON.

A story has long been current which the above letter appears to confirm. It is that the Prince, having asked Lord Houghton one day who was the best after-dinner speaker in England, received from him the courtly reply,

"It rests with you and myself, sir." His letter to his son shows that his opinion of the Prince's powers was a genuine one, whilst his own claim to distinction in the same capacity will be disputed by none who knew him in his prime.

To Henry Bright.

Fryston, March 17th, 1877.

I came down to Fryston to open a bazaar for the purpose of making my church uncomfortable. If they drive me out of my pue (the proper way of spelling it, the meaning being " private "), I join the Nonconformists and return to the faith of my fathers. Lord Acton has delayed the issue of the Philobiblon volume for three months. I hate him as much as the Pope does. I have had some good Saturday breakfasts at 6, Clifford Street. I have another next Saturday; will you come? There is a new French book called " L'Assommoir," which everybody reads, and which makes everybody sick; don't read it. Tennyson has taken a house in town for three months, and will only dine out at 7; and all society has to submit to this idiosyncrasy of the poetical digestion.

Lord Houghton to Mr. Gladstone.

6, Clifford Street, Saturday, March 24th, 1877.

My dear Gladstone,—If you are in town next Wednesday, the 28th, will you dine here with Tennyson? H. P. M. names his own hour, 7. I wish you had mentioned Frederick Maurice in your estimate of preachers; to me it was more apostolic than anything I ever heard.

Mr. Gladstone to Lord Houghton.

73, Harley Street, March 26th, 1877.

My dear Houghton,—Many thanks, I cannot dine, but will, assuming your permission, come in the evening. It was not my intention to describe the greatest preachers or speakers I had heard or the most striking, but those in whom some feature was observable that was imperfect or even open to objection in itself, but yet was tolerable, or even desirable from its contributing to make up a remarkable and excellent whole. But my desultory and scrambling remarks might well mislead you as to my meaning.

Ever sincerely yours,
W. E. GLADSTONE.

Lord Houghton to Mr. Gladstone.

MY DEAR GLADSTONE,—I have to thank you for the pretty volumes of Gleanings from your large field " from the author." I knew the sheaves already. I should like to have had the literary portion which I most affect in a more bibliothecal form. Poet Rogers used to say, " Nobody had written carefully since they had ceased to be printed in quarto."

You may have seen my name attached to a memorial addressed to the authorities at Cambridge, respecting the compulsory study of Greek. I remember dear Lyttelton took an interest in that subject, and would have been much astonished to see that view regarded as implying any disregard of classical studies in general. I should like to see Latin taught as universally as in our old Grammar Schools; but Greek should be the first of accomplishments.

I am,
Yours very truly,
HOUGHTON.

Lord Houghton to his Daughter Florence.

Clifton, Wednesday.

The Duke of —— is here, and is wonderfully improved, as most men are, by having held a prominent position in the world. There is nothing so odious to self and fellows as obscurity.

Travellers' Club, May 1st.

I have just been breakfasting with Gladstone. We talked no politics, mainly Walter Scott and other novel subjects; but he made it very agreeable. He said he had been in a hurry for forty years, which must account for many of his shortcomings.

London, April 11th, 1877.

DEAREST FLORENCE,—I got back from Fryston yesterday evening. The foundations are turning out so bad that there will be a very heavy expense in renewing them. The architect must have been thinking of Venice, for the whole front is built on a wooden base which has gradually decayed, and there are heaps of rotten wood taken out. Placknett says the drawing-room side might have come down with a run. In which of Wilkie Collins's books is the disappearance of a whole house and its contents in a landslip?

Lord Houghton to Henry Bright.

April 15th, 1877.

I have taken a big house to entertain you and the Philos at breakfast in May, and you must come up if the result is your bankruptcy and a lying article in *Truth*. I take possession of 24, Arlington Street on the 20th. Before this I am at 6, Clifford Street. I find my books still more disordered than I expected, hardly any large series complete, and the number of broken volumes most annoying. My fine Dante and Froissart have turned up, but Charles I.'s Spenser is still missing.

To Miss Louisa Milnes.

Fryston Hall, Ferrybridge, May 24th, 1877.

DEAREST LOUISA,—You will like a letter with this date. I came here to see how the building was going on, and found the top all right—that is, the roof is all on—a little higher than before, but nothing to change the front aspect. The bottom—

that is, the foundation—has turned out very bad. The piles were rotten, have to be taken out, and to be replaced by bricks and concrete; going down in some places to the depth of ten feet below the foundation. It is an interesting triumph of masonic skill, but I fear a very costly one without anything to show for it.   The Board School is prospering, and the architect of the Ecclesiastical Commission has been to see the church. There are fortunately not means enough to spoil the outside, so they are going to be content with opening out the roof and re-pewing. I transfer my box to the gallery which gives satisfaction. I have written to-day a somewhat long article in the *Leeds Mercury* against the Bishopric of Wakefield. I might have said they might be content with their "Vicar," but I don't suppose anyone reads it nowadays. I hope to have some peaches for my banquet to General Grant on the 7th. I have the Dukes of Wellington and Argyll, the Marquis of Ripon and Hertford, the six leading Generals, Lords Granville and Rosebery, Kinglake, and Harcourt. This ought to set up the American people. Everybody who supported the North will be there in the evening. I went to Pomfret to see Mr. Hammond about his new vicarage, but he was from home. The Moxons were at Paris, so I consoled myself with Dr. Bisset's excellent sherry. He complimented me both on my politics and my divinity, agreeing with me against Gladstone and the new Bishopric *

The farmers are rejoicing in the high price of wheat in consequence of the War. But it is a curious illustration, that whilst the farmer gains about a shilling per quarter, —— raises her flour at the rate of 10s.

Your affectionate,
HOUGHTON.

Lord Houghton's dinner to General Grant duly took place. Remembering the hospitality he had himself

* Mr. Richard Moxon, who is still happily living, had been one of Lord Houghton's staunchest political friends at the time when he represented Pontefract in Parliament, and he was throughout his life warmly attached to him. Dr. Bisset was Rector of Pontefract.

received whilst in the United States, he was anxious to do his utmost for the distinguished American who was now in England.

His social engagements during the season were, however, interrupted by a slight accident which confined him to his room for a time.

To his Son.

June 22nd, 1877.

DEAREST ROBERT,—I had the oddest accident in the world in the Park yesterday. There was rather a jam of horses, and a Miss Farquhar rode by me with a loose curb rein, which the wind sent under my feet and up my leg. This dragged me back; the stirrup leather gave way, and the pony went from under me. I fell on my face, and luckily the ground was so soft that, though my nose and chin were bruised, the injury was not serious, and the damage not very perceivable. I thought when I got up that I should have a nose like Thackeray's. Poor Amy was in front, and saw my pony without a rider, which was a great shock to her. I went straight to bed, and have not been up to-day. They will let you know how I am going on .

I am your affectionate,

HN.

To Miss Louisa Milnes.

24, *Arlington St., Piccadilly,*

June 29*th.*

DEAREST LOUISA,—You might demur to "many happy returns" of yesterday, but give us as many as you can, not for your sake, but for ours. In one of Henry Taylor's books, he says that old women exercise more beneficent family influence than any other individuals. It is the same socially. London is suffering at this moment distinctly from the absence of any clever and important old ladies. Robert, in my place, went with the Baroness yesterday to open the new Pleasure Ground at St. Pancras, and proposed to some thousand people a vote of thanks to her. Amy says he did it without hesitation, and in excellent taste. There was great applause, and an outcry "God bless the Queen of the Poor!" I am to be carried downstairs this afternoon, but have been obliged to put off a breakfast to the Comte de Paris. It is much the same accident as Robert's at Serlby, but slighter I hope.

Dear love to Jane.

Your affectionate,

HOUGHTON.

To Henry Bright.

Arlington St., June 29th, 1877.

I never wrote to tell you of my accident. I have been in bed and bedroom for a week, hearing nothing of the London June, but the horses of the Piccadilly coaches, which Horace Walpole, who lived here, and Hogarth who painted here, might have listened to in their time. I take my first drive to-day, but shall not be able to ride, which I enjoy in town and dislike in the country; I don't know why.

To Henry Bright.

July 7th.

The Roxburghe dinner went off very pleasantly. I had myself carried to it. The Duke made himself agreeable, as only Dukes can do. I promised them a book for next year.

Mrs. Procter to Lord Houghton.

North Berwick, N.B., July 21st, 1877.

MY DEAR LORD HOUGHTON,—I want very much to know how you and yours are, and what you are going to do with yourself this autumn. Will you punish yourself at some baths, and expiate the sins of good dinners by eating bad ones? I generally find that what is disagreeable is said to be good for one. We are here in a very simple place, and the best thing here is the society of Lady Elizabeth Duncan. She is charming. I go and see her every other day, and should go every day were it not that I am afraid of wearying her. She is a fine old gentlewoman .... I suppose your season has come to an end with the garden parties, which seem to have been good. We are cold here, wearing our winter cloaks. I found Lady Duncan with a fire yesterday, and the rain it raineth every day. I paid Carlyle a visit before I left London. I found him just as he was in 1825, when I first knew him; his eyes are as keen as they were then. We talked of old days, and we both cried as we spoke of our dear, dear Edward Irving. Please send me a line. I love my old friends best, and to me there is nothing so delightful as to speak of those days that are no more. You and I and Mr. Kinglake are all that are left of the goodly band that used to come to St. John's Wood: Eliot Warburton, Motley, Adelaide, Count de Verg, Chorley, Sir Edwin Landseer, my husband.

Your affectionate old friend,
ANNE B. PROCTER

Lord Houghton recovered from his accident in time to enable him to visit Plymouth on the occasion of the meeting of the British Association there in August. He stayed at Mount Edgecombe.

To Henry Bright.

Torquay, August 25th, 1877.

I have been doing the British Association at Plymouth. As I was staying at that "gem of the sea," Mount Edgecombe, I liked it; but in itself it was uneventful and unsocial. The West kept up its character for dulness and not for adventure. We talked a great deal about population and subsistence in my section. It is curious how the Malthusian doctrine seems to rile the English people, for by our facts I am inclined to b' Besantian, especially in this country where any descent in the social ladder is abominable. There is some little improvement in this matter; for instance, Lord —— marries Lady ——; and he is to be a tenant farmer. But you would dislike one of your boys standing behind a counter, and I should not like Robert to keep an hotel, both which in America would be matters of course. What a pleasant book the " Life of De Quincey " is.

To the Same.

August 29*th.*

Page seems to me the best social biographer (after Lord Houghton) of his times. It is really interesting to have one's early writings alluded to as " poems " in the West. It shows one of two things: either the thing is remembered, or someone likes one well enough to pretend that it is so.

Thiers died in the month of September, and Lord Houghton was asked to write about him for the *Fortnightly Review.*

Lord Houghton to John Morley.

Fryston Hall, September 14*th,* 1877.

MY DEAR MORLEY,—Thiers will be talked and written out, and have become a bore, by the time your next number is out, so I would not write about him if I could. The disastrous fire has burnt or lost the few letters I had from him, and which I would have given you, but they were not interesting like Guizot's. Lord Granville told me yesterday that his father said, " All French politicians lie, but with distinctions. Comte Molé lies to keep up the dignity of his country and his own; Thiers lies *de gaieté de cœur*—it is natural to him; M. Guizot only lies when the condition of the State requires it." The best notice of Thiers I have seen is in an odd place—in *Truth.* It is written by Henry Labouchere, one of the few British who know Frenchmen. I said at Sheffield that my intimacy with Thiers convinced me of all the futility of our judgment of foreign statesmen; it was so impossible for such a man to have succeeded with us. Guizot, on the contrary, would have done almost as well as Peel. There is a point in this war no one has noticed; in regular belligerency the whole matter is duty; here on both sides it is real savage appetising *amusement*, the odd duality of kindness and bloodshed; why should it stop? It makes men happy. If you are to have war at all, such ones are the only defensible ones. There is some compensation for the immense discomfort. Have you been abroad with Mr. Chamberlain?

HOUGHTON.

Lord Houghton to Henry Bright.

October 12*th*, 1877.

Please procure for yourself and me Mr. Hall Caine's dramatic study. I am delighted to hear that there is a second man of letters in Liverpool, and he should be made much of. The *Academy* behaves very cruelly; but I respect provincial literature when we can get it.

To the Same.

Fryston, October 20*th*, 1877.

Have you read and reviewed a novel called "Heaps of Money?" If you have not, do so. It is one of the few witty books I have read for an age. . . . . This building process makes this house so cold that I shall not be able to be here in the winter, so we must try to meet at Crewe.

To the Same.

November.

Sumner speaks of me amiably, which is more than I do of him. I like Burnaby very much, but think his book over-praised. The truth is people are amazed at anything but the merest commonplace coming from a soldier, especially a Lifeguardsman !

Failing health hardly diminished Houghton's interest in the men of letters of his time. He was no longer able, indeed, to live on such terms of close intimacy with them as had existed between himself and Carlyle, Thackeray, Tennyson, and Spedding. If no other difference had existed, it would have been impossible to ignore the difference of age. Yet, to the last, he was always curious about the "rising men," always anxious to know them, and, if he could, to give them a helping hand. One day he remarked to his biographer, " I think I know every man of letters now whom I want to know, except one." The exception was Mr. Thomas Hardy, for whom he felt a great admiration. But the momentary expression of satisfaction with the extent of his acquaintanceship in the literary world must have been due merely to a passing fit of depression; for it was only a week or two later that he wrote making eager inquiries about another of the younger novelists, and begging for an introduction to him. At the Beefsteak Club, which he frequented regularly when in London, he was brought in contact with many of the younger actors, and he always had a kind word for them. For Mr. Irving he had a real admiration, and took part with a keen relish in some of the *symposia* for which the Lyceum, under its present management, is famous. His biographer cannot ignore the fact that many of the new generation "knew him not." They could not understand his complex character; they were bewildered by his paradoxes, and inclined to regard them as expressions of his real opinions upon men and things. At times, too, young men who had a full share of the confidence of youth took offence at his humour, and afforded a measure of their own possession of that inestimable quality by the manner in which they resented the light raillrey in which he delighted. Not that this raillery was ever vicious or unkind. But sometimes it pierced a vain soul to the quick; and words which Carlyle would have received with a burst of delighted laughter excited quite another sentiment in the breasts of men who were not worthy to touch the hem of Carlyle's cloak.

But whether appreciated or not, in one respect Houghton never varied—that was, in the real affection which he felt for all who belonged to the literary calling. The humblest man amongst them might have reckoned with confidence upon his friendship and his sympathy. It was not many months before his death that he was entertained by the Birmingham Press Club as its guest at one of its annual dinners. The company was one of working journalists—only distinguished by the fact that they formed part of the great body of the English Press. Lord Houghton spoke to them words of real wisdom, full of kindly feeling, touched, too, with that rare feeling for literature as an art which he had always possessed. When he was leaving the party, the young men composing it rose to their feet and cheered him with an enthusiasm which touched him. He turned round and, with uplifted hand, uttered a single sentence of farewell, "Be brave, my boys! be good!"

There were none present who were not moved by that simple appeal.

It was noticeable all through his life that he had a special regard for those literary workers who lived in the provinces, away from the turmoil and publicity of London. A provincial journalist seemed to him to be in every respect as deserving of friendship and sympathy as a London journalist; and if he saw anything in one of the country newspapers which seemed to have merit, he was generally anxious to know the writer. If at any time he heard of anything being done in literature by a resident in Yorkshire, he would make a special effort to meet the author, and afford him such compensations as he could for the lack of the stimulus to be found in the great centres of literary work. In these pages, of necessity I have had to speak chiefly of his friendships with men who were eminent and successful; for it is only in such friendships that the world at large feels any interest. But a great company of men, many of whom are still living, who have never emerged from obscurity, have never won the applause of the public, heard from him those cheering words of sympathy and appreciation which are so precious to the intellectual worker. And it was seldom that his kindness ended in mere words. Lady Burton, in the letter I have quoted, spoke of what such men as her husband and Mr. Swinburne had owed to Houghton; and the reader of these pages knows something of other cases in which he had been the first to recognise and assist men of undoubted genius. But in the background were a host of other men, for whom he had done as much. He was untiring in his eagerness to help where he believed that help was merited, and would not be given in vain. Little as he liked letter-writing, he was constantly writing to make the names of unknown journalists and men of letters known to the leading writers of the day. If he knew that one of these humbler friends of his was going to any city abroad, he would, unsolicited, forward to him a batch of introductions to the most notable personages in the place. Sometimes he almost embarrassed those whom he liked with his kindness. Before now a provincial journalist has gone abroad bearing with him letters of introduction from Lord Houghton to royal princes, ambassadors, Ministers, and the most renowned of European authors—all given spontaneously, and with no other object but that of helping a man whom he esteemed. Remembering these things, the world may well forget those impetuous utterances which occasionally fell from his lips in moments of irritation, the rare instances in which his humour took an acid form, or his sarcasm was pointed by too keen a personal application.

"A Review of Lord Melbourne's Life" was one of the works of Lord Houghton, penned during the winter. It was written in response to an urgent request from Mr. Morley, and appeared in the *Fortnightly Review*.

"There is no one in England," wrote Mr. Morley, "so exactly qualified to do justice to Lord Melbourne's political position as you are. Nobody else has been at once a vigilant spectator and an actor, knows equally well the people of the rough Northern towns, and the territorial aristocrat (God bless him!), and is equally free from canting formulas of the hustings and the leading article; so, as I say, I hope the friendly task may fall to you, as you are kind enough to be willing to undertake it."

Lord Houghton to John Morley.

Fryston Hall, October 30*th*.

MY DEAR MORLEY,—If the publisher will send a copy of Torrens' book ["Life of Lord Melbourne"] to me at the Travellers' Club, Pall Mall, I will see if I can do anything useful on it. It is, however, with him as with many other notable persons whom I only saw in their decadence; and knowing how age alters men, I am very careful in my judgment of those I have only known in their sere-time. If Mrs. Norton had been alive, she would willingly and powerfully have helped me, and said things through me she could not have said herself. But the Great Silence has come there too.

How Frederic Harrison comes out in his Symposium!

Yours very truly,

HOUGHTON.

When the MS. of Lord Houghton's article reached the printers' hands, it was in such a state that it threw another task both upon editor and compositor.

"DEAR LORD HOUGHTON," wrote Mr. Morley, January 27th, 1878, "I did my very best to make your article correct, down to a comma. If I live longer in this cheerful world than you, I shall be able to tell your biographer that whereas the printers only demand half-a-crown a sheet extra for 'Dean Stanley,' for you they will have nothing less than 50 per cent. to induce them to do their work. But the body is more than raiment, and an article is more than handwriting; and I am really very much obliged to you for one of the most interesting pieces I have ever published. It is a most furnished estimate of a man of singular quality. I suppose you are right in calling him 'the last of the gentlemen ministers.'"

Lord Houghton's handwriting was the terror of his friends. Only one who has been compelled to spend many months in reading the letters and journals of a lifetime can fully estimate the difficulties which the stranger, to whom a MS. in his hand was submitted, had to confront. In his youth, it is true, he wrote legibly; but after middle age, he seemed to suffer from a positive inability to follow the ordinary rules of caligraphy, the result being that his letters were a series of symbols rather than of actual words. Familiarity, of course, enabled his regular correspondents to grasp his meaning, though, even in their case, it was not easy to do so at the first glance; and it is quite possible that in the transcripts of his many letters, printed in these volumes, some serious errors may have crept in from this cause. Many amusing stories have been told of the difficulties occasioned by his peculiar handwriting. A tradition has long prevailed to the effect that the worst English writer of the past generation was Dean Stanley; but Dean Stanley's writing, difficult though it is, cannot be compared with the writing of Lord Houghton in his later days, and the letter I have quoted from Mr. Morley shows that the compositors of London held this opinion. Not the least amusing feature of the correspondence which Lord Houghton left behind him was the number of letters received from friends, containing inquiries as to the meaning of notes he had addressed to them. At the General Post Office, among other curiosities of the same kind exhibited there, is one of the envelopes addressed by Lord Houghton, the decipherment of which was looked upon by the Postal authorities as a miracle of acuteness on their part. He himself was fully sensible of this serious limitation to the enjoyment of his epistolary effusions; but it seemed as though no care on his part could suffice to enable him to write with the plainness of an ordinary mortal. There is no wonder, therefore, that Mr. Morley and the other editors, whose pages he graced with his contributions, looked with almost as much of terror as of gratitude to the favours he thus bestowed upon them.

The year 1878 opened gloomily for Lord Houghton with the death of another old friend, Sir William Stirling Maxwell.

"Stirling Maxwell's death" [he writes to Henry Bright] "is a desolation. He, I, and you were the only real men of letters in Great Britain. I am writing a few words about him in the *Academy.*"

The loss of his friend opened up for Houghton himself a new position of dignity and usefulness, that of Foreign Corresponding Secretary of the Royal Academy.

Sir Francis Grant to Lord Houghton.

21, *Sussex Place, Regent's Park, March* 27*th,* 1878.

DEAR LORD HOUGHTON,—Your name has been submitted to the Council of the Royal Academy as successor to the late Sir William Stirling Maxwell, for the vacant honorary office of Secretary for Foreign Correspondence. I need hardly tell you that the office is almost if not quite a purely honorary one, entitling you to some of the privileges of an Academician. The Council were unanimous in their approval, and if you will intimate to me your willingness to do us the honour of accepting the post, I will have the pleasure of submitting your name to the next General Assembly for confirmation.

I am ever, dear Lord Houghton,

Yours sincerely,

FRANCIS GRANT, P.R.A.

Lord Houghton gave his assent, and the nomination of the President was duly confirmed. Among the privileges attached to this distinction was that of regular attendance at the Royal Academy banquets. Houghton had frequently been the guest of the Academy on these occasions, but he now took his place amongst the Academicians as a matter of right, and for the future, whilst he lived and his health permitted, never failed to be present at their board on the occasion of their great yearly festival.

Another honour was also offered to him during the spring of this year when Sir Rutherford Alcock, the President of the Royal Geographical Society, asked him to allow himself to be proposed as his successor in that important office. This position, however, involved the performance of duties which with the best will in the world he felt to be beyond his strength, now waning with the passage of the years, and he consequently never attained a dignity which in his earlier days he would eagerly have coveted.

Nothing has been said as yet in this memoir of Lord Houghton's friendship for the eminent author who is known to us as George Eliot. It was, however, very real. He had been one of those who from the first had recognised the brilliant talents of the writer of "Scenes of Clerical Life;" and after her identity had been revealed, he was one of the chosen few who knew her intimately in private life.

Mrs. George Lewes to Lord Houghton.

The Priory, North Bank, Regent's Park,
April 9th, 1878.

DEAR LORD HOUGHTON,—I had a little chat with Mrs. M. the morning I met her under your kind auspices, and I think we came to the understanding that I preferred the breach to the observance of such flattering attentions as calls from "Strangers." I have been so constantly declining to accept proposed visits of that kind from American ladies that it would be invidious on my part to make an exception, unless it were warranted by the prospect that I could render some needed service. But Mrs. M. is so well received and appreciated that I can add nothing to her advantages during her stay in London. Visits from friends and from those who are likely to become friends I am very fond of, but I have a horror of being interviewed and written about, and though I would not impute an intention of that sort to Mrs. M., my experience in relation to other American ladies has confirmed me in my churlish habits. Pray interpret me charitably, and believe me

Yours very sincerely,

M. E. LEWES.

Edward Fitzgerald to Lord Houghton.

Little Grange, Woodbridge, April 30, 1878.

DEAR LORD HOUGHTON,—You are as ever very kind to me, not least so in writing me a letter which I find is a hard task to my oldest friends now, partly because of their being oldest I suppose. My dear old Spedding, I can barely screw out a dozen lines once a year from him. I have just had them, almost two months before the year was out, and on them I must try to live another year more.

> " And with the aid such correspondents give
> Life passes on—'tis labour—but we live."

So says Crabbe, only " ships and sailing " in the first line, from his " Borough," which with the rest of him no one now reads except myself I believe. I write at once not only to thank you, but to return you Lushington's corrections. I should have thought they were printers', not copyists', errors. In return for all this I enclose for you one of my works. You see I drew it for myself because I often find myself puzzled about the few dates in the dear fellow's life when reading his letters, as they are now edited: then I thought that some others would like such a " Cotelette d'Agneau à la Minute," as Pollock calls it, and so here it is for you if you please. I am told that the present generation sneers at C. L.—I suppose a natural revolt from their predecessors—*us* who love him so well. But his turn will come again, I feel sure. " Saint Charles," said old Thackeray to me in a third floor in Charlotte Street, thirty years ago, putting one of C. L.'s letters to his forehead. I won't swear to the exact accuracy of my " Cotelette ; " it is not easy to get it all from his biographies—and I am—Paddy, but I believe it is near enough. Pray do not be at the trouble of acknowledging it. You entertained many people at that 26 Pall Mall as I can witness for one, and one of us was a thief. I suppose someone stole a volume I had of Thackeray's drawings which I lent to Anne T. when she was about that best " Orphan of Pimlico." I entreated her to use some of his more graceful drawings, enough caricature already; but she or her publisher listened not, and she never could find my book again. I did not want it again, but I did not wish it to fall into other hands than hers. Now I think you have enough of

Yours very sincerely,
EDWARD
(how many more of the name do you know?)
FITZGERALD.

Surely the Keats should be published. What a fuss the cockneys make about Shelley just now, not worth Keats's little finger.

The enclosure in Fitzgerald's letter was a brief list of the principal dates and events in Lamb's life, just such a list as would be found useful by any reader of his letters.

Early in May Lord Houghton and his daughters went to Paris for a few weeks to visit old friends there.

To his Son.
6, Clifford St., May, 1878.

DEAREST ROBERT,—Write a few lines to me at Hotel St. James, Rue St. Honoré, Paris. . . . I dine with Waddington on Monday to meet H.R.H., and on Tuesday and Wednesday to meet other notabilities; that is what I call hospitality. You will see my Academy speech in the *Observer* to-morrow. I have written it out for once, which I always dislike doing, distrusting my memory more than my improvisation.

To the Same.
Paris, May 10th, 1878.

We have had very nice weather, and the chestnuts—Tennyson's "hyacinth trees"—are in high beauty. The Waddingtons are uncommonly kind. We dined there these two days running,

and do so again on Monday. It is the best amusement the girls have; they do not know enough people to make the balls amusing. I have just been by myself to one at the Marshal's— not one hundred people. All Society cut the old man since he accepted "*cette horrible République.*" I have had interesting conversations with Gambetta and other public men, and am going to-morrow to see Victor Hugo and Zola ("L'Assommoir").
. . . We had the Comte de Paris's box at the Italian Opera last night, and we have the Marshal's to-night at the Grand Opera.

In the summer a sharp attack of illness prostrated his strength, and he was ordered to the baths of Royat, where he spent some weeks, afterwards visiting La Puy Carcassonne and Nimes, and staying with some friends near St. Julien for the vintage.

To Henry Bright.

Royat, August 27th, 1878.

Your letter found me in the centre of France, under the shadow of the mountains of Pascal. I am sent here to a dull place, with beneficial waters and fine air, rather for security than cure, as I may be said to have recovered from my bronchitis. Having my elder daughter with me I do not want company, and one always finds someone to vent one's poor French on. It must produce an odd impression on a Frenchman to hear me speak, as I do, with fluency and a certain wit and grace, and yet making the most terrible blunders of grammar and gender. Our Ministers put the best face on it, but they must by this time feel that the Treaty is very hollow; it could not have been anything else. I shall be here till the 9th of September. I hope to find Fryston in October in the way of becoming habitable.

The Treaty referred to in the foregoing letter was that of Berlin. Lord Houghton had not been a supporter of the strong Anti-Turkish policy of Mr. Gladstone; but he had been even less inclined to support Lord Beaconsfield in his adventurous defiance of Russia. Writing to his aunt on the eve of Lord Beaconsfield's return from Berlin, he said, July 16th, 1878 :—

I hope to be in my place on Thursday, to see the reception of the Great Adventurer. Whether from knowing him so well, or from the sarcastic temperament of old age, the whole thing looks to me like a comedy, with as much relation to serious politics as Punch to real life.

CHAPTER XX.

LAST YEARS.

Marriage of his Son—Letter from Miss Nightingale—The Passion Play at Oberammergau—Visit to Berlin—Conversation with the Austrian Crown Prince—An Annoying Incident—Algernon Swinburne and Landor—Death of James Spedding—Assassination of the Czar—Houghton and Panizzi—Houghton becomes a Trustee of the British Museum—Marriage of his Elder Daughter—Visits her in Egypt—Returns by Athens—Serious Illness at Athens—Kindness of Mr. Ford—Increasing Difficulty of Literary Work—Illness of Henry Bright—Visits him at Cannes—Mrs. Carlyle's Married Life—Lord Houghton Proposes to Visit India—The Project Abandoned—Death of Henry Bright—The Last Gathering at Fryston—Another Accident—Last Days in London—Death at Vichy, August 11, 1885.

CORRESPONDENCE became increasingly difficult to Houghton as time passed. His letters were fewer in number and briefer. Age was creeping upon him; and though his spirit, in spite of his reference to the sarcastic temperament of age, was still young, and his sympathies as quickly moved as in the days of his youth, he was compelled to refrain from many things which had been easier to him in bygone years. Not, indeed, that he gave way to indolence, or allowed himself the repose which the valetudinarian deems necessary. On the contrary, a certain quality of restlessness, which had always been present, now asserted itself more strongly than it had done when his health was better, and he refused to allow any physical infirmity to shut him off from those social enjoyments of which he had partaken so largely, and which he relished so much. That this restlessness was due in part to physical suffering is more than probable. He needed something to divert his mind in his frequent attacks of pain, and he found it in the society of his friends, and in the extension rather than the curtailment of his social engagements. Those who met him for the first time in public during these last years of his life might easily have fallen into strange errors regarding him. They could not know his real physical weakness, the effort which was required to sustain him when he joined in conversation in large and mixed parties, the constant struggle which he had to maintain with disease and pain; yet neither weakness nor pain sufficed to make him dull, or to blunt his interest in men and in affairs. He still shone as one of the best talkers of his time, maintaining his old supremacy in the face of many new comers, who now aspired to be his rivals in the social world. He was still, also, ready to help, with pen or tongue or purse, any cause or any object which enlisted his sympathy. Even during that autumn of 1879 with which I am now dealing, he took part in not a few public engagements in Yorkshire and elsewhere, addressing large and important societies with all his old fertility of fancy and grace of language. One such occasion I can well remember at this period in his life.

In the late autumn of 1879 the Liberals of the West Riding, who were engaged in active preparations for the coming election, held a great demonstration in Leeds. The evening meeting on the day of this demonstration was one of the largest ever held under a roof. Its scene was a vast shed attached to the Steam-Plough Works of Messrs. Fowler and Co., and, at a moderate computation, 25,000 persons were crowded into this improvised hall. The Duke of Argyll was in the chair, and among other distinguished men present were Mr. Forster and Lord Houghton. So vast was the crowd that it was impossible for any one speaker to make himself clearly heard. It was not the speeches, however, but the scene which that immense meeting presented in the great and dimly-lit hall, that moved the imagination of the spectator. Many men, looking across the acre and a half of human faces, were vaguely struck by the magnificence of the spectacle which was offered to them. It was left to Lord Houghton, in a few happily-chosen words spoken towards the close of the meeting, to express with inimitable grace what all had thus felt. He likened the scene before him, with its multitudinous sea of faces stretching away into the dim and cavernous depths of the vast workshop, to one of Martin's grandiose pictures, and the simile at once struck home to all who heard it as being the truest and most apt that could have been used. It was often given to him thus, by a single phrase or a few well-chosen words, to give utterance to thoughts which were struggling for expression in a thousand breasts. He had ceased to write poetry; yet all the feeling and the imagination of the poet would assert itself in many of these little speeches of his.

In the winter he had the great pleasure of seeing

the restoration of his house completed, and his first action, after the Hall had again become fit to receive guests, was to invite a party of friends, old and new, to partake of his hospitality. On the 6th of January, 1879, the reopening of the house, or rather of that portion of it which had been destroyed by fire, was celebrated by a dinner given in the newly-completed drawing-room, which, as the morning-room of old days, had witnessed so many notable gatherings. Among those who were there were two of his oldest and dearest friends, Mrs. Procter and Mr. Venables.

It was shortly after Fryston had been restored that he spoke to me of the state of his health, and of the effect which advancing age had upon his spirits and pursuits. "I feel," said he, "as young as I ever did, and I can enjoy everything I ever enjoyed; besides that, I can do just as much as I ever did. The only difference is, that it takes more time and costs more money than it used to do when I was younger." He could travel as far, he explained, but he could not travel as fast as formerly; and he needed comforts and the attendance of servants which had been unnecessary in the days of his strength. That he would not give in, would not surrender to the advance of age, he seemed fully determined, nor did he ever waver in this resolution to the very last, but fought a brave fight against increasing weakness and infirmity.

A few extracts from his letters to Henry Bright, almost his only regular correspondent outside his family during the year 1879, may be fitly inserted here:—

To Henry Bright.

January 31*st.*

When I was in France they told me the change in their Government would be very easily effected; I did not credit them with doing it in 6¾ hours.

April 10*th.*

Had Bret Harte to breakfast to-day; very light in hand and agreeable; town so thin of letters that it was no use to make a party for him.

June 22*nd.*

Not "poor Prince Imperial," but poor Empress.* That goddess Nemesis is a brute; she is all right in her place, but should not be so savage. I hear the poor lady is dying.

June 30*th.*

Change of scene.† Our patron the Duc d'Aumale arrived on Monday, and wishes to have the Philobiblon Breakfast at Strawberry Hill, on Tuesday the 8th. Prince Leopold has joined the Society.

July 2*nd.*

The Duc d'Aumale has a crotchet about not coming to England at the time the Prince's body arrives; so the Strawberry Hill fête is put off.

Crewe Hall, September 11*th.*

The Bishop of Manchester has won all hearts here. He is a capital specimen of the busy Bishop—something between an Apostle and a bagman. He preached on music yesterday; but told us to beware of singing women, alluding to the old Hebrew Nautch girls, I suppose.

---

* The Prince Imperial had been killed in Zululand.

† The Philobiblon Breakfast was to have been held at his house.

Dunfermline, October 16*th.*

I and Florence are descending to England, having had our Indian summer in magnificent scenery. I spent three days with the painter Millais at Dunkeld, where he was enacting the sportsman with a lovely river without fish and a moorland with moderate grouse. His future son-in-law arrived from Zululand, with the assegai that had wounded him somewhat severely. We go from here to Alnwick Castle.

Oct. 22*nd.*

Yesterday I dined with Prince Leopold, whom I found charming. There was a ball in the evening, where about 300 ladies of the unloveliest appearance paid their respects to Royalty in high dresses, which is as much contrary to etiquette as if we had been in frock coats. It is only permitted to Republicans to be thus punctiliously and over-chastely attired. They must show themselves to monarchy.

During the summer an event of great interest and importance in the history of his family was the engagement of his son to Miss Sibyl Graham, daughter of Sir Frederick and Lady Hermione Graham of Netherby.

In the autumn he paid a short visit to Paris, and in December went to Ireland.

To Henry Bright.

March 22*nd.*

My son's marriage is fixed for the earlier part of June. I met Julian Hawthorne at dinner yesterday, and was much struck with his handsomeness. He talked, too, very intelligently about his father's life at Concord, &c. Lowell is gone back to Spain to his sick wife. He seems delighted with his position, as is Bret Harte with his at Glasgow. I don't understand how the mercantile Americans stand their commercial affairs at great ports being entrusted to these amateurs; the diplomatic posts do not matter, as they have no diplomacy.

The spring of 1880 witnessed the general election with the triumphant return of Mr. Gladstone to power. Lord Houghton sympathised entirely with the Liberals in the conflict, and was delighted at the result.

Letter to his Daughter.

Athenæum Club, April 6th, 1880.

DEAREST AMY,—You see we are all right in the West Riding, and I am not sorry that Sir Andrew Fairbairn heads the poll. I was dining at the Bischoffheim's, in a nest of titled Tories, when Gladstone's victory was announced. Lady A. and I were the only two to cheer. The Queen comes back on the 17th, and will meet her Prime Minister on the 18th. He will, as a matter of form, advise her to send for Granville, who, I believe, will tell her to send for Gladstone. Dilke breakfasted with me this morning, of course in high spirits. He will certainly be in the Cabinet, which will be a hard nut for —— to crack. I am told Lowe is to come into the House of Lords.

Travellers' Club, April 29th, 1880.

DEAREST AMY,—An amusing party at Lady Cork's. The Duke of Bedford says, "My Tory wife has taken office under Gladstone." Most of the appointments are approved, except the Ripon's.* I am sorry personally; it will kill both of them. Hartington said to me, "I should like to change places with him," but there is nobody else. Goschen is much complimented on refusing everything.

To Henry Bright.

May 3rd, 1880.

I do not think ——— has managed the *Pall Mall* business adroitly. Greenwood has many friends in political and social life, and the new régime will start under bad auspices.

* Lord Ripon had been appointed Governor-General of India.

The composition of the Government is generally approved, with the criticism that Mr. Dodson and Lord Spencer are superfluous members of the Cabinet. There is also much surprise at Trevelyan having been offered nothing. It seems Gladstone never forgave his throwing up some small office he held.

Lord Houghton had been a regular contributor to the *Pall Mall Gazette* for many years. It had now passed from the editorship of Mr. Greenwood to that of Mr. Morley, between whom and Lord Houghton a warm friendship existed. The latter, as the reader has seen, had written pretty constantly for the *Fortnightly Review* whilst Mr. Morley edited it, and he was altogether friendly not only to the policy but to the proprietor as well as the editor of the *Pall Mall Gazette* under its new management. But his hand was no longer so facile as it had once been, writing was becoming more and more difficult to him, and with all his good wishes for the paper in its new form, he was no longer able to contribute to it as he had done when it was in the hands of Mr. Smith and Mr. Greenwood. It was about this time that Mr. Morley, writing to him on the subject of a promised contribution to the *Fortnightly*, told a little story which shows how widespread were Houghton's friendships.

"Cobden, I find, had his first interview with Louis Napoleon at your table on his escape from Ham. The next time he saw L. N. was when he converted him to Free Trade as Emperor."

His son's marriage was fixed for the beginning of June. It necessarily occupied not a little of his thoughts.

Among the many letters of congratulation which he received one was from Miss Nightingale, the friend of many years.

Miss Nightingale to Lord Houghton.

London, May 18*th,* 1880.

MY DEAR FRIEND,—I *will* give you joy, I *do* give you joy, and I condole with you too as you desire on your boy's marriage. Such promise—not only promise—such proof of so much being in him, it seems a pity that he should not have served his apprenticeship to hard work, which not alone but generally forms the best foundation for the future edifice if there is plenty of stuff. For that he will do something great for his country— and what times are these?—we do not allow ourselves to doubt for one moment. On the other hand, there is something very inspiring in the faithful love, the early and the late, when two always say "we." I remember when I was a girl, Madame Hoche in Paris, widow of General Hoche, after the first year of marriage (far away be the omen!) to her dying day always said "*nous*," she never called him to her only child "*ton père.*" I think one has known such instances of two in one through a long life together, God in both and both in one; but then the wife must help the husband in work, not prevent him. May such a life be given to our young pair; may all the true blessings be theirs, and may it be theirs to be a blessing to many in these the most stirring times of this or any day! And after these are over may it be given them " world beyond world to visit and to bless " together. Can one wish them more?

What worlds there are even in this world? There is India, which a century of statesmanship and a wilderness of statesmen would not be too much to set even on the first step; what have we done for the people of India? There is a country farther away from us than India. In one end of London there are whole lands unvisited and unblessed by us in England. There is

Ireland, there is Liverpool, and the big towns; there is education; there is pauperism. Suppose this Whitsuntide were a really new Whitsuntide to the world, a new intellectual and moral inspiration, a new creation? How we need it! how we might have it if we chose! Is there any reason but our own fault why we should not have apostles of agriculture now for India, out of whose soil we take twenty millions a year and give nothing back, or to save a thousand a year here or even a hundred there take back the little we have given? Why should there not be a political and an administrative Holy Spirit with a new birth in all these vast vital interests? I agree and I do not agree in what you say about the real education young men get in the society of married women. I think I see creeping over, not only women but men, a forsaking of solid practical administrative things for glittering politics; a belief in substituting a vague general (so-called) "influence" for real practical acquaintance with the ways the world's business is managed, and the ways it might be managed. It is so easy, so attractive, talking and declaiming politics like a German newspaper; it is so difficult, so unattractive, to know really and to administer, whether public or private things, so as to bring about effectively a high end. People actually talk now as if they thought that a good wife would enable a Viceroy of India to reform the crying Land Tenures; and there is something of the breath of magazining in everything, in which the inkbottles, guileless of all accurate knowledge of all but "good motives," gracefully write of what they know nothing about.

But this is a strange "Wedding March." Believe that I would, if I could, contribute the sweetest music to inspire the footsteps of the beautiful marriage pair. My love, please, to the two daughters from the bottom of my heart. You kindly ask after me. After twenty-three years of overwork and illness, of which the last six have been without one day's rest of body or mind, I am quite broken down, more than I knew myself, and have had to go away twice for a little silence. Alas, how work halts! I think I am "done" as to work.

Fare you very well, and believe me,
Ever yours very truly,
FLORENCE NIGHTINGALE.

Lord Houghton to Henry Bright.

June 4*th.*

I send a *Morning Post* of Robert's marriage. It was the most childlike wedding I ever saw. There was a profusion of presents—over two hundred. The tenants sent some beautiful plate and jewellery.

To the Same.

June 19*th (my* 71*st birthday).*

I am fresh (in a proper sense) from a charming Philobiblon, including Lowell and Layard. The Prince of Wales asked me to go with him to Holyhead and Trentham; but my Apostles' Dinner prevented me. I saw Robert and his bride yesterday on his way through town, and I go to the christening of Lord Galway's daughter Violet to-morrow. So the world goes.

A few weeks later he paid a visit to France, and was the guest of the Comte de Paris at the Château d'Eu.

To Miss Jane Milnes.

Château d'Eu, Seine Inférieure, July 23*rd,* 1880.

DEAREST JANE,—You will like a few lines from this royal residence. It was built by the Ducs de Guise, and the trees planted by them are still its chief ornament. Of course, the house is much changed; but the apartment of the Grande Demoiselle remains exactly as she designed it and lived in it, bed and all. During the great Revolution it belonged to the Duc de Ponthièvre, and the poor Duchesse de Lamballe passed her youth here. There is only a small party, the chief person being the Duchesse de Montpensier, who has suffered so terribly in her family. After having lost three sons, she has lost, in the last three years, two daughters, one the young Queen of Spain. She is a noble lady, the picture of dignified sorrow. The Comtesse de Paris is most amiable, and Amy gets on very well with her and a daughter of fifteen. We got to Paris, St. James's Hotel, Rue St. Honoré, on Saturday. The only *désagrément* has been that I was robbed at the Calais Station of my pocket-book with £25 in it, my year's diary, and the only photo I had of Annabel in her younger life.

With Amy's love, I am,
Your affectionate
H^N.

From Paris he went on to Vichy, and after taking the waters there made a round of visits in Germany, including an excursion to Oberammergau, where the Passion Play was being performed.

Lord Houghton to George von Bunsen.

Hotel de Parc, Vichy, Aug. 1st, 1880.

MY DEAR GEORGE,—I am here for a short cure on my way to the Passion Spiel, and I write to you for a practical purpose it is to ask whether you are likely to be in Germany in the earlier half of September. I have half promised Münster to pay him a visit, and I should not like to be near you without seeing you and yours. And I have never seen the new Museum at Berlin, so please give me a line by return of post as to this matter. I have paired in favour of the Irish Bill, which I see has been rejected by a very large majority, as indeed it deserved to be; it had neither principle nor practice to recommend it.

I have been staying with the Comte de Paris, and have seen the chief Buonapartists and Gambetta and others. France has a *mauvais moment* to get over ; but this large Opportunist majority is a great security, especially as it will do much to bring the Senate into harmony with the Chamber.

I cannot but connect Gladstone's illness with our Indian disaster. It is very serious, involving, besides the present loss, a large and novel future difficulty.

Yours affectionately,
HOUGHTON.

Lord Houghton to George von Bunsen.

Vichy, August 15*th*, 1880.

MY DEAR GEORGE,—I look forward with great delight to seeing you again. I see that the great Prussian manœuvres take place the second week of September. Though not a young man, or capable of fatigue like your Emperor or your Moltke, I should not dislike to see a little of them if they took place in the neighbourhood of Berlin, and I would desire my red coat to be sent to me from London to your care.

I go to-morrow to M. D'Haussonville's at the Château de Coppet, near Geneva, to stay a week. Please give me a line there. I spend the following week in Alsace, where I am curious to see something of the state of the population.

With kindest remembrances to Madame.

HOUGHTON.

The Same to the Same.

Oberammergau, August 29*th*, 1880,

MY DEAR GEORGE,—I have a letter from Count Münster saying he has to leave home on the 13th, and does not know when he will return, so I go to him from Friday to Saturday next till I come to you, which I propose to do on the 9th and 10th if that quite suits. I have sent your address to my tailor to send my red coat, on which I suppose Bismarck levies a protective duty. If you have anything necessary to say you can telegraph. The play is different from my anticipations; there is nothing dramatic about it, though the actors are fairly good, but it is wonderfully pictorial, and you see Van Eyck, and Rubens, and Salvador, and Raphael, in life. I am lodging with "Christus," who has nothing of the traditional figure, but much dignity of his own.

Yours affectionately,

HOUGHTON.

The Same to the Same.

Munich, September 3rd, 1880.

MY DEAR GEORGE,—Thanks for your two letters; I shall be with you on the 8th, probably early. . . . . I have been passing the day with Döllinger, old but interesting. He said ultramontanism is dyin out in Germany, which I do not believe.

Yours sincerely,

HOUGHTON.

To his Daughter Florence.

Villa Arco, Tegernsee, September 2nd, 1880.

This is Lord Acton's lovely place, and the Wittgensteins are opposite. Aunt Harriette and Amy were to have come, but —— had an attack which they thought was scarlet fever. It was a false alarm. They go to Salzburg and Linz, and down the Danube to Vienna. I go to the Münsters to-morrow; but it is more safe for you to write to George Bunsen's, 1, Maienstrasse, Berlin, where I shall be the middle of the week I saw the Ammergau play comfortably, being in the house of the man that acts Jesus Christ. He is a delightful man, but too old for the part. The whole thing was rather effective than affecting; few English there, Sir Baldwin Leighton, Lady Tavistock, Lady Stanley, Lady G. Lennox, all I knew.

His elder daughter accompanied her aunt on a long visit to the East during the autumn and winter.

Lord Houghton to his Daughter.

Berlin, September 16*th,* 1880.

DEAREST AMY,—I am thirsting for news of you. I told Aunt Harriette I would pay for a telegram from Pera, which I hoped to have got on Monday, and I might even have had a letter from Vienna by this time. I am *mal tombé* here for social purposes, everybody being absorbed in the manœuvres; and it will gratify your filial fears to know that no civilian is allowed to follow the suite on horseback. I was therefore compelled to witness the two great parades of twenty-five thousand men each from Bunsen's commodious carriage. I have dined with the Emperor and the Crown Prince, full-dress formal banquets, curious to see, but nothing more. I have, however, had conversations with Moltke, and other important people. Bismarck is not here.

The Emperor is wonderful in vigour of body and mind. There is a theory that he lost so much blood in the last shooting that he has had strength enough to develop a new life and may live any time. There is not a sign of languor or suffering about him at eighty-three. The Empress was very kind, and regretted not seeing more of me; she goes to-day to Baden. I return next week, perhaps by Hamburg to Hull, and expect to be at Fryston on Friday. The political event here is the visit of the Duke of Cambridge, the first since the robbery of Hanover. I remember once saying to him that I was sure he would not dine with me for fear of meeting Garibaldi or the King of Prussia, and he said, "It might be so, and he did not know which of the two he hated most." They make a great deal of him here now.

The Connaughts are quite domesticated here. He asked me what I thought of my friend Forster now, and I didn't know what to say.* She is a sweet little woman.

Nothing can be kinder than these dear people (the Bunsens). I have a beautiful room with a four-post bed, and Edward next me. Then he lionises me so intelligently. I am disappointed

---

* Mr. Forster had just made his speech attacking the House of Lords for their rejection of the Compensation for Disturbance Bill.

in the remains from Olympia, hardly worth the trouble of discovering them. Odo Russell is very friendly, but still a Russell.

Best regards to the Goschens. I am glad I have not his work to do, tell him.* You ought to have had delightful weather; it is now autumnal here, but not disagreeable.

Your and Aunt Harriette's affectionate

HOUGHTON.

Berlin, September 18*th,* 1880.

DEAREST AMY,—Yours just arrived, so I write off at once. I go to England Monday by Düsseldorf and Flushing, arriving on Wednesday in London, at Fryston on Friday. I am glad I came here, though the military affairs have absorbed everybody, and I have seen nothing of the Court beyond the formal dinners. But the Moreas (?) and the Greek discoveries at Pergamos and Olympia are worth coming to see of themselves, and the town is now very fine.

Your impression of Stamboul is absolutely correct. There is nothing Oriental about it except the population; it is a huge Greek village, with those ugly monotonous minarets; but I thought the forms of the hills of the Bosphorus very beautiful, and you will, I do not doubt, have moments of glorious colour.

Lothar v. Bunsen arrived from London yesterday. His father is very anxious what to do with him. I think you will find Goschen very busy. They say here he works his people very hard, but Mrs. G. ought to have time to show you about and to enjoy your company. I judge from your story that you did not suffer much from the sea.

HOUGHTON.

To his Son.
Bei G. v. Bunsen, Maienstrasse, Berlin,
September 11*th.*

I have yours of the 8th, so if you give me a line by return I shall get it here. We have Dufferin, very well but rather

* Mr. Goschen was at this time Ambassador Extraordinary to the Porte.

subdued in spirits. . . . After so much not largely-informed fashionable society, I am glad you are going to a house where you must learn something whether you like or no. Lord —— has already sent to Berlin for information for his speech at the Social Science Congress in August next.

He enjoyed his visit to Berlin more owing to his being brought once more into close intimacy with a host whom he esteemed so highly, than for any other reason. Duly wearing his red coat at the great review before the Emperor, he and his friend Mr. von Bunsen found their carriage placed in the front rank of the row of spectators, and he was able to watch the grand military spectacle with the intelligent interest he always displayed on such occasions. Among other eminent men whom he met was Von Moltke, with whom he had a conversation of special interest. There was, however, one unpleasant *contretemps* in connection with this visit to Berlin. He met the Crown Prince of Austria (the ill-fated Prince Rudolph) at dinner. The Prince was delighted with Lord Houghton's talk, and they had a long conversation, which by-and-by turned upon serious political topics. What passed between them was mentioned by Lord Houghton only to a few persons in whom he had confidence, and that merely in a casual manner. But to his great surprise and mortification he subsequently saw a version of his conversation with the Crown Prince published at length in a German newspaper, an exaggerated meaning being attached to the words of the Prince on that ever-burning topic the Eastern Question. Houghton promptly wrote to the

Times to disclaim any part in this violation of confidence, and at the same time to protest against the unfair interpretation put on the words of the Crown Prince. The affair annoyed him seriously.

To George v. Bunsen.

Fryston, November 1st, 1880.

MY DEAR GEORGE,—The Hermes arrived in safety and is now bending that lovely head at me. The enclosed may interest you. I do not know who is ——'s adviser in German politics. You will probably have seen from the foreign correspondence of the *Times*, and my letter, the scrape which the editor of the *Cologne Gazette* got me into by not only repeating but exaggerating and commenting on my conversation with Prince Rudolph. No English editor would have reproduced a private conversation without the permission of the conversee; and I fear that the consequences to me will be serious in my intercourse with both Austrian and Belgian diplomatists. I am never likely to go again to the Court of Berlin or Vienna, so that that does not much matter. Amicia is in Palestine. She has had a most delightful journey, and will think she understands all about the Revelations from having seen Patmos in the distance, and Paul's philosophy from having tasted fish out of the Sea of Galilee. I hope you like Rome better than you thought you should. The slope of the Capitol is ever a home for you.

With kindest regards to your delightful family,

I am, your affectionate

HOUGHTON.

Another of his oldest friends was taken from him in December.

To his Son.

Poltimore, Exeter, Dec. 7th, 1880.

DEAREST ROBERT,—Just arrived here all right. I am much distressed at Colville's death [Sir James Colville]. We only heard of it yesterday at the Literary Society, when we were sitting down to dinner, and expecting him to come in. Both the Lord Chancellor and the Chief Justice seemed much shocked, and spoke very highly of him. . . . I had a pleasant two nights at Mentmore. I do not know whether Harcourt or I talked the loudest. Rosebery is devoted to his baby, whom he carries about all day. . . .

Your affectionate
H^N.

To his Daughter.

Torquay, Dec. 29th, 1880.

DEAREST AMY,—Your letter received yesterday gave great joy to man and womankind. We shall, however, be glad of your next, as the tent-work in Palestine, and the hills of Jericho is a hot-bed of fever, and the banks of the Red Sea are very pestiferous.   I have written about Egypt in my letters to Alexandria, and shall like to fancy you hoisted up the Pyramids and looking at the noseless, melancholy Sphinx. There is no historic doubt that the Pyramid looked down on Joseph just as it does on us, and that Moses, when a theological student, sat under the obelisk of Memphis. How you will delight in the Egyptian evenings! I have a short article on Dizzy's new novel in the *Fortnightly*.

HOUGHTON.

A. C. Swinburne to Lord Houghton.

The Pines, Putney Hill, S.W., Dec. 18th, 1880.

DEAR LORD HOUGHTON,—Though you did not encourage my design when I told you of it on your last visit here, of a memorial poem on Landor, I feel none the less bound in common gratitude to send the first copy I send to anyone of the book which contains it, to the man whose kindness procured me the great honour and delight of being received as a friend by one of the three great men who seemed to me as a schoolboy the three above all others alive whom I should most like when a man to meet and do homage to. To Mazzini Karl Blind introduced me; to Victor Hugo some very boyish articles of my own seemed enough to make me worthy of his notice; but I owe it to you that Landor ever honoured me with the name of his "dear friend." I wish I had something worthier to send in proof of gratitude to you and reverence for him. Do you know the dead cathedral city which I have tried to describe in the last poem in this book—Dunwich in Suffolk? The whole picture is from life—salt marshes, ruins, and bones protruding seawards through the soil of the crumbling sandbanks. What a divine and transcendent poem is Tennyson's "Rizpah"! But you will see what I think of it if you care to look into the *Fortnightly* in ten days time.

Ever yours truly,
A. C. SWINBURNE.

To Henry Bright.

New Year's Day, 1881.

An odious year that 1880. Will the next be any better? I had to write my notes on "Endymion" in a great hurry, and was very poorly, so it is full of printer's blunders, which I will correct in the copy I shall send you. I think that —— is getting duller and duller; but then so is the world, and so, too, perhaps is

Your obedient servant
HOUGHTON.

Letters to his Daughter Amy.

Athenæum Club, Feb. 8th, 1881.

DEAREST AMY,—You will have heard of the Irish Parliamentary storm, which I was not fortunate enough to see, having business at Manchester at the time. There is now a dead calm, and the Home Rulers speak quietly and rationally. Whether there will be another outburst is another matter.

Carlyle's death has been received as an almost national solemnity. The Dean, of course, tried to get him for the Abbey, but he left his sternest injunctions that his body should be taken to the railway without the least demonstration, and that he should be buried, not beside his wife, but by his father and mother at Ecclefechan, in Dumfriesshire. His niece wrote this to me, thinking I might wish to join any solemnity. This is very characteristic. The Dean proposed for him a service in the Abbey without bringing him there, but the family did not think it permissible; he preached, however, a very fine sermon on him. A sort of life, mostly autobiographical, edited by Froude, will come out very shortly. Some of the newspaper articles have been very good, but none written by anyone who knew him long as I did.

We thought of you in your pleasant sunshine in our long snows that we have here at Fryston. We bore the storm very well; no pipes burst, and the drawing-room kept very warm and comfortable. The air was very equable and fairly warm. I thought the general impression of Egypt melancholy; it looks like something intermediate which was stunted before it was destroyed; but it is a thing to be seen once, and cannot be forgotten.

London, Feb. 19th, 1881.

DEAREST AMY,—This is probably the last letter I shall write to Africa, and my next is likely to be to " Naples, *Poste Restante.*" You will hardly resist stopping there when you see it from the curve of the railway from Brindisi to Rome. It will be irresistible even if you only stop to see Pompeii, the third dead world you will have seen—and it is Greek, not Roman. I do not suppose any Roman town was like it. I come up to London next week for two or three days. We expect to have the Irish Bill next week, and a debate, brought on by Lord Lytton, against the abandonment of Candahar. The Grahams are all unhappy at the death of Sir R. Musgrave, a double connection. He dined with the Speaker on Wednesday, and died the Sunday following. Henry Brougham is the guardian of his children.

London, March 11*th,* 1881.

DEAREST AMY,—I hope Aunt Harriette got my telegram sent on Wednesday. I sent it, as it might alter your plans after Greece. I also wrote to her very lately. I have been much shocked at the fatal accident that has befallen my old comrade in life, James Spedding. He was run down by a cab, and died in St. George's Hospital in four days without much suffering. Hanmer died yesterday, hardly a friend.

The talk of the town is the autobiography of Carlyle, printed by Froude. It comes very harshly on the world, as it represents only the critical and satiric side of his character. Nobody is spoken well of but myself and dear mamma, who is "all kindness." The book, however, is most interesting to those who knew him and her as we did. Mrs. Greville's "angel mother" is dead, and I send you Swinburne's lines on her—to my mind very touching, and good verse besides.

I daresay Alexandria is as dirty and dull as ever. There is a pretty sea-place, Ramleh, which you will probably go to for a day or two. I remember the Monteiths spent some months there.

Politics are in a very chaotic state. Forster is somewhat happier, but he has not got out of his battles unwounded. After all, I believe Irish landlords are better off than English; more may be shot, but fewer will be ruined. You will have seen the coast I recommended once, the Isthmus of Corinth, and that beautiful sail under Olympia. I only wish you were both strong enough to take the ride which I describe in my poem of Delphi over Mount P.; it is the most beautiful in the world, with the descent on the Sacred Way. It is, too, a charming sail from Patras to Corfu, through the islands; and from Corfu you have your choice of Ancona, Venice, Trieste and Dalmatia, including the amphitheatre of Pola and the ruins of Spalato. Whistler has done some delightful sketches of Venice; he calls them pastels.

Your affectionate
HOUGHTON.

Manchester, March 16*th*, 1881.

DEAREST AMY,—It is amusing to write from Manchester to Athens, though I do not know that I have anything to add to my last. You seem to have seen Cairo well and leisurely. I am not sorry you missed the Rock Temple, as I did.

This horror of the Czar's murder seems to have no compensation of historic or political advantage. The *Pall Mall* says it is the most causeless regicide since that of Henry IV. The poor Emperor lived in horrible terror. When last at Windsor, he fired a revolver in the night, and hit one of his own servants. I remember him as Czarevitch at the time they said he wanted to marry one of the ——'s. The person I most pity is his second wife, who will be left out in the cold; but he will probably have given her a great deal of money. . . . Athens must be very different from when I last saw it in 1843. I had been there the last year of the Turkish occupation. I remember going to visit the Pasha at that time. There was a mosque in the middle of the Parthenon. The Temple of Jupiter Olympius rests most vividly in my mind; you may remember it is the model of it. The plain of Marathon, with the mound under which the Persians lie, is deeply impressive. I hope there will be no danger of brigands to prevent you from going there. My finances are not prepared to ransom you if there is. My impression is, that the Greeks will not get Joannina—which they call the cradle of their independence—but they will get Thessaly and Crete, which is a great development, and will not mix them up with the confusions of Albania. It will be quite curious to see Greece in arms. I have no doubt it is very theatrical. This Russian murder will shut up the Court. The smallness of Greece will strike you strongly after Egypt.

HOUGHTON.

Mention has already been made of the old feud between Lord Houghton and Sir Antonio Panizzi. Mr.

Fagan's "Life of Panizzi" had appeared about this time, and Lord Houghton reviewed it in the *Academy;* not in an acrid spirit, but with perfect candour as to his own opinion of the distinguished man, whose appointment as the head of a great national institution he had always regarded as a slight upon Englishmen. The following correspondence with Mr. Gladstone paved the way for Houghton's appointment as one of the trustees of the British Museum—a position he would have attained long before, if it had not been for his quarrel with Panizzi:—

Lord Houghton to Mr. Gladstone.

Private. Fryston Hall, April 17th, 1881.

MY DEAR GLADSTONE,—When, after the death of *our* Bishop of Oxford, the Archbishop and other official trustees proposed that I should succeed him at the British Museum, you wrote to me stating that my difference with Panizzi affected your judgment on the matter, and I did not press it further. I never concealed my disinclination to the man, and I have put it in print, with my name, in the enclosed article; the published letters of Merimêe confirm my impression.

I take the opportunity of informing you and Mrs. Gladstone of the engagement of my elder daughter to Mr. FitzGerald, the Director of Finance to the Khedive of Egypt. He is in the Indian Service, in which he has held high posts; and has been lent to the new Khedive to rehabilitate the Egyptian finance, in which it has been said he has been eminently successful.

She is of an age to make her own destiny, but the departure will be very painful to me.

I am yours sincerely,

HOUGHTON.

Enclosed in the letter was a copy of the *Academy* of December 4th, 1880, containing Lord Houghton's review of Mr. Fagan's " Life of Sir Antonio Panizzi."

Mr. Gladstone to Lord Houghton.

10, *Downing Street, Whitehall, April* 18*th.*

MY DEAR HOUGHTON,—I am sure you would not wish to revive our discussion about Panizzi. There is, indeed, on my side a sensible but very slight approximation to you—in one sense rather marked. I quite agree that as to the trusteeship " that which letteth" is thus far taken out of the way as to the present vacancy. I cannot yet say that your name can be brought up for consideration. There is a *Leviathan* in the way. I shall, however, not lose sight of the subject. It would give me sincere pleasure to see you a trustee. Many thanks for your intimation. Your daughter has our warm good wishes; the bridegroom, whom we do not know personally, our not less cordial congratulations.

Ever yours,
W. E. GLADSTONE.

Mr. Gladstone to Lord Houghton.

10, *Downing Street, May* 4*th,* 1881.

MY DEAR HOUGHTON,—I am very glad to have been *at length* enabled to effect an arrangement under which, with the approval of the principal trustees, I am in a condition to propose you on Friday to the electing trustees as a trustee of the Museum. I hope it will be agreeable to you that I should take this step.

Believe me
Very sincerely yours,
W. E. GLADSTONE.

Whatever the Leviathan referred to by Mr. Gladstone may have been, it did not, as it turned out, prevent Lord Houghton's election. On the 6th of May he received an official intimation from the principal librarian that he had that day been unanimously elected one of the trustees of the Museum.

Edward Fitzgerald to Lord Houghton.
Woodbridge, May 10*th*, 1881.

DEAR LORD HOUGHTON,—I think I have sent you a yearly letter of some sort or other for several years, so it has come upon me once again. I have nothing to ask of you except how you are. I should just like to know that, including "yours" in you. Just a very few words will suffice, and I daresay you have no time for more. I have so much time that it is evident I have nothing to tell, except that I have just entered upon a military career in so far as having become much interested in the battle of Waterloo, which I just remember a year after it was fought, when a solemn anniversary took place in a neighbouring parish where I was born, and the village carpenter came to my father to borrow a pair of Wellington boots for the lower limbs of a stuffed effigy of Buonaparte, which was hung on a gibbet, and guns and pistols were discharged at him, while we and the parson of the parish sat in a tent where we had beef and plum pudding and loyal toasts. To this hour I remember the smell of the new-cut hay in the meadow as we went in our best summer clothes to the ceremony. But now I am trying to understand whether the Guards or the 52nd Regiment deserved most credit for *écraséing* the Imperial Guard. Here is a fine subject to address you on in the year 1880! Let it go, for nothing; but just tell me how you are, and believe me, with some feeling of old if not very close intimacy, Yours sincerely,
EDWARD FITZGERALD.

The reference in one of Mr. Gladstone's letters to Lord Houghton's elder daughter calls for a word of explanation. During her stay in the East she had met at Cairo Mr. Gerald FitzGerald, a gentleman occupying a responsible position in the India Civil Service, whose services had for a time been transferred to the Egyptian Government in connection with the Department of Finance. They had, with the consent of Lord Houghton, become engaged, and their marriage was looked for at an early date.

The marriage of his daughter with Mr. Gerald Fitz Gerald, which took place in the summer, was one of the last occasions on which Lord Houghton succeeded in bringing around him a great gathering of the friends of his lifetime. Those who were present at the reception after the wedding can testify to the fact that the company assembled to congratulate the daughter of the host was one of the most remarkable that even London could have witnessed. It seemed as though on this occasion Lord Houghton was anxious that all sides of his busy and varied life should be represented, and accordingly he had brought together, in the house of his relatives the Thornhills, in Bruton Street, friends, old and new, belonging to all classes in society, of all creeds, professions, and opinions. I mention that remarkable gathering here, because, looking back at it, it seems to have furnished, as it were, a bird's-eye view of his social life. Statesmen, and men and women of high social rank, both at home and abroad, mingled with authors, artists, journalists, men of affairs, and others who had no claim to be present, except that which was founded on the kindness of their host. It was, I say, the last occasion on which Lord Houghton played the host on a large scale in that London which he knew so well; and it is pleasant to think that it was connected with an event so closely associated with his domestic happiness—one which for the moment aroused mingled feelings in his own mind, as he saw the daughter who since his wife's death had been his most constant companion, transferred from English life to a distant country, but which more and more, as his few remaining years passed, he recognised as a blessing, both for himself and her.

To Miss Louisa Milnes.

Travellers' Club, July 29*th,* 1881.

DEAREST LOUISA,—I let the young congratulate the old on continued life. I do not care enough about it myself to do so. . . You will have read of the strange murder in the Brighton tunnel. I passed in the preceding train; but there is no fear of a country gentleman being thought to have any money about him.

Your affectionate

H<small>N</small>.

To his Daughter Mrs. FitzGerald.

Manchester, October 26*th,* 1881.

Your pleasant four sheets arrived at Netherby in time for me to read them before I left yesterday morning to come here. You will be grieved to hear that dear Henry Bright is in great danger of lung disease, and is ordered abroad next week. I have strongly advised Madeira; but he so much dreads the voyage, having already broken a small blood-vessel at sea, that Mentone is to be tried. His friends have little hope. It will be a sad loss to me; he is my best friend of latter life.

Lord Houghton had sent Mr. John Bright a copy of the collected edition of his poems.

Mr. John Bright to Lord Houghton.

Kelso, N.B., November 25th, 1881.

MY DEAR LORD HOUGHTON,—It is very kind of you to remember me at this time, and to send me the gift of your two volumes. I thank you warmly for your kindness. I came down here on Monday, and the time of the journey passed rapidly as I read portions of your first volume. I have a great love of poetry, but I suspect few have less capacity for writing it than I have. What makes it easy to some and impossible to others I cannot understand. I console myself with the belief that it is necessary for some of us to write and speak only in prose. And so you are to lose your now only daughter. It is cruel, but inevitable. I have four daughters now scattered and gone, and my house is almost as lonely as yours. My boys remain with me, but they do not make up for the loss of my girls. I hope your daughters will be happy, and that their happiness will do something to lessen the misery of having lost them. I remember the pleasant evenings at Fryston, and I can imagine how changed is now the scene; but I will not further moralise.

Believe me

Always sincerely yours,

JOHN BRIGHT.

His younger daughter Florence was now engaged to the Honourable Arthur Henniker.

Mrs. FitzGerald had accompanied her husband to Egypt, and was at this time in Cairo. Happily for Lord Houghton, though he had suffered the loss of his two daughters, and felt it as much as Mr. Bright anticipated, he found no slight recompense in the society of his daughter-in-law, who did her utmost to brighten his home-life, and who, bringing him into contact with new interests and people, stimulated his social instincts, and enabled him to retain the pleasure he had always experienced in former days when he found himself surrounded by friends at Fryston.

The first child had now been born to his son, and a new generation had thus come into existence in the old house, to carry his thoughts and his sympathies to a point in the future beyond any they had hitherto reached. But his heart clung to his daughters, and early in January, in spite of bodily infirmities which might well have deterred him from such a task, he went to Egypt in order to spend a few weeks with Mrs. FitzGerald. His intention was to return by Athens, which he had not seen for many years, and to which he had a warm invitation from the English Minister, Mr. Ford. Whilst in Cairo he witnessed the beginning of the troubles connected with the insurrection under Arabi Pasha—troubles which were to have consequences so momentous.

To his Son.

Cairo, Jan. 30th, 1882.

DEAREST ROBERT,—As Amy writes to Florence, I will only ask you to thank her for her pleasant letter. I hope to hear something definite as to her destiny by the next mail. FitzGerald will probably arrive from Malta the end of this week or the beginning of next. I have pretty well decided to accept Mr. Ford's invitation for Athens, and should leave this on the 14th February, stay there a week, and return by Naples and Rome. I had a long talk with the Khedive about FitzGerald, of whom he spoke with great esteem, and with gratitude for his services to Egypt; but the position of no European, not of the Controllers themselves, is safe in the present current of public opinion. We have had only one or two invitations to dinner, but several pleasant luncheons to travellers, including M. Lesseps and Count Potocki, and Colonel Clarke with his pleasant wife. But the tide of travellers has been seriously checked by the rumours of disturbances and cholera, quite unfounded. I am afraid the Opposition will make capital of Gladstone's minatory policy here, when Malet recommended silence and conciliation.

Your affectionate
H^N.

To his Daughter Florence.
Cairo, Feb. 6th, 1882.

The revolution—a real one—took place on Friday, when the Notabilities came to Cherif Pasha, and said he must agree to their own constitution or resign, and he did so the next day. The Khedive placed the nomination of the War Minister in the hands of the Assembly, who have made Arabi Minister of War, and filled the other places as they chose. The officers, between two and three hundred, assembled yesterday, when the Prime Minister thanked them, and said they would work together for the liberty and independence of Egypt. It now remains to be seen what the English and French Controllers will do. It is thought that they will say that they can no longer be responsible for the finances of the country, and refuse to continue. The future is quite dark. I do not think FitzGerald's office will be attacked at present, but I cannot think he can remain long. The payments to non-Egyptians amount to near £400,000 per annum— rather a strong order. The political excitement has very much suspended society, so I have been a good deal alone with Amy. I shall be the better for a course of Mary's black chips and stodgy omelettes, and the consequent abstinence, after a month of Battiste's* two dinners a day, in which he has never once

* Mr. FitzGerald's French cook.

repeated himself. Henry [his servant] is getting very fat on truffles and *poulet à la Marengo*, and will feel the change. We have a dinner of ten to-day, the first since my coming, and the same next Monday—a farewell. We dined one day with the Blunts in the desert in a tent, on lambs and pistachio nuts, and three Bedouins eating with their fingers. They remarked how brown and healthy Lady Anne looked from her wild life, and what a contrast Amy was from living in the town.

To his Son.

Cairo, Feb. 13*th,* 1882

DEAREST ROBERT,—I have had my farewell audience of the Khedive. Nothing can be better than his disposition, but that is all. . . . They now call Arabi Bey " le Cromwell Egyptien." I was introduced to him at a fête. He is a powerful-looking man. The troops I have seen are very poor, and could not resist ours or the French a moment. FitzGerald left Charlie Beresford and "the Swell of the Ocean" at Malta; very eager to go to Alexandria. Write " *Poste Restante,* Naples."

Your affectionate,

H^N.

Deeply interested as he was in the great crisis in Egyptian history which had now arrived, Lord Houghton could not linger longer at Cairo, as he had engaged himself to Mr. Ford, the English Minister at Athens, for a particular date. When he left Egypt, affairs seemed, to the outward eye, to be settling down with the appointment of Arabi as Minister of War, but so close an observer as he was could not be deceived by the outward calm, and he distinctly perceived that a great change in Egyptian affairs was at hand.

To his Son.

In Quarantine at Piræus, Feb. 15*th,* 9 *a.m.*

That is, in a room with four bare walls and bare boards, a trestle-bed, a table, and a chair. I remember in my early days that the lazarettos of Ancona, Corfu, and Malta were very comfortable: so cannot understand this savagery. But it is only twenty-four hours of observation, and I shall be in Ford's salon at 7 p.m. In the meantime it is so cold that I am writing in bed, and shall not get up till midday.

I had written thus far when the Vice-Consul came in and said we had *pratique*, probably from my being there; on the contrary, I found that this quarantine was altogether taken off, and that I, with my usual luck in small things, had come in the last day. I am, however, comfortably installed in Ford's house, with the Acropolis in front. It looks higher and steeper than I remembered it, and I miss the Venetian Tower, a very fine piece of brickwork, which improved the outline and did no harm to the Parthenon. I will write an "Athenian Letter" (did you ever read them?) in a post or two, and now shortly answer yours. . . .

Alas! the pleasures which he had promised himself from a renewal of his Athenian life were not to fall to his lot. Hardly had he found himself under the hospitable roof of Mr. Ford than Lord Houghton was struck down by the most serious attack of illness he had suffered from since his boyhood. The attack was one of angina pectoris, and placed his life momentarily in imminent danger. His sister Lady Galway, and his daughter Mrs. FitzGerald, were immediately telegraphed for, and both hastened to him, as did also his son. In the meantime he himself wrote, trying to soften the serious character of his illness, in order to prevent any alarm on the part of his family.

To his Son.

British Legation, Athens, Feb. 22*nd.*

DEAREST ROBERT,—I did not like to state the case precisely in my telegram; but the fact is, that the discomforts I mentioned in my last letter culminated in an attack of angina pectoris on Tuesday evening, which might have ended all, but for timely assistance. A doctor was here in ten minutes, and the spasm gave way to injections of morphia into the blood, after half an hour's intense suffering. I thought of Stanley's description of the death of Dr. Arnold, and many other things—for the head remained quite clear. The result is, that the doctor positively forbids me to leave the room till there is a decided change of temperature, which may not be for a fortnight. I have a delightful hospital, and every care; and I hope you will some day express to Ford your obligations for his attention to me. Dr. Schliemann had organised a banquet of all the rank and scholarship of the place for yesterday, and had to make a tremendous eulogy in my absence, to which Ford had to reply. The main object now is to put off as long as possible the recurrence of the disorder. It is very rarely a single attack; but if I have as much warning another time as this, I may hope to be able to keep it off, or mitigate its severity. As I had been at a ball and a breakfast of all the fashion of the place, my illness is "the new thing" of the Agora, and quite a god-send of gossip. It may get to Europe in any form. Write as much of this as you like to Florence, and the Galways, and the aunts. I will write myself to each in a post or two, when I see my way more clearly. I send a vague paragraph to the *Morning Post,* but you can tell any friends. You can read about angina pectoris in any book of pathology. It is a very curious malady, and said to be rare—no women have it; the heart seems beating, but it does not beat—it only stops.

Yours and your wife's affectionate

H^N.

It is needless to comment upon the manner in which he thus gave his son the news, not only of a most critical illness, but of the fate which too certainly lay before him. Once more the "cheery stoicism" of his order, to which Carlyle had long ago referred admiringly, asserted itself.

To his Son.

Athens, February 25th.

DEAREST ROBERT, — Got your kind telegram yesterday; hoped to have started to-morrow *via* Corfu, but the abnormal "beating of my own heart" still continues in a slight degree, and the doctor will not let me go till it quite subsides. There are no boats in the early part of the week, so I am here till Thursday or Friday. I see by the *Times* that I am still expected in Rome on the Severn business; but for that I should cut Rome altogether. The House of Lords seems to have made a feckless demonstration, which Lord Cairns ought not to have let go to a division. I am quite sorry about the mode of *clôture* the Government recommend, though some is absolutely necessary. The initiative of the Speaker seems to me the worst of all the alternatives; and to stop a man for "repetition or irrelevancy" is to check oratory itself. Mr. Fox said : "Mr. Pitt expatiates; I repeat, and it has more effect of the two." I should like to know what the Duke thinks of it. The Ministry here will be decided next week by the choice of the President, so political is it acknowledged to be. It will be amusing to come in for another political crisis. There is only one very able man, and he is too good for the place. I am

Your affectionate

H^N.

To Miss Louisa Milnes.

March 6th, 1882.

DEAREST LOUISA,—I write this on board the packet, in the hope of posting it at Marseilles to-morrow. Harriette has got out at Naples, having had enough of the sea, and joins us tomorrow evening. I shall find my way to London some time next week. I walk well even here, and have, so far as I know, no paralytic symptoms, but the doctors say they may come on with any active exertion, physical or mental; that is, that I should live the life of a dormouse, which is perhaps pleasant, but not dignified or useful. I was admirably taken care of at Athens by Mr. Ford, our Minister, who took us all into his house. He is a Devonshire man. Amy is very happy at Cairo with her friend Miss Palmer, who is still there.

Writing to another friend about the same time, he described his condition in equally cheerful language, stating that he feared that so far from being able to undertake any mountain climbing, he would not even be allowed to walk up the "eminent descent" of St. James's Street—an allusion to Lord Beaconsfield's slight confusion of language in his recently-published novel of "Endymion."

No words can do adequate justice to the kindness he had received under Mr. Ford's roof at Athens—kindness which he remembered gratefully to the end of his life.

Mr. Ford to Lord Houghton.

British Legation, Athens, March 30th.

MY DEAR LORD HOUGHTON,—I am writing from your old room, and thinking of you, and rejoicing sincerely to think you have made so good a journey so far homeward—for the last I heard of you was from Marseilles. I am sure the change of air must have been beneficial to you, and happily you had good weather for the journey. I dined with the King and Queen last Monday, and they talked to me a great deal of you, and expressed the greatest interest in your welfare. There was a great ceremony at the Palace on the same day when the infant prince was baptised. It was an interesting sight; there were as many as nine Greek Archbishops officiating. The little baby was stripped and ducked three times in a big silver tub, after which some mystic rites were gone through, the nine Archbishops and the baby, carried by the Duke of Sparta, walking round the tub three times. It reminded me of the scene of the witches in *Macbeth*. Next week is Holy Week, and the Greeks give themselves up to prayer and mortifying the flesh. There is no particular news to impart. I hope you will remember me most kindly to your son, and believe me,

Ever yours,
F. C. FORD.

The news of his illness brought many letters of inquiry and sympathy from his friends.

George von Bunsen to Lord Houghton.

Berlin, March 20th, 1882.

MY DEAR LORD HOUGHTON,—I cannot bear not writing to you in your troubles, although it seems a more natural thing to bear them with you in silence, hoping and trusting. You are in our daily thoughts. How often have we blessed your brilliant thought at Vichy to announce yourself here last year, and to witness what interested you infinitely more than it did your hosts—Kaiser Wilhelm's military display! Since then we followed your movements—such, in particular, as when you took luncheon with my Lothar at Berry, or when you found work for young MacCarthy at Cairo. There was much beautiful sentiment, as I thought, in your preparing to bring a companion to Keats; and this, alas! you have been prevented from doing. Our official world has taken Ignatieff and Skobeloff quite as seriously as our public; but they kept their counsel—wisely, I think. It improves our position whatever may come. Strange to say, every " Liberal " Russian fondly imagines that Europe ought to flatter Austria out of Bosnia and Herzegovina—peaceably of course. On the 28th my trial for libel—an action of Bismarck's personaliv—comes on at Hirschberg. On some old friend scolding him for this foolish prosecution, he said, "Leave me my sport." Do not answer this letter.

In true affection yours,
G. v. BUNSEN.

Miss Nightingale to Lord Houghton.

London, Easter Day, 1882.

We have been very anxious about you, dear friend, and have followed you every step of your way with our most fervent wishes. May God bless you and raise you up again, as He *has* done this Easter-tide! Ah, how much we all stand in need of being raised up again every day! The sweet savour of your Egyptian saint abides with me always. Give a wedding blessing to your other daughter from her old namesake; but it is hard for you to have to part with her too, and to Ireland, and I do not know how to give you joy. May all success attend her with a good soldier of professional enthusiasm, which is the right thing. The woes of Ireland almost surpass those of India with which I am always occupied.

Fare you very well, dear friend,
FLORENCE NIGHTINGALE.

He reached Fryston safely, and apparently in somewhat better health, and rested there for a few weeks to recruit himself.

Lord Houghton to Mr. Severn.

Fryston, April 16*th,* 1882.

MY DEAR SEVERN,—I am returned home, very well, but obliged to take good care of myself, which is not pleasant. I am now sorry that I did not carry out my Roman plan at all risks. At the worst, Keats would have lain very pleasantly between his friend and his biographer, with a wreath of fresh Athenian violets over his head. I hope to return to town the end of next week. I am,

Yours very truly,

HOUGHTON.

He wrote during the summer an article on "Endymion," at the request of Mr. Morley, for *Macmillan's Magazine*, of which Mr. Morley had just become editor. It was not an easy task in his state of health, and with the difficulty he now found in exertion of any kind; but he could not resist an appeal from an old friend who was undertaking a new venture, and he did his best. Still, he was compelled to relinquish more than one literary task which he had been anxious to execute. Writing in October to his son, he said:—

I am in a sad humour with myself, not having been able to write an article I promised for the *Quarterly*. I knew that my illness had affected my powers of composition, but I hoped that the Scotch air and quiet life might restore them;* but it has not done so, and I find serious writing next to impossible. I doubt the faculty ever coming back either to limbs or ideas.

Yet, though he was thus crippled, he resolutely pursued his social life, resolved that illness should make as little difference as possible in his ordinary habits. During his stay in Scotland he visited at many of the country houses he had known in earlier days; and whatever other effect his illness might have had upon him, those who enjoyed his society found that his memory

* He was on a visit to Lady Ashburton at Loch Luichart.

was just as good as it had ever been, and that he could talk as delightfully as of old of the people and the places he had known in bygone times. Among the visits he paid this autumn was one to Mr. Gladstone.

To his Son.

Hawarden Castle, Chester, Oct. 15*th,* 1882.

DEAREST ROBERT,—You may be easy about my personal security. We have two detectives in the house (one engaged to the cook), and Lord Spencer brought three more yesterday; this is irrespective of the County Police. Lyttelton, Sir J. Adye's *aide-de-camp,* arrived last night straight from Brindisi, full of the last information and the last sight of Arabi, who, he says, behaves with great dignity. Lyttelton is well. He says there is much typhoid fever at Cairo; he left his servants all there. . . . .   Your affectionate

H^N.

In one of the previous letters Lord Houghton mentioned the serious state of his friend Henry Bright. Mr. Bright had happily rallied somewhat from the grave attack which had alarmed his friends, and was able to add at least one more pleasant letter to the many which he had addressed to Lord Houghton during their long friendship. It contained an invitation to him to join Mr. Bright at Cannes, where he was going to winter. The project was one which suited him admirably; and accordingly, in the early spring of 1883, he went to Cannes, and after spending some weeks there in the society of Mr. Bright, went on to Naples, Rome, and Florence, not returning to England until the summer.

Lord Houghton to Henry Bright.

Fryston, Jan. 25th, 1883.

With two such comrades as Acton and yourself at Cannes, and Miss Chamberlain, whom I don't know, to look at, I don't see how I can keep away from Cannes. But I feel myself bound to stay here till the meeting of Parliament, and if you like to take the Villa Scott, and ask me to occupy Gladstone's apartment,* I don't think I can decline. Of course, call on the G. O. M. He likes you yourself, and, besides, is always glad to shake hands with Liverpool, though that city has never embraced him. Nevertheless, Mrs. G. will die Viscountess Liverpool.

Queen's Hotel, Manchester, Jan. 31st, 1883.

I am fairly well, and only brought my nurse with me because I could not depend on waiters and chambermaids.

Let me know where your hotel is, and whether it has a lift. That is a serious matter with my weak heart, for, if I run up a long stair, I may find the Elysian Fields at the top.

I have been very anxious about my Orleanist friends. As men hardened in the vicissitudes of historic life, they could and would live anywhere; but, as Frenchmen, it would be dreadful for them to have to educate their children anywhere out of France.

If you see Lord Acton, tell him there is a chance of my coming to see him and you some short time after the meeting of Parliament. It looks as if we should have a debate on the Address, most of the Egyptian papers being already delivered.

Feb. 6th, 1883.

Please ask the manager of the Prince of Wales Hotel if I can have two sunny bedrooms and a moderate-sized sitting-room any day the first week of March.

---

* Mr. Gladstone was at this time at Cannes, occupying the Villa Scott.

I go to London on Saturday, and propose to go to Paris on the 26th—Hotel Meurice.

Everybody is sorry that Gladstone does not stay longer with you; but he seems indispensable on the Treasury Bench, as representing the authority of the Party and the House.

Lord Houghton to John Morley.

Cannes, Prince of Wales Hotel, March 2nd, 1883.

MY DEAR MORLEY,—With our friendship you might well have expected a letter from me after the Newcastle election. I may have had something of Goethe's feelings, which prevented him from noticing a friend's marriage. One doesn't congratulate a man on buying a lottery ticket, and the House of Commons is just such a lottery as marriage. But I might have remembered, as I do now, that you were a natural politician, and that the House of Commons is the best political platform to stand on in the world, and that any man holding that function may well be felicitated on getting there. If you go on with the Press (as I hope you will), you will expect a difficulty in the combination of functions, such as Lowe experienced when on the *Times;* but he got over it, and so will you, though it requires much tact. We have here a worse than English March, among desolate orange-trees, astonished palms, and distracted olives. The beautiful vegetation is irreparably injured, and all the invalids are worse for being here. I am only no better. The society of Cannes was shocked by Gladstone's reception of Clemenceau, and men ask how he has liked the serenade his Radical friends have given him on his return. Nothing pleases Frenchmen more than the bits of revolution in England. They always chafe under our supposed immunity. My letters from Egypt urge some distinct announcement of the continuance of the occupation as the only means of credit and security; and would not mind reduction of the force to five or ten thousand, if that were done. The amount of the force is of no importance. Alexandria will not be reliable till that is done.

To his Daughter Amicia.

Cannes, March, 1883.

I have been here ten days, and have had nearly constant cold winds; but with them a few hours of sunshine each day, that has made up for them. This has culminated in a snow storm, and now under my window the palms and azaleas are standing in a foot of snow. They tell you, as they told me when I was with you in the rain of Egypt, that this is unprecedented; but that makes it no better. So one must admire the Esterelles in an Alpine dress; they look beautiful.

Lord Houghton to Henry Bright.

Naples, April 20*th,* 1883.

The "tideless, dolorous Midland Sea," as Swinburne calls the Mediterranean, was the British Lake it ought to be, and landed me here on Tuesday morning in sunshine.

I left Cannes without regret for anything but your and Acton's society.

I *did* Pompeii yesterday, walking for 2½ hours without much fatigue. . . . Vesuvius only smokes, does not blaze.

What a good letter the Duke of Argyll has written from his gouty chair! It reminds me of Cobden saying to me of the country gentlemen, "I will not rest till I crush that *gang.*" We are fairly well *crushed* now.

To his Daughter.

Rome, May, 1883.

You ask about Mrs. Carlyle. The book makes the case worse than it was. She was really very fond of Lady Ashburton, and certainly not jealous in the vulgar sense of the word. She strongly enjoyed being at the Grange, though perhaps *froissée* by the indifferent formality and the fine ladies, whom Carlyle rather liked and admired. She was really attached to me, and I to her. If she had come to Fryston with him, as she intended, and stayed there whilst he was at Edinburgh, she would not have had the accident that proved fatal.

To his Son.

Basle, May 20*th,* 1883.

DEAREST ROBERT,—I am very glad that you and your wife should visit Holmbury, a gem of English nature, with excellent living, the best of company, and a most genial host. In fact, I look on him and Henry Cowper as the two hosts of the intermediate generation between yours and mine. You can tell Lord Granville that when at Rome I had an interesting interview with Cardinal Jacobini. Mr. Errington wanted to take me to see him; so, as I had frequently been to his predecessor, Cardinal Antonelli, in former times, I saw no objection. His Eminence received me almost with *empressement*, and kept me over an hour, talking mainly about Ireland. My observations were probably no more than a repetition of Errington's, but the old gentleman took them very kindly, and seemed pleased at my talking to him in fair Italian. I do not, however, infer that the rebuke to Archbishop Croke is a consequence of my arguments, or even of Errington's. I believe it to be mainly a bid for a direct representation of England at the Vatican, and that rather from political than ecclesiastical motives. I think I must have told you that old Lord Melbourne once said to me, "We Whigs have made two great mistakes: we have always under-rated two powers—the Church of England, and the Pope." As to our relations with the latter, Lord Lyons, who has had the experience, is fond of saying, "It is so difficult to deal diplomatically with the Holy Spirit."

I am your affectionate

HOUGHTON.

Lord Houghton to Henry Bright.

June 26*th*, 1883.

I dined last night at ——, and sat next Mr. G. Trevelyan, who is very agreeable, and quite took my view about Mr. and Mrs. Carlyle—that they were about as happy together as married people of strong characters and temperaments usually are.

Sept. 5*th*, 1883.

The question of precedence at the funeral of the Comte de Chambord had a real political and historical signification. It meant, Who will the Legitimists give their money and their lives to in the coming Revolution? The Comte de Paris kept his own, and has won the game, such as it is.

I quite sympathise with you as to *old letters*. *Teste* my verses on them.

In sorting mine, I have adopted one rule. I have kept one or two letters of everybody. My son or daughter may meet him or her who will say, "I knew your father in 18—; did he ever speak to you of me?" and then may ask him or her to dinner.

It was after his return to England from Italy that a project of a still more daring character than a mere Continental journey took possession of his mind. Despite his growing infirmities, he contemplated a visit to India—a country he had long wished to see; with which many of his friends, including Sir Charles MacCarthy, had been closely connected; and a visit to which he regarded as something in the light of a duty. I mention the fact here to illustrate the extent to which he still was influenced by that eager interest in men and affairs, that earnest desire to learn by personal observation, which had been one of the leading characteristics of his life. His friends and family were, naturally, opposed to his undertaking the risks of such a journey; but he was resolutely bent upon it, and it was only when Sir Joseph Fayrer, whom he had consulted as a medical expert, positively imposed a veto upon the scheme, that he reluctantly abandoned it.

To his Son.

Athenæum Club (? August, 1883).

Change of front! Sir Joseph Fayrer inhibits India, except Calcutta, which is hardly practicable. He suggests the Cape and Australia, which is matter for consideration. Quain behaved with much tact, made his report, and left the K.C.S.I. to decide; he declared a long opinion, which was resolvable into four words, " you are too old "—very disagreeable, but unanswerable. The Orient Line, by the Cape, reaches Melbourne in thirty days, and the return by Singapore and Egypt seems very practicable in February and March. Sir Bartle Frere said, " In this route you never go into the heat or the cold." I never looked on Madras as the tropics.

Your affectionate

H^N.

It should be explained that one of the strong temptations to him to undertake the journey to India was an invitation he had received from Sir Mountstuart Grant Duff, who was at this time Governor of Madras. The project was given up in obedience to Sir Joseph Fayrer's wise opinion, and though he talked for a time of a sea voyage to Australia, the idea did not seem to have for him the attractions which surrounded the vision of a winter in India. In the end he determined to content himself with another visit to his daughter at Cairo, which since he had last seen it had witnessed so many striking events.

In the autumn of 1883 he went to Bournemouth, principally for the purpose of seeing Henry Bright, who was staying there, in declining health. One of his relations (Mr. Percy Thornton) recalls the delight, as of two schoolboys, which the two friends showed in each other's society. Houghton was full of vivacious talk and eager interest in all forms of knowledge when in general company during this stay; but it was in the society of Henry Bright that he specially rejoiced, and with him that he spent the greater part of his time.

It was in March, 1884, that the visit to Cairo was paid, and it passed off pleasantly, in spite of his growing weakness. He bore the fatigues of the long journey successfully, and came home recruited by another peep at that East which he had known so long and loved so well. He returned to find that another and the last of the great sorrows of his life awaited him. The hand of death was laid upon his friend Henry Bright, with whom for a quarter of a century he had been on terms of most affectionate intimacy, and who had in a great measure filled the blank which had been caused many years before by the death of Sir Charles MacCarthy.

Henry A. Bright to Lord Houghton.

Bournemouth, April 5th, 1884.

MY DEAR LORD HOUGHTON,—I have asked —— to act as my secretary, for I know you will be sorry to hear that I have been very seriously unwell for the last two or three weeks—much breathlessness, with a very high pulse—and I must spare myself as much as I can. I am only anxious about getting home, and we hope to go back to Ashfield on the 16th. I hope you have been keeping well, and I trust that we may yet meet again at Ashfield Pray remember me affectionately to your daughter and Robert, and

Believe me ever, dear Lord Houghton,
Yours most faithfully,
HENRY A. BRIGHT.

Should we not meet, let me here thank you for a friendship of nearly twenty-five years, which has added so greatly to the brightness and happiness of my life.

The postscript was written by Mr. Bright himself. Lord Houghton did not arrive in time to see his friend again.

"Henry Bright passed away last Tuesday without suffering and with perfect resignation," he writes to his daughter on May 8th "I look on him as the last of my friends of mature life."

He was so constantly, even to his latest days, surrounded by those who delighted in his friendship, and he himself so cordially responded to every expression of good-will and affection, that even among the general circle of his friends few guessed how deeply he had been attached to one or two, and how greatly he felt their loss. During this summer of 1884 he moved about freely in society, spoke at the annual dinner of the Newspaper Press Fund, and fulfilled engagements numerous enough to have imposed a severe tax upon the strength of a younger man; yet with it all those who were near him saw how steadily his strength was running down and his natural vigour abating. It was towards the close of August that, going to see him at Fryston, I heard him, almost for the first time, complain of being very ill. "What is the matter?" I asked. He looked up quickly, with a flash of intelligence in his eyes. "Death," he answered gravely; "that is what is the matter with me; I am going to die." And then the face was illumined by the beautiful smile which those who loved him knew so well. "I am going over to the majority," he added, "and, you know, I have always preferred the minority."

About a month later Fryston was the scene of the last large party assembled there during his lifetime. It was a political party, the guests having for the most part come to attend a great Liberal demonstration at Pontefract. The meeting was held on the racecourse; but although held in the open air, in the latter part of September, Lord Houghton was able to attend and preside, speaking for some time with all his old grace and impressiveness, and with not a little physical force. He was greatly pleased during the meeting when his old friend and political ally Mr. Richard Moxon, who had been closely associated with him when he represented Pontefract in Parliament, referred to him as "the Grand Old Man of Yorkshire." Kindly recognition of this kind, coming from the warm heart of a friend, was infinitely dearer to him than any praise he could receive from the outer world. One still remembers how at his dinner-table, in spite of the fatigues of the meeting, he talked with all his old vivacity and fulness of knowledge, charming the large party assembled in the house as he had charmed so many of their predecessors in the days that were gone.

A few weeks later he met with a serious accident. He was staying at Lord Rosebery's house near Epsom, and during the night fell from his bed and fractured the collar-bone. The account he gave me was that he had dreamed that he was being pursued by Mr. Gladstone in a hansom cab, and that in his struggle to escape from him he had fallen on the floor. No more striking instance of that rare physical courage which he possessed, that power of endurance which many a stronger man might have envied, could have been given than that which he offered at this time. In spite of his broken collar-bone, and the acute pain it caused him, he travelled from Epsom to Fryston, took part in a meeting of magistrates, and transacted other business, only placing himself in the hands of the doctor on his return to town, where he was staying with Lady Galway, at her house at Rutland Gardens. Even when he was closely confined to the house by the doctor's orders, his old spirit asserted itself, and he received with delight the friends who came to see him.

On one evening in December he had a little dinner-party—Sir Frederick Pollock and Mr. James Payn being his chief guests. None of us who were present on that occasion will forget his high spirits or the delightful flow of conversation, full of reminiscences of bygone celebrities, which made the evening pass so quickly. None of us imagined that one who still lived so thoroughly could be so near his end.

A critical division was expected in the House of Lords, on the question of the Reform Bill, and Hough ton, who was as ardent in his political faith as he had ever been, had resolved, in spite of his doctor's orders, to be present in order to vote "I will go in my Peer's robes," he said, alluding to the fact that he could not wear a coat, "if I am not allowed to go in any other fashion." Fortunately the agreement arrived at between the two political parties obviated the necessity for his appearance in his place in Parliament.

All who saw him at this time must have been struck by the fact that neither age, nor disappointment, nor acute physical suffering had soured his temper, or warped his sympathies, or given him anything of cynical bitterness. Cynical to a certain extent he had always been, but nothing could have been gentler than the cynicism which he had acquired in his youth, and which had clung to him throughout his life.

Literary projects of one kind and another occupied much of his thought during these last months of his life. He wrote a sketch of Henry Bright for the *Philobiblon;* and another—his last piece of work—of the Duke of Albany. In both he showed the fine taste which had always characterised his critical writings, and he took as much pains to be accurate in small details as he had ever done. Much as he had written, he had never scamped his literary work, but had always tried to give the world his best.

In the early spring of 1885 he went to Italy with his sister, and was delighted to see once more the land which had so strong a hold upon his affections. At Naples he found some old friends of his, women of distinction in society; and in writing to his son he tells him what care they had taken of him, and how good their company was in the drives which he was able to take.

Then he came back to town, and was not to be deterred from taking part as of old in the social life of the season, manifestly unequal as his strength was to the part which his spirit compelled him to play. He was greatly cheered at this time by the return of Mr. FitzGerald and his wife to England, the prospect of having his elder daughter once more near him giving him great pleasure.

One of his public appearances was on the occasion of the unveiling of the bust of Coleridge in Westminster Abbey on May 7th. Mr. Lowell delivered an address, and after him Lord Houghton, in response to a call from the Dean, made a brief speech, in which he recalled the fact that when a student at Cambridge he had gone with Arthur Hallam to call on Coleridge, who had received them as Goethe or as Socrates might have done. " In the course of conversation the poet asked us if either of us intended to go to America. He said, ' Go to America if you have the opportunity; I am known there. I am a poor poet in England, but I am a great philosopher in America.' "

Some weeks later he took a still more prominent

part in a similar ceremonial at Cambridge on the 26th of May, when he unveiled a bust of the poet Gray.

His last speech of all was delivered in Lady Galway's house at Rutland Gardens, where he was staying, on the afternoon of Wednesday, July 8th, at the annual meeting of the Wordsworth Society; and it is touching to note how in this speech from which in an early chapter I have given one passage he dwelt upon his earliest association with the great poet, whom he had known as a friend. Looking back to the time when he was himself a student at Trinity College, he said:—

My recollections of that period are sufficiently vivid to enable me to say that I am very proud of having personally in some degree contributed to that great acceptance of, and I might say enthusiasm for, Wordsworth which was generated among the youth of Cambridge at that time. When I look back upon that time, and the, so to say, mental proceedings by which it was made important to the lives of all who shared in it, I find it somewhat difficult precisely to comprehend the cause of that enthusiasm. It was contemporaneous with a burst of interest in the poetry of Shelley and of Keats. With regard to Keats, of whose life I had afterwards the pleasure of being the recorder, we were very proud of having been the means of introducing to English literature the delightful poem of "Adonais." A son of Mr. Hallam the historian, who was the Marcellus of his day, and who, if he had lived, would have been a most distinguished name in English history, the Arthur Hallam of the "In Memoriam," arrived from Italy at that time, bringing with him a copy of the "Adonais," which had been printed at Pisa, under the superintendence of Byron. That copy we reprinted at Cambridge, and, as it were, introduced into British literature.

Lord Houghton went on to tell once more the story of the famous expedition from the Debating Society at

c c

Cambridge to the Debating Society at Oxford, which has already been told in these pages, and after discussing the characteristics of Wordsworth's verse, concluded with the personal confession·—

If I am asked, in that perfunctory way in which one is sometimes asked to write in a lady's album, "What is the greatest poem in the English language?" I never for a moment hesitate to say, Wordsworth's "Ode on the Intimations of Immortality." That poem is to me the greatest emblem of philosophic poetry, which may decorate youth and childhood itself with the years of grave and philosophic manhood; it comprehends the life of man.

It was a happy accident which enabled the old poet and critic in this last summer of his life to join in paying these public tributes of respect to three of his great English compeers in the world of verse.

The Newspaper Press Fund, for which he had done so much, and on whose behalf he had pleaded so often, was again one of the chief objects of his care. The last letter the present writer received from him was an urgent request to be present at the annual dinner of the Fund, in the summer of 1885.

His last public appearance in London, where he had lived so large a life, and where, for nearly half a century, it had almost seemed as though no company was complete without him, was at a dinner given by Mr. Cyrus Field in July at the Crystal Palace.

Almost the last house which he visited was one with which he had been familiar from his boyhood, the well-known and, in a sense, historic mansion on Battersea Rise, which had been the home of his uncle Mr.

Thornton, the Governor of the Bank of England, whose association with Wilberforce and Zachary Macaulay has secured for him a high place in the annals of British philanthropy. Throughout his life Houghton had often beaten a retreat from the bustle of London to the comparative quiet of the old suburban mansion, in the library of which Macaulay in his youth had passed so many hours. The house is now in the possession of Mr. Percy Thornton, and it was to see him that Houghton went thither, almost on the eve of his departure from England. Dr. Butler, the Master of Trinity, and Mr. Weldon, were fellow-guests at Battersea, and Houghton delighted them by the fulness and picturesqueness of his reminiscences of the academic world to which they belonged. There was not a sign of any failure in his mental powers, or in his interest in the men and affairs of his time.

A day or two afterwards he went to Vichy to join Lady Galway, hoping to recover some measure of strength at the watering-place he had so often visited before. Apparently he bore the fatigue of the journey quite well, arriving at his destination on Saturday, August 8th, in good spirits and full of eager inquiries as to the friends whom he hoped to meet there. On Sunday he went with his sister to the English church, but on reaching it found that there was no service. On the following day he dined as usual at the *table d'hôte*, and had an animated conversation with those at table— a party of French ladies and gentlemen—in the course of which he explained to them the services which the

Prince of Wales was able to render to English society. He talked as brightly as he had ever done, and there was nothing to cause the slightest apprehension to his sister. A few hours later the end came. Shortly after he had wished his sister good-night, he came to her room, breathing with difficulty. A violent thunderstorm was raging, and no medical man could be induced to come to the hotel. No remedy that could be applied restored him even momentarily; and his strength swiftly ebbed away. It was early on the morning of the 11th of August that the kindest of human hearts ceased to beat, and the shadow of a great sorrow fell upon a thousand homes of rich and poor, of cultured and simple, scattered throughout the world, in all of which his presence had been welcomed as that of a friend. His body was brought back to England. On the morning on which it left London for Fryston a service was held in St. Margaret's Church, Westminster,* at which many of those who had known him in his later days, as well as one or two of his oldest friends, were present. On Thursday, August 20th, Milnes was laid by the side of his wife in the little churchyard at Fryston. The Archbishop of York, who had known them both throughout their married life, and whose warm affection for them had never changed, conducted the service. All the members of the family were present, as well as a great company of his Yorkshire friends and neighbours, to all of whom he had shown the unvarying kindness which was characteristic of the man.

* Lady Galway's house is in the parish of St. Margaret's.

CHAPTER XXI.

LITERARY AND PERSONAL CHARACTERISTICS.

Lord Houghton's Poetry—His Prose Writings—Contemporary Criticism—The Ultimate Judgment—His Best Poem—Reminiscences of Mr. Locker-Lampson—Mr. Venables on Lord Houghton—Grillion's Club—The Philobiblon Society—The Newspaper Press Fund—An Epitaph which does not Lie.

To the present generation the poetry of Lord Houghton is practically known only in connection with one or two brief pieces, of unimpeachable grace and melody, which have attained a popularity that is literally world-wide. His more important works, as well as many shorter poems that are in every way equal in merit to those that have secured a lasting popularity, are but little known to the readers of to-day. The changes of fashion, which are as marked in literature as in dress, account in part for a fact of which no one was more conscious than Lord Houghton himself. In part, too, we may attribute it to the undisputed pre-eminence in the world of poetry of the great singer who had been Houghton's friend at college, and whose rapid growth in power and fame none had watched with greater pleasure than he had done. Nowadays it may seem strange, almost unintelligible to the ordinary reader, that there was a time when Monckton Milnes was looked upon as the destined successor to the premiership in English poetry. I have mentioned how, at a breakfast at Rogers's, Landor stoutly maintained that he was the greatest poet then living and writing in England; and there were many who shared Landor's opinion. No such estimate of himself was ever made by Milnes, nor will it be set forth here; but this, at least, is certain, that if an opinion which exalted him to such a pinnacle was exaggerated, the comparative neglect into which his poetry has of late years fallen is entirely undeserved. A great singer he may not have been; a sweet singer with a charm of his own he undoubtedly was; nor did his charm consist alone in the melody of which he was a master. In many of his poems real poetic thought is linked with musical words; whilst in everything that he wrote, whether in verse or in prose, one may discern the brightest characteristics of the man himself—the catholicity of his spirit; the tenderness of his sympathy with weakness, suffering, mortal frailty in all its forms; the ardour of his faith in something that should break down the artificial barriers by which classes are divided, and bring into the lives of all a measure of that light and happiness which he relished so highly for himself. Like all other men who write much, he was unequal in his work; and, at times, in his poetry the tricks of conventionalism, alike in substance and in form, were plainly to be seen. But there were other times when it was clear that the song sprang from the singer's heart, and that he had poured forth in it the real inspiration of a soul which could rise above the sordid commonplaces of life.

One of his friends used to tell in later years how, chancing to sit beside Houghton in a company of which Tennyson happened to be a member, the former said, pointing to the Poet-Laureate, "A great deal of what he has done will *live;*" and then added, half, as it were, to himself, "and some things that I have done should live too." It was no overweening estimate of his own merit. Some of the verses he has added to English literature will not easily lose their place in it. The reader in this story of his life has seen Monckton Milnes chiefly as the busy man of society, the ambitious politician in his younger days, the leisured literary expert of his maturity, the kindest of friends both in youth and in age—and perhaps this was all that the later generation saw in him. But nothing could be more unjust than to forget that—at any rate, until he reached middle life—he held a high place in the estimation of his contemporaries as a poet, and that great hopes were cherished for his future by a wide circle of men and women throughout Europe. The season of his activity in the production of poetry was comparatively brief. He first made his appearance before the public, with his "Memorials of a Tour in Greece," in 1834; and it was just ten years later, in 1844, that he published "Palm Leaves" In these ten years he brought forth a remarkable quantity of verse; and though, as I have said, his productions were of unequal merit, it may be confidently affirmed that in the work of these ten years there was much that no lover of English poetry would willingly let die. "The Memorials of a Tour in Greece" were followed in 1838 by " The Memorials of a Residence on the Continent, and Historical Poems," and " The Poems of Many Years," printed in the first instance for private circulation only. In 1840 appeared another volume of poetry collected from the magazines, to which he was then a regular contributor, and including his " Poetry for the People; " whilst four years later appeared his " Poems: Legendary and Historical," which included several pieces published in former volumes, and his little volume of " Palm Leaves." After that date, which coincides with the commencement of his serious political career, he wrote but little poetry, though many of the pieces which subsequently appeared from his pen had all the charm that belonged to his work in his earlier days. He had always maintained that to write poetry was an admirable preparation for the writing of prose; and after 1844 it was in prose, rather than in verse, that he gave his thoughts to the world. He had already, in his remarkable " One Tract More," published in 1841, given proof of the fact that he was the master of an admirable style. He was even then writing regularly in the *Quarterly* and *Edinburgh* reviews, and was doing much to create the taste of that generation for the writings of those younger men upon whom the elder reviewers had frowned persistently. Let it always be remembered to his credit that he was one of the first to tender, through the pages of a great review, the full acknowledgment of the genius of Tennyson. In later years it was his happy lot to make another great poet —Algernon Swinburne—similarly known to the outer world; and again and again, in the course of those critical writings of his, he gave proof of the keenness of his perception where genius was concerned, and of the absolute freedom from jealousy which characterised his critical utterances when he was helping to introduce a new writer to the world of letters.

"One Tract More" was followed in 1842 by his pamphlet entitled "Thoughts on Purity of Election." Two or three years after that time he devoted himself with great thoroughness to a more serious task, the writing of that "Life of Keats" which still maintains its place as a standard biography. This appeared in 1848, and in 1849 came the pamphlet on "The Events of 1848," to which I have referred at length elsewhere. There was a long interval after this, during which his literary labours were almost wholly anonymous, though they comprised many pieces of work of rare merit, such as the short poem on "Scutari" published in the *Times*, the lines on Thackeray which appeared after the death of the great novelist in the *Cornhill Magazine*, the sympathetic notice of David Gray prefixed to his poem "The Luggie," and many articles on the chief books of the time in the *Edinburgh* and *Quarterly* reviews. In 1866 a volume of selections from his poetry appeared, and this revived for a time the poetic fame of his earlier years. Seven years later came the best of his prose works, his volume of "Monographs," a work which in the fulness of its knowledge, derived almost entirely from personal experiences, in the soundness of its critical judgment, and in the charm of its style, has an excellence that is almost unique. In 1876 the collected edition of his poems appeared, and enjoyed a considerable popularity. In addition to his writings in the two great quarterlies, he contributed largely to the *Fortnightly Review*, under the editorship of Mr. Morley, and to the *Pall Mall Gazette*, under that of Mr. Greenwood, whilst in later years he took a warm interest in the *Academy*, and was a not infrequent writer in its pages. One cannot but regret that he never set himself to a task for which he was so well fitted, the writing of a book in which we should have had something like a complete picture of the society of his own time, a picture for which the "Monographs" might well have been regarded as preparatory sketches. Such a work from such a pen would have had an altogether exceptional interest and value; but that inability to make any prolonged or continuous effort from which he suffered in his later days stayed his hand, and although more than once he seriously contemplated a book of this kind, his intentions remained unfulfilled, and not even a fragment of the promised memoirs was discovered after his death. But even as it is, the volume of his literary labours was large, and the substance of undoubted merit.

It is hardly the part of a biographer to assume the critic, and it will perhaps be more to the purpose if I record here rather the judgment of the best critics of his own day upon his writings than attempt to pass any verdict of my own. So far back as 1838 the *Quarterly Review* devoted a long article to the poems of Trench and Milnes, in which full justice was done to the merits of the latter, though the writer was not blind to the desultoriness of his mind, and concluded his review by expressing the earnest hope that he would yet give his talents fair play by devoting himself of set purpose to some serious labour. In the same year another *Quarterly* reviewer rebuked him for having allowed himself to be led astray by the new lights of the hour.

We are quite sure [said this critic, who accurately represented the standard of critical judgment in his time] that Monckton Milnes will hereafter obey one good precept in an otherwise doubtful Decalogue,
"Thou shalt believe in Milton, Dryden, Pope,"
and regret few sins of his youth more bitterly than the homage he has now rendered at the fantastic shrines of such baby-idols as Mr. John Keats and Mr. Alfred Tennyson.

Perhaps, after quoting this remarkable passage, I am hardly doing a service to the subject of my memoir when I say that the critic announced, in conclusion, that "in spite of all their weaknesses and affectations, Milnes's poems contain better English verses than have as yet been produced to the public by any living writer not on the wrong side of the Mezzo Cammin."

Some years later, in 1843, he was again the subject of serious attention from the critics.

Milnes [said a writer in one of the leading magazines] is a true poet for the people, though not of them. He is a scholar, a gentleman, and a Tory of the Coleridgian school. An old *Quarterly* reviewer, in a notice of his poetry, speaks of him as "a leading pupil of that school, which embraced some of the most intelligent politicians and best instructed of the nobility of England. . . . We may add, though it may be considered somewhat irrelevant, that Milnes is besides a poet for the scholar. He has a fine antique imagination of the past, and reverence for the memorials and monuments of national and personal greatness, that cannot fail to awaken the sympathies of the retired student, who knows nothing of political distinctions, but worships all of the remnants of every faded glory. Our poet has a fine chivalry of nature that by no means unfits him for the advocacy of the rights of his fellows, yet which adds an additional grace to the manliness of his thoughts and style, rendering him an attractive author to those who might be repulsed by the homeliness of one class of his productions.

It was in the same year that Christopher North, in *Blackwood*, devoted a pleasant article to his verse, quoting as worthy of special commendation that poem on " The Flight of Youth " which Milnes himself always regarded as his best.

We read these lines [said Christopher] without fearing to let all their pathos fall upon our spirits, for into its depths, should that pathos sink, it will find there a repose it cannot disturb, or a trouble it cannot allay. The truths they tell have been so long familiar there, that we seem to hear but our own voice again, giving utterance to thoughts that for many years have lain silent, but alive, in their cells, like slumberers awakened at midnight by solemn music, lifting up their heads for a while to listen, and then laying them down to relapse into the same dreams that had possessed their sleep. But ye who are still young, yet have begun to experience how sad it is and mournful exceedingly to regret, perhaps to weep over, the passing away of the past, because that something *was* that never more *may be*, ponder ye on the strain, and lay the moral, the religious lesson, it teaches within your hearts. So may the sadness sanctify, and the spirits that God sends to minister unto us children of the dust find you willing to be comforted, when Youth has left you heedless if to despair—for, angel though he seemed, he is not of Heaven; but of Heaven are they, and therefore immortal."

After an exordium such as this, from one who was by no means the kindliest of critics, it is only fair that the reader should have the opportunity of judging Milnes's more serious verse for himself, and I therefore quote his lines on "The Flight of Youth" as being those which not only received the unstinted commendation of the ablest men among his contemporaries, but which, as I have said, seemed in his own opinion to be the best that he had written.

THE FLIGHT OF YOUTH.

No, though all the winds that lie
In the circle of the sky
Trace him out, and pray and moan,
Each in its most plaintive tone,—
No, though Earth be split with sighs,
And all the Kings that reign
Over Nature's mysteries
Be our faithfullest allies,—
All—all is vain :
They may follow on his track,
But he never will come back—
Never again !

Youth is gone away,
Cruel, cruel youth,
Full of gentleness and ruth
Did we think him all his stay ;

How had he the heart to wreak
Such a woe on us so weak,
He that was so tender-meek?
How could he be made to learn
To find pleasure in our pain?
Could he leave us, to return
Never again!

Bow your heads very low,
Solemn-measured be your paces,
Gathered up in grief your faces,
Sing sad music as ye go;
In disordered handfuls strew
Strips of cypress, sprigs of rue;
In your hands be borne the bloom,
Whose long petals once and only
Look from their pale-leavèd tomb
In the midnight lonely;
Let the nightshade's beaded coral
Fall in melancholy moral
Your wan brows around,
While in very scorn ye fling
The amaranth upon the ground
As an unbelievèd thing;
What care we for its fair tale
Of beauties that can never fail,
Glories that can never wane?
No such blooms are on the track
He has past, who will come back
Never again!

Alas! we know not how he went,
We knew not he was going,
For had our tears once found a vent,
We' had stayed him with their flowing.
It was as an earthquake, when

We awoke and found him gone,
We were miserable men,
We were hopeless, every one!
Yes, he must have gone away
In his guise of every day,
In his common dress, the same
Perfect face and perfect frame;
For in feature, for in limb,
Who could be compared to him?
Firm his step, as one who knows
He is free, where'er he goes,
And withal as light of spring
As the arrow from the string;
His impassioned eye had got
Fire which the sun has not;
Silk to feel, and gold to see,
Fell his tresses full and free,
Like the morning mists that glide
Soft adown the mountain's side;
Most delicious 'twas to hear
When his voice was trilling clear
As a silver-hearted bell,
Or to follow its low swell,
When, as dreamy winds that stray
Fainting 'mid Æolian chords,
Inner music seemed to play
Symphony to all his words;
In his hand was poised a spear,
Deftly poised, as to appear
Resting of its proper will,—
Thus a merry hunter still,
And engarlanded with bay,
Must our Youth have gone away,
Though we half remember now,
He had borne some little while
Something mournful in his smile—

Something serious on his brow :
Gentle Heart, perhaps he knew
The cruel deed he was about to do !

Now, between us all and Him
There are rising mountains dim,
Forests of uncounted trees,
Spaces of unmeasured seas :
Think with Him how gay of yore
We made sunshine out of shade,—
Think with Him how light we bore
All the burden sorrow laid ;
All went happily about Him,—
How shall we toil on without Him ?
How without his cheering eye
Constant strength embreathing ever ?
How without Him standing by
Aiding every hard endeavour ?
For when faintness or disease
Had usurped upon our knees,
If he deigned our lips to kiss
With those living lips of his,
We were lightened of our pain,
We were up and hale again :—
Now, without one blessing glance
From his rose-lit countenance,
We shall die, deserted men,—
And not see him, even then !

We are cold, very cold,—
All our blood is drying old,
And a terrible heart-dearth
Reigns for us in heaven and earth :
Forth we stretch our chilly fingers
In poor effort to attain
Tepid embers, where still lingers

> Some preserving warmth, in vain.
> Oh! if Love, the Sister dear
> Of Youth that we have lost,
> Come not in swift pity here,
> Come not, with a host
> Of Affections, strong and kind,
> To hold up our sinking mind,
> If She will not, of her grace,
> Take her Brother's holy place,
> And be to us, at least, a part
> Of what he was, in Life and Heart,
> The faintness that is on our breath
> Can have no other end but Death.

A criticism upon some of his later poems appeared in the *Quarterly Review* from the pen of his friend Mr. W. D. Christie. In this criticism Milnes was compared favourably with any of the young writers of his day. The melody of his verse, we are told, was perfect, "his language chaste, correct, and nervous. Thought, feeling, and fancy abound in his poems; and there are not a few, especially in the earlier volumes, which prove him capable of the highest efforts of 'shaping imagination.'"

I have given these brief extracts from contemporary criticism in order to show how Milnes struck the men of his own day at the time when he was bringing forth his poetry. In later years, when a generation had arisen which knew him well as a social favourite, but hardly knew him at all as a poet, there were still those who maintained the accuracy of the judgment they had pronounced many years before. Among these was Mr. Christie, who, writing in *Macmillan's Magazine*, said:—

If Richard Monckton Milnes had not been a man of the world, and a busy politician, and if he had been able to concentrate his energies on poetry, and gird himself to the building up of some great poem, none who know what poetry he has written can doubt that it was in him to be a great poet; and none who know his "Life of Keats," or any of his many pamphlets and articles in reviews and magazines, will deny that he presents another example of what he himself has lately proclaimed and supported by much good proof, that a good poet makes himself a good prose writer.

A still later critic,* after quoting Landor's estimate of Milnes, "the greatest poet now living in England," added some words of genuine critical insight:—

Startling as this opinion may sound now, there would have seemed nothing surprising in it when it was originally uttered. There were many competent critics who held that you were appreciably Tennyson's superior in the chosen walk of his genius; nor is it inconceivable that if your destiny had been different, you would have done poetic work of imperishable calibre. As it is, you have written much which will always have a place in every anthology of English verse. The originality of your genius declared itself in the extreme freshness, the keen insight, and the vivid truth of your productions. You were as anxious to show men Nature, and as successful in showing it, as was Wordsworth himself. The form taken by your interpretation of the Universal Mother was all your own. When it is recollected that the age in which you accomplished this was wedded to literary artificiality, that it was the epoch of false sentiment, tawdry rhetoric, and spurious imagery, it must be allowed to constitute a considerable achievement. Much indeed that you wrote does not rise above the level of the best album epigraphs of the period; while many of your most exquisite compositions have been set to

* The *World*, August 22nd, 1883.

music, and are cheapened by their associations with importunate piano strummings. But when all deductions on these grounds have been made, there is yet enough in your public writings to vindicate your claim to a respectable niche in the shrine of the Muses. You were the poet of society; you did not, indeed, write in the accepted sense of the term "society verses," but every verse which came from your pen was primarily intended for polite minds. A little more zeal and enthusiasm, a little more of that fire which would have burned less fitfully in a different social atmosphere, would have saved you from that tendency to desultoriness and trifling which was ever your besetting sin. The true charm of your poems is that they furnish those who read them carefully with something like a philosophy of existence; but the philosophy is only partially revealed. You give us glimpses of every kind of life and character, but they are glimpses only. When you touch a deep chord, you suddenly withdraw your hand as if you had been guilty of some breach of good taste. There is something tantalising in the way in which you play with profound problems, and dally with dark enigmas. What is probably your most familiar poem, "Strangers Yet," is also your most characteristic, and in it I read as follows :—

> "Oh, the bitter thought to scan
> All the loneliness of man!
> Nature, by magnetic laws,
> Circle unto circle draws;
> But they only touch when met,
> Never mingle—strangers yet."

To some these lines may seem commonplace because of their familiarity. As a matter of fact there is nothing commonplace about them. They belong to an extremely high order of poetic thought and feeling; but they bear the impress of a hand which, qualified as it is to lift the curtain on the mysteries and contradictions of life, will not do so because it would be a work of some trouble.

When Mr. Forster wrote to a friend describing his

first meeting with Milnes, he spoke of him as a man
" with some small remnant of poetry left in his eyes,
and nowhere else;" but in later years, when Forster
knew his friend better, he would not have repeated that
superficial judgment, the first which naturally occurred
to the man who met the poet for the first time, and who
judged from the outward side of things only. It is true
that as the years passed, and the constant strain of social
life, mingled with those demands of duty and ambition
which he never forgot, pressed upon Milnes, the poetic
side of his nature was driven from the surface, showing
itself outwardly at all events "only in his eyes"; but,
as to the last day of his life he continued to write verse,
so to the end, deep down in his soul, was a well of pure
poetic thought. Its existence, unsuspected by the
multitude, hidden with care from ordinary society, was
known to those who knew him best, and to the last in
their eyes he was not merely the man who had written
poetry, but the poet who could still judge the world
around him from a different and a higher standpoint than
that of his ordinary fellow-creatures. But to what purpose do we dwell here upon what might have been in
the case of a man like Lord Houghton? Of what avail
are regrets for that which never came to pass? Doubtless these questions occur to the mind of the reader;
but no picture of Milnes's life and character would be
complete which did not show how, as in his college days
his old friend Stafford O'Brien had prophesied would
be the case, he came "near something very glorious,
though he never reached it."

And here I may fitly introduce a few lines for which I am indebted to Mr. Frederick Locker-Lampson :—

I knew Lord Houghton for thirty years or more, and had a warm regard for him. He was kind-hearted and affectionate, keen to discover and eager to proclaim the merit of the unrecognised. He had a reverence for genius wherever he met with it, and few people showed a sounder judgment in literary matters when he was seriously called upon to exercise it. Then with his great ability, wide reading, and knowledge of the world, and his air—half romantic, half satirical—he was very attractive. Lord Houghton was whimsical in his wit, and sometimes more than whimsical in his offhand opinions, which those who understood him received as he intended they should be. He was not unduly taken up with his poetry; he was modest about it. I once asked him which of his poems he most esteemed. He at once replied, "The Flight of Youth," "The Long Ago," "The Men of Old," "Never Return," and " Half Truth." I think the literary world has made up its mind that these poems are admirable, and that I am justified in saying that his poetry depended less on the way the thought was expressed than on the thought itself. It is very thoughtful poetry.

Not long before Lord Houghton died I was talking to him of the increased size of London and of his celebrity, and I remarked what an enormous acquaintance he must have. "On the contrary," said he, " I regard London as an old acquaintance who is fast forgetting me." I think if Lord Houghton had not been a delightful humorist he might some day have found himself in the Cabinet, which no doubt would have pleased him. However, he never became cynical; to the end of his life he was always more than kindly disposed to his fellow-creatures, and he accomplished a good deal and in a more charming way; he was an illustrious member of society, he took a foremost part in many important social movements, and he was a remarkably stimulating entity amid the congeries of heavy social atoms. In fine, he was a man of great mark in his crowded generation, and, what is more and still better, I should think his name was still loved in many a retired home (like our own) where his sympathy and many nameless acts of kindness are remembered. It is thus that Fortune makes light of our desires and hopes, but never altogether ignores our deserts. Lord Houghton had a happy spirit, and, like many another, was content to bask in the present. He might have said :—

> " What boots it to repeat
> That time is slipping underneath our feet?
> Unborn to-morrow and dead yesterday,
> Why fret about them if to-day be sweet? "

I first met Lord Houghton at Keir, and it was delightful to see him and William Stirling together. I wish this was a proper place for saying a few words about the latter. I do not suppose I shall ever see Poloc or Keir or Fryston again; and if I did, would not they be full of ghosts, the voices of the dead, and the songs of other days?

Few of Houghton's friends can doubt that something of his verse will live; that his shorter pieces, which, as one of the critics I have quoted says, have become hackneyed by their very popularity, will long linger in the memory; but there is nothing far-fetched in the fancy that a time will come when some of his more serious lines, instinct with a tenderness of heart and fancy which hardly appeared in the outward man in his later days, and impressed by a gravity of thought which most persons believed to be altogether foreign to his nature, will regain their hold upon the ear of the reading public, and will keep his name alive long after the memory of his brilliant life of social success has passed away, and only the recollection of his deeds of kindness survives among those who found in him a helper in their time of need.

Many tributes to his memory appeared in the press at the time of his death. Not a few of these came from the hands of old friends, who were able to speak from real knowledge of the man of whom they wrote. The London of 1885 was a very different place from the London in which, fifty years before, he had made his *début* in society; and the later generation, which had watched him with curiosity and interest as the survivor of a brilliant past, was not to be blamed for the fact that it could not properly appreciate the man himself. It had never known the Monckton Milnes who had been a real power in his own generation; and it saw rather the foibles than the striking talents of the poet and the wit. Though let it be said, in justice to the men and women of to-day, that though they knew but imperfectly the life, the story of which has been told in these pages, they were not blind to the kindness of heart which had been its chief characteristic, and freely recognised Lord Houghton's claim to be regarded as one who had loved and served his fellow-men. Amid much that was written of him after his death one notable tribute to his memory requires mention here. It was from the pen of his trusted friend Venables—one of the few who, having known him in his early days at Trinity College, lived to mourn his death. To no man could the task of writing the Life of Lord Houghton have been entrusted more fittingly than to this brilliant man of letters and trustworthy and sagacious friend; but Mr. Venables had himself reached the age when the labour of reading and preparing for the press the voluminous correspondence of which the reader now knows something, was far too great to be undertaken; and now he has himself passed away from us. Yet no one can read the article which he contributed to the *Saturday Review*, of which periodical he had been so long one of the chief supporters, without mourning the fact that his was not the hand which was called upon to prepare a complete memorial of his dead friend. In that article Mr. Venables sketched some of the chief characteristics of Lord Houghton's mind with equal truth and tenderness, and I cannot do better than quote here one or two of the things he said·—

Both in and out of Parliament [said Mr. Venables] he took an active part in many social movements. He introduced the first Bill for the establishment of Reformatories, and he was the founder and president of the Newspaper Press Fund. He inherited from his father, who had refused Cabinet office at the age of twenty-three, a remarkable command of language, which made him, in conjunction with other gifts, perhaps the best after-dinner speaker of his time, and which characterised his literary compositions; but he failed as a Parliamentary orator through the adoption of a formal and almost pompous manner, which was wholly foreign to his genius and his disposition, though it might have suited the taste of an earlier generation. One of the most humorous of companions, he reserved for the House of Commons a curiously artificial gravity. There were politicians enough to occupy themselves with party conflicts; it was the business of Milnes to study human nature in its most opposite phases at home and abroad. . . . It was literally true, though the statement was probably intended by its author as a mere exaggeration of his wide range of sympathies, that "Vavasour had dined with Louis Philippe, and had received Louis Blanc at dinner." The catalogue of his temporary and permanent acquaintanceships would have formed an almost exhaustive list of the most conspicuous men of action or of letters in Europe and America. From all he acquired the special kind of knowledge which he instinctively valued; and wherever he was placed he gave at least as much as he received. Many years ago a commonplace man of the world, who only knew him slightly, and who shared few of his tastes, remarked, as others must have often said or thought, "Whenever Milnes comes into a room, everybody is in better humour with everybody else." . . . The extraordinary range of his social experience furnished him with an inexhaustible supply of anecdote, which never degenerated into gossip. Every story which he told had a purpose and a point, and it was always seasonable and frequently illustrative, even when it happened to be, in its literal form, absolutely incredible. His copious stores of narrative were not, like those of some of his competitors, his principal qualification as a talker; he was always ready to engage in the give-and-take play of conversation, and he felt keen enjoyment in the exchange of wit and humour, and on fit occasions in serious discussion. Perhaps the greatest charm of his social intercourse was the joyous spirit and unfailing good-humour which would have made a duller companion agreeable and popular. His gifts were cordially appreciated both by ordinary members of society and by remarkable persons, who might have been thought to be separated from him by irreconcilable differences of intellect, of character, and of temperament. Lord Houghton was the intimate friend and favourite associate of Bishop Thirlwall, and his cheerful paradoxes often dissipated the moral indignation of Carlyle. A commentator on Mr. Froude's biography compared not inaccurately the friendly contests of the gloomy prophet and the self-possessed man of the world to a combat between the Secutor and Retiarius of the Roman arena. . . . Two humours as dissimilar to one another as they were to the rest of the world could not be more equally matched. There were probably some serious and unimaginative judgments to which the perpetual versatility and multiform irony failed to approve themselves; but candid observers, who felt an imperfect sympathy with Lord Houghton, might have satisfied themselves that his reputation was well deserved when they saw that he was valued by his friends almost in the proportion of their respective opportunities of understanding his character. . In all relations of life he was unaffectedly and warmly sympathetic. No one could be more exempt from the pretension of austerity, and it was not unfrequently his pleasure to assume an attitude of even excessive tolerance; but if Wordsworth was right in defining the best portions of a good man's life as consisting of

"His little, nameless unremembered acts of kindness
and of love,"

Lord Houghton need not have feared comparison with the most pretentious philanthropist. He never made the general demands of society, which he recognised more fully than others, an excuse for slighting any claim on his attention which might be justly preferred even by those who might be considered as dull or obscure. . His generous and cordial temper, exhibited in all the relations of life, might have atoned for graver faults than the harmless foibles which scarcely formed an alloy to high intellectual gifts and to abundant virtues. Some harmless eccentricities which may be readily acknowledged require rather explanation than excuse. Lord Houghton was a fanfaron—not of vices, but of paradoxical fallacies which seldom deceived himself. Like other genuine humorists, he had some mannerisms which irritated and misled strangers and dull observers. One of his half-conscious peculiarities was a habit of propounding in a tone of earnest conviction any odd paradox which had for the moment passed across his fancy. Dull humours took his off-hand utterances for his real opinions, and resented the intellectual vivacity which found it impossible to rest in commonplaces and truisms. Like Tennyson's Ulysses, he enjoyed all things greatly, though it may be hoped that he had no sufferings beyond the common incidents of humanity.

It is difficult to add anything to this short sketch of Lord Houghton's character, so slight and yet so complete; but before I lay down my pen one or two features in his social life which have not as yet received due attention in this narrative call for notice. More than once in the letters which have been laid before the reader mention has been made of Grillions Club. It is strange that so little of this club is known in London society, where it has long played so great a part. Houghton's connection with it was of such a character that I am justified in saying something here of the club itself. Founded in 1812, mainly for the purpose of allowing the leading members of both political parties to meet together at a board from which all the violence of political controversy was excluded, it has faithfully fulfilled that office down to the present day. Many of the most illustrious men of the century have been associated with it. It is impossible here to give anything like a complete list of its members; for though the club itself is limited in numbers, there has hardly been a man of mark in the political world in recent times who has not been connected with it. Lord Russell, Lord Derby, Lord Shaftesbury, Lord Ashburton, Lord Stanhope, Lord Granville, Lord Canning, Lord Lyttelton, Lord Clarendon, Lord Dalhousie, Mr. Gladstone, Sir George Cornewall Lewis, Sir William Stirling, Mr. Walpole, Charles Buller, Sir James Graham, and Dean Stanley, may be cited as representative of the membership of this small but remarkable body.

Lord Houghton joined it in 1849, and for the remainder of his life was one of its most conspicuous members. The club meets on certain evenings during the Session, when those members who are in town dine together. Each is chairman and vice-chairman in rotation, and it is the duty of the chairman to make an entry in the club minutes of the guests present and of the wine drunk. Once or twice in the course of its history it has happened that only one member has been present at dinner, and these occasions have always been regarded by the club as notable. On March 9th, 1864, Lord Stratford de Redcliffe thus dined alone, and made a minute to that effect in the club book. On the following Wednesday, when another meeting of the club was held, and the minutes of the solitary dinner were read, the Bishop of Oxford being in the chair, Lord Clarendon moved, and Colonel Wilson Patten seconded, a resolution " that Lord Houghton do write an ode on Lord Stratford de Redcliffe's solitary dinner." The title of Poet-Laureate of the club was at the same time conferred upon Lord Houghton. In obedience to the command thus laid upon him he wrote the following lines:—

> Alas! my bishop, you in vain invoke
>   A Muse whose joints are stiff with gout and time,
> To gambol with you in prelatic joke,
>   Or raise to Stratford's height the serious rhyme.
> Rather might you, in your embroidered prose,
>   Draw some fine moral from his wondrous fate—
> How on the worthiest fall the heaviest blows,
>   How never lonely are the really great.

> I will but ask that if this book records
>   Ever again a solitary feast,
> Be he who dines, and he who notes his words,
>   As brave a statesman and as bright a priest.

Nearly twenty years afterwards a similar event did happen. Mr. Gladstone, on April 27th, 1883, dined alone at the club, and having written as chairman in the club book " one bottle of champagne," added the following lines :—

> The mind is its own place, and in itself
> Can make a heaven of hell, a hell of heaven.

Again were the services of Lord Houghton as Poet-Laureate called into requisition, and he penned the following lines :—

> Trace we the workings of that wondrous brain,
> Warmed by one bottle of our dry champagne;
> Guess down what streams those active fancies wander,
> Nile or Ilissus ? Oxus or Scamander ?
> Sees he, as lonely knife and fork he plies,
> Muscovite lances—Arab assegais ?
> Or patient till the foods and feuds shall cease,
> Waits his des(s)ert—the blessed fruits of peace ?
> Yes, for while penning this imperious verse,
> We know that when (as mortals must) he errs,
> 'Tis not from motive of imperious mind,
> But from a nature which will last till death,
> Of love-born faith that grows to over-faith,
> Till reason and experience both grow blind
> To th' evil and unreason of mankind.
>   HOUGHTON, *Poet-Laureate of the Club.*

These were fair specimens of the society verses

which to the last Lord Houghton was in the habit of composing, frequently in response to the invitation of his friends, occasionally at the bidding of some inspiration of his own. Here, for example, are some lines written at Raby Castle:—

> Time was when I could ring a dainty rhyme;
> Now wandering echoes through the distance chime,
> And memory, impotent in words,
> The past reluctantly records;
> Yet clear as in the early time,
> And vigilant in thought, recalls
> The frequent hospitality
> To guests of every quality,
> The multitude of comely faces,
> The choruses of happy phrases,
> The titled and untitled graces
> That peopled those historic halls.

One day, a few years before his death, when he was dining at the house of Mr. James Knowles, the conversation turned upon the relative characteristics of Mr. Gladstone and Lord Beaconsfield, and it was remarked by some one that if Lord Beaconsfield was a good judge of men Mr. Gladstone was a still better judge of mankind. Houghton was asked to turn the epigram into verse, and he did it as follows·—

> We spake of two high names of speech and pen,
>   How each was seeing, and how each was blind;
> Knew not mankind, but keenly knew all men;
>   Knew naught of men, but knew and loved mankind.

In a lighter mood were the following lines penned on some social occasion:—

> The first of September, one Sunday morn,
> I shot a hen pheasant in standing corn,
> Without a licence; combine who can
> Such a cluster of crimes against God and man.

A word or two must be said with regard to that Philobiblon Society, of which he was the founder, and throughout its life one of the most active members. The club was established in 1853, the number of its members being limited to thirty, and the qualification for membership being the interest taken by the candidate in the history, collection, or peculiarities of books. The members, as the reader will have gathered from many of Lord Houghton's letters, were in the habit of breakfasting together, when it was expected that such of them as possessed rare books or other literary treasures should bring them forth for inspection by their fellow-members. The club published a number of volumes of transactions, which were for the most part edited by Lord Houghton, and to which he contributed largely. In the first instance the secretaries were Mr. Sylvain Vandeweyer, the Belgian Minister in London, and Milnes; subsequently Sir William Stirling replaced Mr. Vandeweyer, though the latter continued until his death to be deeply interested in the meetings of the society. Prince Albert was for a number of years its president; afterwards the Duc d'Aumale was closely connected with it, enjoying the position of patron; and one of its later presidents was the Duke of Albany, who held that post at the time of his death. One of Lord Houghton's last labours was the preparation of a sketch of the Duke in his character as president. It was after the death of the young Prince that the society itself fell upon somewhat evil days. Most of the original members had passed away, and it was difficult to secure worthy successors to them, so that in the end it was resolved that the society should cease to exist. On Christmas Day, 1884, the last Christmas Day of his life, Lord Houghton penned a little valedictory notice with which to close the last volume of the Philobiblon Transactions.

It is not without personal emotion [he wrote] that I dissociate myself from this good company, with which I have worked and talked for over thirty years. I would desire especially to record three names with which I have been associated as Honorary Secretary during this period—Sylvain Vandeweyer, whose courageous and judicious participation in his country's felicitous revolution, and the establishment of its honest dynasty, was duly rewarded during his lifetime, and has been commemorated by a public monument after his death; William Stirling Maxwell, whose works will hold their place in our literature as the results of a sincere historical spirit, united with fine artistic tastes and precise antiquarian accuracy, and the greater part of which, privately printed and illustrated at his own cost, he liberally distributed among his personal friends in the Society; and Matthew Higgins, the "gentle giant," who, under the sobriquet of "Jacob Omnium," was one of the clearest and wittiest writers on the subjects of his time.

Too soon Lord Houghton himself was to be added to the list of those members of the society who had passed away.

As little akin in its character to the Philobiblon as the Philobiblon was to Grillions, was another institution of which special mention must be made in these closing pages of the record of Lord Houghton's life. This was the Newspaper Press Fund, the immediate object of which is to provide for the working journalists of the United Kingdom a fund to which they and their families, in seasons of distress or of bereavement, may resort for assistance. The Newspaper Press Fund has long since established itself so thoroughly that it no longer need fear unfriendly criticism; but the case was very different when it was first established. Many of the most influential members of the Press not only stood aloof from it, regarding its establishment as a blow at the dignity of the profession to which they belonged, but offered it their most strenuous opposition. Lord Houghton, who during his life had seen and succoured so many cases of distress among intellectual workers, and who had already taken a valuable part in connection with the Royal Literary Fund, threw the whole weight of his personal influence into the scale on behalf of the Newspaper Press Fund. He became its first President, and retained that office to the day of his death; and it is no exaggeration to say that the Fund owed more to him than to any other man. He never lost his interest in it—never ceased to take as much part as he could in the administration of its affairs; and every year used his great social influence for the purpose of making its annual dinner a success. I have given special prominence to these three bodies, because they appear to be singularly representative of three phases of Houghton's character. In Grillions he met that political society in which at one time he took a prominent part, and with which from the day when he entered Parliament he was so closely associated. At the breakfast-table of the Philobiblon he met those who shared his cultivated literary tastes, and who, like himself, were as eager in the pursuit of a rare book as many men are in the pursuit of wealth; whilst his long connection with the Newspaper Press Fund illustrates that side of his life on which now one loves best to dwell—his unfailing consideration for the distress too often (though happily in an ever-decreasing degree) incident to the calling of letters.

Many men of Lord Houghton's time, including some who started on the battle of life with him, achieved a far more brilliant worldly success. Some have done to the State those great services which he was never privileged to render to it; whilst one or two have achieved that literary immortality which was long one of the objects of his ambition. But if the life, the story of which I have endeavoured to tell in these pages, was marked by no great achievements, by none of those brilliant successes which the world prizes so highly, it was none the less a life which made its mark upon its own generation; a life, the record of which might have been carried forward, if I had so chosen, along a shining track of deeds of love and kindness, and which is now made fragrant by the best of all the memories which can surround the name of the dead. Of Houghton himself it may be said, in the words of Landor, that he "warmed both hands before the fire of life." But this also may be truly claimed for him by his biographer, that from first to last no object was dearer to him than the sharing of the pleasures and the blessings which he himself relished so keenly with those who were less happily placed. "Other people," he once said to a neighbour at Fryston, "like to give their friends bread; I like to give them cake." And the whimsical saying was absolutely true. He never stinted his deeds of kindness and goodwill, even when prudence might have led him to do so. It was his greatest delight to give, not the savourless bread of charity, but the rich fruits of sympathy and love to all who stood in need of them. "Write me as one that loved his fellow-men" was an epitaph he would never have thought of claiming for himself; for cant and the affectation of virtue were alike hateful to him. But it may justly be claimed for him by his friends; and if those words had been written upon his tomb, for once an epitaph would not have lied.

> Adieu, dear Yorkshire Milnes! we think not now
> Of coronet or laurel on thy brow;
> The kindest, faithfullest of friends wast thou.*

* W. Allingham, August 11th, 1885.

APPENDIX.

Some extracts from the Commonplace Books deserve to be included in this volume. I have selected, in addition to some interesting sayings by Sydney Smith, Carlyle, and others, a number of Milnes's own reflections, jotted down in these volumes from time to time.

Sayings of Sydney Smith.

"Melbourne used to begin by damning the subject of conversation. I used to say, 'Well, well, suppose it damned, and proceed with the discussion.'"

"Lord Melbourne's accession to the Government reminds me of the letter which one lady of easy virtue wrote to another when Bolingbroke was named Minister. "Rejouissez-vous, ma chere! B. est Ministre! 500,000 francs de rente, et tout pour nous!'"

In the debate on the Education question in the Lords there was some good play between Dick of Dublin and the Devonshire Champion.

Sydney Smith speaking with some severity of the sporting clergy to H——, Archbishop of York "Mr. Smith, do I understand that you object to the clergy riding?" "Not in the least, your Lordship, provided they turn out their toes."

"I am not fond of expecting catastrophes, but there are cracks in the world."

"If you are every day thinking whether you have done anything for the Flowers of History, of course you will be unhappy."

"It is a great matter for a man to find out his own line and keep to it—you get so much further and faster on your own rail."

"Are you always expecting the day when the ledger against Mr. M. Milnes will be brought out?" ("Read Mr. Milnes's ledger in life.") "Please, sir, there is no ledger of Mr. Milnes, only a waste book."

Rogers calling on S. S. very late, writing in the morning · "If I had known it was you, of course Mrs. Smith and myself would have got up to receive you."

Sydney Smith introduced by O'Connell after one of his Irish sixpennys to a large party: "I must present to you the ancient and entertaining defender of our faith."

"Lady Holland going with all her cooks and stew-pans to Holland House like the Homeric gods to Ethiopia."

"Babbage's treatise a decided minus quantity for his fame."

"B. always seeming at a white heat, ready to scorch up some rival man of science."

Murchison giving not *swarries*, but *quarries;* ladies all with ivory-handled hammers and six little bottles for each, to test the different stones.

"I cannot cure myself of punctuality."

"I suppose the creatures we see in the solar microscope tear one another to pieces for difference of opinion."

Discussion whether Macaulay was better to hear or read. Rogers says the former, because you need not listen. S. S.: "Oh! I'm for the latter, because you can't dogs-ear and interline him and put him on the shelf when he's talking."

A lady sitting between two Bishops—"Her name is Susanna, I assume?"

Some one of somebody: "He will let nobody talk but himself." Sydney Smith: "Why, who would if he could help it?"

S. S. always exercises his jokes in society before he runs them upon paper.—*R. M. M.*

Sydney Smith offering to call somewhere: "We shall be on our knees to you, if you come." "I'm glad to hear it. I like to see you in that attitude, as it brings me in several hundreds a year."

"A Bishop should marry a comely woman of a certain age, not such a shamefully pretty girl as the Bishop of Hereford [Musgrave] has done, who looks himself like the waggoner that drives the heavy waggon from Hereford to London."

"The integumental charity that covers so many sins."

Having some articles charged at the Custom House, asking under what head: "Unmentioned articles." "I suppose you would, then, tax the 39."

"In the country I always fear that creation will expire before tea-time."

"At Coombe Flory I am always in the condition of saying with Scripture, 'Go into the village over against you, and straightway ye shall find an ass.'"

"Selling correct cards, and getting sent to gaol because they prove incorrect!"

People putting about that Wyndham Smith bet for his father on commission.

"No railroad will be safe till they have made a Bishop *in partibus*."

Asked to dinner at the Duchess's when engaged to Whitbread, writing, "Dear Duchess, sorry I can't; engaged to the fermentarian." Misdirecting the letter to W., who was furious.

Calling the railroad whistle "the attorney," as being suggestive of the shriek of a spirit in torment, and "you have no right to assume that any other class of men is damned."

"In a wet summer, using the anti-liquid prayer, Allen put up a barometer in the vestry, and remained there during the rest of the service to watch the effects, but, I am sorry to say, did not find them very satisfactory."

"Lady Davy is *blue* to her very bones."

My saying Wakley had so pleasant a manner, S. S., "Off the body?"

"In my younger days mustard was never eaten with roast

beef, only with boiled; I can't find out when gooseberries ceased to be eaten with goose, and apple-sauce began: Luttrell can't tell me; it is beyond him."

"Macaulay's letter refusing to subscribe to the Edinbro' races was very foolish; if indeed they had asked him to ride—in a tight silk dress—talking to his opponent jockey all the race, and showing him how Lord Godolphin rode, and both up to the fetlocks in sand!"

"The only practical way of abolishing slavery in the U.S. is for Morpeth to marry a black woman."

"That most solemn and terrible duty of a Bishop, the entertainment of the clergy."

At the Geological Society: "How is Murchison to-day?" "In matter of conversation, I wish he was cut for the stone."

Lord M.: "I think I may assert without fear of contradiction," &c. S. S.: "Are you acquainted, sir, with Mr. Hallam?"

"Palmerston's famous peroration about the zones was all like Mrs. Marcet, where Charlotte says, 'Mamma, what is the use of zones?'"

Palmerston's manner when speaking like a man washing his hands, "the Scotch members don't know what he is doing."

"I wish Macaulay would see the difference between colloquy and soliloquy."

"What a pity it is that we have no amusements in England but vice and religion!"

"You can't stand Macaulay always, any more than a Budelight under your eyes."

Walking with the Bishop of Exeter by a shop written up, "Tongues cured here." "Shall we go in, my lord?"

To his company sitting down to dinner, "Now, are you crystallised?"

On MacCulloch's stating that the burials were no test of the number of deaths: "Do you mean that people keep private burying-grounds, like skittle-grounds?"

"Lady A. M. Donkin has so much the manner of a bore

that it is only after long acquaintance that you discover her to be a pleasant and clever woman."

"I don't care about the marriage with one's sister-in-law; I want an Act to prevent widows marrying the tutors in the family. They see handsome young men declining and conjugating with the dear orphans, and are caught instantly; if I'd been a tutor, under such circumstances I could have married any given widow."

"The average duration of Bishops in modern times is twelve years."

Puseyite dating a letter to him from some feast of the Church, he dating his answer "Washing-Day."

S. Smith calling the fire-bell rope the *rector*, and the cord beside, for pulling, the curate.

S. Smith begging another canon to do the Church business for him, saying he was "so rheumatic in his *professional* joints."

S. Smith saying Hallam was so contradictory that when the watchman called out, "Half-past three o'clock!" he jumped out of bed, and said from the window, "It's four!"

"Why is a horse in good condition like a greyhound in bad? Because they neither turn a *hare*."

Somebody writing to S. S. for his autograph: "I regret, madam, that your collection should have descended so low as, &c.—S. S."

S. Smith at a dinner party to his next neighbour: "Now, I know not a soul here present except you and our host; so if I by chance insult or dishonour any of their brothers, sisters, aunts, uncles, or cousins, I take you to witness it is unintentional."

S. Smith to some one who had grown fatter. "I didn't half see you when we met last year."

Some one comparing S. Smith's declaration of orthodoxy to the conduct of a Jew in Spain or Portugal, who is always known by the quantity of pork he swallows to conceal his tenets.

"God preserve to us that purity of style which from our

earliest days we have endeavoured to gather in great schools of ancient learning."

S. Smith writing to Brougham when the Whigs came in, that he should like to have a good Prebendary or something in that line, that a bishopric would neither suit his friends to give or him to receive, &c. Brougham replying that here he showed, as always, his complete commonsense. "Leave the fortresses of the Church for others; be content with the snugnesses for yourself."

S. Smith protesting that he followed the health of all the Deans with anxiety : " Westminster was better this morning, but Durham has had a wretched night."

Rogers asking Sydney Smith what attitude he recommended him to be painted in : "There is a very expressive one we of the clergy use in first getting up into the pulpit which might suit you very well" (holding both his hands before his face)

Young man asking S. Smith how he liked his preaching : "If you must know, I like you better in the bottle than in the wood."

"Has W. increased his library?" "Yes, it has overflowed all the lower rooms, and has crawled up the staircase, and covers the walls like an erysipelas."

Sydney Smith contradicted at some church meeting by the Dean, who afterwards said, " Mr. Canon Smith, I now see you were in the right." " Mr. Dean, I have the habit of being so."

Sydney Smith at dinner where H. Reeve was expected: "We are so sorry poor H. R. is laid up with the gout." " H. R. with the gout ? I should have thought rheumatism was good enough for him."

Sydney Smith much amused by somebody calling him "a handsome preacher."

Sydney Smith and Mrs.———. She says "if she began her life again, she would come out as a good listener as the best means of success; that is, she would win Heaven through Purgatory."

She told him Macaulay had not talked so much as usual

to-day. S. S. : " Why, my dear, how could he ? Whenever I gave him a chance, you cut in."

S. S. to Mrs. Grote : " Go where you will, do what you please, I have the most perfect confidence in your *indiscretion*."

S. S. of Egerton Harcourt : " He always looks like the amiable Joseph of the family, who had been taken out of the pit and sold by his worldly elder brothers."

S. S. at Lady Essex's private theatricals saying he watched with intense anxiety for the slightest approach of impropriety, that he might carry off the Archbishop of York as the pious Æneas did his sire.

S. S. feeling so ill and confused that he could not remember whether there were nine Articles and thirty-nine Muses, or the contrary.

S. S. of the Archbishop of York's accident : " He has sprained the tendon Athanasii, which in laymen is the tendon Achillis."

Of General Cleveland when publicly reproved by the Duke of Wellington : " He can't live, you know ; his wife and children will be always in tears, his pointers will bite him, the pew-opener won't give him a seat, the butcher won't trust him, his horse will always kick him off, prussic acid will be too good for him."

Mrs. Norton fanning S. S.: " Is Eastlake here ? What a picture he would make ! Beauty fanning Piety—happy Piety ! "

S. S. of Arnold : " He seems to have been a learned, pious, virtuous person, without five grains of commonsense."

Of Lord Eldon : " He spent all his life in encouraging men in their most mischievous prejudices, and in making money by them."

" You see, the Duke says what comes uppermost ; Peel, what comes undermost."

" Never gamble at the game of life; be content to play for sixpences ; marriage is too high a stake for a wise man to risk."

" People seem to imagine that life-making is an art as easily taught and learned as watch-making, but they are wrong."

S. Smith of Cornewall Lewis : " If he ever does go to

Hades, his punishment will be to sit book-less for ever, treaty-less, pamphlet-less, grammar-less; in vain will he implore the Bishop of London, sitting aloft, to send him one little treatise on the Greek article, or one smallest dissertation on the verbs in $\mu\iota$."

Some M.P. saying that if the corn-law was repealed "we should return to the food of our ancestors." "What did he mean?" "Thistles, to be sure," said Sydney Smith.

"Popham would die for his game; he is a pheasant-minded man."

"It is admirable of you to send game to the clergy; that's what I call real piety; it reminds one of the primitive Christians."

"When I went to Church at Kensington, they took me for Lord Holland; he was not known by sight at his parish church."

"Some people are born out of their proper century. Brougham should have lived in the Italian Republic, Lyndhurst under Charles II."

Sydney Smith of Milner's "History of Christianity": "It's a mistake altogether in our friend—no man has a right to write on such subjects, unless he is prepared to go the whole *lamb*."

"The great advantage to the farmer in having his tithe taken by the black parson instead of the white, is that the former knows so much less about the business."

Allen asking Sydney Smith if he ever wrote poetry "Rarely, but next Whit-Sunday I will attempt an Ode to Religion, and dedicate it to you."

S. Smith's indignation at Granville Vernon explaining to the company what he meant by some joke: "You see, he means so-and-so."

S. Smith of Rogers's refusals to invitations: "He has a quantity lithographed, all beginning 'Pity me!' He asked his servant for one the other day, who said, 'Sir, all the "pity me's" are used up.'"

Curious scene of S. S. sitting like an accountant looking over the schedule of Wyndham's debts, who lay on the sofa by the fire, and remarked as his father read each name, "That's a rascal, pay him half"; "That must all be paid"; and so on. When concluded, W. left the room, and S. S. drew his chair to the fire, and was heard slowly repeating the Lord's Prayer to himself, and when he came to "forgive us our trespasses," saying it twice over.

Sterling saying somewhere, "If you Whigs send Campbell Chancellor to Ireland, you will drive them mad." S. Smith: "And a very short stage to go, my lord, and no postillions to pay."

S. Smith saying, "There was not the least use in preaching to anyone, unless you chanced to catch them ill."

S. Smith, overhearing Mrs. Austin saying she was no relation to Miss Austin, saying, "You are quite wrong; I always let it be inferred that I am the son of Adam Smith."

Jeffreys coming in late to breakfast at Rogers's. S. S · "Ah! we know you have been detained trying the case of Hallam v. Everybody." Hallam present.

S. Smith saying the great use of the raised centre, revolving on a round table, would be to put Macaulay on it, and distribute his talk fairly to the company.

Macaulay that "talk-mill."

Sayings of Carlyle.

"I daresay Lord Raglan will rise quite quietly at the last trump, and remain entirely composed during the whole day, and show the most perfect civility to both parties."

Carlyle of the fireworks in the Peace · "There is something awful, and something childish, too, in them—a sort of hell and Tommy affair."

"The product of happiness is to be found not so much in increasing your numerator as in lessening your denominator."

"Palmerston, the chief Anarch of England at this given time."

"I look on Carlyle's religion as Calvinism without Christianity."—*W. Harcourt.*

"I plant cypresses wherever I go, and if I am in search of pain I cannot go wrong."

Of Leigh Hunt: "He is dishonest even for a Cockney—he has learnt from that kind of up-bringing to regard shoemakers and tailors as *feræ naturæ*—creatures that you are authorised to make any use of without notion of payment."

"You may forgive for seventy times seven, but the unforgivable will always come at last."

"Macaulay is well for a while, but one wouldn't *live* under Niagara."

Carlyle saying of Sterling's mind "that it went like a kangaroo."

"Harriet Martineau is a remarkable kind of product, not without strength."

"Puseyism is a very nice Claude picture, but it won't do to drive a plough into it and work it. That's the worst; you can't raise food out of a Claude, and a man hungry for religion will find little comfort in Puseyism."

"We must make people feel that heaven and hell are not places for drinking sweet wine, or being broiled alive, some distance off, but they are here before us and within us, in the street, and at the fireside."

"Harriet Martineau is indignant because she can't light her pipe at the lightning."

"A happy man seems to me a solecism; it is a man's business to suffer, to battle, and to work."

"Your horse is going such a pace as if it was following the funeral of the British Constitution."

Sydney Smith "as coarse as hemp."

"French books have most dancing-dog thought about them; ours are like the quiet intelligent meditation of an elephant or a horse."

"Miss Martineau is a good deal more talkative than is good for her."

"Burns's songs are just a jet of pure poetry springing out of the universal depths of things."

"The *Beggar's Opera* is a mere pouring of bilge-water and oil of vitriol on the deepest wounds of humanity—a miserable mockery; while there is a true *Beggar's Opera* getting itself acted every day in many a cottage of these kingdoms."

"Trial by jury and a town funeral seem to me the two pitifullest shams and lies that the world has ever yet invented; and which must be thrown into the sea together, if any good is to come to us."

"These are busy days for religion. Puseyism puts on its beaver and walks abroad; the old kirk shakes herself and gets up, ashamed to have lain so long among the pots."

"Purgatory, a sort of gentleman's waiting-room, till the train comes by."

"Some day or other people will look on our Christianity much as we look on Paganism."

"Some persons are trying to get up a worship within a dark crypt roofed over with the fragments of the fallen Church."

"The French are great indeed as cooks of everything, whether an idea or a lump of meat; they will make something palatable of the poorest notion and the barest bone."

"The motto of the English people is cure or endure."

"A certain falsehood of exaggeration is the consequence of the velocity of London life. A man has only a minute to speak to you, and you to hear; and unless he say something surprising and emphatic, you have no chance of remaining in his mind an hour beyond."

Carlyle when a child having saved in a tea-cup three bright halfpence, a poor old Shetland beggar with a bad arm coming to the door, C. giving him all his treasure, saying, "The feeling of happiness was most intense; I would give £100 now to have that feeling for one moment back again."

"The prose of Goethe brings to mind what the prose of Hooker, Bacon, Milton, Browne, would have been, had they written under the good, without the bad, influences of the French precision, which has polished and attenuated, trimmed and impoverished, all modern languages, made our meaning clear, and too often shallow as well as clear."

Landor says Carlyle made a few ideas go further than anyone had ever done before. "If you see a heap of books thrown on the floor, they look ten times as many as when orderly on the shelf."

"A man may have a very true morality of his own, though he seems to go crashing through etiquettes and ten commandments and such like."

"A school for public speaking! I wish we had a school for private thought!"

Carlyle preaching "silence" through a trumpet, and proclaiming "good-will to man" by mouths of cannon.—*Sterling*.

"I wish, when you start on a railroad, that they would sell you stupefiers, made of opium or some such thing, to make you unconscious till you get to the end of your distance—stupefiers to Derby, to Edinburgh, and so on—or if they won't do this, at least they may let you smoke."

"You look on this world as a thing made of musk and honey, and forget the pain there is in it entirely."

"If you're afraid of pain and such like, I loo on you just as on a rabbit."

Carlyle's *cinerous* language—all ashes and sackcloth in the face of the summer sun.—*R. M. M.*

"An industrious man seeing a great strong man perfectly idle —a squatting, pumpkin-eating black—has the best right to make a slave of him and make him work at something.

"I only wish some competent man would come and make a slave of me. The chief use of freedom is to be able to enslave yourself."

"This Puseyism in the Church reminds me of our graziers, who always come to Dumfries market in a new pair of boots when they are hard up and likely to get into quod. This Puseyism is the new boots of the Church of England."

"All history should aim at resembling the Iliad, remembering it is a greater task than the human mind is capable of, really and literally to present the smallest fact as it itself appeared."

"Brougham's tongue seems to be a mere wooden clapper pulled up and down by anybody for any time, and to have nothing of a reasonable member about it."

"They may talk as they like of the pangs of remorse, but why am I, Thomas Carlyle, who have never consciously hurt anyone, suffering like Judas Iscariot?"

"I would rather have one real glimpse of the young Jew face of Christ than see all the Raffaelles in the world."

"We have lost all sense of right and wrong in these putrid ages; we are in a perfect puddle of benevolence; we must have recourse to Citizen Lynch at last, if this goes on."

MISCELLANEOUS.

Thackeray's proposed work: "The Young Gormandiser's Guide; or, Eating in Paris Made Easy."

"Tegg's shop is the limbo of fate to which we authors are all tending—critics themselves shall not be saved; and he has now bought half the *Quarterly Review.*"—*Thackeray.*

"There goes Wordsworth browsing on life, ruminating and cud-chewing for everlasting."—*Thackeray.*

"If Goethe is a god, I'm sure I'd rather go to the other place."—*Thackeray.*

I to Thackeray: "Was not your audience with Goethe very awful?" "Yes, like a visit to a dentist."

Thirlwall's character as drawn by the newspapers. *Bell's Weekly Messenger* says, "he had given lectures at Cambridge which some persons admired, but he was estimated by graver men as a flashy and frothy declaimer." A correspondent of the *Times* concluding with, "thus we see that this new Whig Bishop was expelled from Trinity College for refusing to give

Divinity lectures to his pupils." The *Cambrian* calling him "the golden melodist of Cambridge."

"Whewell's humbug and imbecility reciprocally limit each other."—*Venables.*

Charles Buller telling Ben Stanley at Lord Melbourne's dinner that "he was jealous of me, that he feared to be only known to posterity as the contemporary of Milnes."

"O'Brien's face is always to me like a black cloud with his features indistinct on it."—*Rio.*

"Brougham's reputation fifty years hence will probably be much what that of Lord Somers, or Pulteney's is now—known to have been the best speakers of their day, and to have written much which was thought good, but which nobody reads now."—*Macaulay.*

"The Tories wishing to uninvent printing and undiscover America."—*A. De Vere.*

Canning said to me, "No Ministry can be a powerful one whose head is not in the House of Commons."—*R. P. Milnes.*

"The National Gallery would make a capital warehouse for foreign corn."—*R. P. Milnes.*

My saying to Peel, after making his appointments in 1841, "You must have been so busy the last weeks." "Busy indeed, and with most *odious* and *disgusting* business."

Rogers to me: "Don't you be so hard on Pope and Dryden, you don't know what we may come to."

Someone asking a common workman if M. Lamennais lived in that house: "Oui, là, au cinquième, tout près du ciel."

Southey of Coleridge: "He is the best of men, but can never do a duty." C. of S.: "I never can think of S. but with a pen in his hand."

"Wordsworth does more to unidealise himself than any man I know."—*Kenyon.*

Wordsworth introduced to the Wedgwoods by Coleridge. Wedgwood to C.: "Why, W. could not hold a candle to you." "Sir, a man like Mr. W. passes men like you and me so far that he is dwarfed by the distance."

Louis Philippe to me: "If it is by the Treaty of Utrecht that you prevent a son of mine from marrying the Queen of Spain, I claim the condition of the Treaty which only permits a Queen of Spain at all on the extinction of both the Spanish and Neapolitan branches of the Bourbons."

"Do you want a German king of Spain? Have you not had enough of the kings of Greece and Portugal?"

Louis Philippe to me: "*J'ai occupé le trône de la France parcequ'il était vide, et les trônes vides sont les trônes brisés.*

Louis Philippe of M. Guizot, "*Il a le courage de l'unpopularité au plus haut dégré.*"

Louis Philippe to me (May, 1843, at Neuilly) : "Remember, whenever you come to France you will always be welcome here —that you will always be received with regard and with confidence."

"My policy has always been to return slight for slight to Russia, Spain, and every other country."—*Louis Philippe.*

"The high sense of personal honour and the low feeling of public duty which distinguishes our political men and the English aristocracy in general."—*C. Buller.*

C. Buller to me: "I often think how puzzled your Maker must be to account for your conduct."

My proposing to pay the Irish clergy, D'Orsay calling out, "L'Église Catholique en Irlande ! C'est impayable !"

Lady Holland saying, "she never could see the difference between the resurrection and the ascension—she could not understand those subtle distinctions."

Macaulay coming to the conclusion that God must be limited by law, as Jove was coerced by Fate—that evil was something in itself necessary and beyond His jurisdiction. Thompson saying "this was such a Whig notion of a *constitutional* God."

Napoleon before his abdication abusing Talleyrand most furiously in full council, saying there was a Judas here, and he knew who he was, " c'est vous—ne m'avez-vous pas conseillé la mort du Duc d'Enghien ? ne m'avez-vous pas conseillé l'invasion d'Espagne ?" &c.—T. all the time standing utterly unconcerned. (Related by Molé, who was present.)

"How many persons will dance over Brougham's grave, but they will be very sure he is in it first!"—*Rogers*.

"I have told Venables it surely is not necessary that he should enter every drawing-room with the feelings of Prometheus prepared to defy the vulture."—*Lady Ashburton*

March 14th, 1852.—Sir A. Rothschild bet me 100 sovereigns to one, Fleming 100 shillings to one, Baroness Charles 100 doz. pairs of gloves to one, that Dizzy did not carry the Jew Bill before January, 1854.

Talking of something twenty years hence, Lady Ashburton, "What does it matter? I shall be dead, and you will be living in the country, too fat to be moved up to town."

The same of me, "I cannot fancy you looking sad; I have seen you grave and dignified, but never unhappy."

"As I get old, I economise my pleasures so as to get more into a day than I used to do into a month; I have to separate enjoyments which I have not had in the vigour of life. I have a game of play every day with children in the streets by means of looks and gestures. You young men can talk of meeting annihilation, but those who are so near the change as I am look on it far otherwise."—*Rogers*.

Mr. Smith, in proposing vote of thanks to me at the City of London Institution, speaking of "that writer who sent out Palm Leaves, which came back Laurel."

A Charade on R. M. M.

My first in dark seclusion dwells
'Mid shadowy aisles and cloistered cells.
My second 'mid the glare of light
Is worshipped by the fair and bright;
The proud, the great, the rich, the free
Before its altar bend the knee.
My third is useful to prepare
The food we eat, the clothes we wear;

APPENDIX.

> And like the stone so sought of old
> Can turn most substances to gold.
> My whole is part of that which rules
> The court, the camp, the church, the schools,
> And meddles in all sorts of things,
> From beggars' meals to rights of kings.
>
> I was a Tory; am a Whig;
> Once Sairy Gamp, now Betsy Prig.

Made on me by Archdeacon Marcus Beresford, at Headfort, after my acting in the Charade of Mu-sic.—December 6th, 1846.

"Sir R: Peel is always tossing himself up, and does not know whether he will come down heads or tails."—*Fonblanque.*

Brougham writing to Allen in 1810, "The Secretaryship of War is being hawked all over the town, young Milnes having refused, and at last they have given it to that foolish young courtier, Lord Palmerston."

"When I think of the Cimetière Montmartre, I always see a pair of shoes or boots, pumps or slippers, at the foot of each tomb, ready for the sleepers; lying in the light, clean-brushed by the hands of the angels, those boots of the great world-hotel."
—*Heine.*

Gladstone saying "he felt strongly that the statesman was becoming every day more and more the delegate, and less the leader of the people."

When you have to choose between alternatives all objectionable, begin at the bottom, striking off what is worst, and going on that way till you get the residuum nearest to good.

Miss Chough's character of Gladstone, solely from his handwriting:—"A well-judging person, a good classic, considerate, apt to mistrust himself, undecided, if to choose a profession would prefer the Church, has much application, a good reasoner, very affectionate and tender in his domestic relations, has a good deal of pride and determination, or rather obstinacy, is very fond of society, particularly ladies', is neat and fond of reading."

Lord Houghton's own Sayings.

It is not the spirit of obedience that is wanting in man; he is not only willing to obey, but there is a necessity on him to do so. In his maddest dreams of freedom he enthrals himself to a Marat; in his widest theory of individual judgment he makes a Pope of Chalmers or Wesley or Channing. Only let a man see what he ought to obey. Here rather is the difficulty. "I will not obey the Church," says one, "for the Church does not exercise any power over me; I do not acknowledge its authority; I do not feel its superiority." "I am not a loyal subject," says another, "because I know that the Queen is an inexperienced little girl, no wiser than one of my daughters." It is only by attesting their divine mission that institutions can be, or it may be ought to be, obeyed.

It is not the amount of genius or moral power expended, but concentrated, that makes what the world calls a great man; the world never sees a man but in *one* capacity.

Life may be but too long for any motions of confusion and ambition, but it is very short for the enjoyment of tranquil happiness and elevated repose; it is for these things only one wishes to have it prolonged into heaven.

We do not know how essential an ingredient even of our best pleasures their transitoriness may be; everything delightful is perhaps, *ipsa natura,* too short—regret is a continual symptom of the natural death of every gratification—if it perish not thus, it only lingers on to be killed by Time at last.

It is perhaps impossible for any truth to make its way to the general human heart, unless winged or pointed with more or less of lie.

What a rare thing is a grown-up mind!

The worst part of affectation is that there is generally so little art in it.

I face the world under singular disadvantages; the excitement of sporting and the calm of smoking are both strange to

APPENDIX. 487

me. I severely wounded my best friend in attempting the first, and I took the trouble of going to Berlin and taking a master to learn the second, but in vain. But my hardest case is that I am unable to hate easily or to revenge myself at all. I pity the man who injures me, and do not see how I better the ease by injuring him in return. I see that revenge is pleasant to others, but to me it is only a necessity or duty to society, and I perform it grudgingly.

I will be responsible for no other war than one in which our success shall be a benefit to the human race, and in which defeat itself shall not be dishonour.

I can hardly conceive a case in which war for England shall be anything better than a lesser evil.

No wonder we were friends, for we had found ourselves in a moral quarantine together.

I looked at the coffins in the vault till they seemed to me to become transparent, and to show the dead lying within them in victorious quietness over this tremulous and spasmodic life, and gently subsiding into the large lap of catholic Nature.

That strange fantastic nervous organism which is the outward expression of life.

The two chief medicines of the poor, beer and ale.

What a flush of Art was that of Venice in the eleventh century!

Is not all our life of affection spent in finding out one another? We do not know how much love we owe to the stimulus of curiosity; if all our sympathy was clear and direct, how little love would have to do, and how do we know it could subsist in merely idle enjoyment?

From the Splügen you behold the glaciers on either side in which the Rhine and the Adige rise. How small a space determines whether the river belongs to the Adriatic or the German Ocean! And they never come so near again. Thus was it with these two lives.

There are some minds that seem merely frightened into folly by the solemnities of Nature, to whom truth is simply terrible and confounding, and who seek refuge for it in any distraction or littleness of their own thoughts.

The most beautifully sincere people will seldom be found quibbling about verbal truth; this is so strongly felt by the instinct of public opinion that the formalism of verbal truth among the Quakers has been sufficient to inspire the sense of their insincerity; the evil of attaching so much importance to this superficial veracity probably is, that people get content with the truth that is in the bubbles of the well, and don't care for what is at the bottom.

Trust in leaders has the same relation to politics that credit has to commerce.

The poetical periods of a nation have always been those of internal prosperity and external honour. The reigns of Pericles and Augustus, of Louis Quatorze, of Elizabeth, and of Anne are plain examples. It is a curious question whether in the uneasy and degraded epochs it is the poets that are wanting or the power of appreciating them.

Most history is like that large portion of Africa in Arrowsmith's map, " dry country abounding in dates."

In my old age I return to my classics, and they fit me now better than they did in my youth. I leave the romantic, with its activity and variety, to youth and to manhood, and find in the calm and monotony of these great masters of form something becoming the staid repose and sculptural tranquillity of closing existence.

All the other English dramatists give you events and persons just as they were, and in the best way; but Shakespeare suggests an hundred things to his reader, and his reader suggests them to others, and thus the moral chain will go on for ever.

Certainties in religion have become probabilities; probabilities, possibilities; and possibilities are dogmatically denied.

Surely it is as well to call pain and sorrow the *will* of God as anything else, but we must take care not to consider these things as God's *pleasure* and *satisfaction,* as the Calvinists do.

No intensity of literary starlight can make a moral noonday.

There is nothing so wearing as continually playing at superiority.

Often the shadows of the past rise up about the present, and clothe it in their mist, and at last hide it altogether.

How little of the real life of a thoughtful man gets into words! How much is there that passes through hundreds of minds unuttered, and every now and then indirectly betraying itself! The mine of truths is deep in many hearts, though only openly worked here and there.

Life is a jest—not witty, but humorous.

You may generally divide the goodness of your joke by the number of your auditors. A joke good enough for half a dozen people will be too good for an hundred; you must coarsen your humour for the House of Commons or any other mob.

Every man who finds himself in the wrong has learnt something.

A *paix armée* is peace without comfort, and war without energy.

The worst of self-government is that everybody is trying to govern his neighbour, and nobody to govern himself.

Our youth, thank God! has felt no such keen political disappointment as must have fallen upon those who religiously believed in the French Revolution. What a crash of hopes! What a triumph of base and brutal and ignorant enemies! What a humiliation, not of oneself, but of all that is good or exalted, before the basest of policies and most selfish of systems! It was the hardest shock the ideal has ever had to suffer.

The Carlton Club, that political scullery.

How often people's books are better than themselves, how often their conversation! Is it not that these things are in fact the souls of those persons, and what they would be but for some contingent circumstances that make them otherwise? These things are the men without their persons and passions and personal weaknesses.

Nobody talks well just before dinner; as Solomon says, "Out of the abundance of the mouth the heart speaketh."

American life is like its standard—all stripes and stars.

It is in my temperament to prefer receiving benefits from the love and friendship, rather than from the necessities and self-interest, of my fellow-creatures.

I believe evening prayer to be more frequently regular than that at morning; the mind feels its dependence on the Unknown and Invisible more strongly when committing itself to the mysterious world of sleep and dream, than when waking into the action of daily life, with a will apparently free, and energies apparently independent.

Religion is the science of hope; till mankind possess a present that satisfies their whole being, so long religion must exist.

In India we talk of allowing so much to the native princes, as if this were not a miserable part of their own property, which we have still left them.

I have a strange liking for poor and weak books. Is the conviction agreeable that I could have written a better on the subject myself? have avoided such and such errors, supplied such and such deficiencies? Or is it a pleasant occupation of the fancy, to remedy and supply as it goes along—or, at least, to believe that it does so?

A man's thought is always better than his act—*i.e.*, his book than his life.

There are many men who have a sort of lyrical facility in their youth, which makes and proves them to be poets, who in manhood become utterly prosaic, and even incapable of poetical susceptibilities.

Second childhood is childhood without its discipline, without its improvement. Do not call it childhood, merely because it is querulous, unreasoning, and exacting.

When in trouble, think of the troubles you have been saved from. A friend of mine said he kept the circumstance that he wanted to marry a woman who afterwards went mad, and all but had a child hideously deformed, as a sort of store of consolation.

Is not Hope another name for the faculty of present enjoyment? If we are fully happy to-day, we can have no gloom on our thoughts of to-morrow.

An unsuccessful speech of Disraeli's, "the Hebrew language without the points."

That grove of barren fig-trees commonly called London Society.

He lost both dinners and flattery, both his bread and his butter.

Character of Himself.—He (R. M. M.) was a man of no common imaginative perceptions, who never gave his full conviction to anything but the closest reasoning; of acute sensibilities, who always distrusted the affections; of ideal aspirations and sensual habits; of the most cheerful manners and of the gloomiest philosophy. He hoped little and believed little, but he rarely despaired and never valued unbelief, except as leading to some larger truth and purer conviction.

Solitude on me has at once an irreligious and an immoral effect—it makes me set great store by sensual pleasures, and in exciting my critical faculty checks the sentimental instincts, and drives me to the acutest logical distinctions. I think the tendency of solitary reflection is rather towards making the sceptic than the enthusiast.

I like to feel my own height, but not as contrasted with the inferiority of others. I do not like ruling other men, because I do not like to think them only fit to be ruled.

I, a Puseyite sceptic—Carlyle, a Free-Kirk infidel.

A man's sympathy for his fellow-creatures will depend entirely on his starting-point as to the destiny and condition of humanity: if he takes the lowest state for the normal one, and everything above it to be the exception (himself included), he will end by caring little about mankind generally; if he looks upon the rich as the real men whom the others are lagging after, he will then have the deepest feelings for every neglected creature below him in wealth.

Oh! how wide is the diapason of my mind—from what a height to what a depth!

In England we have often comfort without luxury—oftener luxury without comfort—rarely the two combined, as the East has them.

Life is so full in London that it is nothing against any occupation to say it fails to get a hold there.

Christianity is the consummation, the perfection of idolatry.

The man who chooses to be a politician without a Party, or a religionist without a Church, ought to know what he undertakes, the strength of individuality required in him, and the self-sufficiency of his own mind; he will not be compromised by others, but then no one will compromise himself or him.

An honest man cannot retract what has been honestly said or done—he may learn something else which may lead him to another conclusion, but he must maintain that, as far as he then knew, he was right.

What is great in Patriotism comes not from the love of one's own country to the exclusion of others, but from the forgetfulness of one's own self in the possession of a larger idea of humanity. Christ as a patriot would have been adored by the Jews, and probably recognised as the Messiah. They hated Him because He loved the Gentile.

Poetry leaps and bubbles forth out of the heart of youth; in later years it sinks deep inwards and filtrates through life and the world around, and sometimes, but not often, it flows forth in latter years in a calm clear stream.

There is no saying how much character is developed by antagonism to convictions. A man sees his inclinations are sentimental; he therefore, to avoid excess and keep the balance in his mind, throws himself into utilitarian objects; he feels himself naturally irreverent, and therefore tries to cultivate and profess religious feelings; and all this implies no want of sincerity, rather a true and sincere knowledge of his own deficiencies.

The Anglo-Saxon race has so much of the devil in it that it rebels against the decrees of Nature, will have its own way, and ends by making a new Nature of its own.

I really have not room to pity everybody—I'm not God Almighty.

Poetry keeps a man from ambition by extending the range of his aspirations further than ambition can reach, but it may incline him to selfishness, by so diminishing the value, and exhausting the meaning of other objects, that the instincts which protect and elevate Self make it mighty in comparison.

Why may we not look on a state of things as possible where scientific and moral truth should be obligatory on every individual, but religious belief and theory should be as free and as individual as æsthetic or political opinions now are?

God has given us the gift of Faith, it is true, but He has given us the gift of Doubt as well.

The first victory of Protestantism was the right to read the Bible, the next must be the right to interpret it.

To a Theologian.

> Because your nature can't extend
> Its sight beyond a needle's end,
> And you with self-sufficient air
> Tell us how plain you see God there,
> You must not murmur that mine eye,
> Moulded and trained to reach the sky,
> Views Him in yon far star as clear
> As ever you can find Him near;
> And, if my vision is more true,
> I feel His presence more than you.

I am always trying to place myself in the highest class in the School of Life, and impose upon myself the duty of doing the highest work my faculties can possibly perform, forgetting that if I do not do the school business, I must get flogged for idleness.

Curious dream that I had drowned myself with the intention of coming back to life when I had seen what it was like, but had found it impossible to do so.

My life is as public as that of a waiter at a large inn.

I feel so much more pain in the presence of an evil than pleasure in my power to remedy it.

The pursuit of fame is either our duty or a pitiable weakness unworthy of a man.

It is certainly much easier to be a pure-minded and unselfish Liberal than Tory.

This existence is melancholy with all its splendours—a life of immense acquaintance without friendship and without love.

In England we rarely take society for its own sake; it is almost always either regarded as a means of getting on in life or settling oneself.

Grote to me· "If we are to have a new religion, I hope you may be the prophet of it, as it will be the only good-natured and benevolent one the world has yet seen."

One may look on Shelley as the head of the benevolent and reverent atheists as opposed to the French and Byronic schools.

The doctrine of plenary inspiration reduces the Bible to an Act of Parliament.

Hold over your head the umbrella of religious reverence, and though you get damp with infidelity you will not be wetted through.

You calculate the spiritual advancement of the people by the number of church and chapel sittings; you might just as well decide the amount of food consumed in a house from the number of square feet occupied by the kitchen.

I can be humble enough, but, alas! I always *know* that I am so.

One can't help feeling that one's Maker must have a humorous pleasure in the absurdities and inconsistencies of one's existence.

Mrs. Grote to me: "Young England, with all thy faults I love thee still."

Men of poetical temperament seem to be rarely of strong *natural* affections; the imagination seems to overpower the instinct, and substitute its own objects.

Why is the present English social system like the Ptolemaic system of astronomy? Because it is full of circles which *cut* one another.

I prefer to read by the faint and clouded sunlight of a great truth than by the accumulated starlight of small ones.

A man is none the worse for casting a good many asses'-skins before his own comes fairly out—that is, provided he does really cast them entirely.

A man may be superficial without being a pretender—surface may be just as true a thing as substance; if you take the one for the other, the fault is yours.

Having no duties to perform, I am obliged to put up with pleasures.

My father saying "good dandy roads were only fit for a villa, he liked his guests to feel themselves *in* the country."

The worst effect on myself resulting from attendance on Parliament is that it prevents me from forming any clear political opinions on any subjects.

The Tories have the past, the Radicals the future, and the Whigs the poor narrow uninteresting present.

You might fancy by his remarks that my father had just been introduced to his family.

Originality must be more or less unsympathising, and therefore unamiable; the salient points of character cannot touch other minds and hearts as a smooth impassive surface can.

Yes, we may be all mad together, but the philosopher will only discern the madness of others, that knows, estimates, and controls his own.

Experience! Nonsense! What a man has done once, that he'll do again—with a difference.

Good conversation is to ordinary talk what whist is to playing cards.

Don't grumble when your friends go on half-pay by marrying

or settling themselves on interests apart from your own; be thankful that they do not quit the army of Affection altogether, or even go over to the enemy.

"You are a man of a large heart," said Lady Waldegrave to me. "That may be," I answered, "but it is not near so useful as a narrow mind."

I look on the intimate and independent conversation of important men as the cream of life.

My love knows no more of forgetfulness than children do of death.

Good conversation is the small change of vested powers which implies the possession of more precious coins.

In this age of ours we have all the facilities of locomotion, but, on the other hand, we have the impossibility of rest; we have all the conveniences of machinery, but, on the other hand, are always talking of the dignity of rank; we have the anæsthesia of chloroform and relief from the inequalities of position, but there is the perpetual sense of unended responsibility, which keeps us in continual doubt and difficulty.

I understand the gods taking the young and fresh and hopeful for the sake of their society, but what can they do with an old used-up soul like mine?

I am anxious to preserve the Constitution of my country unimpaired, as I would that of my own body; but I do not think I should secure that object by stagnation or privation, but rather by good food and sufficient exercise, by healthy circulation and nutritive digestion.

Gladstone's method of impartiality is being furiously earnest on both sides of a question.

Is it to be wondered at that persecution fascinates and obscures the minds of the best men? Fancy the united pleasures of the exercise of cruelty and the satisfaction of the love of Truth !

Yes, I live for Pleasure and for Power: for Pleasure that injures no one, and Power that benefits Mankind.

The great value of the Bible is that it is not, like the Koran, the work of one god, but of many—from the fierce patriot-God of the Jews, to the universal human God, Christ.

I always wish that Christianity had come later into the world, so that it should have been the highest ideal of life and manhood as it is to come, rather than of what has been and is passed away.

The worst part of failure in life is the envy of the successful. It is almost impossible to be just at once to them and to ourselves.

It is undeniable that the acts of my life that I look back to with the greatest regret as having impeded and damaged my means of usefulness and exertion of talents and occasions of improvement, have, in the main, been the result of good, high, and honourable motives; whereas many of the so-called successes in life have been founded on poor and vain principles of action, and often prosecuted by unworthy means.

I believe there is nothing so rare as a happy life between thirty and fifty, in the years when the hopes vanish and the realities come out clear, when the failures of life become distinct, and the limitations of success visible, when the past, which was so lightly prized when passing, is looked back on with envy, and the future is regarded with tremulous uncertainty, it may be with dread.

I look on the Parable of the Talents as the Law and the Gospel, and could almost be contented to lose my faculties in the consideration that I was relieved from the responsibility of employing them.

There will be always cross-lights troubling every earnest mind.

INDEX.

"A Yorkshire River," poem by Lewis Morris, referred to, i. 6 (note)
Aberdeen, Lord, i. 235, 248, 272, 333; Gladstone's letters to, 451; Prime Minister, 478; defeat of his Ministry, 501; Gladstone's opinion of his Ministry, 502, 503
About, Edmond, ii. 169
Academy, The, Lord Houghton's articles on Lord Russell, ii. 303, 338, 374; Panizzi, 404
Acland, Mr., i. 204, 205, 218, 222
Acton, Cardinal, i. 291
Acton, Lord, ii. 212, 394, 421
Acton, Sir John, ii. 143
Adams, Mr., American Minister, i. 464; ii. 317, 334
"Adonais," Shelley's, its first publication in England, i. 77, 83
"Adventures of a Younger Son," Trelawny's, i. 145
"Advice to Servants," Swift's, i. 115
Aidé, Hamilton, i. 464; ii. 321
Aire, River, i. 2, 6
Alabama Question, ii. 261
Albert, Prince, i. 514; death, ii. 74, 356, 463
Albrizzi, Count, i. 106, 136
Alcock, Sir Rutherford, ii. 375
Alford, Henry (afterwards Dean of Canterbury), i. 75; one of the "Apostles" at Cambridge, 81, 83, 177; ii. 161, 243
Alford, Lady Marian, ii. 23
"All fair things have soft approaches," poem by R. M. Milnes, i. 120
Allen, John, i. 75
Allingham, William, lines on Lord Houghton, ii. 467
Almack's, i. 109
Althorp, Lord, i. 100, 111
Alton, i. 161
Amberley, Lord, ii. 135

America, Lord Houghton's visit, ii. 307—335
American War, R. M. Milnes's adhesion to the Republican side, ii. 65, 66, 128
Ampthill, Lord, ii. 296
Ancona, i. 129; detention of R. M. Milnes in the lazaretto, 136
ANECDOTES: Mr. R. P. Milnes's wager with a friend for £100, i. 11; Mr. R. P. Milnes's refusal to take office in the Ministry, 13; Duke of Wellington before the Battle of Waterloo, 25; Mr. R. P. Milnes and his addiction to gambling, 30; Mr. R. P. Milnes and Lord Foley, 31; Mr. R. P. Milnes and the poachers, 32; the Queen's carriage drawn by the rabble and accident to Milnes's sedan chair, 33; effect of a passage in Gray's "Elegy" on Mr. R. P. Milnes, 33; R. M. Milnes at Dieppe, 34; want of intelligence in English farmers, 36; Rodes, Milnes, and Lord Glasgow, at York races, 37; Mr. W. E. Forster and R. M. Milnes, 44; Lord Tennyson and R. M. Milnes, 63; R. M. Milnes and Dr. Wordsworth, Shelley deputation, 77; Duke of St. Albans and the Siamese boys, 94; Prince Leopold and the British Plutarch, 94; Alfred Tennyson, Spedding, and Dr. Whewell, 105; R. M. Milnes and Swift's "Advice to Servants," 115; Niebuhr and the French Revolution of 1830, 115; R. M. Milnes and his sister, 117; R. M. Milnes, Wordsworth, and the Queen's masked ball, 119; Miss H. Milnes and the scorpion at the Venetian concert, 137; R. M. Milnes, Trench, and C. J.

MacCarthy on the Strada Giulia, Rome, 156; the whale and the calf, 163, 164; Thackeray and smoking in R. M. Milnes's room, 167; origin of the song, "I wandered by the brook-side," 175, 176; R. M. Milnes and his breakfast visitors, 187; Carlyle, and the one "post" for which R. M. Milnes was fitted, 187; Carlyle and Macaulay at Samuel Rogers's, 191; Lord Houghton and Goethe, 201; R. M. Milnes's, rejoinder to the closing words of Disraeli's maiden speech in the House of Commons, 202; "Keys of St. Peter" —Mr. Disraeli, the Attorney-General, and the House of Commons, 204; R. M. Milnes and Sydney Smith at Holland House, 213; R. M. Milnes with reference to a letter of Sydney Smith on jocular titles, 214; R. M. Milnes and Disraeli, 216; S. Rogers and Lady Parke, 218; Sydney Smith (or Lockhart) and Landseer, 218; S. Rogers and Jane Davy, 218; Carlyle and R. P. Milnes in the drawing-room at Fryston, 254; squib by R. M. Milnes and Charles Bullar on a report of an imaginary French debate on a fancy ball at Buckingham Palace, 280; R. M. Milnes singing on the Nile, 290; R. M. Milnes and Carlyle on Tennyson's pension, 296; R. M. Milnes and Peel, on Tennyson, Sheridan Knowles, 297; Sydney Smith and Apostolic Succession, 300; Sir Robert Peel and Gladstone's "Church and State," 316; Prince of Schwarzburg Sondershausen and the deputation asking for a Constitution, 342; the Duke of Albany and Lord Houghton at Claremont, 379, note; Thackeray and the fall of the tree at Fryston, 427; Mrs. Disraeli at Lord St. Germans', 491; Sir Frederick Thesiger and Lord Campbell, 496; Lord Lyveden and R. M. Milnes at Paris, 518; the Dean of York and the candidate for ordination, ii. 22; Bishop of Exeter and R. M. Milnes, 39; the request to R. M. Milnes for £50 from a man of letters, 44, 45; Milnes and the accident to the prelate's wife, 93; Milnes, and the "immeasurable gulf" between a peer and a commoner, 98; Lord Stanley and Lord Houghton, 120; Disraeli's idea of amusement, 120; Lord Clarendon and Lord Houghton, 136; Carlyle and Kirkstall Abbey, 148; "Home sweet Home," and Madame Pasta, 259; Gladstone mistaken for Disraeli, 276; Mr. R. P. Milnes and Mrs. Proctor, 357; the Prince of Wales and Lord Houghton, 359; Cobden, Lord Houghton, and Louis Napoleon, 388; S. T. Coleridge and Lord Houghton, 432; Grillion's Club and Lord Houghton, 460; Grillion's Club and Gladstone, 461

Anglesea, Lady, i. 151
Anglesea, Lord; his government, i. 60
Anne, Queen, ii. 356
Anonymous Club (*see* Sterling Club)
Antonelli, Cardinal, ii. 189, 424
Antrim, Lord and Lady, i. 112, 113
"Apostles," The, i. 80; description of this Association by W. D. Christie, 82; essay read by R. M. Milnes, 91, 146, 193
Appleton, Miss (married to Mr. Longfellow), i. 303
Archduchess of Austria, The, i. 101
Argyll, Duke of, i. 496, 522, ii. 179, 333; presides at a Liberal Demonstration at Leeds, 383, 423
Arnold, Matthew, writes to R. M. Milnes on the Italian question, and his pamphlet on the subject, ii. 40, 41
Arta, i. 128
Ashburton, Lady, ii. 220, 251
Ashburton, Lord, i. 187, 270, 280; friendship with R. M. Milnes, 478; death of Lady Ashburton, and Carlyle's opinion of her, ii. 25, 26, 93, 95; death, 122; Lord Houghton's opinion of him, 123
Ashley, Lord, and Factory Legislation, i. 324, 325, 332, 453
"Atalanta in Calydon," Lord Houghton's article in the *Edinburgh Review*, on Swinburne's, ii. 136, 138
Athenæum, The, i. 60, 61, 79: started by Mr. James Silk Buckingham, and edited by Frederick Denison Maurice, 81; the *Literary Chronicle* merged into it, 81; ii. 141, 264, 265, 272, 303, 338, 354

INDEX.

Athenæum Club, i. 221; ii. 78; dinner to Longfellow, 193, 195
Athens, i. 129, 130, 132, 133; R. M. Milnes, description of, 134, 282; illness of Lord Houghton there, ii. 413—416; a baptism, 417
Austria; effect of Revolution in Paris of 1830, i. 100; severe measures in Milan, 101; rule in Lombardy, 111, 137, 431; the Emperor at the opening of the Suez Canal, ii. 20; Crown Prince of, ii. 397

Baggs, Dr., i. 291, 293
Bagot, Sir Charles, i. 272
Baiæ, i. 113
Bailey, Archdeacon, i. 408, 434
Baines, Matthew Talbot, Chancellor of the Duchy of Lancaster, ii. 24
Baker, Sir Samuel, ii. 211
Balloon ascent of Mr. R. M. Milnes, i. 65—68
Bamford, Samuel, ii, 44
Bancroft, Mr. and Mrs., ii. 256
Barham, Lord, i. 109
Baring, Lady Harriet, i. 437
Barnard, Governor of Paris, i. 28
Barrett, Miss (see Browning, Mrs. Barrett).
Baur, Monseigneur, ii. 209
Bawtry, Pemberton Milnes's estate at, i. 5; inherited by his daughter, Viscountess Galway, 5; Mr. Pemberton Milnes (2) becomes the owner of the estate, 38; return of the Milnes family, 158, 317, 407; ii. 118; the old Meeting House, 312
Beaconsfield, Lord, frequenter of Gore House, i. 185; maiden speech in the House of Commons, 202; "keys of St. Peter," 204; mouthpiece of the "Young England" school, 319; letter to R. M. Milnes on the latter's criticism of "Coningsby," 320; visit to Fryston, 337; his conception of R. M. Milnes as "Mr. Vavasour" in "Tancred," 337—339; R. M. Milnes's opinion of him, 352; becomes the implacable antagonist of Peel, 369; remark of Carlyle on his "Jewish jackasseries," 436, 444; tergiversations, 453; leader of the Conservative party, 479; ii. 13, 120; the Reform question, 159; Gladstone's opinion of him, 175; recommended by Lord Derby to the Queen for Prime Minister, 186; illness of Mrs. Disraeli at the opening of Parliament, and Gladstone's speech of sympathy, 187-189, 191, 196; "Lothair," 223, 260, 298; accepts a peerage, 339; Treaty of Berlin, 380, 399; "Endymion," 416; lines of Lord Houghton on a comparison of him with Mr. Gladstone, 462

Beauclerk, Lady Di, ii. 199
Beaumont, Gustave De, Criticism on Montalembert by, i. 246; visits London, 408; ii. 30
Bedford, Duke of, ii. 296
Beecher, Henry Ward, ii. 322
Beef-steak Club, ii. 368
Beelzebub, and the Manchester Athenæum, A remark of Carlyle on, i. 435
Belfast, i. 110
Belgrave, Lord, i. 95
"Beneath an Indian Palm a Girl," poem by R. M. Milnes, i. 120
Benevolence, Unbeneficial, Opinion of R. M. Milnes on, ii. 4
Bentinck, Lord George, i. 401, 408; ii. 118
Benzene, Countess, i. 136
Béranger, Reference of W. S. Landor to, i. 181
Berlin, i. 153; R. M. Milnes's visit to, 340—345; ii. 397
Bernal, Ralph, i. 75
Bernard, General, ii. 18
Berne, i. 145
Bernstorff, Count, Prussian Ambassador, ii. 126, 235, 239
Berrys, The Miss, Lord Houghton's sketch in his "Monographs" of, i. 188, 234; "the link between the society of the nineteenth century and that of the eighteenth century," 233, 319, 383; article by Miss Martineau, 511
Biarritz, ii. 154, 157
Bigelow, Mr., ii. 317
Binns, Mr., private tutor to R. M. Milnes, i. 47
Birmingham, i. 161
Birmingham League, The, ii. 283
Birmingham Press Club, Lord Houghton's reception at the, ii. 369
Bismarck, Prince, ii. 127, 157, 173, 231; his Erastianism, 285
Bisset, Dr., ii. 362
Blackburn, Mrs., ii. 292
Blackwood, criticism on Trench's poems in, i. 159; attack on W. S.

Landor, 182; review of R. M. Milnes' poems, 230; ii. 444
Blair, Mrs. Hunter, i. 150
Blake, William, i. 220; ii. 221, 222
Blakesley, J. W., i. 49, 75; one of the "Apostles" at Cambridge, 81, 83, 90; commences a new debating society, "The Fifty," 106; letter to R. M. M. on subscribers for "Sartor Resartus," ii. 162, 200; candidate at the Athenæum Club, 221; Sterling Club, 222
Blane, Louis, visit to London, i. 455
Bland, Sir John, i. 455
Blessington, Countess of, and Gore House, i. 185
Blücher, i. 23, 26.
"Blue Ruin," i. 31
Bodenham, Delabarre, i. 317
Bognor, Visit of Mr. P. Milnes and family to, i. 23
Bolingbroke, i. 88
Bologna, i. 107
Bolton Street, Mayfair, i. 13
Bonn, Mr. R. M. Milnes's first and subsequent impressions of, i. 97; frequency of duels, 98; ii. 133, 181
Bordeaux, ii. 154
Bosquet, General, ii. 9
Botham, Mrs., i. 150
Boulogne, i. 21, 22, 56, 57, 59, 60, 65, 68; ii. 8
Bournemouth, ii. 427
Bowen, Sir George, recollections of his visit to America with Lord Houghton, ii. 328
Brandis, Professor, i. 97; ii. 78
Brazil, Emperor of, ii. 262
Breakfasts, R. M. Milnes's, i. 185, 228, 461, 473
Bright, Henry, friendship with Lord Houghton, ii. 141, 172, 176, 196, 205, 242, 251, 269, 271; his pamphlet, "Unpunished Cruelties on the High Seas," 273, 279, 281, 283, 289, 297; "Year in a Lancashire Garden," 304, 318, 327, 384; visit to Cannes with Lord Houghton, 420; Lord Houghton visits him at Bournemouth, 427; death, 1884, 427, 431
Bright, John, his Free Trade doctrines, i. 369, 513; ii. 13, 16; meeting with Lord John Russell, 38; sympathies during the American war, 65, 143, 144; the Franchise Bill, 150, 151; speaks at the Reform banquet at Manchester, 157, 178;

illness, 226, 271, 333; on Lord Houghton's poems, 409
British Association, i. 146; meeting at Plymouth, ii. 365
British Museum, i. 234; the Trusteeship, ii. 277, 279, 406
Brittany, i. 231
"Broad Stone of Honour, The," by Kenelm Digby, i. 117
Brontë, Charlotte; friendship with R. M. Milnes and Thackeray, i. 428, 429; Milnes's kindness to her relations, 429; Mrs. Gaskell's interest in her, 476, 527; ii. 283
Brookfield, Rev. C., i. 489, 523; ii. 170, 297
Brooks's Club, i. 19, 501
Brougham, Lord; friendship with the King of Hanover, i. 301; against the Factory Bill, 325; the O'Connell Appeal Case, 335; his opinion of Milnes's "Letter to Lord Lansdowne," 414, 415; his attack on Lord Palmerston's policy, 419; remarks on the Apostles and the Times, 433; Social Science Congress, ii. 25; at Cannes with Lord Houghton, 121, 122, 281, 401.
Broughton, Lord, i. 43; visit of R. M. Milnes to Tedworth, ii. 120
Broughton, Miss, ii. 338
Browning, Mrs. Barrett, i. 279
Browning, Robert, "Strafford," by, i. 196; intimacy of R. M. Milnes with, 383; ii. 10, 70; the Athenæum Club, 78; the Queen and, 198, 243, 244; stories of him by S. Kirkup, 249, 256, 264; on the death of Lady Houghton, 291
Bruce, Mrs., ii. 190
Bruges, i. 24
Brummel, Beau, i. 32, 37; his fallen fortunes, 244
Brunow, Baron, Russian Ambassador in London, i. 487
"Brunswickers," The (Cambridge University), i. 59, 61
Brussels, i. 24, 25, 97
Bryant, Mr., President of the Century Club, ii. 329
Buccleuch, Duke of, ii. 252
Buchanan, Mr. Robert, befriends David Gray, the Scotch poet, ii. 54
Buchanan, Sir Andrew, i. 464
Buckingham, Duke of, i. 271
Buckingham Palace, Wordsworth and R. M. Milnes attend a masked ball at, i. 119

INDEX. 503

Buller, Charles, i. 49, 81, 83; fails to make an impression in Parliament, 99, 171; R. M. Milnes's rival in wit, 189, 272; *jeu d'esprit* on a fancy ball, 280, note; 303, 324, 375; death, 409; R. M. Milnes's tribute to, 414, 489; ii. 29, 196
Buller, Mrs., i. 99
Bulwer, Lytton (*see* Lytton, Lord)
Bulwer, Sir Henry, English minister at Madrid, i. 391, 396, 399, 400
Bunsen, Chevalier, i. 124, 126, 151, 153, 173, 228, 305, 340, 343, 344, 439; Milnes's visit to, ii. 19, 20, 21; death, 66
Bunsen, George, i. 473; ii. 18; reminiscences of R. M. Milnes, 67, 68, 123, 126, 153, 154, 173, 230, 281, 285, 343, 392, 397, 417
Burdett-Coutts, Baroness, ii. 179, 202, 260; 364
Burghersh, Lord, i. 23
Burnaby, Captain, ii. 367
Burns Anniversary, The, i. 506
Burns, Robert, Unveiling of statue of, ii. 355
Burton, Lady, ii. 301, 302, 370
Burton, Sir Richard, i. 462; article by R. M. Milnes in the *Edinburgh Review*, ii. 76, 300
Busk, Miss Rachel, i. 6
Busk, Mr. Hans, i. 6
Bute, Lord, i. 315
Butler, Dr., i. 53; Master of Trinity, ii. 435
Buxton, ii. 250
Byron, Lord, i. 72; revolt at Cambridge University against this poetry, 74, 77; Moore's "Life" of him, 88, 89, 104; acquaintance with Madame Guiccioli, 136; influence on the wane, 1836, 171; Leigh Hunt's opinion of him, ii. 203
"Byzantium," subject of Cambridge prize poem for 1830, i. 93

Caine, Hall, ii. 367
Cairo, i. 282; R. M. Milnes's visit to, 289; ii. 410, 427
Cairns, Lord, ii. 240, 415
Calder, River, ii. 2
Calvin, ii. 134
Cambridge Amateur Dramatic Club, i. 84
Cambridge, Duke of, i. 507; ii. 395
Cambridge House, i. 7
Cambridge Union Society, i. 50, 52, 53, 57, 58, 59, 61, 62; its use as a preparation for parliamentary speaking, 71; debate on Wordsworth and Byron, 72; leading men who took part in its proceedings in 1829, 74-75; A. Hallam, Milnes, and T. Sunderland, sent as a deputation to the kindred society at Oxford, to maintain the superiority of Shelley to Byron, 77; R. M. Milnes's account of the visit and discussion, 78; "Transactions," 83; R. M. M. states his inability to lead it, 92; two speeches by R. M. M., 93; "nearly at death's door," 1831, 106; opening of new rooms by Lord Houghton, ii. 159-166.
Campbell, Charles, i. 50
Campbell, Lady, i. 106, 107, 110
Campbell, Lord, the O'Connell Appeal Case, i. 336; ii. 71
Campbell, Miss (sister of Thomas Campbell the poet), i. 48
Campbell, Sir C., i. 509
Campbell, Thomas, the poet, i. 96; acquaintance with R. M. Milnes and his father, 121, 171, 173; death (1844), 329, 333; R. M. Milnes secures an appointment in the Civil Service for the nearest relative, 329
Canada, Lord Houghton's visit, ii. 308
Canaletti, i. 106
Cannes, ii. 121, 184, 420
Canning, Lord, Governor-General of India, i. 512; ii. 3
Canning, Mr., Secretary of State, 1806, i. 9, 80
Canning, Sir Stratford, i. 272; friendship with R. M. Milnes, 282
Canrobert, Marshal, ii. 268
Canterbury, Archbishop of, i. 465; "Essays and Reviews," ii. 131
Canterbury, Lord, i. 203, 270
Captain, Loss of the, ii. 233, 235, 236
Cardwell, Mr, resignation of office, i. 503; ii. 25
Carleton, Dudley, ii. 178
Carlisle, Lord, i. 301; ii. 133
Carlton Club, Withdrawal of R. M. Milnes from the, i. 401, 501
Carlyle, Mrs., i. 333; and Lady Ashburton, ii. 423
Carlyle, Thomas, Goethe's influence upon, i. 116; residence at Cheyne Row, 171; acquaintance with R. M. Milnes, and appreciation of his merits, 172; the "post" for which R. M. Milnes was fitted, 187; as a dinner-table talker, 190; visitor at

S. Rogers's, 190; completes the "French Revolution," and appears as a lecturer, 192, 193; "Sartor Resartus," 200, 293; letter to R. M. Milnes, 209, 217: lectures, 220; reported statement about him by R. M. Milnes, 224; Emerson's "Nature," 224; meeting with Thirlwall, 228; growing intimacy with R. M. Milnes, 229; projects the London Library, 234, 236; visit to Fryston, 251-259, 268; letter to R. M. M. on the York Courthouse, Scotch people, suggesting Milnes should found a "priest's cell" at Fryston, 265—268; letter to R. M. M., on the Copyright Bill, &c., 276—278; letter to the same on the Chartist Riots, &c., 281, 282; letter to the same on the latter's return from the East, 290; Tennyson's pension, 296; visit to the Bishop of St. Davids, 302, 303; letter to R. M. M. on Cowper's "Crow," and asking for information relative to the Darley family, 308, 309; "Cromwell," 308, 360; letter to R. M. Milnes, March, 1844, on "Palm Leaves," Mahomet, &c., 323, 324; visit to Mr. W. E. Forster at Rawdon, 386, 387; his opinion of Milnes's "Letter to Lord Lansdowne," 416; his "Sayings" from R. M. Milnes's Commonplace Book, 435, 436; his advice to Milnes at being passed over by Sir Robert Peel, 437; article in *Fraser* on Slavery, 439; opinion of Lady Ashburton, ii. 26; "Frederick the Great," 94, 127; his wife's illness, 112, 127; Lord Rector of the University of Edinburgh, 144; death of Mrs. Carlyle, 149; his visit to Fryston (1866), 148; on his wife's qualities, 149; *Punch*, 153; Biography of Stirling, 161, 250; on Lord Houghton's cheery stoicism, 345, 369; his death (1881), 401; happiness of his married life, 425; his "Sayings" from Lord Houghton's Commonplace Books, Appendix, 477—481

Carné, M., on the Paris fortifications, i. 742
Carnival at Rome, i. 151
Casa Arconati, i. 107
Caserte, i. 125

Castlereagh, Lord, i. 23
Catesby, Monsignore, ii. 300
Catholics; proposed .Parliamentary measure of relief defeated in 1806, i. 9; R. M. Milnes's sympathy in early life with them, 118; the gulf separating them from the Protestants in Ireland, 120; endowment of the Church in Ireland, 300, 301, 320; aggression in England, 445, 446; effect of the Maynooth grant on the clergy, ii. 198
"Cave of Adullam," ii. 150
Cavendish, seventh Duke of Devonshire, i. 53, 62
Cavendishes, The, i. 5
Cavour, Count, ii. 10; 124
Century Club, ii. 329
Ceylon: Governorship of Charles MacCarthy, i. 123
Chamberlain, Miss, ii. 421
Chambers, Mrs., i. 150
Chambord, Comte de, ii. 425
"Characteristics, August, 1875," notebook of Lord Houghton, containing a record of his visit to America, ii. 309—312
Charade, by W. S. Landor, i. 183
Chaucer, i. 119
Chesham, Lord, ii. 294
Chester, Bishop of, ii. 17, 137
Chesterfield, Lord, i. 291
Chicago, ii. 309, 312
Childers, Mr., ii. 250, 259
Choate, J. H., ii. 334
Cholera in Italy, i. 161
Chorley's novels, ii. 282
Christ and London; a remark of Carlyle, i. 435
Christ, the silence of, a remark of Carlyle on, i. 435
"Christian Art," M. Rio's, i. 158, 292
Christian, Princess, ii. 190
Christie, W. D., describes the association of the "Apostles" at Cambridge, i. 82; ii. 449
Christmas Annuals, i. 177
Church, General, i. 133
Church and State, Lord Houghton's opinion on the connection of, ii. 192
Circourt, Comte and Comtesse, accompany R. M. Milnes on a tour through Northern Italy, i. 143, 151; ii. 145, 234
Civil Service Reform, Carlyle's opinions on, i. 494, 495
Civita Vecchia, i. 122

Clarendon Lord, i. 484, 525; ii. 9, 127, 135, 176, 460
Clanricarde, Lord, i. 92, 473, 499
Clarke, Colonel, ii. 411
Cleveland, Duke of, i. 96; ii. 135
Clifford, Sir Augustus, ii. 22
Clinton, Lady Susan, i. 524
Cloth and woollen trades of Leeds and Wakefield, i. 1, 2
Cloth manufacture, the oldest English industry, i. 1; monopolised in Wakefield by the Milneses in the eighteenth century, 3
Clôture in Parliament, ii. 415
Clough, Arthur Hugh, i. 463, 490
Cobbett, William, lecture at St. Ives, i. 94, 101
Cobden, Richard, Free Trade doctrines, i. 369; intimacy with R. M. Milnes, 377, 383; remark on the French Socialists, 434; remark of Carlyle, "an inspired bagman," &c., 436, 513, ii. 16; Russell's opinion of his Budget, 24, 423
Cockburn, Sir Alexander, ii. 135
Codrington, General, i. 509
Coleridge, S. T.; his "Ancient Mariner," i. 61; definition of a gentleman, 80; on "Church and State," 88, 146; dinner-table talker, 190; unveiling of bust at Westminster Abbey, 432
Coliseum, The, Rome, i. 122
Collins, Wilkie, i. 463; ii. 79; visits Fryston, 127, 183, 361
Collyer, Dr. Robert, ii. 312
Colville, Sir James, a friend of R. M. Milnes, i. 199, 229, 284, 292, 322, 382, 409; ii. 38, 73, 75; death, 398
Combermere, Lord, i. 29
Commonplace Books, Extracts from Lord Houghton's i. 419—422, 423, 424; sayings of Carlyle, 435, 436; contains also sayings of Guizot, Bulmer, King Louis Philippe, De Tocqueville, Grote, Pusey, Spedding, Thackeray, Lord Morpeth, Bunsen, Macaulay, Charles Buller, Tennyson, Sir David Brewster, Professor Airy, Whewell, and others, 436; sayings on Milnes's own foibles, 437; note on Peel's accident and death, 443; ii. 276; sayings of Sydney Smith, Carlyle, and others, Appendix, 469—497
"Complaint of Glenquoich, The," poem by Lord Houghton, ii. 241

"Coningsby," R. M. Milnes's criticism in *Hood's Magazine* on, i. 319
Constant, B., i. 70
Constantinople, visit of R. M. Milnes to, i. 282
Conversation, the true art of, i. 190
Convocation, attack on "Essays and Reviews," ii. 128—131
Conyngham, Lady, i. 152
Cook, Eliza, ii. 354
Copenhagen, i. 14
Copyright Bill, 1838; letter from Wordsworth to R. M. Milnes, i. 226, 227; (1842) R. M. Milnes's interest in it, 275, 276
Corfu, i. 126, 128, 129, 130
Corinne, i. 113
Cork, Lady, i. 95; ii. 387
Corn Laws, The, i. 278; meeting at Covent Garden, 322, 359; the crisis of January, 1845, 366, 367; their repeal, May 15, 1846, 371
Cornhill Magazine, Poem by Milnes in, ii. 64, 112
Cornish, Mrs., ii. 321
Cornwall, Barry, Allusion by Charles Sumner to, i. 327
Cosmopolitan Club, i. 44
Cottenham, Lord; the O'Connell appeal case, i. 336
Court of Ultimate Appeal, Views of R. M. Milnes on the, i. 335
Courtenay, Lord, i. 332
Courvoisier, i. 187, 426
Cousin, V., i. 70, 72; ii. 121
Coventry, Lady, i. 151
Cowley, Lady, ii. 204
Cowley, Lord, i. 514; ii. 170
Cowper, Lady, ii. 61
Cowper, Spencer, i. 513 515
Cowper's "Crow," Carlyle's allusion to, i. 308
Cowper's Grave at Olney, Sonnet by R. M. Milnes on, i. 194
Cranbourne, Lady, ii. 177
Cranbourne, Lord, ii. 177
Craven, Mrs., "Récit d'une Sœur," by, ii. 156
"Crescent and the Cross, The," Eliot Warburton's, i. 109
Crewe, the Honourable Annabel, Marriage of R. M. Milnes to, i. 447, 450
Crewe, Lord, i. 447, 497; ii. 240
Crimean War, i. 486; sufferings of the British troops, &c., 493; Miss Nightingale's Mission, 493, 509;

want of medical stores, 500; proclamation of peace, 1856, ii. 8
Croker, J. W., i. 111, 391
"Cromwell," Carlyle's, i. 308, 360
Crowle, Mr. Charles, i. 455
Crowquill, Alfred, i. 179
Croy, i. 146
Crystal Palace; Lord Houghton's last public appearance in London at a dinner given by Cyrus Field, ii. 434
Cullen, Cardinal, i. 124, 498
Cunliffe, Mrs., i. 159
Cuningham, Lord, i. 24
Curzon, Robert, i. 445
Custine; his abuse of Russia, i. 325, 326
Cuvier, Baron, i. 68

Daily News; contributions of Miss Martineau, i. 525; ii. 32; article on Thomas Sunderland, 166; memorial to Leigh Hunt, 206, 240, 281; Bulgarian horrors, 340
Daily Telegraph; article on R. M. Milnes's accession to the peerage, ii. 101, 102
Dalrymple, Sir Hugh, i. 24
Darley, George, i. 200
Darrell, Captain, i. 417
Dashwood, Colonel, i. 24, 25
Daudet, ii. 168
D'Aumale, Duc, i. 463; member of the Philobiblon Society, 509; ii. 131, 251, 255, 266, 268, 385
D'Auvergne, Latour, ii. 134
Davoust, i. 27
Davy, Lady, i. 291
De Broglie, Duc, ii. 10; 31; 238; 251; 293
De Chartres, Duc, i. 463
De Flahault, M., ii. 10
De Grey, Lord, i. 271
De Lhuys, M. Drouyn, i. 515
De Vere, Mr. Aubrey, Reminiscences of R. M. Milnes's youth, by, i. 113—120; 177; 180; letters from R. M. Milnes, 193—197
De Vere, Sir Vere, i. 114
De Walden, Lady Howard, ii. 310
Deal, i. 21
Delancey, General, i. 28
Delane, J. T., guest of Mr. and Mrs. Milnes, i. 473; battle of Alma and the Times, 500; ii. 109, 133, 175, 186, 192, 204, 255
Denison, Mr., ii. 191
Denman, Lord, the O'Connell Appeal Case, i. 336
Derby, Lord, i. 204; end of his first Administration, 478; Prime Minister, ii. 149, 187, 189
Derbyshire, The Milneses sprang from, i. 3
Devonshire, Duke of, i. 229; Chancellor of Cambridge University, ii. 161
Dickens, Charles, reference by C. Sumner, i. 281, 306, 333; as an actor, 358; ii. 80, 139; death and interment in Westminster Abbey, 227–229; his grandmother and the Crewe family, 227, 256, 257, 289
Dieppe, i. 34
Digby, Kenelm, "The Broad Stone of Honour," and "Mores Catholici," by, i. 117
Dilke, Sir Charles, ii. 256, 303, 387
Dinner-table talkers, Distinguished, i. 190
Disraeli, Benjamin (see Beaconsfield, Lord)
Dissenters, The; missionary enthusiasm, i. 159; bitterness and fanaticism, 294, 300; the Tahiti affair, 334
"Dobbin, Major," i. 75
Dobell, Sydney, befriends David Gray, ii. 50, 51
Dodson, Mr., ii. 388
Dolby, Mrs. Sainton, ii. 193
Doncaster, i. 30
Donizetti, ii. 259
Donne, W. B., ii. 127
Doré, Gustave, ii. 176
D'Orsay, Count, at Gore House, i. 185, 228, 377, 432
Douglas, Sir Charles, i. 205
Doyle, Richard, i. 465
Doyle, Sir Francis, i. 77; refers in his Reminiscences to the Shelley deputation to Oxford, and the honours which fell to Milnes, 86; visitor at Fryston, 256, 279; marries Miss Wynn, 330, 354
Dublin, i. 110, 112
Dublin Review, Review of Milnes's poems in the, i. 262
Ducrot, General, ii. 268
Dudley, Lady, ii. 191
Dudley, Lord, ii. 208
Duelling at Bonn, i. 98
Duff, Sir Mountstuart Grant, ii. 426
Dufferin, Lord, ii. 83, 397
Dufour, Arles, ii. 134
Duncan, Lady Elizabeth, ii. 365
Duncan, Lord, i. 71
Duncombe, Tom, i. 202, 324

INDEX.

Durgan, Mr., i. 185
Duty on foreign books, motion of R. M. Milnes for the abolition of, i. 480

Earthquake at Rome, i. 122
Eastlake, Mrs., i. 431
"Ecce Homo," The author of, ii. 178
Edgeworth, Miss, i. 113; Memoirs, ii. 183
Edinburgh, i. 47, 242
Edinburgh, Duke of, marriage, ii. 276
Edinburgh Review, i. 106; R. M. Milnes' article on Russia, 317, 325, 369; other articles by R. M. M., 446; article by R. M. M. on Sir Richard Barton, ii. 76; Lord Houghton's article on "Atalanta in Calydon," 136; Houghton's review of "The Spanish Gypsy," 192, 220; Lord Houghton's article on Landor, 221; Lord Houghton's article on "Lothair," 223, 282
Education Bill, Mr. Forster's, i. 388
Effingham House, i. 7
Effingham, Lord, lines on Pemberton Milnes, i. 5
Egerton, Francis, i. 159
Eldon, Lord, "Life" of, i. 340
Elgin, Lord, i. 408, 431
Eliot, George, ii., 193, 283; friendship with Lord Houghton, 376
Eliot, Lord, i. 271
"Ellen Middleton," Gladstone's review of, i. 335
Ellenborough, Lord, i. 382
Ellesmere, Lord, i. 527
Ellice, Edward, i. 84, 96; ii. 241
Emerson, R. W., correspondence between R. M. Milnes and Carlyle on the works of, i. 224, 225; his history and character, 237—239; his letter to R. M. Milnes on the latter's review of his essays, 241, 242, 323, ii. 307; entertains Lord Houghton at Concord, 318
"Endymion," Article by Lord Houghton in *Macmillan's Magazine* on, ii. 419
Englishman, The, Hallam's criticism of Tennyson's poems in, i. 117
"Eothen," i. 340, 346
Epaminondas, i. 129
Epilogue to *Much Ado About Nothing*, written by R. M. Milnes, i. 84
Errington, Mr., ii. 424
"Essays and Reviews," Attack in Convocation, and debate in the House of Lords on, ii. 128, 129; Lord Houghton's speech in defence of, 129; Lord Westbury's speech on the attack of Convocation, 130, 131
Eugenie, The Empress, at the opening of the Suez Canal, ii. 207, 209, 210, 234, 235, 239, 385
"Eustace," i. 113
Evarts, Mr., ii. 322, 323
"Events of 1848, The," by Lord Houghton, ii. 441
Ewart, Mrs., ii. 20
Examiner, The, i. 517
Executions, Substitution of private for public; Lord Houghton's advocacy of the change, ii. 280
Exeter, Bishop of, Humorous allusion of Sydney Smith to the, i. 300; ii. 39, 260
Exeter Hall and Popery, i. 434
Eyre, General, i. 509

Factory Education, i. 294
Factory Legislation; Lord Ashley's proposition, i. 324
Fairbairn, Sir Andrew, ii. 387
Fane, Julian, i. 465; "Tannhauser," ii. 69, 176, 178, 226
Farrar, Archdeacon, ii. 182
Fawcett, Henry, i. 465
Fayrer, Sir Joseph, ii. 426
Fenian attempt to blow up the House of Detention, ii. 188
Fenwick, Miss, i. 192
Fesch, Cardinal; sale of his pictures, i. 72
Field, Cyrus, ii. 434
Fielding, i. 222
Fiesole, i. 144
"Fifty, The," a debating society at Cambridge, i. 106
Fitzclarence, i. 96
Fitzgerald, Edward, ii. 263, 377
Fitzgerald, Lord Edward, i. 110, 270
FitzGerald, Mr. Gerald, Lord Houghton's son-in-law, ii. 407, 432
FitzGerald, Mrs. Gerald, Lord Houghton's elder daughter, i. 473, 486, 517; ii. 10, 19, 60, 81, 158, 169, 171, 181, 198, 201, 294, 298, 387, 395; marriage, 407, 408, 413, 416, 432
Fitzroy, Augustus, i. 49, 62, 84, 91, 96, 97
Fitzroy, H., i. 489
Fitzwilliams, The, i. 5, 479; ii. 153, 327

Flaubert, ii. 168
Fleury, General, ii. 268
"Flight of Youth, The," R. M. Milnes's, i. 117; ii. 445
Florence, i. 107, 144, 155: tragic incident at a ball, 155; the cholera, 161
"Flower of the Levant, The" (Zante), i. 130
Foley, Lord, i. 31; ii. 23
Foljambes, The, i. 5.
Follies of Fashion, The, a comedy, by Lord Glengall, i. 91
Fonblanque, i. 517
Ford, Mr., English Minister at Athens, ii. 410, 412, 416
Forster, John, Friendship of Mrs. Procter with, i. 306; as an actor, 358, 506; sympathies during the American War, ii. 65; and Seymour Kirkup, ii. 249
Forster, Mr. W. E., Opinion of Mr. Richard Monckton Milnes of, i. 44; ii., 451; visit of R. M. M. to, i. 385; R. M. M.'s friendship with, 387; meets R. M. M. in Paris, 1848, 404; ii. 221, 226, 250, 252, 259; the Birmingham League, 283, 303, 333; the Leeds Demonstration, 1879, 383; attack on the House of Lords, 395
Fortnightly Review, ii. 152, 366; Lord Houghton's Review of Lord Melbourne's "Life," ii. 371, 399
Forum, The, Rome, i. 122
Fox, General, ii. 250
Fox, W. J., M.P. for Oldham; his appearance in the House of Commons, ii. 6
Fox, Mrs. Lane, ii. 18
Fox, Rt. Hon. C., supported in politics, and assisted in payment of debts by Mr. Slater Milnes, i. 7; defeat in 1806, 9, 97; ii. 358, 415
Franco-Prussian War, ii. 219, 230, 233, 235, 237
Franklin, Lady, ii. 15; Sir John, attempt in the House of Commons for the despatch of a final expedition in search of, ii. 15
Fraser's Magazine, Publication of "Sartor Resartus" in, i. 200, 262; Carlyle's article on Slavery, 439; ii. 50
Frederick of Schleswig-Holstein, Prince, ii. 202
French at Rome, The, i. 418
"French Revolution, The," Carlyle's, i. 171, 192, 196, 220

Frere, Sir Bartle, ii. 426
Frimont, General, i. 107
Froude, Mr. J. A., i. 172; reference to Carlyle and R. M. Milnes, 187; reference to Carlyle and Thirlwall, 228; his "Thomas Carlyle, History of his Life in London," 253 (note); "Nemesis of Faith," 433
"Froude's Remains," i. 218, 220
Fryston estate, i. 4; purchased by Mr. Slater Milnes, 6; its surrounding beauties, 6; left by Mr. Slater Milnes to his widow, 9; Mr. R. P. Milnes resides there, 18; visit of Mr. R. M. Milnes, 94, 103, 148; charades, 164, 165, 200, 201, 214; visit of Carlyle, 251–259, 293, 317, 333; visit of Mr. and Mrs. Disraeli, 1844, 337; Mr. and Mrs. C. J. MacCarthy spend their honeymoon there, 407, 433; description of the house, the library, pictures, social life, and parties of distinguished visitors, 454–466, 523; ii. 18, 34, 127, 191, 242; the biographer's personal experience there, 245—248, 289; American visitors, 336; partly destroyed by fire, 345—354; its restoration, 353, 384, 418, 430; Lord Houghton buried in Fryston churchyard, 436

Galignani, ii. 32, 186
Galt, Scotch novelist, i. 95
Galway, Dowager Viscountess, i. 38; death, 153, 424
Galway, Viscountess, ii. 125, 167; i. 48, 51, 52, 57, 69, 91, 98, 110, 112; R. M. Milnes's affection for her, 117, 121, 206, 122, 127; her singing at Venice, 137, 154; illness, 193, 195; marriage, 206, 378, 229—233; Carlyle's description of her, 257, 260; ii. 155, 268, 270, 276, 413, 430, 435
Galway, Viscount (5), marries daughter of Robert Pemberton Milnes, i. 5; colleague of Mr. R. S. Milnes in the representation of York, 7, note
Galway, Viscount (6), husband of R. M. Milnes's sister, i. 206; ii. 14; death, 338
Galway, Viscount (the present), i. 351, 378; ii. 305
Gambier, Sir James, i. 24, 25
Gambetta, M., ii. 268, 293, 379
Gambier, Charles, i. 150
Garden, Francis, letter to R. M. M., i. 146, 150, 523

INDEX.

Garibaldi, Guiseppe, ii. 124, 185, 208, 395
Garibaldi, Ricciotti, i. 463 ; ii. 124, 208
Garrison, William Lloyd, ii. 177
Gaskell, Mr. James Milnes, i. 57; describes R. M. M.'s talents as a debater, 58, 72, 78, 92; Member of Parliament for Wenlock, 202; office in Peel's Administration, 272; the Brontë papers, 527; ii. 178, 199, 252
Gaskell, Mrs., her interest in Charlotte Bronte, i. 476 ; censorious reception of " Ruth," and Milnes's sympathy, 481
Gem, The, i. 108
Genlis, Madame, Reference of W. S. Landor to, i. 181, 182
Genoa, i. 122
Gentleman, Coleridge's definition of a, i. 80
George IV., Death of, i. 99
Gerbet, Abbé, ii. 134
Germans, Lord St., i. 483
Giant's Causeway, The, i. 112
Girardin, Emile, ii. 173
Gladstone, Robertson, ii. 193, 288, 319
Gladstone, W. E., extracts from letters from Arthur Hallam on J. M. Gaskell and R. M. M., i. 57, 58; an undergraduate at Oxford, 77 ; R. M. M.'s opinion of him, 78 ; a talk with R. Monteith about R. M. M., 191; letter to R. M. M. on his sister's illness, &c., 199; visit to Scotland, 200 ; " Young England," 218, 226 ; London Library, 237 ; letter to R. M. M. on " One Tract More," 260, 261; appointment to the Board of Trade, 271, 272 ; letter to R. M. M. advising him respecting his position in Parliament, 312—314; article on Puscyism and Sir R. Peel, 316, 330 ; letter from R. M. M. asking for a copy of the review of " Ellen Middleton," &c., 335 ; letter to R. M. M. on French affairs, &c., 336 ; his railway policy, 345, 359, 372, 444 ; his Naples letters to Lord Aberdeen, 451 ; his translation of Farini's " History of the Roman State," 452; duty on foreign books, 480; appealed to by R. M. M. to join the Liberal party, 501—503 ; resigns office, February, 1855, 503, 507, 517, 524 ; ii. 13, 25 ; Ionian Question, 38 ; Oxford election, 142 ; the Reform agitation, 152 ; contrast between him and Palmerston, 152; on Reform agitation, 153, 154, 162, 172; opinion of Disraeli, 175, 179; Italian view of him, 189, 198; Irish Church, 199, 233 ; correspondence with Lord Houghton on the Franco-Prussian War, 237—241, 247, 252, 261 ; lecture at the Liverpool College, 271, 272 ; Trusteeship of the British Museum, 277, 279 ; dissolution of Parliament, 1874, 288 ; Bulgarian horrors, 340 ; the Turks in Greece, 341, 342, 361 ; triumphant return at the General Election, 1880, 387; illness, 392 ; British Museum Trusteeship and Lord Houghton, 404, 405 ; Lord Houghton's visit to Hawarden, 420, 422, 430 ; at Grillion's Club, 461 ; lines of Lord Houghton on a comparison of him with Lord Beaconsfield, 462
Glasgow, Meeting of the British Association at, 1855, i. 521
Glenarm Castle, i. 112
Glengall, Lord, comedy *The Follies of Fashion*, i. 91
Glynn, Stephen, ii. 240
Goderich, Lord and Lady, i. 473, 477
Goethe, i. 98 ; R. M. M.'s admiration for, 116, 201, 217 ; ii. 160
Goldsmith, Oliver, at Leyden, ii. 203
Gordon, Dr., i. 48, 49
Gordon, Lady Duff, introduces R. M. M. to Heine, i. 250
Gore House, resort of literary celebrities, i. 185
Goschen, Mr., ii. 387, 396
Gough (Commander-in-chief in India), i. 430
Goulbourn, Mr., i. 95 ; Chancellor of the Exchequer, 270
Gower, Lord F., i. 497
Gower, Lord Ronald, ii. 236, 254
Graham, Sir Frederick, ii. 386
Graham, Sir J., i. 95, 321 ; his warrant to open Mazzini's letters, 330, 473 ; resignation of office, 503 ; ii. 280
Grant, General, ii. 315, 325 ; visits Fryston, 362.
Grant, R., i. 108
Grant, Sir Francis, ii. 374
Granville, Lord, i. 473 ; ii. 185, 226, 260, 261, 387
Grattan, i. 96
Gray, son of the Bishop of Bristol, i. 125

Gray, David, the Scotch poet; the story of his efforts, illness and death, and of R. M. M.'s sympathy and benevolence towards him, ii. 46—59, 135, 312, 331
Gray, Mr., editor of the *Buffalo Courier*, ii. 312
Gray, Thomas, the poet; unveiling of his bust at Cambridge by Lord Houghton, ii. 433
Great Houghton Hall, formerly the residence of Strafford, acquired by the Milnes family, i. 4; left by Mr. Slater Milnes to his widow, 9; ii. 97
Greece, Mr. R. M. Milnes's tour in 1832, i. 128—136; struggle with Turkey, 135
Greek Church, the, in Athens, i. 135
Green, Mr., the aëronaut, i. 65; bears testimony to R. M. Milnes's courage, 68
Greenwood, Mr., ii. 387
Greg, Mr., ii. 22
Grenfell, Pascoe, ii. 177
Greville, Charles, i. 515; ii. 171
Greville, H., ii. 9
Greville, Mrs., ii. 200, 402
Grey, Lord, i. 301; declines to hold office with Lord Palmerston as Foreign Secretary, 359, 408, 409, 431, 439, 469; ii. 3
Grey, Mrs., ii. 281
Grey, Sir George, ii. 20
Grillion's Club, ii. 459
Grotes, The, i. 325, 434, 499; ii. 190
Guardian, The, ii. 303
"Guesses at Truth," Julius and Francis Hare's, i. 116
Guiccioli, Madame, acquaintanceship with Lord Byron, i. 136
"Guide to Rome," Mrs. Starke's, i. 152
Guizot, M., i. 244—248; letter from R. M. Milnes on the state of political feeling in England, 270—272, 292, 324; letter from R. M. Milnes on English political affairs, &c., 325, 326, 354, 404; an exile in London, 414, 420, 422, 434; remark of Carlyle, 436; growth of friendship with R. M. Milnes, 441, 518; Milnes's visit to, ii. 17, 18, 156, 239, 251
Gully, Mr., M.P., i. 139, 263
Gurney, Mr., ii. 317

Haddington, Lord, i. 270

Hadleigh, i. 146
Halifax, Lord, ii. 167, 240
Hallam, Arthur H., i. 57; extract from letter to Mr. Gladstone on Mr. J. M. Gaskell, and Mr. R. M. Milnes, i. 57—59, 62, 65; writes to R. M. Milnes on the latter's balloon ascent, 67; doubts R. M. Milnes's courage, 67, 68; his reported injustice towards Milnes, 68, 70; quotation from sonnet, 72, 75; one of the deputation to Oxford to maintain the superiority of Shelley to Byron, 77, 78; one of the "Apostles" at Cambridge, 81, 83, 84, 88, 91, 93, 95; his declamation prize read in the presence of Wordsworth, 105; listens to the preaching of Irving with R. M. Milnes, 109; criticism in the *Englishman* on Tennyson's poems, 117, 146; death, 147; "Remains," 157; ii. 161, 162, 432, 433
Hallam, Henry, i. 108; R. M. Milnes dedicates his "Memorials" to him, 147; his son's "Remains," 157, 173, 192, 228, 235
Halle, Charles, ii. 321
Hanmer, Sir John, i. 307
Hanover, King of, visit to London, and Brougham's friendship with him, i. 301
Harcourt, Colonel, ii. 22
Harcourt, Sir W. V., i. 492; ii. 362
Hardinge, Lord, i. 430
Hardy, Thomas, ii. 368
Hare, Augustus, i. 152
Hare, Francis, i. 116
Hare, Julius, i. 49, 59, 62, 70, 73, 74, 93, 107, 108; "Guesses at Truth," 116, 142; sermon at the Protestant Chapel, Rome, 142, 144, 148, 150; death of his brother Augustus, 152, 177; Biography of Sterling, ii. 160
Hare, Miss, i. 152
Harris, Admiral, ii. 201
Harrison, Frederic, i. 465; ii. 372
Harrow, i. 35
Harte, Bret, ii. 385, 386
Hartington, Lord, chosen to lead the Liberal party, ii. 303
Hatherley, Lord, ii. 240
Havelock, General and Lady, ii. 27.
Hawarden Castle, visit of R. M. Milnes to (1855), i. 524
Hawes, Sir Benjamin, i. 380, 391; ii. 3, 42
Hawkshaw, Mr., ii. 210, 211, 217

INDEX. 511

Hawkstone, Captain, ii. 16
Hawthorne, Julian, ii. 386
Hawthorne, Nathaniel, i. 497; ii. 76; and Mr. H. Bright, 141, 242, 318
Haydon, "Life" of, i. 486
Hayward, Mr. A., i. 463, 473; ii. 261
"Head-money" in the Pontefract poll-book, i. 198
"Heaven and Hell Amalgamation Society, i. 187
Heidelberg, i. 90; ii. 19.
Heine, i. 116
Helps, Sir Arthur, ii. 244, 245
Henniker, The Hon. Arthur, son-in-law to Lord Houghton, ii. 409
Henniker, Mrs., ii. 3, 85, 180, 260, 266, 267, 269, 361, 386, 409
Herbert, Sidney, i. 271, 496; resigns office, 503, 521; death, ii. 72
"Herodotus, The Essential Dualism of," i. 62
Heytesbury, Lord, i. 57
Higgins, M. J., i. 463; member of the Philobiblon Society, 508
Higgins, Matthew, ii. 464
Hilliard, George S., i 279
"History of England," Lord Macaulay's, i. 411; its great success, 432
"History of Greece," Thirlwall's, i. 162
"History of Greece," Grote's, i. 375
"History of the Roman State," Gladstone's translation of Farini's, i. 452
Hoche, Madame, ii. 389
Holland, Dr., i. 473
Holland, Lady, i. 184; "Life of Sydney Smith," 214
Holland, Lord, ii. 10
Holland, Sir Henry, ii. 92, 179
Holland, Queen of; Lord Houghton a guest of the, ii. 185, 186; 195, 196; 199—203; 220; 304
Holland House, society of, i. 184; 213; ii. 40; 236
"Home, sweet Home," Controversy on, ii. 258
Homespun material of the West Riding, i. 2
Hood, Thomas, R. M. Milnes's services to, i. 347—351; *Hood's Own*, 347; death of, 349; subscription for the family of, 350; 408; ii. 111
Hood's Magazine, Criticism on "Coningsby" by R. M. Milnes in, i. 319; 347
Hook, Theodore; "Maxwell," i. 104; Sydney Smith's rival as a talker, 210

Horsman, Edward, i. 75
Houghton, Lady, Tribute of George von Bunsen to, ii. 68; 157; death, 287—290
Houghton, Lord (Richard Monckton Milnes); ancestry, i. 1—10, tells the story of his father's wager respecting the office of Chancellor of the Exchequer, 11; birth, 13; first visit when a boy to the House of Commons, 33; placed under a tutor at Dieppe, 34; his precocity, 34; taken to the Rev. W. Richardson's school at Hundhill Hall, near Pontefract, 34; serious illness, 35; education carried on by private tutors up to the time of going to the University, 35; lack of close attachment to his father in youth, his fondness for paradox, 35; anecdote—want of intelligence in farmers, 36; enters Trinity College, Cambridge, 36, 49; urges his father to accept a peerage offered by Lord Palmerston, 41; letter of sympathy on his father's death from Lord Palmerston, 42, 43; Mr. W. E. Forster's opinion of him, 44; the keynote of his character and career —"a good man to go to in distress," and "a good man to go to in disgrace," 44—46; early years and education, 47; letter to his mother, August, 1825, 47—49; his tutor and friends at Trinity College, 49, 50; influence upon him of Connop Thirlwall, afterwards Bishop of St. David's, 50; letter to his mother, November, 1827, 50; dislike of the chapel system at the University, 51; letter to his mother, December 4, 1827, on his phrenological development, and a Scotch definition of metaphysics, 52; letter to his father on—Cavendish, afterwards seventh Duke of Devonshire, 53; letter to his mother on "wearing a hat," his speech at the Union, &c., 53, 54; royal descent through the family of the Duke of Rutland, 54; loyalty to his college, 54; letter to his father on Senior Wranglership, and college examinations, 54; letter to his father proposing to keep terms at an Inn of Court, 55; family embarrassments, 55; letter to his father asserting his industrious habits, 56;

THE LIFE OF LORD HOUGHTON.

Houghton, Lord (continued).
spends the long vacation with his family at Boulogne, 56; letter to his mother on the "flush of noblemen" at the University, and the Presidency of the Union, 57; Arthur Hallam's opinion of him, 57, 58; one of the principal orators at the Union, 58; letter to his father on the disappointment owing to his father's embarrassments, the Union, Clubs, &c., 58, 59; friendship with John Sterling, 59, 60; spends Christmas at Boulogne, 60; the *Athenæum* "men," &c., 60; writes to his father on Mr. Peel's view of Irish affairs, the debate on the "Ancient Mariner," and Mr. Martin's Acts, his progress in mathematics, contributions to the *Athenæum*, his poem, "Timbuctoo," &c., 60 - 62; writes to his father on the speakers at the Union, 62; early friendship with Lord Tennyson, 63; writes to his father on his failure at an examination and dislike of mathematics, 64, 65; balloon ascent, 65, 66; describes the adventure in a letter to A. H. Hallam, 66, 67; affection for A. H. Hallam, 68; joins his family at Paris, is introduced to Lafayette, Baron Cuvier, and others, and proceeds to Switzerland and Italy, 68, 69; attachment to Italy, 69; conversation with Cousin, 70; his "Walpoliana," 71; plans for study at Cambridge, 71; thinks the Cambridge Union may have an injurious tendency, 71; reference to Lady Morgan's views on legislators, 71; quotation from a sonnet by Hallam, 71; proposes an economical method of living in London, 72; sale of Cardinal Fesch's pictures, 72; takes part in the debate on Wordsworth and Byron, 72, 73; enthusiasm for Wordsworth, 73; views on the poetry of Wordsworth, Shelley, and Keats, 73, 74; contemporaries at Cambridge, and his opinion of Thomas Sunderland, 75; his story of the Shelley deputation to Oxford, 77; account of the debate at Oxford on the comparative merits of Shelley and Byron, 78; his Homeric essay, his opinion

Houghton, Lord (continued).
of his father's definition of an orator, his views on Parliamentary influence, and on entering Parliament, 79, 80; contributes to the *Athenæum*, 81; member of the association of the "Apostles," 81; his "Memorials" of his stay at Cambridge, 82-84; takes prizes for English Declamation and English Essay, 83; writes an epilogue to *Much Ado About Nothing*, and takes the part of Beatrice, 84; Stafford O'Brien's high opinion of him, 85, 86; one of the best-beloved of the "Apostles," and one whom his contemporaries expected would accomplish great things in the future, 86; enrols himself at the University of London (1830), 86; associates in London with Maurice, Stirling, J. S. Mill, and the Kembles, and attends the church of Edward Irving, 87; distinction as an amateur actor, 87; letter to his father on the Shelley mission to Oxford, and new books read, 88; discussions with his father on a Parliamentary career, 89; reference to "Bob Milnes's second speech" in Moore's "Life of Byron," 90; proposes to visit Germany, 90; reads an essay at the "Apostles" Society, 91; intimacy with Fitzroy and O'Brien, 91; his general view of politics (1830), 92; unable to lead the Union, 92; speeches at the Union, 93; opinion of F. Tennyson's position, 93; writes for the prize poem, "Byzantium," 93; farewell to Trinity, 94; hears Cobbett lecture at St. Ives, 94; stories of Duke of St. Albans and the Siamese boys, and Prince Leopold and the British Plutarch, 94; goes to Fryston, 94; considers the possibility of representing Pontefract, 95; goes to London, visits the House of Commons, and mingles in society, 95; criticism on certain Parliamentary speakers, 95; fêted during a visit to Cambridge, 96; declines to enter Parliament by patronage, 96; goes to Germany, and stays at Bonn, 97; introduced to Madam Schopenhauer and Schlegel, 98, 99; a proposal to

INDEX. 513

Houghton, Lord (*continued*).
represent Pontefract in Parliament, 99; extract from a letter on the Revolution in Paris, 100; leaves Bonn, and joins his family at Milan, 100; sympathy with the Italians, 101; attends a Court ball, 101; attachment to his aunts, Misses Louisa, Caroline, and Jane Milnes, 102, 103: opinion of Italian men and women, 104; regrets the arrest of O'Connell, 104; perplexities, and lack of entire sympathy between him and his father, 105, 166, 167; impressions of Venice and the Venetians, 106; a proposed visit to Rome, 107; opinion of the Reform Bill, 108, 116; reference to Lord Macaulay, 108; sketch of W. S. Landor in "Monographs," 108; returns to England, and takes his degree at Cambridge, 108, 109; in company with Hallam listens to the preaching of Edward Irving, visits Ireland, and has his first experience of railway travelling, 109, 110; impressions of Dublin, 110; remarks on the House of Commons debates, &c., 111; difference between his father and himself on Parliamentary Reform and Austrian rule in Lombardy, 111; acquaintanceship with Lady Morgan, 112; reminiscences of his youth by Mr. Aubrey de Vere, 114—120; love and knowledge of books, 115; his Toryism, 115; devotion to German literature, 116; estimation of art in poetry, 116; admiration for Schiller and Goethe, 116; "Flight of Youth," 117; affection for his sister, 117, 206; Mr. Aubrey de Vere's estimate of his character, 118, 119; leaning in early life towards the Catholic Church, 118; sonnet, "To search for lore in spacious libraries," 118; goes to a masked ball at Buckingham Palace in the character of Chaucer, 119, 326; the character of his poetry, 119; goes to Rome (1832), 121; acquaintanceship with Thomas Campbell, 121; friendships formed in Rome, and impressions of the city, 122—127; friendship with Christopher Wordsworth, 126; arranges for a tour in Greece, 125—127; tour in Greece with Christopher Words-

Houghton, Lord (*continued*).
worth, 128—136; his "Memorials, chiefly Poetical," 128; affection for the Turkish character, 131; return to Venice, and popularity there, 137; attachment towards Rodes Milnes, 138, 139; declines to become a nominee of the Duke of Newcastle for a seat in Parliament, 139, 141; self-depreciation, 143; tour through Northern Italy, June, 1833, 143; serious illness, during which he is nursed by Mr. and Mrs. W. S. Landor, 144; goes to Switzerland, 145, and then to London; his "Impressions of Greece," 147; estimate of A. H. Hallam's character, 147; returns to Italy, 148; society in Rome during the Carnival, 150—152; goes to Venice, Munich, the Salzkammergut, and Florence, 153 — 155; returns to Rome, 155; returns to England, (1835), 156; effect on his mind and character of his sojourn on the Continent, 157; kind-heartedness, 157; arranges for the English publication of M. Rio's "Christian Art," 158; tour in Ireland (1835), 158; "wasting his fine talents and good heart on things that win him neither respect nor love," 160; leanings towards the Catholic Church, 140, 160; intimacy with Dr. Wiseman, 162; goes to Bawtry and Fryston, 162; intimacy with Connop Thirlwall, 162; charades at Fryston, 164, 165; visit of Thackeray to R. P. Milnes's house at Fryston, 167, 264; begins his London career (1836), 167; prospects, temptations, and aims, 167—169; great love for his fellow-men, 170; social and literary parties at South Street, 170; makes the acquaintance of Carlyle, 172; Carlyle's appreciative references to him, 172; Landor's high estimate of him as a poet, 172, 181, 183 distinguished friendships and social gifts, 173; antipathy towards him in literary circles, 174; rooms at 26, Pall Mall, 174; origin of his song, "I wandered by the Brookside," 175, 176; subsequent popularity of the song, 176; produced most of his poetry between 1830

h h

Houghton, Lord (*continued*).
and 1840, 176; prepares "The Tribute," 177; contributions of the Tennysons and of Landor to "The Tribute," 177, 183; frequents Lansdowne House, Holland House, Gore House, and the house of Samuel Rogers, 184, 185; member of the Sterling Club, 186, 222; his breakfasts, 185, 228, 461; catholicity of temperament and sympathy, 186; Carlyle's jest on his cosmopolitanism, 187; views on "the true art of conversation," 188, 189; distinguished for his dinner-table talk, 189, 190; needed sympathy more than admiration, 190; popularity in Italy of his lines on "Venice," 192; friendship with Carlyle, 193; sonnet on Cowper's Grave at Olney, sent to Mr. Aubrey de Vere, 194, 195; elected member of Parliament for Pontefract, 197, 198; his Conservatism, 199; admiration for Goethe, 201; maiden speech in the House of Commons, 202—205; publication of "The Memorials of a Residence on the Continent, and Historical Poems," and "Poems of Many Years," 207, 208; acquaintance with Sydney Smith, 209—215; remonstrance with Sydney Smith respecting certain jocular titles, 213, 214; titles applied to him—"Cool of the Evening," "London Assurance," "In-I-go Jones," 214; non-success of his speeches in Parliament and his political earnestness, 216, 217; Charles Sumner's description of him, 223; reported statement respecting Carlyle being unknown, 223, 224; Emerson's "Nature," 224; growing intimacy with Carlyle, 228, 229; trip to the Pyrenees with Colvile, 229-233; friendship with the Miss Berrys, 233, 234; helps to establish the London Library, 234—237; interest in Emerson, 237; visit to Scotland, 1839, 242; visit to Paris, 244, 250; introductions to Guizot, Thiers, Lamartine, De Tocqueville, and King Louis Philippe, 244—246; article in the *Quarterly Review* on De Tocqueville, 245; entrusted with messages from the King to Sir Robert Peel, 247, 248; intro-

Houghton, Lord (*continued*).
duction to Heine, 250; review of Heine's poems in the *Edinburgh Review*, 251; Carlyle at Fryston, 251—259; his "One Tract More," 260—262; address to the electors of Pontefract at the dissolution of 1841, 262; re-elected for Pontefract and his desire for office, 265, disappointment at no office being offered to him in Peel's Administration, 268, 269, 310; writes to M. Guizot on English political affairs, 270, 271; political ambition, 273; fitness for controlling English Foreign Policy, 274; interest in the Copyright Bill, 275, 276; independence of action in the House of Commons, 278; Corn Laws, 278; correspondence with Mr. Sumner, 279; his "Thoughts on Purity of Election," 279; journey to the East, 282—290; "Palm Leaves," 282, 283, 288, 290, 308, 318, 322, 323, 325, 345; his benefactions, 294; Tennyson's pension, 295; Sheridan Knowles, 297; pension to Mrs. Southey, 298, 299; proposal for the endowment of the Catholic Church in Ireland, 301; friendship with Charles Buller, 304; friendship with Mrs. Procter, wife of Barry Cornwall, 306—308; discouragement in the House of Commons, and proposal to give up his seat, 310—315; Mr. Gladstone's advice to him, 312—314; determines to remain in Parliament, 315; article on Russia in the *Edinburgh Review*, 317; publication of "Palm Leaves," 318; criticism on "Coningsby" in *Hood's Magazine*, 319; sides with Lord Ashley on the Factory Bill, 324, 325; De Tocqueville thinks he returned from the East "too much the Mussulman," 328; his portrait as "Mr. Vavasour" in "Tancred," 337—339; Lectures at Pomfret, 337; his liking for acting, 337; visits Berlin, 340—345; the *Quarterly Review* on "Palm Leaves," 345; services to Thomas Hood, 347—350; his pamphlet on the "Real Union of England and Ireland," 353; interest in the railway agitation, 355; severe disappointment in not obtaining the office of Under-Secretary for Foreign

INDEX. 515

Houghton, Lord (*continued*).
Affairs, and his loss of sympathy with the Conservative party, 360—365; his middle position on the question of the Corn Laws and Protection, 370; introduces a Bill for the establishment of Reformatories for juvenile offenders, 373; becomes a Liberal on the accession of Lord John Russell to the Premiership, 376, 377; death of his mother, 378; thoughts on death, 379: contest at Pontefract, 380, friendship with Robert Browning and W. E. Forster, 383, 385, 387; friendship with the Duke of Wellington, 388—390: tour in Spain and Portugal, 391—401; stay in Paris, 400; returns to London and withdraws from the Carlton Club, 401; his Liberalism, 402, 403; visit to Paris at the Revolution, 1848; meets W. E. Forster, 404; refuses to condone the *coup d'état* of the 2nd December, 405; begins his "Life and Letters of Keats," 406; "A Letter to the Marquis of Lansdowne," and the hostile criticism in the pamphlet provoked from Lord Brougham, and the *Morning Chronicle*, 410—416; challenges Mr. George Smythe, the writer of the article in the *Morning Chronicle*, but agrees to accept an apology, 417, 418; extracts from his Commonplace Book on Thiers, &c., 419—422; incorrect story in Lord Malmesbury's "Recollections" respecting Milnes and Louis Philippe, 423; states in his notebook, "I have become Republican," 424; close friendship with Thackeray, 425—429; tries to secure a magistracy for Thackeray, 427; makes the acquaintance of Charlotte Bronte, and befriends her relatives after her death, 428, 429; "Sayings of Carlyle" extracted from Commonplace Books, 435, 436; review on the state of Europe, 438; advanced opinions on the condition of Ireland, 438; again visits Paris, 1850, 440, 441; his position during the Papal Aggression agitation, 445, 446; writes for the *Edinburgh* and other reviews, 446; connection with the Royal Literary Fund, and the Yorkshire

Houghton, Lord (*continued*).
Union of Mechanics' Institutes, 447; his marriage to the Hon. Annabel Crewe, 1851, 447—450; growing intimacy with Lord and Lady Palmerston, 448, 449; goes with his wife to Vienna, 451; revises Gladstone's translation of Farini's "History of the Roman State," 452; his large collection of books at Fryston, 455—458; pictures, social life, visitors' book at Fryston, 458 — 466: his love for the streets of London, for Italy and the East, 460; town residence, 16, Upper Brook Street, 467; loss of his friend, Eliot Warburton, 467; his note in the book of guests at Upper Brook Street, 472; birth of a daughter, Amicia, 473; motion in the House of Commons on the subject of foreign refugees, 473; confidence in Palmerston as a leader, 474; acquaintance with Miss Florence Nightingale, 475, 493, 509; in conjunction with Mrs. Gaskell, befriends Charlotte Bronte, 476; acquaintance with Macaulay, 477; friendship with Lord and Lady Ashburton, 477, 478; carries a measure for the abolition of duty on foreign books, 480; sympathy with Mrs. Gaskell at the hostile reception of "Ruth," 481; visit to Ireland during the Exhibition, 1853, 483; a round of visits, 489—492; opposed to Civil Service reform, 495, 496; appeals to Gladstone and the other Peelites to join the Liberal party during the Crimean crisis, 501, 502; declines Palmerston's offer of a Lordship of the Treasury, 504; helps to establish the Philobiblon Society, 507; visit to Miss Martineau, 510; offers Tennyson a portion of the house at Fryston as a residence, 513; again visits Paris, 1855, 513—519; writes his poem, "A Monument for Scutari," 519; attends the meeting of the British Association at Glasgow, 521; the "Red Lion" dinners, 521, 522; visits to Crewe Hall and Hawarden, 524; addresses meetings on behalf of the Nightingale Fund, 527. II. Dis-

Houghton, Lord (*continued*).
appointed in his position and prospects, 2; disappointment at his father's rejection of a peerage, 2; birth of a second daughter, Florence, 3; efforts to establish Reformatories for juvenile offenders, 6; Miss Nightingale on his love for children, 7; visit to Paris, 1856, 8—10; acquaintance with Hudson, whom he befriends in adversity, 11, 12; supports a motion in the House of Commons in the case of Lady Franklin, 14, 15; asked to stand for Manchester and Chester, but is re-elected for Pontefract, 16; speaks at the Free Library banquet at Liverpool, 17; visit to France, 1857, 17—19; visits Bunsen at Heidelberg, 19; visits Baron Rothschild, Lord Lansdowne, &c., 21, 22; interest in various literary meetings, the Social Science Congress and the Sheffield School of Art, 24, 25; visit to Lord Ashburton after Lady Ashburton's death, 26; birth of his son, Robert Offley Ashburton, the present Lord Houghton, 26; begins to lose interest in political affairs, 28; visit to France and M. de Tocqueville, 29—31; death of his father, 33; ceases to take an active part in politics except in philanthropic matters, 37; secures the Governorship of Ceylon for Sir Charles MacCarthy, 42; his ready assistance to brokendown men of letters, 43, 44; befriends David Gray, 46—59; friend of young poets, 59; article in the *Quarterly Review* on Beaumont's "Life of De Tocqueville," 63, 64; poem in *Cornhill*, 64; espousal of the Republican side in the American War, 65, 66; wins popularity, 66; friendship with the Bunsens, 66—69; Robert Browning and the Athenæum Club, 78; severe illness and visit to Buxton, 1862, 81; Mr. Coomara Samy's visits to Fryston, 87, 89; rumours of his peerage, 91; marriage of the Prince of Wales, 93; visits Lord Ashburton in Paris, 93; entertains Thackeray and Spedding at Fryston, 94; raised to the peerage under the title of Baron Houghton of Great Houghton, 97; the "im-

Houghton, Lord (*continued*).
measurable gulf" between a peer and a commoner, 98; congratulations of the *Times*, *Daily Telegraph*, 99—102; takes leave of his constituents, 102—106; congratulations from friends, 107—111; Thackeray's last letter and farewell Christmas greeting to Milnes, and death, 112; humorous lines by Planché on the pronunciation of Lord Houghton's name, 114—117; visit to Broadlands (Lord Palmerston's), 119; and to Lord Broughton's, 120; goes to the Riviera, 1864, 120—125; interests himself in the Newspaper Press Fund, 125; visit of George von Bunsen to Fryston, 127; attacks Convocation respecting its condemnation of "Essays and Reviews," 128—131; death of his friend Sir Charles MacCarthy, 132; goes to Vichy, 133—135; seconds the Address to the Queen's Speech in the House of Lords, 135; article in the *Edinburgh Review*, on "Atalanta in Calydon," 136, 137; friendship with Mr. Henry Bright, 141; Carlyle again visits Fryston, 144, 147; presides at a great meeting at Leeds in favour of reform, 151; goes to Vichy, Bordeaux, and Biarritz, 1866, 154; attends a Reform Banquet at Manchester, 157, 158; delivers the inaugural address at the opening of the new rooms of the Cambridge Union Society, 159 — 166; one of the jurors at the French Exhibition, 167, 168; joins the movement in favour of the suffrage of women, 178; goes to Bonn and Wildbad, 179; takes Lady Houghton to the South of France, 183; attends the autumn session of Parliament, 1867, 185; visit to Rome with Lady Houghton, 188; interest in the Leeds Exhibition of Fine Arts, 190; friendship with Mr. Watkiss Lloyd, 190; Longfellow's visit, 193; visit to Strathfieldsaye, 195; visit to the Queen of Holland, 197; death of his aunt, Miss Caroline Milnes, 197, 199; unveils the monument of Leigh Hunt, 204; present at the opening of the Suez Canal, 205—207, 210, 211; report to the Royal

Houghton, Lord (*continued*).
Geographical Society on the Suez Canal, 214—218; articles for the reviews and *Pall Mall Gazette*, 219—221; review of "Lothair" in the *Edinburgh*, 223; bet with Mr. Trollope, 224—226; death of Dickens, and connection of Dickens's grandmother with the Crewe family, 227—229; sympathy with Prussia in the Franco-Prussian War, 230—232; correspondence with Gladstone on the War, 237—241; visit to Scotland, 241; admiration for N. Hawthorne, 242; visit of Browning to Fryston, 244; friendship with Sir Arthur Helps, 244, 245; visit to Buxton, 250; leader of the movement for legalising marriage with a deceased wife's sister, 251; the transaction of business in the House of Lords, 255; friendship with Mr. Edmund Yates, 256—258; letter to the *Athenæum* on "Home, sweet Home," 258; visit to Torquay, 1872, 259, 260; the Alabama question, 261; gives up his house in Brook Street, 262; receives the Order of the Rose of Brazil, 262; correspondence with Edward FitzGerald, 263; friendship with the ex-Emperor Napoleon III. and the Prince Imperial, 265; visit to Paris and M. Thiers, 266—268; visits to Vichy and Venice, 268—270; Gladstone's lecture at the Liverpool College, 271, 272; Mr. H. Bright's "Unpunished Cruelties on the High Seas," 273; publication of "Monographs," 273—276; illness, 276; Mr. Joaquin Miller, 276; the trusteeship of the British Museum, 277—279; President of the Social Science Congress at Norwich, 279—282; supports W. E. Forster in his struggle with the Birmingham League, 283; death of Lady Houghton, 287—292; goes to Vichy, 292—296; acquaintance with Lady William Russell, 296, 297; friendship with Sir William Stirling Maxwell, 299; acquaintance with Sir Richard Burton, 300—302; his preface to the works of Thomas Love Peacock, 302; his son wins the prize-poem at Cambridge, 305; incident respect-

Houghton, Lord (*continued*).
ing a *jeu d'esprit* of Sir Wilfrid Lawson, 306; visit to the United States (1875), 306—335; article in the *Quarterly Review* on England and America, 337; elected an Honorary Fellow of Trinity College, Cambridge, 339; his view of the Eastern question, 340—344; burning of Fryston Hall (1876), 345—352; rebuilding of Fryston Hall, 353, 354; unveils a statue to Robert Burns at Glasgow, 355, 356; opinion of the Prince of Wales's powers, 359; dinner to General Grant, 362; accident, 363; visit to the meeting of the British Association at Plymouth, 365; admiration for Mr. Thomas Hardy and Mr. Henry Irving, 368; address to the Birmingham Press Club, 369; kindness to journalists, 370, 371; his review of "Lord Melbourne's Life" in the *Fortnightly*, 371, 372; his handwriting, 372—374; made Foreign Corresponding Secretary of the Royal Academy, 374, 375; offered the presidency of the Royal Geographical Society, 375; friendship with George Eliot, 376; visit to Paris and Royat (1878), 378, 379; failing health, 381, 382, 384; attends a Liberal demonstration at Leeds, 382, 383; engagement of his son to Miss Graham, 386, 388; visits to Paris and Ireland, 386; sympathy with the Liberals in the victory of 1880, 387; contributions to the *Pall Mall* and *Fortnightly*, 388; visit to the Comte de Paris, 391; visit to Germany, 392; at the Berlin Review, 397; review of the "Life of Panizzi," 404, 405; appointment as a trustee of the British Museum, 404, 406; engagement and marriage of his elder daughter to Mr. G. FitzGerald, 407, 408; engagement of his younger daughter to Hon. A. Henniker, 409; visit to Egypt and Athens, and illness, 410—418; return to Fryston, 1882, 418; article on "Endymion" for *Macmillan's Magazine*, 419; visit to Scotland, 419; contemplates a visit to India, 425; visits to Bournemouth and Cairo, 427, 428; speaks at the meeting of the Newspaper Press

Houghton, Lord (*continued*).
Fund, 428; presentiment of approaching death, 429; attends a Liberal demonstration at Pontefract, 429; accident at Lord Rosebery's, 430; sketches of Henry Bright and the Duke of Albany, 431; visit to Italy, 432; speech at the unveiling of the bust of Coleridge in Westminster, 432; unveiling of a bust of Gray at Cambridge, 433; his last speech, 433; Newspaper Press Fund, 434; last public appearance in London, 434; last visits in London, 434, 435; goes to Vichy, 435; death at Vichy, 11th August, 1885, 436; service at St. Margaret's, Westminster, and interment at Fryston, 436; his poetry, 437—440; prose writings, 441, 442; contemporary criticism, 443—449; later criticism, and tributes to his memory, 449—459; features of his social life, 459—464; connection with the Philobiblon Society, and the Newspaper Press Fund, 464—466; an epitaph that does not lie, 467; *Appendix*, Sayings from his Commonplace Books, of Sydney Smith, 469—477; sayings of Carlyle, 477—481; miscellaneous sayings, 481—497
Houghton, Lord (the present), i. 4; ii. 26, 34, 122, 170, 202, 206, 270, 298, 305; wins the prize poem at Cambridge, 305, 355; visit to America with his father, 314, 364; marriage, 388—391
House of Lords, Transaction of business in the, ii. 255
Howard, Lady Edward, ii. 199
Howe, Dr., the mesmerist, i. 301
Howe, Julia Ward, ii. 317
Howick, Lord, i. 324
Hudson ("The Railway King"), i. 433; befriended by R. M. Milnes, ii. 12
Hughes, Mr. Thomas, i. 463; ii. 142, 180
Hugo, Victor, i. 116; ii. 32, 379
Humboldt, Baron, Hospitality to R. M. Milnes of, i. 340, 344
Hume, Joseph, i. 202, 375
Hundhill Hall School, i. 34
Hungary, Queen of, i. 102
Hungary, The Russians in, i. 419; R. M. Milnes stopped on the frontier of, 451

Hunt, Leigh, R. M. Milnes's acquaintance with, ii. 10, 11; Monument in Kensal Green Cemetery unveiled by Lord Houghton, 204, 206; his opinion of Byron, 203
Hunt, Mr., i. 111
Hurlbert, Mr., *New York World*, ii. 311 319, 320, 321
Huskisson, i. 95
Huxley, Professor, i. 466; ii. 145, 152
Hyacinthe, Father, i. 465; ii. 243, 262
Hyères, ii. 120, 122

"I had a Home," poem by R. M. Milnes, i. 120
"I wandered by the Brookside," song by R. M. Milnes, its origin and popularity, i. 175, 176
Imperial, The Prince, ii. 236, 265, 385
"Impressions of Greece," R. M. Milnes's, i. 147, 150, 152, 153
"In-I-go Jones," origin and application of the term, i. 214
Indian Mutiny, ii. 13, 20
"Influence of Homer," prize essay by R. M. Milnes, i. 83
Inglis, Sir R., i. 324, 375
Interviewers, American newspaper, ii. 313—315
Ionian Islands, i. 129
Ireland, Visit of R. Milnes, in 1831 to, i. 109—113, 120; second visit of Milnes, 175; pamphlet of Milnes on the Union, 353; Milnes's advanced opinions on the condition of, 438; Milnes's third visit to, 483—485; visit of Queen Victoria to, 438, 484, 485; Lord Houghton's visit, 1876, ii. 344
Irving, Edward, i. 87, 109, 140, 160, 365
Irving, Henry, ii. 368
Isle of Man, i. 92
Italy, long residence of the Milnes family in, i. 68; sympathy of R. M. Milnes with Italians, 101; treatment of Mazzini in England, 330; R. M. Milnes on Italian liberty in his "Letter to Lord Lansdowne," 411—414; the Poor Law, 439
Ithaca, i. 129
Ives, St., i. 94

Jacobini, Cardinal, ii. 424
James, G. P. R., i. 154
Jameson, Mrs., i, 515
"Jane Eyre," i. 477
Jeffrey, Francis, Reference of Carlyle

to, i, 258; opinion on Milnes's "Letter to Lord Lansdowne," 416
Jersey, Lady, ii. 22
Jews, The, i. 263
Jex-Blake, Miss, ii. 281
John, Lord St., i. 71
Johnson, Reverdy, i. 465.
Jowett, Professor, and "Essays and Reviews," ii. 129

Kean, Charles, i. 218
Keats, interest in his poetry roused at Cambridge University, i. 73; R. M. Milnes's acquaintance with his poetry, 116, 127; growth of his influence (1836), 171; R. M. Milnes's "Life" of him, 406; remark of Carlyle on his "hungering after sweets," 435; a lock of his hair at Fryston, 457, ii. 263, 433
Kemble, Fanny, i. 87, 93, 96, 498, ii. 85, 182
Kemble, J. M., i. 49, 58, 60, 71, 83, 84, 87, 90, 91, 93, 104, ii. 161
Kenealy, Dr., ii. 188, 305
Kennedy, C. R., i. 75; one of the "Apostles" at Cambridge, 81
Kent, Charles, ii. 257
Kenyon, Mr., i. 220
Kerry, Knight of, i. 113, 115, 120
Kerry, Lord, brother of the fourth Marquis of Lansdowne, i. 57, 108
Khedive of Egypt, ii. 206, 209, 410, 412
Kildare, Bishop of, i. 110
Kildenbee, S., i. 111
"Kingdom of Christ, The," F. D. Maurice's, i. 197
Kinglake, A. W., i. 83, 307; author of "Eothen," and a criticism in the *Quarterly Review* on R. M. Milnes's "Palm Leaves," 346, letter to R. M. Milnes, promising to assist Hood, 347, 348, 352; quest of Milnes, 473; the battle of Alma, 499, ii. 161, 365
Kingsley, Charles, and Dr. Newman, ii. 354
Kinnaird, Lord, i. 29
Kirby Underdale, i. 162
Kirkup, Seymour, ii. 222; on Browning, 249
Kitson, Sir James, ii. 145
Knatchbull, Sir Edward, i. 271
Knight, Charles, A remark of Carlyle on, i. 435
Knight, Mr. and Mrs. Gally, i. 326
Knowles, Mr. James, ii. 256, 462

Knowles, Sheridan, Pension for, i. 296, 297

Labouchere, H., ii. 12, 366
Lafayette, General, i. 68, 70
Lalande, i. 70
Lamartine, M. de, i. 245, 292, 328, 421
Lamb, Charles, his adopted daughter, ii. 248, 285, 292, 298
Lamb, Sir Frederick, i. 232
Lamennais, Abbé de, i. 123, 124, 141, 151
Landor, Walter Savage, i. 107; acquaintance with R. M. Milnes, 108, 116; nurses R. M. Milnes during a serious illness at Fiesole, 144; R. M. Milnes's opinion of him, 145; intends to settle in England, 159; letter to R. M. Milnes on verses for "The Tribute," 181—183; two letters to R. M. Milnes on Southey, his works, &c., 297—299; congratulates Milnes on his elevation to the peerage, and writes of his own helpless condition, ii. 110, 111; death, 111, 136; tribute to him in "Atalanta in Calydon," 138, 249, 438
Landseer, Sir Edwin, i. 434; guest of Milnes, 473
Lansdowne, (Fourth) Marquis of, i. 57, 88, 184, 192, 235; "A Letter" to the, by R. M. Milnes, 410, 506; Milnes's visit to, ii. 22, 92
Lansdowne House the home of literary society, i. 184
Laplace, 79
Larissa, i. 129
Lawrence, Sir Henry, ii. 18
Lawson, Edward, ii. 257
Lawson, Sir Wilfrid, ii. 306
Layard, Sir A. H., i. 506, 508; ii. 10, 84
Leeds, competition with Wakefield for commercial pre-eminence, i. 1; railway projects in, 394; Reform Meeting in the Cloth Hall, ii. 149; Exhibition of Fine Arts, 1868, 190; Liberal Demonstration, 1879, 382
Leeds Mercury, The, on the burning of Fryston Hall, ii. 349, 350; article by Lord Houghton, 362
Lemoinne, John, ii. 155
Leonidas, i. 129
Leopold, Prince, i. 90, 94; ii. 385, 386, 431
Lepanto, Gulf of, i. 129
Lesseps, M. de, ii. 216, 217, 234, 235, 411

"Letter to the Marquis of Lansdowne, A," R. M. Milnes's, i. 410; extracts from, 411—414

Letters, and extracts from letters, from Arnold, Matthew, to R. M. Milnes, on his pamphlet on the Italian question, ii. 40, 41

Berry, Miss, to R M. Milnes, on the criticism in *Hood's Magazine* on "Coningsby," 319

Blakesley, J. W, to R. M. Milnes, on subscribers for "Sartor Resartus," i. 200; to the same, on his election to the Athenæum Club, Tennyson, Trench, &c., 221; to the same, on the Sterling Club, 222

Bowen, Sir George, to the Dowager Viscountess Galway, on Lord Houghton's visit to America, ii. 328

Bright, Henry, to Lord Houghton, on Mrs. Hawthorne, &c., ii. 242; to the same, on the "Life of Hawthorne", &c., 271; to the same, on his "Year in a Lancashire Garden," 304; to the same, on the Fryston fire, 351; to the same, on his illness, 427

Bright, John, to Lord Houghton, July, 1865, on the elections, &c., ii. 143; to the same, on the House of Lords, &c., 144; to the same, on the latter's poems, 409

Brougham, Lord, to R. M. Milnes, on the latter's letter to Lord Lansdowne, i. 414, 415

Browning, Robert, to R. M. Milnes, March, 1847, on the secretaryship to a British Minister at Rome, i. 384, 385; to the same, October, 1861, on his admission to the Athenæum Club, ii. 78; to the same, on the same subject, 79; to the same, on an invitation to Fryston, 243; to the same, with New Year's wishes, 244; to the same, on Lady Houghton's death, 291

Buchanan, Robert, to R. M. Milnes, on David Gray, the Scotch poet, ii. 54

Bunsen, George von, to Lord Houghton, on German affairs, ii. 230; to the same, on the latter's speech at Norwich, 281; to the same, on the Catholic Church in Prussia,

Letters (*continued*).
285; to the same, March, 1882, 417

Burton, Lady, to Lord Houghton, ii. 301

Carlyle, Mrs., to R. M. Milnes, on her husband declining to take a holiday at Easter, ii. 94; to the same, March, 1866, on an invitation to Fryston and Mr. Carlyle's Lord Rectorship, 145, 146; to Lady Houghton, two letters, on an invitation to Fryston, and her illness, 146, 147

Carlyle, Thomas, to R. M. Milnes, i. 209; to the same, on Emerson's "Nature," and American bookselling, 224, 225; to the same, accepting an invitation, 227; to the same, inviting him to ride with him, 229; to the same, on the formation of the London Library, 236; to the same, on the latter's review of Emerson's Works, 239, 240; to the same, on the same subject, 240; to the same, accepting an invitation to Fryston, 252; to his wife, describing his Fryston visit, 252, 253; to the same, on the same subject, 255—258; to R. M. Milnes, on the Scotch Moors, &c., 259, 260; to the same, July, 1841, on the Courthouse at York, the "terrible" Scotch, suggesting Milnes should found a "priest's cell," &c., 265, 268; to the same, April, 1842, on the Copyright Bill, 276, 277; to the same, August, 1842, on the Chartist riots, &c., 281 282; to the same, May, 1843, on the latter's return from the East, 290; to the same, on Darley's notes of the Long Parliament, Cowper's "Crow," &c., 308, 309; to the same, on "Palm Leaves," Mahomet, &c., 323, 324; to the same, in reply to an invitation to visit Fryston, 357; to the same, asking for a meeting, 386; to the same, on the duty on foreign books, 480; to the same, March, 1854, on Civil Service Reform, 494, 495; to the same, October, 1855, on the "Johnson Goddaughter Case," 526; to the same, on his visit to Scotland,

INDEX. 521

Letters (*continued*).
&c., ii. 41, 42 ; to the same, August, 1861, expressing his attachment, &c., 73, 74 ; to the same, expressing his opinion of Thackeray's qualities, referring to his wife's illness, &c., 112—114; to the same, August, 1864, on his wife's illness, and "Frederick the Great," 128, 129 ; to the same, November, 1865, on an invitation to Fryston, 144, 145

Collins, Wilkie, to Mrs. Milnes, apologising for not attending her "At Home," May, 1862, ii. 79

Colvile, Sir James, to R. M. Milnes, on his experience at Calcutta, &c., i. 382, 383

De Tocqueville, A., to R. M. Milnes, on "Palm Leaves," and Mahomedanism, i. 327, 328 ; to the same, April, 1850, on his illness, &c., 442, 443 ; to the same, February, 1852, on the prospects of war, &c., 470, 471 ; to the same, April, 1858, congratulating him on the birth of a son, ii. 26, 27

Delane, J. T., to R. M. Milnes, October, 1854, on Kinglake's account of the battle of Alma in the *Times*, sending Mr. Macdonald as treasurer of the Patriotic Fund, &c., i. 500; to the same, September 1855, on Milnes's verses, "A Monument for Scutari," and the failures of the English in the Crimea, 520, 521 ; to the same, congratulating him on his accession to the peerage, ii. 109; to the same, on French affairs, 255

Dickens, Charles, to Mrs. Milnes, July, 1862, thanking her for a photograph of a picture executed by her, ii. 80 ; to Lord Houghton, declining an invitation, ii. 140

Disraeli, Benjamin, to R. M. Milnes, on the latter's criticism on "Coningsby," i. 320 ; to R. P. Milnes, March, 1853, on debates in the House of Commons, &c., 479 ; to the same, on the Vienna Note, Lord Palmerston's article in the *Morning Post*, &c., 488

Emerson, R. W., to R. M. Milnes, on the latter's review of the writer's Essays, i. 241 ; to the

Letters (*continued*).
same, inviting him to Concord, ii. 318

Fane, Julian, to R. M. Milnes, on "Tannhauser," &c., ii. 69

Fitzgerald, Edward, to Lord Houghton, on Keats, ii. 263 ; to the same, on Tennyson, 264 ; to the same, on Spedding, &c., 377 ; to the same, on the Battle of Waterloo, 406

Ford, Mr., to Lord Houghton, on a Greek baptism, ii. 416

Forster, W. E., to Lord Houghton, on the Fryston fire, ii. 350

Franklin (Lady) to R. M. Milnes, thanking him for his speech in the House of Commons in favour of a final attempt to discover Sir John Franklin, ii. 15

Garden, Francis, to R. M. Milnes, on Cambridge news, i. 146, 147

Gaskell, J. Milnes, on R. M. Milnes's talents as a debater, i. 58

Gaskell, Mrs., to R. M. Milnes, Oct., 1852, on befriending Charlotte Brontë and her husband, i. 476 ; to the same, on the criticisms on "Ruth," 481

Gladstone, W. E., to R. M. Milnes, June, 1837, on the approaching dissolution, &c., i. 199 ; to the same, on the Copyright Bill, 275, 276 ; to the same, with advice on his position in Parliament, and the "uneasiness" of members who act independently, 312—314 ; to the same, on the latter's "Letter to Lord Lansdowne," 415; to the same, Oct., 1855, on Milnes's "A Monument for Scutari," 521; to the same, July, 1863, on Milnes's elevation to the House of Lords, ii. 108; to the same, on Reform agitation, 153 ; to the same, Oct., 1870, 240 ; to the same, on the failure of Greece, 341 ; to the same, on the "greatest preachers," 359 ; two letters to the same, on the latter's election to the Trusteeship of the British Museum, 405

Grant, Sir Francis, to Lord Houghton, with the offer of the Foreign Secretaryship to the Royal Academy, ii. 374

Gray, David, to R. M. Milnes, asking him to look at one of his poems, ii. 46 ; to the same,

Letters (continued).
on his "posthumous existence," and a proposed visit to Torquay, &c., 50, 52; to the same, accepting the latter's offer to send him to Torquay, 52, 53; to the same, on the guarantee money for the Torquay Institution, 53; to the same from Scotland, on his new poem, his hasty departure from Torquay, &c., 54, 55; to the same, on his new poems, 55, 56; to the same, on his right lung being affected, his "crown laid in the dust," &c., 56, 57

Gray, senr., David, to R. M. Milnes, on his son's illness in London, &c., ii. 49; to the same, announcing his son's death, 57; to the same, on the latter's kindness and sympathy, 58

Guizot, M., to R. M. Milnes, January, 1850, on the state of affairs in France, i. 441, 442

Hallam, A. H., to R. M. Milnes, on the balloon ascent, i. 67

Hallam, H., to R. M. Milnes, on his son's "Remains," i. 157

Hare, Julius, to R. M. Milnes, on the latter's return to England, i. 156

Hawes, Sir Benjamin, to R. M. Milnes, on the appointment of Sir Charles MacCarthy to the Governorship of Ceylon, ii. 42

Hayward, A., to Lord Houghton, on the Alabama question, ii. 261

Heine, to Lady Duff Gordon, on Milnes's friendship, i. 251

Helps, Sir Arthur, to Lord Houghton, on an invitation to Fryston, ii. 245

Holland, Queen of, to Lord Houghton, with an invitation to the Hague, ii. 197; to the same, on his visit, 204; to the same, 220; to the same, on the Stuarts, &c., 304

Houghton, Lord (Milnes, R. M.)—
to his mother, August, 1825, from Edinburgh, 47—49; to his mother, Nov., 1827, on Thirlwall, Sterling, Simeon, &c., 50, 51; to his mother, Dec., 1827, on his phrenological development, a humorous definition of metaphysics, &c., 52, 53; to his

Letters (continued).
father, Dec., 1827, on Cavendish, seventh Duke of Devonshire, 53; to his mother, on "wearing a hat," his speech at the Union, &c., 53, 54; to his father, Jan., 1828, on the Duke of Sussex, Perry, Senior Wrangler, De Vere, &c., 54, 55; to his father, proposing to keep terms at an Inn of Court, 55; to his father, exonerating himself from lack of industry, 56; to his mother, Oct., 1828, on the "flush of noblemen" at the University, the Presidency of the Union, &c., 57; on his anatomical studies, the Debating Society, &c., 57; to his father, Dec., 1828, on his father's embarrassments, the Union, Clubs, &c., 58, 59, to his mother, on John Sterling, &c., 60; to his father, on Mr. Peel, debate on the "Ancient Mariner," and Mr. Martin's Acts, contributions to the *Athenæum*, "Timbuctoo," &c., 60—62; to his father. Feb., 1829, on the speakers at the Union, 62; to his father, on his failure at an examination, and his dislike of mathematics, 64, 65; to A. H. Hallam, on the former's balloon ascent, 66, 67; to his father, on a conversation with Cousin, 70; to his father, Oct., 1829, on his plans for study, the utility of the Cambridge Union as a preparation for Parliamentary speaking, Hallam's genius, &c., 72; to his mother, Nov., 1829, on the debate on Wordsworth and Byron, 72, 73; to his mother, Dec., 1829, on the debate at Oxford on the comparative merits of Shelley and Byron, his Homeric essay, his father's definition of an orator, making a start in Parliament, &c., 77—80; to his father, Jan., 1830, on the Shelley Mission to Oxford, &c., 88; to his father, Feb., 1830, on a passage in Moore's "Life of Byron," his proposal to study in Germany, the characteristics of T. Sunderland, &c., 89—91; to his mother, on his friendships at Cambridge, his political views, &c., 91, 92; to his father, on

Letters (continued).
speeches at the Union, F. Tennyson, Fanny Kemble, &c., 92, 93; to his father, March, 1830, describing the leading features of his poem, "Byzantium," the subject for the prize poem, 93, 94; to his mother, on Cobbett's lecture at St. Ives, and current anecdotes, 94; to his father, referring to speeches in Parliament by O'Connor, Lord Belgrave, and others, his mingling in London society, his reception on a visit to Cambridge, &c., 95, 96; to his sister, from Bonn, July, 1830, on the frequency of duels near Bonn, his introduction to Madam Schopenhauer, &c., 98, 99; to ——, referring to the failure of Charles Buller to make an impression in the House of Commons, 99, 100; to his father, on the Revolution in Paris, 100; to Miss Caroline Milnes, Milan, Feb., 1831, on the Milan opera, Italian men and women, arrest of O'Connell, &c., 103, 104; to his father, Venice, March, 1831, on Venetian society, a proposed visit to Rome, the Reform Bill, &c., 106–108; to his mother, Dublin, Aug., 1831, on his first railway experience, buildings in Dublin, Lady Campbell, debates in the House of Commons, &c., 110, 111; to his sister, on the Giant's Causeway, writing a journal, &c., 112, 113; to his mother, on his Irish trip, 120; to his grandmother, Rome, Jan., 1832, 121; to his father, Rome, June, 1832, asking consent to visit Greece, &c., 125, 126; to his father, on his plans for a tour in Greece, &c., 126, 127; to Miss Caroline Milnes, Zante, Aug., 1832, 129, 130; to Miss Jane Milnes, Athens, Oct., 1832, on his tour in Greece, 132-135; to his mother, on Greece, 135, 136; to his father, expressing solicitude with regard to the family embarrassments, 138, 139; to his mother, from Fiesole, during an illness, 144; to his father, on W. S. Landor, "Adventures of a Younger Son," &c.,

Letters (continued).
145; to Miss Caroline Milnes, 1833, on his Büchlein, &c., 148; to his mother, Rome, Jan., 1834, on English society in Rome, 150, 151; to Miss Caroline Milnes, on the Carnival at Rome, the death of Augustus Hare, English people in Rome, &c., 151, 153; to his aunt, February, 1835, on the termination of the residence of his family on the Continent, 154; to ——, on society and ballet dancing in Florence, 154, 155; to C. J. MacCarthy, on Trench's poems, &c., 158, 159; to Aubrey de Vere, March, 1837, on his poems, Dr. Newman's book on the prophetical character and verses, &c., 193, 194; to Aubrey de Vere, May, 1837, on reunion after death, Browning's "Strafford," Miss Martineau's "America," the Newmanites, &c., 195—197; to C. J. MacCarthy, saying he was intended by nature for a German woman, 201; to C. J. MacCarthy, on magnetism, Disraeli's speech against Lord John Russell, his own maiden speech, &c., 203-205; to C. J. MacCarthy, March, 1838, on "Froude's Remains," London gossip, &c., 217—219; to Aubrey de Vere, on Carlyle's lectures, "Froude's Remains," &c., 219—221; to his sister, Lady Galway, 1838, on a projected Continental trip, reviews of his poems, Parliamentary affairs, &c., 229—231; to the same, on Continental Travels, &c., 231, 232; to the same, on the same subject, 232, 233; to C. J. MacCarthy, from Edinburgh, October, 1839, 242; to Sir Robert Peel, on King Louis Philippe and the French Government, 247-249; to C. J. MacCarthy, on "One Tract More," &c., 261, 262; to C. J. MacCarthy, on the Pontefract election, Lord John Russell's Bribery Bill, &c., 263; to C. J. MacCarthy, on the Pontefract election, 264, 265; to M. Guizot, Sept., 1841, on the state of political feeling in England, 270, 271; to the same, on wintering at Fryston,

Letters (continued).
273 ; to W. E. Gladstone, on the Copyright Bill, 275 ; to C. J. MacCarthy, Smyrna, November, 1842, on Eastern travel, &c., 284, 285 ; to Sir Robert Peel, on political affairs in the East, &c., 285—288 ; to C. J. MacCarthy, May, 1843, on political affairs, English society in Rome, London gossip, &c., 290 — 294 ; to the same, on Puseyism, the Roman Catholic Church in Ireland, the King of Hanover, &c., 300, 301 ; to the same, on the Rebecca riots, Queen Victoria's visit to France, Bunsen, &c., 304, 305; to W. E. Gladstone, Oct., 1843, on his discouragement in Parliament, and application for the post of Secretary of Legation in Paris, 311, 312; to the same, on his decision to remain in Parliament, 314, 315; to C. J. MacCarthy, on Sir Robert Peel, O'Connell, Gladstone, &c., 315, 317; to the same, on the O'Connell trial, 317; to the Mayor of Pomfret, on the Bill for the Maynooth Grant, 321 ; to C. J. MacCarthy, February, 1844, on O'Connell's re-appearance in the House of Commons, "Palm Leaves," &c., 321, 322; to the same, on Factory Legislation, French affairs, &c., 324, 325; to M. Guizot, on English political affairs, &c., 325, 326; to his aunt, on the State Fancy Ball, 326 ; to C. J. MacCarthy, on Thomas Campbell and a Ministerial crisis, 330 ; to his father, on the state of affairs in the House of Commons, 331 ; to the same, on the failure of Peel to manage affairs, 331, 332 ; to the same, on new Ministerial appointments, &c., 332; to the same, on the Government opening letters, &c., 332, 333; to M. Guizot, Aug., 1844, on English political affairs, 333, 334; to W. E. Gladstone, on the review of "Ellen Middleton," and the Court of Ultimate Appeal, 335; to C. J. MacCarthy, on Louis Philippe's visit to England, "Young England," "Lord Eldon's Life," Stanley's "Life

Letters (continued).
of Arnold," &c., 339, 340 ; to his father, January, 1845, on his experiences in Berlin, 343—345; to C. J. MacCarthy, on Thiers, Disraeli, the Maynooth College, &c., 351, 352; to the same, on the Maynooth Bill, and his Parliamentary work, 353, 354 ; to his sister, Lady Galway, on his father, &c., 355; to C. J. MacCarthy, on railroad speculation, the Maynooth "storm," &c., 355, 356; to the same, on Parliamentary affairs, &c., 357, 358; to the same, on Newman's secession to the Church of Rome, the resignation of Peel, Lord John Russell's futile attempt to form a Government, Peel's return to office, Carlyle's "Cromwell," &c., 358—360; to his father, declining to stand for North Notts, 361; to W. E. Gladstone, requesting his influence in obtaining the office of Under-Secretary of Foreign Affairs, 361, 362; to the same, on his disappointment at failing to secure the Under-Secretaryship, 364, 365; to M. Guizot, on the state of political affairs in England, 367—369 ; to his father and to C. J. MacCarthy, on the defeat of the Protectionists, 370, 371 ; to C. J. MacCarthy, May 15, 1846, on the repeal of the Corn Law, &c., 371—373; to the same, on the fall of Peel, the accession of Lord John Russell to office, &c., 374—376 ; to the same, on the Pontefract election, and various friends, 380—382 ; to his father, on his projected tour in Spain, &c., 391, 392; to Miss Caroline Milnes, September, 1847, on the same subject, 392, 393; to his father, from Lisbon, on Portuguese affairs, 393, 394 ; to the same, on the same subject, 395 ; to the same, describing Seville, 395, 396; to his sister, on his Spanish experience, 397—399 ; to the same, on society in Madrid, &c., 399, 400 ; to C. J. MacCarthy, Dec., 1847, on his "breaking off the last link of Peelery, the Carlton Club," 401,

Letters (continued)..
402; to his sister, Lady Galway, on the arrival of Louis Philippe and the ex-Queen in England, &c., 406, 407; to C. J. MacCarthy, Sept., 1848, on Fryston, European politics, &c., 407, 408; to Mrs. MacCarthy, on Buller's death, Macaulay's "History," &c., 409, 410; to C. J. MacCarthy, Jan., 1849, on the French in Rome, the Russians in Hungary, &c., 418, 419; to the same, on the Sikh War, Peel's proposal for the re-settlement of Ireland, &c., 429, 430; to Mrs. MacCarthy, on the advance of the French on Rome, Froude's "Nemesis of Faith," visit to Paris, &c., 430—434; to C. J. MacCarthy, on English and French political affairs, 438—440; to the same, on Samuel Rogers, 440; to Mrs. MacCarthy, July, 1850, on the death of Sir Robert Peel, "In Memoriam," &c., 444, 445; to C. J. MacCarthy, July, 1851, on his approaching marriage, 450; to the same, on his wife, Gladstone's Naples Letters, &c., 450, 451; to W. E. Gladstone, on revising Gladstone's translation of Farini's "History of the Roman State," &c., 452, 453; to the same, on Louis Napoleon, Disraeli, &c., 453, 454; to C. J. MacCarthy, January, 1852, on the death of Eliot Warburton, the dismissal of Lord Palmerston, the French *coup d'état*, &c., 468—469; to the same, February, 1853, on the Emperor Napoleon's marriage, Italian affairs, &c., 479, 480; five extracts from letters to his wife during his visit to Ireland, 483—485; to C. J. MacCarthy, on Turkish affairs, &c., 485, 486; to his wife, on Parliamentary business, 489; eight extracts from letters to his wife, on Lord Radstock, Maurice, the *Times'* politics, Lord Palmerston, Florence Nightingale, Mrs. Disraeli, W. Harcourt, and containing lines of congratulation on the New Year, 489—492; six extracts from letters to his wife,

Letters (continued).
1854, on the Crimean war, Florence Nightingale, Nathaniel Hawthorne, Lord F. Gower, &c., 496—498; to the Chevalier Bunsen, asking for information on German affairs, &c., 498; to Mr. Gladstone, February, 1855, appealing to him to join the Liberal Party, 501, 502; to C. J. MacCarthy, on the changes in the Government, &c., 504; six extracts from letters to his wife on the Ministerial crisis; a Philobiblion breakfast; the Burns anniversary, W. E. Forster, &c., 505—507; to his father, on his refusal of Palmerston's offer of a post in the Treasury, 508; to his wife, on Lord Palmerston, 508, 509; two extracts from letters to his wife, on John Bright, the death of Charlotte Brontë, Miss Martineau's article in the *Daily News* on Charlotte Brontë, &c., 510, 511; to C. J. MacCarthy, on English politics, Tennyson's "Maud" and "Balaklava Charge," &c., 511, 512; to his wife from Paris, on Palmerston, &c., 513; to his father, on H. Lushington, the Paris Exhibition, &c., 513, 514; eight extracts from letters to his wife from Paris and Vichy, on the Exhibition, French politics, Queen Victoria's visit to Paris, Tennyson, &c., 514—518; five extracts from letters to his wife from Scotland, on the British Association meeting, Monteith, &c., 522—524; three extracts from letters to his wife from Hawarden Castle, Crewe, and Fryston, on Gladstone, Miss Martineau's illness, &c., 524, 525; three extracts from letters to his wife, on Madame Mohl, Lady Ellesmere, Mrs. Gaskell, &c., 526, 527. II. To C. J. MacCarthy, February, 1856, on family matters, his father's refusal of a peerage, &c., 3; to the same, on benevolence that does little good, his father's rejection of a peerage, &c., 4; to his wife, on a rumoured dissolution, &c., 5, 6; to his wife, Boulogne, on the birth of a French

Letters (continued).
prince, &c., 8; to the same, Paris, on M. Rio, &c., 9; to the same, Paris, on his French friends, 9, 10; to the same, on his meeting with certain French celebrities, 10; to C. J. MacCarthy, on pensions for Colonial Governors, &c., 13; to the same, on Palmerston after his defeat, 14; to his wife, on his address at the Liverpool Free Library banquet, 17; to the same, on the Manchester Fine-Art Exhibition, 17; to the same (three letters) from France, on his visit to M. Guizot, &c, 18, 19; to the same, on his visit to Baron Bunsen, 19, 20; to C. J. MacCarthy, Oct., 1857, on the Indian Mutiny, &c., 20, 21; four extracts from letters to his wife, on visits to Baron Rothschild, Lord Lansdowne, Colonel Harcourt, &c., 21—23: to Miss Jane Milnes, on Lady Russell, &c., 23; to Miss Caroline Milnes, on theatricals at Lord John Russell's, Woburn, Lord Russell's opinion of Cobden's budget, &c., 23, 24; three extracts from letters to his wife, on the Sheffield School of Art, a party at Strawberry Hill, and Lady Ashburton's death, 25, 26; to George von Bunsen, March, 1858, on the writer's article in the *Quarterly* on the siege of Lucknow, 27, 28; to his wife (two extracts), on Palmerston at the dinner of the Royal Literary Fund, and the death of Buller, 28, 29; to the same (four extracts), on his visit to De Tocqueville, &c., 30—32; to C. J. MacCarthy, on French and English political affairs, 32, 33; to the same, November, 1858, on the death of his father, &c., 34; to his wife, January, 1859, with New Year's congratulations, &c., 37, 38; to C. J. MacCarthy, on Lord John Russell and Mr. Bright, &c., 38, 39; to his wife (extracts), on the Bishop of Exeter's surprise at the Milnes family being Dissenters, &c., 39, 40; to ——, with advice as to cultivating poetical gifts, 59,

Letters (continued).
60; to his elder daughter, December, 1859, on Christmas Day, Miss Nightingale, &c., 60; to his wife, on a country-visit, 61; to C. J. MacCarthy, October, 1860, on Lord Palmerston, the Italian question, &c., 62; to the same, on the Duke of Newcastle, Cardinal Wiseman, Beaumont's "Life of De Tocqueville, 62, 63; to George von Bunsen, on the illness of Baron Bunsen, 66, 67; to C. J. MacCarthy, June, 1861, on the American War, &c., 71, 72; to the same, on the death of Sydney Herbert, &c., 72, 73; to Lady Galway, on the meeting of the Blind Asylum at York, &c., 74; to C. J. MacCarthy, on Prince Albert's death, &c., 74, 75; to the same, on the American War and his article on Burton, in the *Edinburgh Review*, 76, 77; to George von Bunsen, on the American War, &c., 77, 78; to his sister, on his visit to Buxton, 81; to his eldest daughter, Aug., 1862, on the natural times for taking food, &c., 81, 82; to C. J. MacCarthy, on the Exhibition of 1862; the Diplomatic Service, &c., 83, 84; to the same, on his second daughter as a verse-writer, the Cotton Famine, &c., 85, 86; to the same, January, 1863, on the prospect of a peerage, Mr. Coomara Samy, &c., 89, 90; three extracts from letters to his wife, on the Prince of Wales's marriage, Lord Lansdowne, &c., 91, 92; to C. J. MacCarthy, on French news, 95; to the same, on a proposed visit to Ceylon, Turkish baths, Prince and Princess of Wales, &c., 95, 96; to his wife (five extracts), on the death of Thackeray, his visit to Broadlands, and Lord Broughton's, 118—120; to the same (four extracts), on his visit to the Riviera, the death of Lord Ashburton, &c., 120—122; to George von Bunsen, April, 1864, on Lord Brougham, Lord Ashburton, &c., 123, 124; to his wife, on his visit to Turin, 124, 125; to George

INDEX.

Letters (*continued*).
von Bunsen, inviting him to visit Fryston, 126, 127; to his wife, on the debate on "Essays and Reviews," 131; four extracts from letters to his wife, on his visit to Vichy, 133, 134; to his wife (two extracts), on the preaching of Liberal divines, the Bishop of Chester, &c., 135, 136; to Henry Bright, on Liberal apathy, &c., 141, 142; to Comte de Montalembert, on the English elections, &c., 142, 143; to his wife (two extracts), on the appreciation and admiration of Carlyle towards his late wife, 149; several extracts from letters to the same, on political events, &c., 151, 152; to Mr. Gladstone, March, 1866, on the agitation for the Reform Bill, &c., 152, 153; to G. von Bunsen, on the change of Ministry, &c., 153, 154; to the same, on the Italian Question, &c., 155; to Lady Galway, on his visit to Biarritz, 156, 177; to his wife, on his Manchester speech, 158; to Henry Bright, on his Manchester speech, 158; to his wife, 167; several extracts from letters to his wife on his Paris visit, 169—171; to his daughter, on the same subject, 171; to H. Bright, 172; to Mr. Gladstone, on Rio, &c., 172, 173; to G. von Bunsen, on Bismarck, &c., 173, 174; six letters to his wife, on political affairs, &c., 174—177; to his daughter, on the Sultan, 177, 178; to G. von Bunsen, on his German visit, 179, 180; to his youngest daughter, on the same subject, 180, 181; several extracts from letters to his wife (October—December, 1867), on the Fenian conspiracy, &c., 184—188; to Miss Jane Milnes, on his visit to Rome, 188; several extracts from letters to his wife (1868), 189—192; to H. Bright, on Church and State, 193; four extracts from letters to his wife, on his visit to Strathfieldsaye, 193—196; to his daughter, from the Hague, 198; to H.

Letters (*continued*).
Bright, February, 1869, 198, 199; to C. M. Gaskell, on a bereavement, 199; to his wife, on Dean Stanley, 200; to Mr. Gladstone, 200, to his wife, on his visit to Holland, 201; to his daughter, on the same subject, 201; to his son, on the same subject, 202; to his wife, on the same subject, 203; to H. Bright, on his Suez journey, 206; to his son, on the same subject, 206, 207; five extracts from letters to his wife, 207—211; to his son, from Cairo, 211; to his wife, from Rome, 211; two letters to his son, from Rome, 212, 213; to Lady Galway, 221; to his aunts, March, 1870, 221; to H. Bright, on Disraeli's novels, 223; to his wife, on J. Bright's illness, 226; to his son, 229; to H. Bright, 232; to his daughter, on the Franco-Prussian War, 233; to the same, 233; two letters to Lady Galway, 234; to his wife (five extracts), on the French in London, &c., 235—237; to Mr. Gladstone (two letters), on the Franco-Prussian war, 237—240; to his wife, 243; to Mr. Gladstone, on the Moxon pension, &c., 248; to his wife, February, 1871, 250; to H. Bright, on Lady W. Russell, &c., 251; to his wife, 252; to Mr. Gladstone, on the latter's Whitby speech, &c., 252, 253; to his wife, from Scotland, 254; to his son, on his Scotch visit, September, 1871, 254; to H. Bright, 259; to his wife, 260; to his son, 260; to his wife, on his visit to Thiers, 266—268; to his sister, from Vichy, 268; to his wife, from Venice, 269; to his son, from the same place, 270; to Mr. Gladstone, on the latter's lecture at Liverpool, 270, 271; to the same, on the same subject, 272; to Lady Galway, on the Duke of Edinburgh's marriage, 276; to Mr. Gladstone, on Joaquin Miller, &c., 277, 278; to the same, on the Trusteeship of the British Museum, 278, 279; to his wife, 281; to H. Bright, on sleeping at a lunatic asylum, &c., 283; to the

Letters (continued)
same, on Charles Lamb's adopted daughter, 284; to Mrs. Tennyson, December, 1873, 284; to G. von Bunsen, on Bismarck, 284, 285; to his son, February, 1874, on the General Election, 288; to H. Bright, on his wife's illness, &c., 289, 290; to H. Bright (two letters), on the pension to Lamb's adopted daughter, &c., 292; to John Morley, June, 1874, on French politics, 292, 293; to his son, on M. Thiers, &c., 293; to his elder daughter, 294; to his son, on competing for prizes, 294, 295; to H. Bright (two extracts), on Lady W. Russell, &c., 297; to the same (several extracts), on his visit to Scotland, the defeat of Forster, &c., 298, 303, 304, 305; to his son, June, 1875, on the prize poem, 306; to H. Bright, from Emerson's house at Concord, Oct., 1875, 318; to the same, from Washington, 327; to his daughter, 327; extracts from letters to H. Bright, chiefly on political matters, 338, 339; to Mr. Gladstone, September, 1876, on the Turks, 341; to the same, on the failure of Greece, 342, 343; to G. von Bunsen, on Turkish affairs, &c., 343, 344; to H. Bright, 344; to Miss Jane Milnes, on the burning of Fryston, 347, 348; to his son, on the same subject, 348; to H. Bright, on the same subject, 349; to C. M. Gaskell, on the same subject, 349, 350; to H. A. Bright, on the books lost at the fire, 354; to his son, on the latter's poem, "Harold," 355; to the same, 356; to Mr. Gladstone, on the latter's article on the Prince Consort, &c., 356, 357; to H. Bright, on "the Great Crusader," Mr. Gladstone, &c., 358; to his son, on the Prince of Wales, 358; to H. Bright, March, 1877, 359; to Mr. Gladstone, on F D. Maurice, 359; to the same, on "Gleanings," 360; Extracts, to his daughter Florence, on Fryston, &c., 360, 361; to H. Bright, 361; to Miss Louisa Milnes, May, 1877, on

Letters (continued).
Fryston, 361, 362; to his son, on an accident in the Park, 363; to Miss Louisa Milnes, on the opening of the St. Pancras Pleasure Ground, 363, 364; several extracts, to H. Bright, on the British Association at Plymouth, &c., 364, 367; to John Morley, on Thiers, &c., 366; to the same, on the "Life of Lord Melbourne," 372; two extracts, to his son, on his visit to Paris, 378, 379; to H. Bright, from Royat, August, 1878, 379; several extracts, to H. Bright, on French affairs, &c., 385, 387; to his daughter, April, 1880, on Gladstone's triumph at the General Election, 387; two extracts, to H. Bright, on his son's marriage, &c., 391; to Miss Jane Milnes, from the residence of the Comte de Paris, 391, 392; to G. von Bunsen (four letters), on German affairs, &c., 392, 394; to his daughter Florence, 394; to his daughter (two letters), on the Berlin review, &c., 395, 396; to his son, 396; to G. von Bunsen, on his daughter's visit to Palestine, &c., 398; to his son, on Sir James Colvile's death, 398, 399; to his daughter in Palestine, 399; to H. Bright, on his notes on "Endymion," 400; four letters to his daughter Amy, on Carlyle's death, Spedding's death, Carlyle's Autobiography, the Czar's murder, &c., 400—403; to Mr. Gladstone, April, 1881, on British Museum trusteeship, 404; to Miss Louisa Milnes, 408; to his daughter Mrs. FitzGerald, on H Bright's illness, 408; to his son, from Cairo, 410, 411; to his daughter Florence, on the revolution in Cairo, February, 1882, 411; to his son, 412; four letters to the same, on being in quarantine at Piræus, his illness at Athens, &c., 412—415; to Miss Louisa Milnes, 415, 416; to Mr. Severn, from Fryston, April, 1882, 418; to his son, on the detectives at Hawarden Castle, &c., 420; four extracts, to H. Bright, on his illness, &c., 421,

Letters (*continued*).
423; to John Morley, March, 1883, on society in Cannes, &c., 422; to his daughter, Amicia, 423; to his daughter, from Rome, 423; to his son, on Cardinal Antonelli, &c., 424; to H. Bright, on Mr. and Mrs. Carlyle, &c. 425; to his son, 426

Hunt, Leigh, to R. M. Milnes, declining an invitation to dinner, ii. 11

Hurlbert, W. H., to Lord Houghton, Aug., 1875, ii. 320; to the same, 321

Imperial, The Prince, to Lord Houghton, ii. 266

Kinglake, A. W., to R. M. Milnes, on assistance for Thomas Hood, i. 347, 348

Kirkup, Seymour, to Lord Houghton, on W. Blake, &c., ii. 222; to the same, on W. S. Landor, &c., 249

Landor, W. S., to R. M. Milnes, on poetical contributions for "The Tribute," i. 181, 183; to the same, April, 1843, on Southey and his works, i. 297—299; to the same, on Southey, Napier, &c., 299; to the same, on Milnes's elevation to the peerage, and his own illness, ii. 110, 111

Lewes, Mrs. George, to Lord Houghton, ii. 376

Longfellow, H. W., to Lord Houghton, welcoming him to America, ii. 317

MacCarthy, C. J., to R. M. Milnes, on the latter's mental depression, &c., i. 140, 141; C. J. MacCarthy, to R. M. Milnes, on Hare's sermon in the Protestant chapel, Rome, &c., 142, 143; to the same, on Milnes's self-depreciation, 143; to the same, 177; on R. M. Milnes's maiden speech, 205; to R. M. Milnes, on the latter's disappointment at not being offered a post in the Peel Administration, 268, 269

Macaulay, T. B., to R. M. Milnes, November, 1852, on an invitation to breakfast, i. 477

Maxwell, Sir William Stirling, to Lord Houghton, on converts to Romanism, &c., ii. 300

Member of Parliament, A, April,

Letters (*continued*).
1807, on Pemberton Milnes's famous speech in the House of Commons, and wager respecting the office of Chancellor of the Exchequer, i. 10, 11

Mill, J. S., to Lord Houghton, on the Women Suffrage movement, ii. 178: to the same, on the same subject, 179

Milnes, R. M. (*see* Houghton, Lord)

Milnes, R. P., to his wife, Brussels, July, 1815, on the defeat of the French at Waterloo, i. 24—26; to the same, Paris, July, 1815, on the same subject, 26—30; to Lord Palmerston, declining a peerage, 40, 41; to the same, shortly before the writer's death, 42; to his son, Nov., 1847, on the sixty millions sunk in railways, &c., 399, 400; to his sister, Miss Jane Milnes, on the speakers in the House of Commons, &c., ii. 6

Montalembert, Count de, to Lord Houghton, August, 1866, ii. 156

Monteith, R., to R. M. Milnes, on old friends at Cambridge, the "Fifty" debating society, the Union, &c., i. 105, 106

Motley, J. L., to Lord Houghton, on the Fryston fire, ii. 351

Murchison, Sir Roderick, to Lord Houghton, ii. 205

Newcastle, Duke of, to R. M. Milnes, on the appointment of Sir Charles MacCarthy to the Governorship of Ceylon, ii. 42

Nightingale, Florence, to R. M. Milnes, on working men and atheism, i. 475; to Milnes's sister, on Milnes's love for poor children, ii. 7; to Lord Houghton, May, 1880, on his son's marriage, &c., 389; to same, on his illness, 418

O'Brien, Stafford, to C. J. MacCarthy, on R. M. Milnes's maiden speech, i. 205

Palmerston, Lady, to R. M. Milnes, on his marriage, i. 449; to the same, Dec., 1853, on the plans of her husband, Russian affairs, &c., 487, 488; to the same, on her husband's resignation, &c., 488, 489: to the same, Sept., 1862, on the marriages of the Prince of Wales and Lord Dufferin, ii. 82, 83

Letters (*continued*).
Palmerston, Lord, to Lord Malmesbury, on the Perceval Ministry, i. 14; to Mr. R. P. Milnes, offering a peerage, 39; to R. M. Milnes, on the death of the latter's father, 42, 43; to the same, on Hudson, ii. 12
Perceval, Mr., to Mr. R. P. Milnes, urging acceptance of office in the new Administration, i. 15
Procter, Mrs, wife of Barry Cornwall, to R. M. Milnes, Oct., 1843, on Carlyle, Thackeray, &c., i. 306, 307; to the same, on "Palm Leaves," &c., 307, 308; to the same, on the appearance of Dickens and Forster on the stage of St. James's Theatre, 358; to Mrs. Milnes, on the Crimean War, A.W. Kinglake, Thackeray, Mrs. Grote, Fanny Kemble, &c., 499; to R. M. Milnes, on Robert Browning, &c., ii. 70, 71; to the same, on Adelaide Ann Procter, Fanny Kemble, &c., 84, 85; to the same, on "Henrietta Temple," &c., 181; to the same, Nov., 1871, 256; to the same, 282, to the same, on "Bothwell," &c., 295; to the same, on Tennyson, &c., 320; to the same, 357; to the same, on Lady Elizabeth Duncan, &c., 364
Samy, Coomara, to R. M. Milnes, on the latter's hospitality, ii. 88; to the same, on the same subject, 89; to the same, 298
Sherman, General, to General Badeau, on Lord Houghton's reception at St. Louis, ii. 313
Smith, Sydney, to R. M. Milnes, 1838, 1840, 1841, i. 210—214
Spedding, James, to R. M. Milnes, on Carlyle's lectures, &c., i. 192; to the same, on the formation of the London Library, 234, 235
Spencer, Herbert, to Lady Houghton, April, 1872; on his visit to Fryston, i. 466
Stanley, Lady Augusta, to Lord Houghton, on the interment of Charles Dickens in Westminster Abbey, ii. 229
Stanley, Dean, to R. M. Milnes, congratulating him on his elevation to the peerage, ii. 110; to the same, on the interment of

Letters (*continued*).
Charles Dickens, 228; to the same, on Père Hyacinthe, 262
Sumner, Charles, to R. M. Milnes, on Emerson, i. 237—239; to the same, on Tennyson's poems, &c., 279—281; to the same, thanking him for his hospitality to American friends, 303; to the same, on the latter's poems, &c., 326, 327
Swinburne, A. C, to Lord Houghton, on his introduction to W. S. Landor, ii. 136—139; to the same, on his memorial poem to Landor, 399
Tennyson, Alfred, to R. M. Milnes, 1833, on Milnes's "Impressions of Greece,' &c., i. 149; to the same, declining to contribute to "The Tribute," 178; to the same, Jan., 1837, consenting to send something for "The Tribute," 179, 180; to the same, on Lady Houghton's death, ii. 290
Thackeray, W. M., to R. M. Milnes, July, 1841, arranging to meet him at York, &c., i. 263; to the same, arranging with R. M. Milnes to see a man hanged, 426; to the same, on the same subject, 427; to the same, on his wish to secure a London magistracy, 427, 428; to the same, inviting him to meet Miss Brontë at his house at dinner, 429; to the same, bidding him farewell on departing for America, ii. 112
Thiers, M., to R. M. Milnes, Jan., 1852, in response to an invitation to Fryston, i. 469, 470
Thirlwall, Connop, to R. M. Milnes, on the "Captain's" story of the whale and calf, &c., i. 162—164; to the same, on Milnes's Conservatism, 198, 199; to the same, on the endowment of the Irish Catholic clergy, &c., 301, 302; to the same, July, 1843, on Carlyle, &c., 302, 303, to the same, on the latter's approaching marriage, 447, 448; to the same, on his acceptance of a peerage, ii. 108, 109; to the same (two letters), on Swinburne's tribute to Landor, in "Atalanta in Calydon," 138—140
Trench, R. C., to R. M. Milnes,

Letters (*continued*).
  March, 1838, on the latter's new volumes, and Tennyson's poem in "The Tribute," i. 208
  Trollope, Anthony, to Lord Houghton, on "The Warden," ii. 155; to the same, on the largest price for a novel, 224; to the same, enclosing a cheque for his lost bet, 225
  Various Correspondents to R. M. Milnes; Jan., 1855, on Florence Nightingale's work at Scutari, i. 509; to R. M. M., on David Gray, ii. 50; to Lady Houghton, on her husband's popularity in Genoa, 125
  Venables, G. S., to Lord Houghton, on political affairs, ii. 158, 159
  Warburton, Eliot, to R. M. Milnes, reminding him of his failure to correspond, i. 243; to the same, on the review of "Palm Leaves," in the *Quarterly Review*, 345, 346; to the same, on Milnes's secession to the "Johnian faction," 403; to the same on the latter's marriage, 449
  Ward, F. O., to R. M. Milnes (four letters) on Thomas Hood's illness, circumstances, death, &c., 348—350
  Ward, S., to Hon. Robert Milnes, on Lord Houghton's visit to New York, ii. 322; five letters to the same, on Lord Houghton's reception in America, 322—324; to Lord Houghton, 337
  Wellington, The Duke of, to Mr. Edkins, July, 1847, on the equestrian statue at Hyde Park Corner, i. 389, 390
  Wiseman, Dr., to R. M. Milnes, on his tour through England and Ireland, &c., i. 160, 161
  Wordsworth, Wm., to R. M. Milnes, on the Copyright Bill, i. 226, 227
"Letters from Italy," i. 113
Leven, Lord, describes Mr. R. P. Milnes's handsome and intelligent appearance, i. 30, 31
Lewis, Cornewall, i. 237
Liberalism in Europe in 1848, i. 411
"Life and Letters of Keats," R. M. Milnes's, i. 406, 408; ii. 263, 441
"Life in Death," R. M. Milnes's, i. 142
"Life of Arnold," Stanley's, i. 340
"Life of Dr. Bell," Southey's, i. 298

"Life of De Tocqueville," Beaumont's, ii. 63, 64
"Life of Sydney Smith," Lady Holland's, i. 214
Lind, Jenny, i. 434
Lister, Mr., author of "Granby," i. 96
Literary Chronicle, i. 81
Liverpool Free Library and Museum, ii. 17
Locke, "loathsome infidelity," i. 60; 116
Locker-Lampson, Frederick: opinion of Lord Houghton, ii. 453
Lockhart, i. 173, 391
Loftus, Lord A., ii. 231
Logan, Dr., i. 317
Lombardy, i. 68, 100, 111, 413; ii. 40
London, Bishop, ii. 39
London Library, Projection and formation of the, i. 234—237
Longfellow; reference by C. Sumner, i. 281; marriage to Miss Appleton, 303, 326, ii. 71; visit to England, 193—195; meets Lord Houghton in America, 317
Lonsdale, Lord, i. 23
"Lothair," ii. 223; Lord Houghton's review in the *Edinburgh*, 223
Lotos Club, ii. 327, 332
Louis, St., ii. 312
Louis XVIII., i. 25, 26. 103
Louis Philippe, King; friendship with R. M. Milnes, i. 246, 292; Queen Victoria, 305; proposed visit to England, 333; visit to England, 335, 339, 377; at the Revolution, 405, 421
Lowe, Robert (*see* Sherbrooke, Lord)
Lowell, J. R., ii. 317, 386; address at the unveiling of Coleridge's bust at Westminster Abbey, 432
Lowther, James, ii. 177
Lowther, Lord, visits Paris with Mr. Pemberton Milnes in 1814, i. 21
"Luggie, The," poem by David Gray, ii. 47, 57
Lushington, E. L., i. 62, 75; one of the "Apostles" at Cambridge, 81
Lushington, Godfrey, ii. 181
Lushington, Henry, i. 75, 381, 513, 514
Lyndhurst, Lord; the O'Connell Appeal case, i. 335
Lyons, Lord, ii. 30, 177, 424
Lyttelton, Mr., attacks Mr. Canning, i. 9, 222
Lytton, Lord, "Life of Palmerston": extract on the Perceval Ministry,

i i 2

i. 14 ; estimate of Pemberton Milnes's character, 16 ; member of Parliament, 202 ; play, 218, 237 ; at the Colonial Office, ii. 33, 182, 257, 260, 409
Lytton, Robert, "Tannhauser," ii. 69

Macaulay, Lord, i. 108, 109 ; as a dinner-table talker, 190 ; return to London from India, 190 ; visitor at S. Rogers', 190 ; "The Right Honourable Tom," 101, 277 ; article on Barère, 325 ; at Edinburgh, 380 ; "History of England," 410 ; great success of the "History," 432 ; intimacy with R. M. Milnes, 477 ; death, ii. 160, 435 ;
Macaulay, Mr. (cousin to Lord Macaulay), i. 146
MacCarthy, Sir Charles J. ; friendship with R. M. Milnes, i. 123, 140, 151 ; ii. 132 ; extract from journal recording an incident in Rome about R. M. Milnes, Trench, and himself, 155, 156 ; Milnes's maiden speech, 205, 261, 264, 268, 269, 284, 285, 290—294 ; assisted by R. M. Milnes, 294, 304, 305, 315—317, 321, 322, 351—356 ; appointed Governor of Ceylon, 378, ii. 42 ; marries the daughter of Sir Benjamin Haines, i. 380 ; knighted, ii. 13 ; visit to Fryston, 42 ; illness, 121, 126 ; death, 132 ; Lord Houghton's "In Memoriam" in the *Times*, 134. 425
Macdonald, Mr. (of the *Times*), treasurer of the Patriotic Fund, i. 500, 518
Maclellan, General, ii. 145
Maclennan, J. F., ii. 135
MacMahon, Marshal, ii. 293
Macmillan's Magazine, ii. 419, 449
Macready, i. 326
Madeley, i. 450, 517
Madrid, R. M. Milnes's visit to, i. 397—400
Magnetism, R. M. Milnes's experience of, i. 203, 204
Mahomet, Allusion of Carlyle to, i. 323 ; De Tocqueville's opinion of, 328
Mahon, Lord, i. 276
Malakhoff, ii. 30, 31
Malet, Sir Alexander, ii. 181
Malmesbury, Lord, extract from letter from Palmerston on the Perceval Ministry, i. 14 ; reference to letters from Palmerston on Pemberton Milnes's refusal to take office, 16 ; reference to his "Recollections of an Ex-Minister" relative to a remark of R. M. Milnes to Louis Philippe, 422, 423
Manchester, Fine Art Exhibition, ii. 17 ; Reform banquet at the Free Trade Hall, 157
Manchester Athenæum and Beelzebub, A remark of Carlyle on, i. 435
Manchester, Bishop of, ii. 385
Manners, John, Lord, i. 301 ; confidence in O'Connell, 302 ; philanthropic efforts, 313 ; one of the "Young England" party, 340, 383
Manners, Lady John, ii. 187
Manning, Dr., ii. 355
Marie Louise (wife of Napoleon), i. 102
Marriage with a deceased wife's sister, ii. 251
Marsh, Miss, ii. 254
Martin, Mr., Acts to prevent cruelty to animals, i. 61
Martineau, Miss, "America," by, i. 196 ; canvasses for subscribers for "Sartor Resartus," 200 ; friend of Emerson, 224 ; reference of Carlyle, 266 ; her copy of "Palm Leaves," 283, 288 ; a remark of Carlyle on, 435 ; illness, 510, 511, 525 ; Lord Houghton's tribute to her, ii. 280 ; on Lord Houghton's prose, 282
Mary, Princess (of Cambridge), ii. 23
Mason and Slidell, Capture of, i. 464 ; ii. 75, 174
Mathew, Father, Allusion of R. M. Milnes to, i. 316, 317
Maurice, F. D., connection with the *Athenæum*, i. 79 ; editor of *Athenæum* and *Literary Chronicle* when the two were merged, 81 ; one of the "Apostles" at Cambridge, 81, 87, 197 ; associate of R M. Milnes, 160, 172 ; the Sterling Club, 186, 222 ; the "Kingdom of Christ," 197 ; remark of Carlyle, 256 ; guest of Milnes, 473 ; King's College Council, 490, 498 ; ii. 161, 190, 355, 359
Mavrocordati, i. 286
Maxwell, Sir William Stirling, member of the Philobiblon Society, i. 508 ; ii. 299 ; death, 374, 464
"Maxwell," Theodore Hook's, i. 104
Mayne, Sir Richard, ii. 188
Maynooth College, Proposed grant to, i. 320, 321, 324, 352 ; visit of R. M.

INDEX. 533

Milnes to, 484; ii. 105; effect of the grant, 199
Mazzini; his letters opened by the English Government, i. 330; his conversion to Protestantism attempted, 333; ii. 400
McHale, Bishop, i. 124
Mehemet Ali, Interview of R. M. Milnes with, i. 289
Melbourne, Lord; Lord Houghton's review of his "Life" in the *Fortnightly Review*, ii. 371; remark to Lord Houghton on underrating the Church of England and the Pope, 424
Melville, Lord, i. 270
"Memorials, chiefly Poetical," R. M. Milnes's, i. 128
"Memorials of a Residence on the Continent, and Historical Poems, The," R. M. Milnes's, i. 207
"Memorials of a Tour in Greece," by Lord Houghton, ii. 439
"Memorials of a Tour on the Continent, and Historical Poems," by Lord Houghton, ii. 440
"Men of Old, The," poem by R. M. Milnes, i. 120
Merchants and weavers of the West Riding in the 18th century, i. 2
Meredith, George, i. 465
Merivale, Chas., one of the "Apostles" at Cambridge, i. 81
Merivale, Hermann, i. 465; ii. 161
Merivale, Morton, i. 146
Metaphysics, A humorous definition of, i. 52
Metternich, i. 100, 230, 422, 434; ii. 19
"Mexico," Prescott's, i. 322
Mezzofanti, i. 127, 140
Mignet, M., ii. 10
Miguel, Don, i. 393
Mill, J. S., i. 62, 87; ii. 142; the suffrage of women, 180
Milan, Residence of the Milnes family at, i. 68, 69, 100; Austrian severity, 101; characteristics of the people, &c., 104, 111, 124, 127, 136
Millais, Mr., ii. 386
Miller, Joaquin, ii. 276, 277, 317
Milman, Dean, ii. 190
Milnes, Amicia (*see* FitzGerald, Lady)
Milnes, Caroline, sister of Mr. R. P. Milnes, i. 102, 103, 129, 130; R. M. M. on the Roman Carnival, &c., 151—153, 525; ii. 23.
Milnes, Florence (*see* Henniker, Mrs.)
Milnes, Harriette (*see* Galway, Lady)
Milnes, Henry, i. 25

Milnes, Jane (1) i. 51
Milnes, Jane (2), sister of Mr. R. P. Milnes, i. 102, 103; ii. 23, 188, 294, 391
Milnes, Louisa, sister of Mr. R. P. Milnes, i. 102; the first of the family to abandon Unitarianism, 103, 152, 260
Milnes, Pemberton, i. 5; Lord Effingham's lines on, 5
Milnes, Richard, marries daughter of Mr. John Pemberton, i. 4
Milnes, Richard Monckton (*see* Houghton, Lord)
Milnes, Richard Slater, i. 6; marries Miss Rachel Busk, 6; acquires Great Houghton estate and elected Member of Parliament for York, 6; purchases Fryston Estate, 6
Milnes, Robert Offley Ashburton (*see* Houghton, Lord, the present)
Milnes, Robert Pemberton (1) i. 5
Milnes, Robert Pemberton (2), father of Richard Monckton Milnes, first Baron Houghton, i. 7; early days and remarkable qualities, 8; career at Trinity College, Cambridge, 8; Member of Parliament for Pontefract, 9; famous speech in defence of Canning's policy, 10; lays a wager that he would be Chancellor of the Exchequer, 11; marries the Hon. Henrietta Maria Monckton, daughter of Viscount Galway, 11, 13; declines a seat in Mr. Perceval's Cabinet, 11, 13; letter from Mr. Perceval urging acceptance of office, 15; reasons for his refusal to take office, 16; the "brilliant political meteor of Bolton Row" transformed into the country gentleman, 17, 18; political influence in Yorkshire and interest in the land question, 18, 19; journal of tour in Italy, 19—21; membership at Brooks' Club, 19; reasons for his Toryism, 19, 20; description of Pitt as an orator, 20, 21; visits Paris with Lord Lowther in 1814, 21; letter to his wife from Paris, April, 1814, 21; interview with Blücher, 23; goes to Brussels and Paris after the Battle of Waterloo, 24; two letters to his wife, 24—30; resides at Thorn Hall, 30; addiction to gambling, 30; favourite in society, 30; his handsome and intelligent appearance described by

Milnes (continued).
Lord Leven, 30, 31; skill and courage in the hunting field, &c., 31; anecdote—selling a hunter to Lord Foley, 31; encounter with poachers, 32; friend of Beau Brummel, 32; passage in Gray's "Elegy" recalls his early triumphs in the House of Commons, 33; visits Dieppe and Paris, 1820, 34; takes his son, Richard, to Hundbill Hall School, 34; leaves Thorne, and resides with family on the Continent, from 1828 to 1835, 36—38, 56; pays his brother Rodes Milnes's debts, 38; becomes the owner of the Bawtry estate, and other property, in 1835, and takes up his residence at Bawtry, and afterwards at Fryston, 38, 153, 158; offered a peerage by Lord Palmerston, which is declined, 39—41; severance from the Tories and re-union, 40; considers no position higher than that of an English country gentleman, 42, 158; dying message to Lord Palmerston, 42; death, 1858, 42 (ii. 34); the "Admirable Crichton" of his day, 43; wishes his son to make a great figure in the House of Commons, 89, 166; residence at Milan, 68, 69, 96; friendships amongst the Milanese and Austrians, 101; lack of sympathy with his son's literary tastes, 105, 166; differences with his son on politics, 111, 112; visit to Rome, 121—124; visit to Switzerland, 145; residence at South Street, Hyde Park, 166; incidents connected with Carlyle's visit to Fryston, 254—258; sale of his property in Leeds for railway purposes, 394

Milnes, Mrs. Robert Pemberton (née Henrietta Maria Monckton), marriage, i. 11, 13; character and talents, 11, 12; writes the history of her married life, 12; her literary gifts inherited by her son, Richard Monckton Milnes, 12; extract from her Journal on her husband's refusal of a seat in the Cabinet, 13; letters from Mr. Milnes, at Paris, 21—23; two letters from the same, written at Brussels and Paris, July, 1815, 24—30; extract from Journal, 1820, on her visit to London en route for the

Milnes (continued).
Continent, 32, 33; extract from same on R. M. Milnes's precocity, 34; extract from same on R. M. M.'s entry at Trinity College, 49; story in Journal of residence at Milan, 68, 69, 96; extract from Journal on the court balls at Milan, 101; extract from Journal on social life at Venice, 136; record in Journal of parties at South Street, 170; extract from Journal on Beau Brummel, 244; Carlyle's description of her, 253; entry in Journal on her son's journey up the Nile, 290; illness and death, 377, 378; born at Claremont, 379

Milnes, Rodes, i. 8, 30; reckless extravagance, debts, and losses, 37; anecdote — York races and Lord Glasgow, 37, 100; popularity and poverty, 138, 139, 394

Milnes, Mrs. R. S., i. 121; death, 153

Milneses, The, belonged originally to Derbyshire, i. 3; migration to Wakefield, 3; their monopoly of the cloth trade of Wakefield in the eighteenth century, 3; their substantial residences, 4; influence and reputation in Yorkshire, 4; intercourse with the aristocracy, and acquisition of Great Houghton Hall, 4; alliance with the Monckton family, 5; resided at Egremont House, Piccadilly, 7; supported Mr. Fox, 7; numerous family, 7

Milton, Lord and Lady, ii. 324
Minto, Lord, i. 270
Missionary enthusiasm, i. 159
Missolonghi, i. 129
Mohl, Madame, i. 515, 526, 527; ii. 170, 184, 237, 295
Molesworth, Lady, i. 484
Moltke, Count, ii. 393, 395, 397
Monckton Family, The; alliance with the Milneses, i. 5, 11
Monckton, Carleton, i. 29, 60
Money, Mr., British Consul at Milan and Venice, i. 101, 106
"Monographs," R. M. Milnes's, i. 108; reference to Cardinal Weld, 122; reference to Cardinal Wiseman, 162; the Misses Berry, 188; Lady Ashburton, 478; its publication and contents, ii. 273-276, 441
Monson, Lady, ii. 10
Monson, Lord, purchases Cardinal Fesch's collection of pictures, i. 72, 96

Montalembert, Count de, i. 123, 124, 141, 158; remarks on King Louis Philippe, 246, letter on Puseyism, &c., 340; ii. 9, 34, 142, 157, 171
Monte Casino, Convent of, i. 125
Monteagle, Lord, i. 275
Monteith, Robert, i. 75, 84; letter to R. M. Milnes from Cambridge, 105, 106, 150, 523, 554; ii. 176
Monteith, A talk with Mr. Gladstone about R. M. Milnes, i. 191
"Monument for Scutari, A," R. M. Milnes's poem, i. 519
Moore, Thomas; "Life of Byron," i. 88, 89, 104; "Life of Lord Edward Fitzgerald," 110, 171, 173
Morea, The, i. 129
"Mores Catholici," by Kenelm Digby, i. 117
Morgan, Lady, 70, 71; acquaintanceship with R. M. Milnes, 112
Morley, John, 1. 465; ii. 372; edits the *Pall Mall Gazette*, 388, 419, 422
Morning Chronicle, Report on Mr. Disraeli's speech, Dec. 8, 1837, in the, i. 204; endowment of Irish Catholic clergy, 202; Mr. George Smythe's review of Milnes's "Letter to Lord Lansdowne," 416—418, 497; ii. 357
Morning Post, i. 232; ii. 281, 391, 414
Morpeth, Lord, i. 202, 281
Morris, Lewis, poem, "A Yorkshire River," referred to, i. 6 (note); ii. 264
Motley's "Dutch Republic," ii. 63
Motley, Mr., ii. 300, 351
Mount Edgecombe, ii. 365
Moxon, Mrs. (Charles Lamb's adopted daughter), Government pension, ii. 248, 285, 292
Moxon, Richard, ii. 362; refers to Lord Houghton as the "Grand Old Man of Yorkshire," 429
Much Ado About Nothing performed by Cambridge undergraduates, i. 84
Munich, i. 153, 159, 161
Munster, Count, ii. 393
Murat, Madame, ex-Queen of Naples, i. 155
Murchison, Sir Roderick, ii. 195, 205
Murray, John, ii. 270
Musgrave, Sir R., ii. 401
"My Youthful Letters," poem by R. M. Milnes, i. 120

Napier, Mr., makes a motion in the House of Commons in favour of a final attempt to discover Sir John Franklin, ii. 15
Napier, Sir Charles, W. S. Landor's allusion to, i. 299; R. M. Milnes at Lisbon, 394, 395
Naples, i. 113, 122, 124, 125, 128, 220
"Naples Letters," Gladstone's, i. 451
Naples, Queen of, i. 102
Napoleon I., i. 21; his improvements in Paris, 23; defeat at Waterloo, 26, 27; subject of debate at the Cambridge Union, 52, 83, 107
Napoleon III., i. 185; President of the French Republic, 405; ii. 29, 30, 432, 440; ii. 231, 233, 239, 265
Narvaez, General, i. 399
"Nature," Emerson's, i 224
Neander and his sister, i. 343
Negropont, The natural beauty of, i. 133
"Nemesis of Faith, The," i. 433
Nemours, Duc de, at Buckingham Palace, i. 355, 420
Neot's, St., i. 66
Newark, i. 199
Newcastle, Duke of, i. 139, 141; ii. 42, 62, 63, 72, 96
Newman, Dr., Book on the prophetical character, and verses by, i. 194; contribution to "Lyra Apostolica," 197; refers in the "Apologia" to Milnes's "One Tract More," 260; secession to the Church of Rome, 359; and Kingsley, 354
Newmanites, The, i. 197
Newspaper Press Fund, The interest of Lord Houghton in the, ii. 125, 428, 434, 465; Prince Imperial, 265
Niagara, ii. 308
Nicholas, The Emperor, i. 326, 487, 245
Nicholls, Rev. A. B., i. 476, 477
Niebuhr, i. 71, 97, 100; death, 104; grief at the French Revolution of 1830, 115
Nightingale, Florence; acquaintance with R. M. Milnes, i. 475, 491; her mission during the Crimean War, 493, 497, 500; work in the hospitals, 505, 509, 524; on Milnes's love for poor children, ii. 7, 83, 251; congratulates Lord Houghton on his son's marriage, 389; on Lord Houghton's illness, 418
Nile, The, R. M. Milnes' journey up, i. 289

Noel, Emma, i. 92, 490
Noel, Hon. and Rev. Baptist, ii. 24
Nonnenwert, i. 98
North, Christopher, ii. 444
North American Review, Article on R. M. Milnes in the, i. 279
Northampton, Lord, i. 67; publication of "The Tribute," 177, 178; London Library, 235
Northumberland, Duke of, ii. 189
Norton, Mrs., i. 174, ii. 119; marriage to Sir W. S. Maxwell, 299, 372
Norwich, i. 279

Oberammergau, ii 392
O'Brien, Augustus, i. 194
O'Brien, Sir E., i. 110
O'Brien, Stafford, i. 49, 84; his high opinion of R. M. Milnes's abilities, 85, 91; President of the Cambridge Union, 106, 110; meets R. M. Milnes at Rome, 150, 158; on Milnes's state of mind, 160; wishes to bring Milnes into the Catholic Church, 160; as "Nicholas Nickleby," 164, 175, 204; letter to C. J. MacCarthy on R. M. Milnes's maiden speech, 205, 220; changes his name, 381
Observer, The; Academy speech of Lord Houghton, ii. 378
O'Connell, i. 101; his arrest, 104, 202, his meetings, 300, 305; failure of his trial, 317; appeal to the House of Lords, 335, 336, 352
O'Connor, Charles Feargus, i. 95; influence in the House of Commons, 432
"Ode on the Intimations of Immortality," considered by Lord Houghton to be the greatest poem in the English language, ii. 434
Œcumenical Council, ii. 206
Oliphant, Lawrence, i. 464
"One Tract More," R. M. Milnes's, i. 260—262, 266, 293
Orange, Prince of, ii. 201
Orford, Lord, ii. 170
Orloff, Count, ii. 10
Orsini Conspiracy, ii. 32 (note)
Osborne, Mr. Bernal, i. 75; ii. 21
Osborne, Mrs. Bernal, ii. 295
Ostend, i. 24.
Otho, King, R. M. Milnes's description of, i. 284
Otranto, i. 128
"Ottoman Empire, Stability of the," i. 285

Oudinot, General; advance on Rome, i. 431
"Outline of History," i. 113
Owens College, ii. 304
Oxford, Bishop of, i. 433, 473, 477; ii. 22; "Essays and Reviews," 131, 188, 195, 251, 460
Oxford University, the Shelley mission, i. 77, 78, 88; ii. 162

Paley, Dr., i. 53, 60, 80
Palgrave, Mr., ii. 243
Pall Mall Gazette, ii. 141; articles by Lord Houghton, 155, 219, 273; new management, 387; on the Czar's murder, 403
"Palm Leaves," R. M. Milnes's, i. 282, 290; humorous sketches by Thackeray, 283, 288; Mrs. Procter's allusion, 308, 322; Carlyle's opinion of, 323; De Tocqueville's opinion, 328; criticism in the *Quarterly Review*, 345; ii. 341, 439
Palmerston, Lady, ii. 82, 108; death, 204
Palmerston, Lord, i. 7; admission into the Ministry on the refusal of Mr. Pemberton Milnes to take office, 13; maiden speech in reply to one of Mr Milnes's, 14; his "Life," by Bulwer, 14; extract from letter to Lord Malmesbury on the Perceval Ministry, 14; reference to letters to Lord Malmesbury on Pemberton Milnes's refusal to take office, 16; offers Mr. Pemberton Milnes a peerage, 39; Mr. Milnes's letter, declining the offer, 40, 41; supported by R. M. Milnes, 41; Mr. Pemberton Milnes's dying message, 42, 92, 95, 202; foreign policy, 248, 249, 272; slave-trade speech, 334; attacked by Lord Brougham, 419; Sicilian papers, 434; intimacy with R. M. Milnes, 448; dismissal by Lord John Russell, 468; Milnes's confidence in him as a leader, 474; Home Office Secretary, 478; resignation and resumption of office, 1853, 486, 491; forms a Ministry, 501; offers a post to R. M. Milnes, 504; prosperity of his Government, 512, ii. 4, 5; the length of his speeches, 6; defeat, 1857, 13; triumphant return at the General Election, 13; Royal Literary Fund, 28; the Orsini conspiracy, 32; opinion of Per-

signy, 61 ; Yorkshire progress, 62, 63, 84 ; offer of a peerage to R. M. Milnes, 91, 96 ; visit of R. M. Milnes to Broadlands, 119, 135 ; death, 150 ; contrast between him and Gladstone, 152; opposition to Suez Canal, 216, 238
"Pamela," Madame de Genlis's, i. 110
Panizzi, Sir Antonio ; differences with Lord Houghton, ii. 277, 279 ; Lord Houghton's review of his "Life," 404
Paris ; Visit of Lord Lowther and Mr. Pemberton Milnes in 1814, i. 21 ; state of, after the defeat of Napoleon, 22 ; improvements carried out by Napoleon, 23 ; Revolution of 1830, 100 ; R. M. Milnes's visit in 1840, 244—247 ; the use of the fortifications, 246, 247 ; Milnes's visit, 1855, 513—518 ; Exhibition, 1855, 516 ; visit of Queen Victoria, 517, 518 ; Exhibition, ii. 167 ; review of troops by Emperor of Austria, 183, 236, 266, 378
Paris, Comte de, ii. 25, 135, 255, 364, 379, 391
Parke, Baron, ii. 3
Parke, Lady, i. 218
Parkyns, Mansfield, i. 490
Parthenon, The, i. 134
Pasquier, Chancelier, ii. 18
Pasta, the actress, i. 104 ; ii. 258
Patmore, Mr., ii. 357
Patten, Colonel Wilson, ii. 460
"Paul Ferrol," 522, 525
Paul, Sir John Dean, i. 525
Paul, St., i. 96
Paulet, Lord W., i. 497
Payn, Mr. James, ii. 430
Payne, Mr., ii. 212
Peacock, Thomas Love, Lord Houghton's preface to the works of, ii. 302
Pedro, Don, i. 109
Peel, Frederick, ii. 5 ; his appearance and speaking in the House of Commons, 6
Peel, Sir Robert, i. 60, 62, 70, 141, 187 ; leader of the Opposition in the House of Commons, Nov., 1837, 202 ; remark on R. M. Milnes's maiden speech, 204 ; letter from R. M. M. on King Louis Philippe and the French Government, 247—249 ; on the representations of M. Guizot, 250, 252 ; formation of his Ministry, 1841, 262 ; allusion of Carlyle, 267, 270, 272 ;

Corn Laws, 278 ; letter from R. M. M. on political affairs in the East, 285—288, 291 ; ignorance as to Tennyson and Sheridan Knowles, 297 ; Maynooth Grant, 321 ; threatens resignation, 330 ; decline of his influence, 331—334 ; resignation, and return to office, 359 ; his prejudice against admitting men of letters into the Administration, 363, 364 ; announces his conversion to Free Trade doctrines, 369 ; his fall, 374—376 ; speech on the resettlement of Ireland, 430, 439 ; death, 1850, 443, 444
Peel, Sir Robert (2) ii. 72
Pemberton, Mr. John, i. 5
Pembroke, Lady, i. 487
Perceval, Mr., presses Mr. Pemberton Milnes to accept the office of Chancellor of the Exchequer, i. 11, 13 ; letter to Mr. Milnes urging him to take office, 15 ; requested by Mr. Milnes to increase the allowance of the schoolmaster of Pontefract, 17
Perry, James, ii. 357
Perry, Mr., Senior Wrangler at Cambridge, i. 54, 55
Persigny, Duc de, ii. 61, 237, 240
Peter's, St., Rome, i. 122, 155
Petrarchi, Madame, i. 232
Petre, Mr., and the St. Leger, i. 37
Pharsalia, i. 129
Philobiblon Society, i. 506, 507; ii. 131, 299, 385, 391 ; Lord Houghton's sketch of H. Bright, 431, 463
Pitt, Mr. ; defeat in 1806, i. 9 ; description of his oratorical powers by Mr. Pemberton Milnes, 20, 21 ; his appearance in the House of Commons, ii. 6, 415
Planché, J. R. ; lines on the pronunciation of Lord Houghton's name, ii. 114—116
Platen, Count, i. 124, 201
"Poems : Legendary and Historical," by Lord Houghton, ii. 440.
"Poems of Many Years," R. M. Milnes's, i. 141 ; quotation, 148, 207, 440
"Poetry for the People," by Lord Houghton, ii. 440
Pola, i 107
Poland, i. 413
Pollington, Lord, i. 263 ; ii. 267, 288
Pollock, Mr., ii. 243.

Pollock, Sir Frederick, ii 430
Pomfret (see Pontefract)
Pompeii, i. 124
Pontefract, Mr. Pemberton Milnes one of its representatives in Parliament, 1806, i. 9, 11; Mr. Milnes petitions for an increased allowance for the schoolmaster, 17, 34, 95; proposal that R. M. M. should represent it in Parliament, 99, 139, 143; election of R. M. M. to Parliament, 198; poll-book revelations, 198, 199, 204, 311, 320; letter of R. M. M. to the Mayor, 321; re-election of R. M. M. (1857), ii. 16; Milnes's farewell address to his constituents on his being raised to the peerage, 102—107; Liberal demonstration at, 429
Pope, The, and the Turks, ii. 213
Portland Administration, The, i. 9
Portsmouth, Lord and Lady, ii. 350
Potter, T. B., ii. 158
Praed, W. M., i. 59, 83; ii. 160
Praslin, Duc de, ii. 18
Prescott, i. 322, 440
Prim, General, ii. 232
Procter, Adelaide Ann, ii. 84
Procter, Mrs., wife of Barry Cornwall; friendship with R. M. Milnes, ii. 306—308, 358, 468; guest of Mr. and Mrs. Milnes, 473, 527; ii. 10; congratulatory lines on Milnes' elevation to the peerage, 108, 109, 181, 256, 282, 295, 320, 384
Protestants, the gulf separating them from the Catholics in Ireland, i. 120
Poulett, Lady W., ii. 120
Punch; Florence Nightingale, i. 497; Carlyle, ii. 152
Pusey, Dr.; heretical sermon, i. 293, 300, 305
Pyrenees, R. M. Milnes's trip to the, i. 229—233

Quarterly Review, Article on De Tocqueville by R. M Milnes in the, i. 245, 262; criticism on "Palm Leaves," 345; Milnes's article on the Siege of Lucknow, ii. 27; Milnes's article on Beaumont's "Life of De Tocqueville," 63, 64; Lord Houghton's article on the social relations of England and America, 337; articles by Gladstone and A. Hayward, 338; Criticism on Lord Houghton, 443, 449
Radowitz, General, i. 498

Radstock, Lord, and F. D. Maurice, i. 490
Radziwill, Princess, i. 341
Raglan, Lord, i. 501
Railway agitation, i. 354, 355, 394
Railways, R. M. Milnes's first experience of, i. 109, 110
Ramsden, Sir John, ii. 288
Ranke, Remark of Carlyle on, i. 435
"Rapture," poem by R. M. M., i. 120
"Rascals" in the Pontefract poll-book, i. 198
Rassam, ii. 194
"Real Union of England and Ireland," R. M. M.'s pamphlet on the, i. 353
Rebecca Riots, i. 302, 304
"Recollections of an Ex-Minister," Lord Malmesbury's reference to an interview between Louis Philippe and R. M. Milnes, i. 423
Red Lion Club, i. 521, 522
Redcliffe, Lord Stratford de, ii. 460
Redpath, Mr., ii. 311
Reform Bill (1831); R. M. Milnes's opinion respecting it, i. 107, 108, 116; Lord Russell's attempt to bring in a Bill (1866), ii. 150; meeting at Leeds, 151; banquet at Free Trade Hall, Manchester, 157, 172; motion in the House of Lords, 431
Reformatories for juvenile offenders, R. M. Milnes succeeds in passing a Bill for the establishment of, i. 373; ii. 6, 7; 280
Refugees, Foreign; motion in Parliament by R. M. Milnes, i. 473
Regent, The Prince, i. 37
Regnier, M., ii. 239
Reminiscences of R. M. M.'s youth by Mr. Aubrey de Vere, i. 113—120
Renan, M., ii. 267
Renaud, Mrs., i. 48
Rendlesham, Lord, i. 24.
Rice, Spring, i. 95; a freshman at Cambridge, 147, 202, 220
Richardson, Rev. W., i. 34
Richardson, Mr., i. 47
Richmond, Duke of, i. 25; 331
Rio, M., i. 124; his "Christian Art," 158, 191, 292; ii. 9, 93, 121, 170, 172, 267
Ripon, Lord, ii. 260, 299, 300, 387
Ritualists, Lord Houghton on, ii. 199
Riviera, The, Visit of Lord Houghton to, ii. 120—124
Robertson, i. 126
Robinson, Crabbe, extract from Diary referring to Milnes as a poet, i. 184,
Rodes, Sir Godfrey, i. 458

INDEX. 539

Roebuck, J. A., visitor at Fryston with Carlyle, i. 256; motion of censure, 501, 506, ii. 31
Rogers, Samuel, i. 171; his breakfasts at St. James's Place, 185, 186, 192; friendship with Sydney Smith, 210, 218, 222, 235; estranged from R. M. M., 322, 440
Rome: a proposed visit of R. M. Milnes, i. 107, 113; R. M. M.'s visit (1832), 121; friendships formed there by R. M. M., 122—124, 142, 150; the Carnival, 151—153, 161; society in, 291; the French in, 418; Lord Houghton's visit (1868), ii. 188, 211
Rosebery, Lord, ii. 299, 430
Rossetti, W. M., i. 465; ii. 264
Rosslyn, Lord, ii. 296
Rothschild, Baron, ii. 21, 152, 235, 267
Rouher, M., ii. 185, 293
Rous, Admiral, i. 497
Royal Academy; Lord Houghton made Foreign Corresponding Secretary, ii. 374
Royal Geographical Society, ii. 214
Royal Literary Fund, The, i. 447; Milnes presides at the annual dinner, ii. 28
Royal Society, The, Lord Houghton elected a Fellow of, ii. 195
Ruskin, John, ii. 25
Russell, Arthur, Lord, ii. 9, 30, 33, 285, 296
Russell, Edward, ii. 25
Russell, Hastings, ii. 32
Russell, Lady W., ii. 61, 251, 298
Russell, Lord John, leader of the House of Commons, Nov. 1837, i. 202; reference to his Bribery Bill, 263, 324; a possible co-operation with Sir Robert Peel, 332; reference to his article on Lords Grey and Spencer, 332; failure to form a government on the resignation of Peel, 359, 368; becomes Prime Minister, 375, 439; dismisses Lord Palmerston, 469; Foreign Secretary to Lord Aberdeen, 478, 496; resignation as Lord President, 501, 508; reference to the part played by his wife in politics, 512, 515, ii. 5; R. M. M.'s visit to Woburn, 23, 24; opinion of Cobden's Budget, 24; meeting with Bright, 38, 84, 96; attempt to introduce a Reform Bill, 150, 152; Lady Russell and Wentworth Beaumont, 175

Russell, Lord Odo, ii. 396
Russell, Lord W., ii. 296
Russia, its commerce with Wakefield, i. 1; article by R. M. Milnes in the *Edinburgh Review* on, 317, 325; invasion of Hungary, 419; demands the passage of the Dardanelles, 430; references to the Crimean War, 492—527; murder of the Czar, ii. 403
"Ruth," Mrs. Gaskell's, i. 481
Rutland, Duke of, Mr. R. M. Milnes traces his descent from royalty through the family of the, i. 54.
Rutson, Mr. A. O., ii 357

Sabine, General, ii. 195
Saldanha, Marshal, i. 394
Salisbury, Lord and Lady, ii. 303
Salzkammergut, The, i. 153
Samy, Mr. Coomara, Hindoo barrister; visit to Lord Houghton, ii. 87, 297, 298
Sand, Georges, ii. 10
Sandwich, Lord, i. 71, 97
Sardinia, King and Queen of, i. 102
"Sartor Resartus," Difficulty in getting a bookseller to reprint, i. 200
Saturday Review, ii. 182; on Lord Houghton, by G. S. Venables, 456
Scarborough, i. 13
Schiller, R. M. Milnes's admiration for, i. 116; a remark of Carlyle on, 435
Schlegel, i. 71; exalted idea of rank and political eminence, 99, 100, 116
Schopenhauer, Madam, i. 98
Schwarzburg - Sondershausen, Prince of, i. 342
Scott, Lady John, ii. 254
Scott, Rev. G. Wyndham, i. 65, 66
Scott, Sir Gilbert, ii. 190
Scott, Sir Walter and Lady, i. 48; the "Waverley Novels," 171
Scutari, i. 475
Sebright, Lady, ii. 198
Seebohm, Frederick, ii. 282
Senlis, i. 26, 29
Serlby Hall, i. 378; ii. 118, 304
Severne, i. 127, 307; ii. 211
Seymour, Danby, ii. 9
Seymour, Sir H., i. 394
"Shadows," poem by R. M. Milnes, i. 120
Shaftesbury, Lord, i. 88
Sharpe, "Conversation," i. 96
Shaw-Lefevre, Mr., ii. 271
"She had left all on earth for him," poem by R. M. Milnes, i. 120

Sheffield School of Art, ii. 25
Shelbourn, Lady, ii. 22
Shelley: interest in his poetry roused at Cambridge University, i. 73; deputation of Cambridge undergraduates to Oxford to maintain his merits against those of Byron, 77, 78; ii. 163; first publication in England of "Adonais," 77, 83; R. M. Milnes's acquaintance with his poetry, 116; growth of his influence, 171; Carlyle on, 435
Shenstone the poet, ii. 163
Shepherd, Mr., schoolmaster of Pemberton and Rodes Milnes, i. 8.
Sherbrooke, Lord, his remark respecting the literary appearance of Fryston Hall, i. 456; leader of the Whig section in the House of Commons, ii. 150, 151, 387, 422
Sherman, General, entertains Lord Houghton at St. Louis, ii. 313
Sherwood, Mrs, ii. 323.
Shiel, Mr., M.P., i. 334
Siddons, Mrs., i. 48, 87
Simeon, Dr., i. 51
Simeon, Sir John, ii. 143
"Simpkinson and the Woolsack," i. 11
Sinclair, Sir George, ii. 73
Slave Trade, Lord Palmerston's speech, i. 334
Smith, Dr. William, ii. 127
Smith, Goldwin, ii. 312
Smith, Sir Culling Eardley, i. 197
Smith, Sydney, and Holland House, i. 184; as a dinner-table talker, 190; friendship with R. M. Milnes, and six characteristic letters to him, 209—215; not happy in the company of other distinguished talkers, 210; provokes R. M. M.'s anger by certain jocular titles attributed to him, 213, 214; rejoinder to Landseer, 218; apostolic succession, 300, 327, 523; his sayings, from Lord Houghton's Commonplace Books, Appendix, 469—477
Smith, Vernon, i. 479, 518, 525
Smyrna, i. 282
Smythe, Mr. George (afterwards Lord Strangford), i. 364; review in the *Morning Chronicle* of Milnes's "Letter to Lord Lansdowne" by, 416, 417; challenge from Milnes to, 417, 418
Social Science Association, ii. 278
Social Science Congress, ii. 24; Presidency of Lord Houghton, 279

Society under the Regency, i. 37
Solferino, Battle of, ii. 40
Somnambulist in Paris, The clairvoyance of a, i. 434
Southey, Robert, i. 171, 178, 297—299
Spada, Count, ii. 125
Spada, Monsignor, i. 127
Spain, R. M. Milnes's visit to, i. 391—401
"Spanish Gypsy, The," Lord Houghton's review in the *Edinburgh Review* of, ii. 193
Spectator, The, ii. 243
Spedding, James, i. 75; one of the "Apostles" at Cambridge, 81; prize declamation, 105, 108, 177; letter to R. M. Milnes on Carlyle's lectures, &c., 193; Sterling Club, 222; meeting between Carlyle and Thirlwall, 228; helps to establish the London Library, 234, 235; ii. 10, 94, 127; editor of "Bacon," 161, 377; fatal accident, 402
Speke, the African explorer, ii. 134
Spencer, Herbert, i. 465; ii. 338
Spencer, Lord, ii. 388
Spencer, Rev., i. 122
Spurzheim, Dr., i. 52
Stafford, Augustus, efforts of R. M. Milnes on behalf of, i. 118, 439; visit to the Crimea, 505; ii. 23, 24, 29
Standard, The, ii. 281
Standish, Lady Lucy, i. 154
Stanhope, Lord, ii. 193
Stanley, Dean, i. 465; ii. 110, 190; entertains the Queen, 200, 228, 243, 262, 373; sermon on Carlyle, 401
Stanley, H. M., ii. 267
Stanley, Lady Augusta, ii. 229, 295
Stanley, Lord, i. 202, 321, 331, 359, 431, 433; ii. 33, 120, 154
Stanley of Alderley, Lord, ii. 15
Stanley, W. M., Parliamentary candidate for Pontefract, i. 197
Stansfeld, Mr., i. 463
Stapleton, Miles, ii. 327
Starke, Mrs., "Guide to Rome" by, i. 152
Stephen, Fitzjames, i. 465
Sterling Club, The, i. 186; its formation, 222
Sterling, John, i. 49, 50; friendship with R. M. Milnes, 59, 60, 72, 81, 83, 87, 156, 160, 172; the Sterling Club, 186, 222, 279; ii. 5; death,

and biographies by Hare and Carlyle, 160
Sterling, Sir William, i. 465
"Stones of Venice, The," i. 484
Stourton, Mr., i. 154
Strafford, Lord, residence at Great Houghton, and mementoes of his execution, i. 4
Strangford, Lady, ii. 151, 182
Strauss, ii. 272
Strawberry Hill, ii. 25, 190, 385
Stuarts, The, ii. 304
Suez Canal, Lord Houghton at the opening of the, ii. 205, 206; Lord Houghton's report, 214—218
Sultan, The Fête in honour of the, ii. 177, 178
Sumner, Charles, reminiscences of English society and of R. M. Milnes, i. 223; letter to R. M. Milnes on Emerson, 237—239, 279—281, &c., 326, 327, 513; ii. 307
Sunderland, Thomas, i. 49, 58, 61, 75; melancholy career, 76; one of the deputation to Oxford 77—79, 83, 88, 92, 95; ii. 162, 166
Sussex, Duke of, i. 54
Sutherland, Duchess of, and the State Fancy Ball, i. 326; ii. 120, 133, 135
Sutherland, Duke of, ii. 124; Visit of Lord Houghton, 220, 254, 305
Sutton, —, son of the Speaker, i. 57
Swift, Dean, and his "Advice to Servants," i. 115
Swinburne, A. C., i. 463; ii. 121; admiration for his genius by Lord Houghton, and his review of "Atalanta in Calydon" in the *Edinburgh Review*, 136, 177; ii. 265, 331, 370, 399, 423
Switzerland, Tour of R. M. Milnes in, i. 68; visit of R. M. Milnes and family, 145
Sykehouse and Fishlake Estates, i. 30
Symons, Mr., i. 61

Taglioni, i. 155
Tahiti affair, Indignation in England owing to the, i. 333; attitude of the Dissenters with regard to the, 334; settlement of the, 335
Talbot, Monseigneur, ii. 192
Talfourd, Serjeant, ii. 226
Talleyrand, i. 22, 27
"Tancred," R. M. Milnes as "Mr. VaVasour" in, i. 337, 339
Tankerville, Lady, ii. 119

"Tannhauser," poems by Julian Fane and Robert Lytton, ii. 69
Taylor, Bayard, ii. 322, 332
Taylor, Sir Henry, "Autobiography" of, i. 184, 186, 192, 220; "The Virgin Martyr," 445, 489, 363
Tempe, i. 130
Temple, Dr., Master of Rugby, ii. 22 · "Essays and Reviews," 129
Temple, R., i. 88, 464
Tennent, Sir E., i. 381; ii. 257
Tennyson, Charles, i. 65, 75; poem on the expedition of Napoleon into Russia, i. 83, 149, 180
Tennyson, Frederick, i. 75, 93, 149, 180
Tennyson, Lady, ii. 284
Tennyson, Lord, prize-winner in the Cambridge poem competition, i. 63; friendship with R. M. Milnes, 63, 171; opinion of R. M. Milnes's character, 63, 67, 75; one of the "Apostles" at Cambridge, 81; a couplet by him on title-page of Milnes's prize essay, 83, 93; remark on Spedding, 105; review of his poems in the *Westminster Review*, 106, 108; poems in the *Gem*, 108; Hallam's criticism in the *Englishman*, 117; poems, and sonnet "Check every Outbreak," 117, 146; letter to R. M. Milnes declining to send verses for "The Tribute," 178; letter to the same, consenting to contribute to "The Tribute," 179, 180; lines in "The Tribute," and the poem of "Maud," 181, 192, 208, 220, 221; criticism of Charles Sumner, 279, 280; pension, 296, 297; "In Memoriam," 445, 473; "Maud" and the "Balaclava Charge," 512, 516; a portion of Fryston offered him for residence, 513; ii. 136, 161; visit of Lord Houghton to, 176, 221, 256, 264; on the death of Lady Houghton, 290; Allusions to, 321, 331, 359, 439
Thackeray, i. 75, 83; remark on R. M. Milnes's father, and anecdote, 167; with R. M. Milnes, in Paris, 251; letter to R. M. Milnes, 263, 264 Visit to Fryston, 167, 264; humorous sketches in "Palm Leaves," 283, 306, 358; close friendship with R. M. Milnes, 425—429; "Going to see a man hanged," 426; frequent guest at Fryston, 427; acquaintance with Charlotte Brontë, 428, 429;

wishes for a magistracy, 427; success in society, 432, 490; ii. 10, 22, 94; Christmas greeting to Milnes, and death, 111, 112, 118, 148, 377

Thackeray, Miss Minnie, ii. 151
Thalberg, i 137
Thebes, i. 130
Thermopylæ, i. 129, 130, 133
Thesiger, Sir Frederick, i. 496
Thiers, M., i. 245, 249, 350, 354; visit to England, 369; his Version of the Affair of February, 419. 420, 469; ii. 170, 174, 234, 239, 266, 268, 293; death, 366
Thirlwall, Connop, afterwards Bishop of St. David's, tutor at Trinity College of R. M. Milnes, i. 49, 52, 59, 62, 74, 93, 96, 97, 146, 150, 156; accepts the living of Kirby Underdale, 162; "History of Greece," 162; letter to R. M. Milnes, 162—164; as "Squeers," 165; lifelong friendship with R. M. Milnes, 172, 193; meeting with Carlyle, 228, 237; début as Bishop in favour of the Jews, 263; letter to R. M. Milnes on the endowment of Irish Catholic clergy, &c., 301, 302; letter to the same on Carlyle, &c. 302, 303; speech in the House of Lords, 356, 477, 505; ii. 108; Lord Houghton's article on "Atalanta in Calydon," 138—140
Thompson, W. H., i. 75; one of the "Apostles" at Cambridge, 81, 463
Thorne Hall, i. 30; removal of the Milnes family in 1828, 36
Thornton, Mr. Percy, ii. 427, 435
Thorpe, Dr., i. 33
"Thoughts on Purity of Election," by Lord Houghton, ii. 441
Tieck, i. 116
Tilden, S. J., ii. 333
"Timbuctoo," Cambridge University prize poem, 1829, i. 62; poems by Alfred Tennyson and Hallam, 83
Times, The, opposition to Sir Robert Peel's Government, &c., i. 356; startling announcement in Dec., 1845, with regard to the Corn Laws, 367, 433, 490, 497; battle of Alma, 499, 500, 502; Milnes's poem "A Monument for Scutari," 519; the Johnson god-daughter case, 526; ii. 9; story of Lucknow, 22; article on R. M. Milnes's accession to the peerage, 99—101, 134, 157, 186, 204, 255, 281, 303, 415, 422
" To search for lore in spacious libraries," sonnet by R. M Milnes, i. 118
Tocqueville, M. de, i. 245; letter to R. M. Milnes on "Palm Leaves" and Mohammedanism, 327, 328, 419; ii. 9, 27; Milnes's visit to, 29, 30; his "Life," by Beaumont, 63, 64
Toogood, Mr., ii. 260
Tories, after the election of 1833, i. 141, 142
Torquay, i. 103, 467; ii. 50—55, 259
Torrington, Lord, ii. 133
Tourgenieff, ii. 168
Tree, The Misses, i. 48
Trelawny's "Adventures of a Younger Son," i. 145
Trench, Richard Chenevix, i. 49, 58, 75; one of the "Apostles" at Cambridge, 81, 83, 90, 109, 110, 146; at Rome with R. M. Milnes and C. J. MacCarthy, 156, 177, 180; letter to R. M. Milnes on the latter's "Memorials," &c., 208, 221, 222; ii. 161, 339
Trevelyan, Mr. G., ii. 425
"Tribute, The," i. 177, 183, 196, 208
Trinity College, Cambridge, i. 8, 36, 49, 51, 74, 83, 114; ii. 339
Trochu, General, ii. 234, 235
Trollope, Anthony, i. 465; ii. 142, 152; "The Warden," 155, 182; bet on the price of "Lothair," 224—226
Truth, ii. 361; article on Thiers, 366
Turin, ii. 124
Turkish Government, The, Mr. Gladstone's views, ii. 341
Turks, R. M. Milnes's affection for the character of the, i. 131
Turk's Island, i. 301
Tyndall, Professor, i. 466; ii. 145, 147, 152, 236

Union League Club, ii. 334
United States, Lord Houghton's visit, ii. 306—335
University of Edinburgh, ii. 144
University of Leyden, ii. 203
University of London, i. 86, 95
"Unpunished Cruelties on the High Seas," pamphlet by Mr. H. Bright, ii. 273

Val Richer, ii. 18
Valentia, Island of, i. 113

INDEX.

Vambéry, Arminius, i. 465
Vandeweyer, M., i. 473; Philobiblon Society, 507; ii. 25
Vatican, The, i. 122
Vatry, M., ii. 10
Vaughan, C. J., i. 465; ii. 135
Vavasour, Sir E., i. 161, 359
Venables, G. S., i. 75; one of the "Apostles" at Cambridge, 81, 83, 237; guest of Milnes, 473, 490, 514; ii. 10, 127, 159, 161, 182, 355, 384; article on Lord Houghton, 456
Vendée, La, i. 231
Venetia, i. 68
Venice, i. 98; Visit of R. M. Milnes, 106, 129; social life in, 136, 137, 153; ii. 268, 270
Vesuvius, i. 113, 124
Vichy, ii. 134, 142, 155, 268, 292, 392; Lord Houghton dies there, Aug. 8, 1885, 436
Victoria, Queen; Visit to France, 1843, i. 305; visit to Scotland, 334; opens Parliament, Jan., 1846, 369; Visit to Ireland, 438, 484, 485; Visit to Paris, 1855, 517, 518; ii. 20; meeting with Napoleon III. at the opening of the French Naval Docks, 29; death of Prince Albert, 74; the guest of Dean Stanley, 200; Allusions to, 237, 298, 387
Vienna, R. M. Milnes's visit to, i. 451
Vigoureux, Colonel, i. 24, 25
Villiers, Charles, i. 391, 392; ii. 186
Villiers, Hyde, i. 100
Voltaire, i. 57, 58; remark of Carlyle on "Ecrasez l'Infame," 435

Waddington, Mr., ii. 39
Wager, Mr. Pemberton Milnes's, respecting the office of Chancellor of the Exchequer, i. 11
Wakefield, Commercial prosperity at the beginning of the eighteenth century, i. 1; prominent position of the Milnes family, 3; brick manufactory of Mr. Pemberton Milnes, 5; lion-fight, 49; Lunatic Asylum, ii. 283
Wakley, Dr., opposes the Copyright Bill, i. 276
Wales, Prince of, i. 518; ii. 19, 83, 93, 95; visit to Yorkshire, 190, 227, 252, 358, 391, 436
Walewski, i. 514; ii. 169
Walpole, Horace, "Letters," i. 145; visits to Fryston Hall, 455
Warburton, Eliot, i. 84, 110, 112; letter to R. M. Milnes, 243, 307, 329; letter to R. M. Milnes, on the review of "Palm Leaves" in the *Quarterly Review*, 345, 346; Milnes's second in a projected duel, 417, 418; château in Switzerland, 419; death at sea, 467, 468; ii. 365;
Ward, F. O.; four letters to R. M. Milnes, on the illness, death, and funeral of Thomas Hood, 348—350
Ward, Samuel, ii. 319, 322—324
Ward, Sir C, ii. 61
Ward, Sir H., ii. 38
"Warden, The," ii. 155, 182
Waterloo, i. 23—30, 97
Waterton, Edmund, i. 465
Watts's hymns and Greek children, i. 135
Weavers of the West Riding in the eighteenth century, ii. 2
Weed, Thurlow, ii. 333
Weld, Cardinal, acquaintanceship with R. M. Milnes and his father, i. 122, 123, 127, 151
Weldon, Mr., ii. 435
Wellesley, G., i. 62, 71
Wellington, Duke of, i. 25, 28, 29, 70, 272, 321; friendship with R. M. Milnes, 388, 389, 497
Wellington, (the second) Duke of, friendship of R. M. Milnes with, i 388, 389, 390; ii. 189; visit of Lord Houghton to, 195
Wenlock, i. 78 (note), 202
Wensleydale, Lord, i. 464
Wentworth, Mr., i. 62
West Riding of Yorkshire, i. 1; early cloth manufacture, 1, 2; settlement of the Milneses, 3; political part played by Pemberton Milnes, 5, industrial growth of the present century, 6
Westbury, Lord, speech in the House of Lords on the condemnation of "Essays and Reviews" by Convocation, ii. 130
Westminster Review, review of Tennyson's poems, i. 106, 108; review of R. M Milnes' poems, 230; R. M. Milnes' review of Emerson's works, 240
Westmoreland, Lord, i. 343, 344, 488
Wetherell, Mr., i. 111
Wharncliffe, Lord ("the dragon of Wantley"), remark of Carlyle, when visiting Fryston, about, i. 256, 257; on the O'Connell Appeal Case, 336

Whately, Archbishop, i. 498
"When lying upon the scales of fate," poem by R. M. Milnes, i. 119
Whewell, Dr., senior tutor at Trinity College, Cambridge, i. 49, 55, 61, 66, 70, 74, 105, 177, 477
Wildbad, ii. 179, 204
William IV., Death of, i. 193
Wilmot, Mr. Eardley, i. 509
Wilson, Sir R., Governor of Gibraltar, i. 397
Windischmann, Fritz, i. 159, 230
Windsor, Dean of, ii. 196
Wingfield, Mr., i. 151
Winthrop, Mr., ii. 176
Wiseman, Dr., afterwards Catholic Archbishop of Westminster, friendship with R. M. Milnes, i. 123, 127, 140, 141, 142, 158, 160, 161, 317, 330; made Cardinal, 445; ii. 63; his lectures at the Royal Institution, 92
Women, Suffrage of, Lord Houghton's sympathy with the question of the, ii. 178
Wood, Sir Charles, ii. 16
Woodford, General, i. 130
Woollen and cloth trades of Leeds and Wakefield, i. 1, 2
"Words that tremble on your lips, The," poem by R. M. Milnes, i. 120
Wordsworth, Christopher, afterwards Bishop of Lincoln, i. 74, 125; friendship with R. M. Milnes, 126; accompanies R. M. Milnes on a tour in Greece, 128; ii. 212, 433
Wordsworth, Dr., Master of Trinity College, Cambridge, i. 49, 62, 74, 77
Wordsworth, William, i. 62, 72; enthusiasm for him at Cambridge generated by R. M. Milnes, 73, 98; attends a masked ball at Buckingham Palace, 119, 326; beginning to be appreciated in 1836, 171, 178, 192, 445

Wordsworth Society, i. 73; last speech of Lord Houghton, ii. 433
World, The, Description of Fryston Hall in, i. 455; criticism on Lord Houghton, 450; ii. 257
Worsley, Mr., i. 142
Wortley, Lady Emmeline Stuart, i. 392, 393
Wrangham, Archdeacon, ii. 22
Wren, Sir Christopher, i. 94
Wrottesley, Lord, ii. 15
Wynn, Miss, i. 293, 330, 471, 527; i. 183
Wyvil, Mrs., ii. 13
Wyvile, Mr. Marmaduke, i. 333 (note)

Yarmouth, Lord, i. 22
Yates, Edmund, ii. 256; friendship with Lord Houghton, 256—258
York, represented in Parliament by Mr. Slater Milnes, i. 6
York, Archbishop of, i. 463, 509; ii. 436
York, Dean of, ii. 22
Yorkshire, West Riding of; prosperity of Wakefield as a commercial centre, i. 1; the Milnes family in, 2, 3, 17—19
Yorkshire Union of Mechanics' Institutes, i. 447
Young, Sir J., ii. 38
"Young England" party, The, i. 206, 231, 315; Disraeli its mouthpiece, 319; Lord John Manners, 340
"Young Ireland," i. 352
"Young Italian" descent on Italy from Malta, i. 330.

Zante, i. 128, 129; "the flower of the Levant," 130, 132
Zara, i. 107
Zola, ii. 168, 379
Zucchi, General, i. 107